# MURDER AT THE SLEEPY LAGOON

# MURDER AT THE SLEEPY LAGOON

Zoot Suits, Race, and Riot in Wartime L.A.

## EDUARDO OBREGÓN PAGÁN

THE UNIVERSITY OF NORTH CAROLINA PRESS

*Chapel Hill & London*

© 2003
The University of North Carolina Press
All rights reserved
Set in Charter, Eagle, and Meta types
by Tseng Information Systems, Inc.
Manufactured in the United States
of America

The paper in this book meets the guidelines
for permanence and durability of the
Committee on Production Guidelines for
Book Longevity of the Council on Library
Resources.

Library of Congress
Cataloging-in-Publication Data
Pagán, Eduardo Obregón, 1960–
Murder at the Sleepy Lagoon : Zoot suits,
race, and riot in wartime L.A. /
by Eduardo Obregón Pagán.
    p. cm.
Includes bibliographical references (p. )
and index.
ISBN 0-8078-2826-2 (alk. paper) —
ISBN 0-8078-5494-8 (paper : alk. paper)
1. Mexican Americans—California—Los
Angeles—Social conditions—20th century.
2. Mexican Americans—Legal status, laws,
etc.—California—Los Angeles—History—
20th century.   3. Sleepy Lagoon Trial, Los
Angeles, 1942–1943.   4. Zoot Suit Riots,
Los Angeles, Calif., 1943.   5. Discrimination in criminal justice administration—
California—Los Angeles—History—20th
century.   6. Violence—California—Los
Angeles—History—20th century.   7. Los
Angeles (Calif.)—Race relations.   8. Los
Angeles (Calif.)—Social conditions—20th
century.   9. World War, 1939–1945—
California—Los Angeles.   10. World War,
1939–1945—Social aspects.   I. Title.
F869.L89M566   2003
979.4′94052—dc21      2003048891

A portion of this work appeared earlier, in
somewhat different form, as "Los Angeles
GeoPolitics and the Zoot-Suit Riot, 1943,"
*Journal of Social Science History* 24:1
(Spring 2000): 223–56, and is reprinted
here with permission.

cloth     07 06 05 04 03   5 4 3 2 1
paper    07 06 05 04   5 4 3 2

FOR JORDAN, LARA, STEPHEN, AND DANIEL

# CONTENTS

# ILLUSTRATIONS

# TABLES AND MAPS

# ACKNOWLEDGMENTS

This work could not have reached completion without the financial assistance and support of the Hispanic Scholarship Fund, the Princeton University Department of History, Dean Eugene Lowe and the Princeton University Office of the Dean of Students, Dean David Redman and the Princeton University Graduate College, the Princeton Society of Fellows of the Woodrow Wilson Foundation, the Association of Princeton Graduate Alumni, the Minority Academic Careers Program of the New Jersey Department of Higher Education, the National Endowment for the Humanities Fellowship for College Teachers and Independent Scholars FB 35241–98, the Dean of the Faculty at Williams College, the Center for Humanities at Wesleyan University, and the Center for U.S.-Mexican Studies at the University of California, San Diego.

I thank the many librarians who have generously offered their knowledge and assistance: Emily Belcher, Anne Caiger, Richard Chabran, Sarah Cooper, Pam Dunn, Linda Long, Dan Luckenbill, Donna McLish, Octavio Olvera, Dace Taube, Roberto G. Trujillo, Mary Tyler, and Yolanda Retter Vargas. I have been fortunate to work with students and others who have shared an excitement about the topic and period and provided valuable support and research assistance: Judith Burchard, Yolanda Davila, Felipe Pérez, and Christopher Wells. Desiree García, Mylene Moreno, Joseph Tovares, and the rest of the Zoot Suit Riot project for the PBS series *The American Experience* were especially helpful in collaborating with me and in sharing their research. I am particularly indebted to the historical actors and their families whose stories I attempt to tell, who welcomed me into their homes, took the time to be interviewed, read and commented on drafts of this manuscript, provided assistance, or allowed access to personal papers and documents: Socorro Díaz Blanchard, Lino Díaz, Ted Encinas, Lupe Leyvas, Rudy Leyvas, Alice McGrath, Theresa D. Torres, Henry Ynostroza, and Mary Jane Zamora.

I am grateful to the many colleagues who have generously offered their time, insights, suggestions, and criticism on various drafts or portions of this work: Jane Aiken, Peter Andreas, Elaine M. Beretz, Albert Camarillo, Leonard Dinnerstein, John Dwyer, Edward Escobar, Elizabeth Escobedo, Desiree García, Ignacio García, Mario García, Karen H. Gardner, Susan

Green, Michael Hall, Gary Hewitt, Meredith Hindley, Walter Johnson, Karen Eileen Kampwirth, Steven Kantrowitz, Ben Labaree, Daniel Liljenquist, Ruth Liljenquist, Jan Logan, Kenneth Maffitt, Lisa Magaña, Mauricio Mazón, Karen Merrill, Joseph Neville, Margarita Obregón Pagán, Nell Irvin Painter, Keith Pezzoli, Jerry Podair, Catherine Ramírez, Daniel Rodgers, Renee Romano, Ricardo Romo, Joel Schwartz, Howard Shorr, Donald Stokes, Julia J. Thompson, Joseph Tovares, Elizabeth Traube, Richard Ulman, Ulrik Vangstrup, Eric Van Young, Gareth Williams, K. Scott Wong, Russell Wyland, and Henry Yu. Lew Bateman, Chuck Grench, Ruth Homrighaus, and Amanda McMillan were encouraging throughout the manuscript review, and Matt García, David Montejano, and the anonymous readers for the University of North Carolina Press provided invaluable comments and criticisms. Finally, I can never express enough gratitude to Margarita Obregón Pagán, Ruth Liljenquist, and Nell Painter for their rigorous but unfailing support throughout this project. Con safos.

The views expressed in this book are those of the author and do not necessarily reflect the views of the National Endowment for the Humanities or of the author's colleagues at the Endowment, and endorsement by the federal government should not be assumed.

# MURDER AT THE SLEEPY LAGOON

# Prologue : The Sleepy Lagoon Mystery

*Dies irae, dies illa calamitatis et miseriae;*
*dies magna et amara valde.*

Day of wrath, this day of calamity and misery;
a great and bitter day.

The blows cracked hard against his head and body, bruising him like someone had picked up a two-by-four and flailed against him mercilessly.[1] Twenty-two-year-old José Díaz tried to duck under his lean arms to shield himself from the punishing beating, but he could feel his strength slipping away. He struggled to defend himself, punching into the dark night at the men who surrounded him, but his aim was bad. Fear surging through his mind caused him to swing wildly, and he was almost too drunk to keep his balance. He hit someone, though, three or four times, hard enough to skin his knuckles and break his finger.

What did they want? Why had he ever come to this party? He had told his mother earlier that evening that he had a strange feeling about going. His neighbors, Amelio and Angela Delgadillo, had spent weeks preparing their small shack for the birthday of their twenty-year-old daughter, Eleanor Delgadillo Coronado.[2] The Delgadillo and Díaz families were friends and lived about a hundred yards away from each other in bunkhouses clustered around a small pond, where Italian, Chinese, and Mexican farm workers made their homes on the Williams Ranch in rural Los Angeles County.[3] Several weeks earlier friends and neighbors had helped the Delgadillos pour a slab of cement on the patio, and they were eager to put it to good use dancing and eating good food on Saturday night, 1 August 1942.

José was one of the invited guests, and although he was not normally one to attend parties, this was his last weekend at home, and this party would be the last time he would see his friends and neighbors. Because he was born in Mexico, he was not subject to the draft, but he felt it was his duty to fight on behalf of his adopted country, and he was to report to the army recruitment center for his induction the following Monday. After confiding his uneasiness about attending the party to his mother, he walked down the footpath along the pond that led to the Delgadillos' home.[4]

José rarely drank, but on this night he accepted the free-flowing beer offered from friends and co-workers at the party.[5] By one o'clock in the morning the dance orchestra had packed up and left the celebration. So, too, had most of the guests, including José in the company of a couple of men. The Delgadillo girls wanted to continue dancing, so they moved their Victrola radio onto the patio and tuned in to a music program.[6] Victoria Delgadillo began dancing with Dominic Manfredi, and Josephine Delgadillo Reyes, nicknamed "Lola," danced with her husband, Cruz.[7] The parents turned their attention to cleaning up the house, and a small cluster of young men gathered outside the fence, smoking cigarettes.

José began to weave his way home, drunk and feeling a bit ill. But when he was far enough away from the Delgadillos' single porch light to be hidden in the shadows of the tall trees and shrubbery, he was viciously attacked. José withstood several blows to his face with fists and to his arms and head with a club. He finally collapsed face forward onto the road when someone stabbed him twice in the stomach with an ice pick.[8]

José was found about thirty minutes later. His swollen eyes were half open, and blood gurgled in his throat as he breathed. He was bleeding profusely from his left ear and through his shirt around his upper abdomen. His pockets had been turned inside out. A neighbor ran to arouse José's younger brother Lino from bed, who awakened and rushed to find his mortally wounded brother surrounded by the Delgadillos, Coronados, and others.[9] In the distance someone ran off to call an ambulance.

An hour and a half after José Díaz entered Los Angeles General Hospital, he quietly died, without regaining consciousness.[10]

The following Monday morning, the city of Los Angeles learned of Díaz's death through an unassuming report about weekend violence printed on the front page of the *Los Angeles Times*. This was not the first time that tales of violence from the Eastside found their way into the Los Angeles newspapers, and both the positioning and the tenor of the report reflected the attitudes that many Angelenos held toward Mexicans in the United States. The story of José's death made front-page news, but only as part of a larger story about an unusually heavy weekend of street brawls in East Los Angeles. The tone of reporting revealed concern over growing violence in Los Angeles but did not suggest any particular alarm at one more Mexican casualty.

The public at large in Los Angeles had a history of holding a complicated set of views toward Mexico and its citizens. Southern Californians in general tended to value facets of Mexican culture that were good for ambience

2

and for tourism and the hard work that they could command for paying "Mexican wages" to racialized nonwhite laborers. But at the time of Díaz's death, the echo had barely quieted from the previous decade, when white Californians called for the mass deportations of Mexican refugees and their American-born spouses and children in order to save the state from having to provide relief to unemployed immigrants during the Great Depression.[11] This reactionary refrain of the 1930s, of course, followed on the earlier cant of Americanization in the 1920s, when armies of social workers, educators, and philanthropists in Los Angeles fought against the imagined danger of cultural diversity that Mexican expatriates threatened in failing to embrace American values and lifestyles quickly enough.

In late 1942, the governor's office sent a memo to the law enforcement agencies of Los Angeles County ordering them to crack down on street violence and youth gangs. As a result, what ordinarily would have been a routine police investigation of the death of José Díaz skyrocketed in political significance for the Los Angeles County District Attorney's Office. The Los Angeles Police Department launched a much publicized war on juvenile delinquency and turned the investigation into a major media event. In the months that followed, Californians would again revive the discourse on "the Mexican problem" and debate whether Mexican citizens and their American-born children were culturally, politically, intellectually, and biologically capable of living within a white, civilized, democratic society.

The outcry in editorials and letters to the editor that followed the growing press coverage of the investigation was as swift as it was angry over the problem of juvenile delinquency in Los Angeles. But the cries for justice came not so much because Díaz or his peers personally meant something to those who called for a strong police showing against juvenile gangs. Had he survived his wounds, José would have remained, in all likelihood, virtually invisible to the public. Instead, his death represented a horrible truth that the white reading public would rather not recognize: the sometimes violent and often unforgiving "City of Angels."

In the weeks that followed the death of José Díaz, the LAPD conducted mass dragnets throughout the neighborhoods of Los Angeles, targeting those areas heavily populated by Mexican Americans and African Americans. More than six hundred young men and women were taken into custody as a result, and the Los Angeles press hailed the police as heroes. Shortly thereafter, through their often brutal interrogations of adolescent youths, the police proudly announced that they had found those responsible for José's death—the young people of 38th Street.

But were they?

# PART I
# MAKE NOISE
# BROKEN WINDOWS

# I : Introduction

or many Americans, World War II was "the good war," both at the time of the conflict and in popular memory today.[1] Although the war may have seemed "good" for some, it was not for all. The nation celebrated a kind of patriotism that was layered with troubling assumptions about power, race, and culture.[2] Indeed, those who looked too foreign or who failed to conform to the celebrated "American" ideal often paid the price. Cultural difference was confused with political dissent, and Japanese Americans, for example, were interned not for crimes committed but for criminality suspected.[3] Race riots, furthermore, raged from Los Angeles to New York, ultimately serving to reinforce the racial barriers of a segregated nation.[4] Of these home front tensions that revealed the social cleavages of American society, none attracted more national and international attention during the war than two events in Los Angeles: the "Sleepy Lagoon" murder trial of 1942 and the Zoot Suit Riot of 1943.

The riot followed the trial during a climate of growing public concern that the children of refugees from the Mexican Revolution, who were increasingly called "Pachucos," were becoming juvenile delinquents in their failure to conform to American social standards. Open confrontation along racial fault lines for this generation began as early as 1940, when mostly Mexican American youths aggressively challenged the intrusion of white military men into their social spaces as they passed through Los Angeles by the thousands. What educators, policy makers, social workers, law enforcement authorities—even members of their own community—were unable to see in viewing these children through the lens of social propriety was that part of their failure to conform came from a direct refusal to accept the racialized norms of segregated America. But in refusing to concede to the privileges of whiteness they were not resisting American culture in its entirety, as contemporary observers believed and some still contend. Rather, they embraced the uniquely American cultural invention of jazz as a means of negotiating their sense of place on terms of their own choosing. Their assertions of self found multiple expressions, from the music to which they danced, the slang they spoke, and the clothing they wore to refusing to defer to the privileges of whiteness and physically assaulting whites in order to maintain the integrity of their social spaces.[5]

The Sleepy Lagoon murder trial and the Zoot Suit Riot are familiar to students of the American home front during World War II. Among Chicanos, the zoot-suited Pachuco captured the imagination of a generation of poets, artists, dramatists, and writers, who envisioned the social crises of the murder trial and riot as a kind of Pachuco passion play that transformed the children of Mexican refugees into the forerunners of the politicized Chicano. As a consequence, what Carlos Jiménez characterized as "the zoot suit years" has enjoyed the attention of numerous scholarly articles, books, works of art, poetry, fiction, movies—and even a Broadway musical—since the time that noted Hollywood screenwriter Guy Endore wrote *The Sleepy Lagoon Mystery* in 1944.[6]

The most detailed discussions to date about the Sleepy Lagoon murder and the Zoot Suit Riot come from the work of Mauricio Mazón and Edward Escobar.[7] Mazón's extraordinarily nuanced work *The Zoot-Suit Riots* (1984) has shaped current understanding of the events by utilizing psychoanalytic theory to explain mob behavior. Escobar's excellent study *Race, Police, and the Making of a Political Identity* (1999) places the Zoot Suit Riot within the larger historical context of Mexican American tensions with the Los Angeles Police Department since the turn of the century. The dominant explanation for why the trial and riot occurred draws from the basic premise argued by Carey McWilliams and Guy Endore in the 1940s, that publishing magnate William Randolph Hearst intentionally used his Los Angeles newspapers, the *Los Angeles Evening Herald and Express* and the *Los Angeles Examiner*, to promote "anti-Mexican hysteria."[8] As a causal explanation for the Zoot Suit Riot, anti-Mexican hysteria was a favored theory of the Left in Los Angeles during World War II and afterward. Progressive activists of the period such as Endore and McWilliams viewed the trial and riot through the lens of conspiracy and corruption, discovering in the sequence of events the machinations of wealth and power unfettered. The appeal of this interpretation was that it simplified the complicated social dynamics and contradictory alliances of wartime Los Angeles by locating the origins of the social conflicts solely within white irrationality stirred by Hearst's profascist designs. Although the notion of riot as irrationality certainly holds merit from a historical and psychoanalytic perspective, it obscures more than it illuminates in relegating the actors in this social crisis to the roles of hapless victims of inflammatory rhetoric. Both white military men and

8

Mexican Americans exist in this interpretation only as pawns of manipulating industrialists. Such casting worked well for the purposes of the leftist polemic of the day because it provided a kind of bloody shirt—or bloodied zoot suit, as it were—that they could wave in condemnation of concentrated wealth and power.

The anti-Mexican hysteria thesis proved supple enough for Chicano historians to continue utilizing it as an explanation for the conflicts as they began to write their own histories thirty years later. But rather than locate the origins of hysteria in the manipulations of corporate interests, Chicano scholars saw anti-Mexican hysteria deriving from the pathology of American society. The appeal of this interpretation was that it moved away from Guy Endore's Hollywood view of sinister men controlling the puppet strings of society and highlighted the pervasiveness of racism and the propensity toward violence in American society. Yet this interpretation rests on a circular line of reasoning, that anti-Mexican hysteria caused news reporters to write unfavorable stories about Mexicans, which led to anti-Mexican hysteria. Furthermore, *how* racial animosity transformed into a murder trial and riot at that particular moment in that particular manner has yet to be adequately explained. In looking to "the press" as the instigator of racial violence, one must assume that riot is the natural and uncomplicated outcome of unfavorable news reports.

The anti-Mexican hysteria thesis, as the singular explanation for the social tensions, disregards critical aspects of the social dynamic before the outbreak of rioting.[9] If widespread and long-standing anti-Mexican tensions led to the murder trial, why did the Los Angeles County District Attorney's Office vigorously prosecute the death of a Mexican national when white authorities could have easily ignored brown-on-brown violence as their counterparts in the South did with black-on-black violence? Why did military men riot when they were only temporarily stationed in Los Angeles on their way overseas and had little prior interaction with Mexican Americans, instead of longtime white residents who would have been the most saturated with and invested in anti-Mexican animosity?[10] The anti-Mexican hysteria thesis also obscures much by placing the actions and motivations of white Los Angeles within the realm of widespread madness and irrationality. I do not seek to dismiss the reality of racial animosity in California, and I have no quarrel with seeing violence as madness, particularly racial violence. My point is that the anti-Mexican hysteria thesis does not account for why rioting *sailors* targeted *zoot-suited* young men across the color line, and not all or even most Mexican Americans in Los Angeles. Nor does it account for why some Mexican Americans responded at least in tacit support of the sailors.

The field of Chicano studies has increasingly moved away from the paradigm of "victimology" to explore the ways in which Mexican Americans have exercised historical agency and fashioned their lives within the confines of their times, however unintended the consequences. My hope is to contribute to this trend in probing the articulations of key factions in Los Angeles that played critical roles leading up to the riot. I ask how popular culture both articulated and shaped the tensions that exploded into riot, how jazz facilitated the negotiation of place for working-class youths, and what their engagement with jazz meant to Mexican Americans and white Angelenos. Through my exploration of popular culture, I shift the origins of the trial and riot away from a monocausal explanation toward a multivalent theory that looks at competing social tensions deriving from demographic pressures, city planning, racism, segregation, and an incipient, street-level insurgency against what Tomás Almaguer called "the master narrative of white supremacy."[11]

A closer look at this specific moment in time reveals a complex social dialogue. Among the young men tried for murder in the Sleepy Lagoon case were white working-class youths, such as Victor "Bobby" Thompson and Hungarian American John Matuz, who socialized, dated, and sided with Mexican American peers through the cultural language of mostly black music, manner, and fashion.[12] At the same moment, Mexican American professionals such as Manuel Ruíz Jr. looked askance at these "Pachucos," sided with the LAPD, and defended the actions of the rioting servicemen. White activists such as LaRue McCormick, Carey McWilliams, and Alice McGrath defied political allegiances to work tirelessly on behalf of the predominantly black and Mexican American communities targeted during this crisis. Accounting for the complicated cross loyalties during the Sleepy Lagoon murder trial and the Zoot Suit Riot requires a rethinking of power and power relations during this period. Indeed, what does it mean for the Chicano historical memory when the young men and women directly involved in the quintessential "Pachuco" moment spoke English exclusively, never wore zoot suits, and did not identify as Pachuco?[13]

The trial and riot were two episodes in a larger struggle over the structures of power and privilege in America, played out through contests over culture and social propriety. The public spaces of Los Angeles served as the arena where the very definitions of who constituted "the public," who could lay claim to those spaces, who could enforce social behavior in those spaces, and who could define the terms of propriety and delinquency all were hotly contested. One unintended consequence of segregation was that it produced a social, cultural, and political fluidity among families thrown together, and a significant outgrowth of that exchange was that young people across the color line, mostly of the working class, discovered and increasingly embraced what Michael Bakan termed "the jazz lifeworld." The jazz music, language, clothing, and behavior that were elements of this black urban subculture expressed aesthetic tastes and sympathies clearly in opposition to the normative social values of mainstream America, as well as to the aspirations of racial uplift and socioeconomic mobility embraced by many parents of the wartime generation. Certainly jazz was not new to American culture in the 1940s; neither were tensions between parents and youths over popular culture. Although both developments played important roles in shaping social tensions in Los Angeles during the war years, they would likely not have led to riot by themselves. Robin D. G. Kelley argues that black zoot-suited hipsters who frequented jazz clubs in eastern cities openly criticized "the white man's war" and prided themselves in evading the draft. It is tempting, therefore, to conclude that military men attacked zoot-suited civilian youths in Los Angeles because of their opposition to the war. Yet jazz never developed into a vehicle for defining, articulating, or communicating an opposition to the war, although some contemporary observers alleged as much. Indeed, as Burton Peretti shows, the successful appropriation of swing jazz and jazz musicians by the national war effort sufficiently divested jazz of its controversial origins as it became mainstream. Working-class youths in Los Angeles engaged swing jazz in qualitatively different ways than black youths in the East, refashioning the politics of black hipsters into a more complicated view of patriotism and civic disobedience as they refashioned the zoot suit into the more conservative "drape." Rather than resisting the war, they were eager to do their part through working in defense industries or proving their valor on the battlefield, but they also found ways of undermining white privilege that underwrote home front social relations in the public sphere.[14]

A parallel development in Los Angeles, wholly unrelated to the growing popularity of swing jazz, created the context for the demonization of the drape as competition between young civilians and military men over social space escalated into open conflict. With the coming of war, city planners imposed a million-dollar training facility for white sailors in an area of town long occupied by working-class and immigrant families. Raúl Villa's observation that "the experience of being displaced in multiple ways from a perceived homeland has been an essential element of Chicanos' social identity in this country" could well describe the reaction that many young people had in the neighborhoods that were directly affected.[15] Their responses to these changes provide another window into the ways in which they interacted with American society. A year before the outbreak of riot, young men living in the neighborhoods surrounding the naval facility, the majority of whom were Mexican or Mexican American, began a guerrilla campaign on the streets that consisted of harassment, intimidation, and resistance to the ideals of white privilege. Social workers, police, city officials, news reporters, and concerned citizens responded by characterizing this increasingly acrimonious contest as the work of misfits, malcontents, and delinquents who posed a threat to wartime stability, and they fixated on the flamboyant drape as the marker of delinquents. The confrontation that erupted into riot between these working-class youths of color, military men, and civilians across the color line was a spontaneous and violent exercise in power to re-inscribe the contested boundaries of public space, public safety, and social propriety.

This study develops Neil Foley's observation in *White Scourge* that perception and behavior played a role in the racialization of laborers in rural Texas. But unlike the tenant farmers in Foley's study, whose "whiteness" derived from a fusion of manhood, politics, and land tenure, young urban laborers underwent a racialization process in an inverse relationship to their exercise of manhood, politics, and material possession. If whiteness can be defined as possessing maximum access to social, economic, and political privilege, then land ownership was less directly a factor in "white" status in Los Angeles of the 1940s because renting was a more common phenomenon among city dwellers. In the anonymity of the city, clothing, bearing, presentation, and behavior were more instantaneous markers of status and affiliation. For urban laborers, their racialization came in direct relationship to their displays of consumption because, as Stuart Cosgrove notes, the clothing they wore and the manner they presented challenged dominant expectations of decorum and deference.[16] Clothing and behavior became political arenas for larger contests between cultural hegemony and self-expression, segregation and inclusion, racism and the rejection of white privilege.

The supremacy of whiteness, held together by a powerful mortar of belief systems, social customs, and laws, was under direct assault at multiple levels during World War II. Through their simple refusal to conform to the dominant expectations of what good, racialized minorities should be—not heard and often not seen by the white middle class—working-class African American and Mexican American youths openly challenged the assumptions of white privilege on the streets of Los Angeles. Through self-representations of their choosing, they also participated in larger and more subtle efforts by Mexican American professionals and white activists to undermine the imposed boundaries of racial identities and racial allegiances. Bobby Thompson, for example, although phenotypically white, chose to dress, talk, and act like his Mexican American friends of 38th Street. It is telling that he was treated as a Pachuco by the police, the press, and the public at large, who presumed deviance in the self-fashioned difference he shared with his peers. At the same time, Manuel Ruíz Jr., although phenotypically Latino, preferred to identify as "an American of Mexican descent" and dress, talk, act, and socialize like a middle-class professional.[17] Equally telling, he was treated accordingly by the police, politicians, the press, and the public at large, who presumed respectability and leadership from his appearance and behavior.

Thompson's and Ruíz's stories allow for an exploration of some of the ways in which racial constructions of identity interact with social standing and political power during particular moments in time. In addition to Foley's study of the historical process of racialization for Mexican Americans, Tomás Almaguer and David Gutiérrez have explored the relationship between racial constructions and social standing.[18] In my own efforts to think through the complicated dynamics of the Sleepy Lagoon murder trial and Zoot Suit Riot, it is clear that in this moment of social crisis race was more of a situational construction of social position than what has been acknowledged thus far in scholarly study. Rodolfo Acuña's observation—that in contemporary California "Mexican acceptability in Los Angeles varies according to the Mexican's appearance and socioeconomic status"—could well describe the phenomena of racial and social positioning in the 1940s.[19] Racial categories have not always been defined by an empirical reality but at times by a *perceived* reality. In other words, the racialization of an individual or group did not always correspond with skin pigmentation but drew from dominant ideas about behavior, clothing, music, culture, and symbols. Because behavior and cultural expression could be altered and manipulated, there were moments when race categories became elastic and unstable because of the time, place, and context of the particular social dialogue between peoples.

This study explores how some Mexican Americans found themselves in a historical context that allowed them to renegotiate the terms of their social dialogue. Manuel Ruíz Jr. and his company of middle-class professionals redefined themselves as "Latin Americans," not to pass for white, or to assimilate American culture, as some have criticized, but to gain political leverage denied them as "Mexicans." At the same time, working-class Mexican American youths also chose to redefine themselves. They crafted an identity that was neither "Mexican" in the manner that their parents' generation would have them nor "American" in the manner that the dominant society would have them. Mexican poet Octavio Paz interpreted this as a cultural ambivalence deriving from spiritual vacuity, and Cosgrove similarly viewed it as the mark of a "disinherited generation" whose members were "stripped of their customs, beliefs, and language."[20] I argue, instead, that this generation of Mexican Americans actively sought to renegotiate their social positioning in ways of their own design and choosing, in dialogue with their peers, their heritage, their times, and their social surroundings.

I use the term "power" in this study to refer to the ability to exercise control over one's life and livelihood through full and equal access to political participation, economic opportunities, and social standing. Privilege differs from power in that it is the selective conferring of power as a particular benefit or advantage attached to political and social affiliation. Thus, although members of the Mexican American middle class were denied full and equal access to power because of their racial status, they enjoyed certain privileges based on their behavior, comportment, social connections, political views, and willingness to work with the powers that be. This elite status for racialized minorities, although connected to color and class, was at the same time not entirely absolute and fixed depending on these criteria but relative and malleable enough to incorporate those whose talents, interests, or political and social affiliations supported those with full access to power.

This is not to say that power in society was fully open to or held equally by elite members of the various racialized communities of Los Angeles. Quite to the contrary, whites who constituted the racial and economic elite of Los Angeles, as well as most of the United States, jealously guarded power and employed a variety of means to separate themselves physically, economically, and politically from large portions of the populace—segregation being the most common. Segregation writ large, which includes economic segregation, was wider ranging in its impact than simply dictating who lived where. The written and unwritten codes of segregation sought to define how, when, and why disfranchised peoples, including working-class whites, interacted with the enfranchised in almost all facets of everyday life. At the same time, elites depended on the cooperation of "leaders" among the disfranchised to maintain order, and these appointed leaders enjoyed greater privileges than others because of their status as "reasonable" or "respectable" members of the community.

Manuel Ruíz and his cohort of professionals during this period depended on and used the construction of "proper Mexican" to gain access to power and that of "improper Mexican" to distance themselves from and explain "Pachucos."[21] Indeed, one of the ways in which power networks tied community elites together despite color differences was through a code of cultural behavior and social propriety. The relationship between power and behavior rested, in part, on a larger set of assumptions about social respectability and cultural propriety—as well as disrespectability and impropriety, which were heavily racialized. For many Americans at midcentury, being "white" had to do with more than just phenotype—it also meant acting "white," which was a particular mode of behavior deemed mannered, decorous, and deferential to white authority and power. Conversely, social behavior in the opposite manner reflected qualities and characteristics especially reserved for racial stereotypes, as several studies since the pioneering work of John Herbert Nelson and Sterling Brown have shown.[22] Social conditions during the Sleepy Lagoon trial and the Zoot Suit Riot polarized around the proper behavior of youths, which allowed various Mexican Americans to become "whitened" and others to become "blackened." Indeed, much of the public discourse drew on dominant assumptions about "blackness" and "Orientalism" to frame how it conceptualized "the Pachuco problem."

Previous scholarship on the period has received criticism for being too focused on the experiences of men, to the exclusion of Pachucas and women activists. This work weaves throughout the narrative the significant roles that women played in the incident at the Sleepy Lagoon, the murder trial, the appeal effort, and the discourse of juvenile delinquency, rather than bracketing their experiences in a separate chapter. At the same time, it is clear that the law enforcement agencies, social agencies, newspapers, reformers, activists, and the public at large overwhelmingly focused on juvenile delinquency as an especially male problem.[23] All the young men of 38th Street who were in the vicinity where José Díaz was found mortally wounded were tried for conspiring to commit murder, but the young women who were also present were charged with the lesser crime of rioting. Although some young women in Los Angeles wore drapes and prompted a handful of exposés of Pachuca life, the fashion appears to have been most widely popular among young men, and the published denunciations of the Pachuco were voluminous. Moreover, during the Zoot Suit Riot, military men targeted only young civilian males.

Why this was so, and why these events developed in these ways, deserve continued scholarly attention. Escobar argues that the arrest rates for Mexican Americans during the war years rose primarily among males because of the selective and concentrated enforcement in the barrios of Los Angeles of changes in statutes regarding immigration, the draft, and curfews.[24] The implication of his argument, by extension, is that the LAPD played a direct role in framing the perception that the so-called crime wave was a particularly male phenomenon. I argue that commonly shared constructions of masculinity—what Mike Donaldson describes as "hegemonic masculinity"—also shaped the gendered ways in which social conflicts were negotiated and where they occurred.[25] Men across the color line seemed to share the view that violence was an appropriate response for their gender to challenges of privilege. They also shared a similar conviction that the public sphere was their domain and that other responses to confrontation, such as ignoring the challenge, backing away, or conceding the moment, were tantamount to the surrender of social place within that domain. Even though there is evidence that women were present during some of the street confrontations between military men and civilian youths, military and civilian witnesses focused instead on what was likely seen as the greater of two evils: the breech of segregation practice in public by "uppity" young men of color.

At the heart of this study lies the story of the young people whose lives were forever altered by the social conflicts of the period, told in revisiting the incident at the Sleepy Lagoon from different vantage points. In the prologue I begin the narrative by reconstructing the moment that sparked a sequence of unforeseen events and draw from forensic evidence to suggest how José Díaz might have experienced the fight after the Delgadillo party. In Part I, I seek to establish the cultural and political context that gave rise to the public reaction to the Sleepy Lagoon murder trial and to the riot that followed. Chapter 2 explores how, while Mexican refugees and expatriates in Los Angeles created the romanticized discourse that Arturo Rosales termed México Lindo (Beautiful Mexico), white city boosters and politicians created their own version of the lost Mexico.[26] The stylistic celebration of Mexican culture in Los Angeles through architecture, city planning, and public events was in part inspired by the México Lindo discourse, but it was also far removed from it in critical ways. The sanctioned celebration of Mexican culture was a kind of Mexicanism made acceptable to white, middle-class tastes, interests, and agendas. Chapter 3 contrasts these competing and sometimes complementary dialogues between city boosters and Mexican expatriates with the cultural life of Mexican American youths on the street level. Wartime production created newfound opportunities for working-class youths to experiment with the material culture of U.S. society, and the styles they adopted suggested that they were eager to explore the perimeters through the jazz lifeworld of music, language, and fashion.[27] For the young people of 38th Street, their youth would come to an abrupt halt in August 1942 when they stood accused of conspiring to commit José Díaz's murder, and I reconstruct the fight as they described it.

Part II looks at the undoing of the romantic myth of Mexico and the persecution of unapproved difference among disfranchised youths. Chapter 4 probes the fundamental assumptions about the presumed relationships between race and conformity, culture and social propriety, and fashion and criminality that underlay the police investigation of José's death and the murder trial. I explore how the state viewed the fight and argue that police intimidation and coercion of the witnesses skewed the evidence presented during the trial and that an uncoordinated team of defense lawyers proved inadequate to the task of defending the young men of 38th Street.

Chapter 5 shows how the questions that Angelenos brought to bear on the so-called Pachuco problem shaped the discursive creation of the Pachuco as delinquent. As different factions sought to understand this generation of minority youths in East Los Angeles, the name "Pachuco" expanded beyond its original usage within the Mexican American community to assume a sinister meaning within the larger public discourse of Los Angeles. The imagined Pachuco as a zoot-suited delinquent took on life and meaning independent of the young people who inspired the myth. In truth, the zoot suit was far from being the uniform of youthful criminals, or necessarily of the Pachuco. In tracing the origins of the style to African American hipsters and jazz artists, I argue in Chapter 6 that working-class youths in Los Angeles adopted, modified, and reinvented the zoot suit into "the drape" as a partial identification with the jazz artists they admired. It was an act greater than simple imitation, however. Jazz music and clothing became parts of the first countercultural expressions among Mexican American youths that sprang into life amid the pressures of wartime conformity. In the process of refashioning their own identities out of the cultural resources at hand, blending elements of African American styles together with Mexican and American culture, they created something uniquely their own. Susan Green argues that the reasons that young men and women embraced the zoot suit "varied from person to person, from place to place, and from time to time."[28] Although I agree that the reasons for their choices varied, the net effect of their choices was a countercultural expression that challenged the dominant ethos of segregation. Jazz culture held out the possibilities of celebration and social transformation in the ways that it skirted the edges of social propriety in transgressing the boundaries of gender, class, and race.

Part III explores how social tensions moved from the discursive to the physical plane. The defiance of racialized norms led to a growing number of confrontations between military men and civilian youths near the downtown area from 1940 to the outbreak of rioting early in the summer of 1943. Although these increasingly hostile encounters had little in common with the death of José Díaz, I argue in Chapter 7 that they had much to do with the perceived problem of juvenile delinquency among Mexican American youths. The young people living in the neighborhoods that lay between the Naval Reserve Training School and downtown Los Angeles increasingly challenged the intrusive presence of military men in what they saw as their space. Thus, in Chapter 8 I argue that the "Zoot Suit Riot" was not necessarily the result of conspiracy, irresponsible journalism, or racism unleashed. Certainly these elements played a role as social relations spun out of control, but the riot was more an act of vigilantism by military men in response to the perceived inability of the LAPD to make tolerable what surely seemed to the rioters as an intolerable state of affairs. It was a particular kind of vigilantism that was designed not only to reassert the authority of the state but also to shore up the segregated boundaries of race and class transgressed by an increasingly assertive generation of young people.

Part IV considers the short- and long-term effects of the riot. Politicians publicly dismissed the racialized nature of the riot but privately struggled to tame the unleashed social tensions. Community leaders and city politicians sought out leaders in the black and Mexican American communities to address the problems that they believed to have been the most responsible for generating violence. Chapter 9 explores how the riot created new opportunities for Mexican American activists to operate within the sphere of city government and civic organizations previously denied to them. The riot also gave new impetus to the grassroots work of like-minded activists and concerned citizens of different colors, ethnicities, and politics who rallied behind the effort to appeal the conviction of the young men of 38th Street. As the war drew to a close and the city moved on to other concerns, the zoot suit fell out of fashion as jazz moved from swing to be-bop. The mystique of the Pachuco changed through the years, however, from a symbol of derision and fear to a symbol of heroic defiance. José Díaz and the youths of 38th Street faded from view in barrio lore, and instead the zoot-suited Pachuco evolved within Chicano literary and scholarly production as a Chicano freedom fighter who struggled to defend what one Chicano poet described as a "will-to-be culture."[29] The epilogue returns to the fateful party at the Williams Ranch in August 1942 and reexamines the evidence to offer a new interpretation of what happened the night that José Díaz died.

## 2 : Genealogy of a Crisis

ocial crises are never orphans in time; their genealogy reveals the many historical influences and forces from which they descend. The public outcry over juvenile delinquency arose like keening at the death of José Díaz, and like mourners hired for the wake, the public lamentation had little to do with him. The discourse on juvenile delinquency in World War II Los Angeles, with its all too common references to the imagined biological proclivities of racialized immigrants, reflected reawakened fears among white Californians of the rapidly expanding population of racial minorities in Los Angeles. The citizens of Los Angeles, however, hardly sounded with a singular voice on the matter, and their competing responses shaped how the events of the period unfolded. The thrust of nativism was to expel the foreign from the American social body, but the aim of the Americanization movement mediated against the worst of nativist fervor in trying to absorb the foreign into American life. At the same time, the marketing imperative of Los Angeles competed with the efforts to erase the cultural distinctiveness of Los Angeles's ethnic population. The mission myth of Old Mexico, celebrated in pageantry and literature and built into the architecture and city planning of Los Angeles, depended on the presence of enough native Mexicans to play the part. Indeed, in addition to Mexican culture, the economic infrastructure of Los Angeles depended on the labor, consumerism, and revenues of Mexicans.

Although evidence suggests that Americanization met with little success among Mexican Americans, one could conclude that in one respect it succeeded far beyond the dreams of reformers.[1] The children of Mexican expatriates grew up fluent in American popular culture; as a result, when they came of age, they began to chart their own course in ways that clashed with the values and expectations of their parents as well as with those of the dominant society. In learning to negotiate American culture on their own terms and in their own ways, second-generation Mexican Americans increasingly undermined the norms of segregation and white supremacy

through cultural expressions of their own choosing. This assertive generation destabilized the romantic myth of Old Mexico and the ongoing work
for racial uplift by middle-class Mexican American activists. It was as if the
packaged image of Mexican life and culture in Los Angeles that city boosters and entrepreneurs long worked to produce for tourism began to unwrap
itself.

Amid such social tensions, the coming of war in December 1941 profoundly affected the demographic pressures in Los Angeles that had been
steadily on the rise since the early twentieth century. The presence of thousands of military men stationed in and around greater Los Angeles from 1942
to 1945 further complicated the growth problems of the area by adding a
highly transient and unstable population to the mix. Military men roaming
in the working-class neighborhoods of Los Angeles increasingly came into
conflict with young people called "Pachucos," the majority of whom were
Mexican American. Through their very visual and public appropriation of
jazz music and culture, working-class youths defied the code of segregation
by blurring the lines of racial identities and challenging the norms of social
propriety.

### Demographic Pressures

In the first decades of the twentieth century, Los Angeles was a city in
profound social flux, and demographic changes dramatically affected social relations. Within the space of thirty years, Los Angeles became one of
the most racially diverse cities in the country, if not *the* most racially diverse. In the era of segregation, such a population boom of foreign, nonwhite racial minorities invariably produced shock waves of racial anxiety
and unrest among white Angelenos who lived in restricted neighborhoods
and communities. For the racialized communities of Los Angeles, the growing numbers of these minorities aided in organizing, in establishing critical
networks, and in lending numerical weight to their ongoing efforts to dis-
mantle the ideology of white supremacy and segregation.[2]

Mexicans were not always the largest group of immigrants in Los Angeles.
Prior to 1910, immigrants from Germany, Canada, and England came to the
city in far greater numbers. From 1890 to 1910, the size of the Mexican immigrant population was almost equal to that of Italians, Russians, and Swedes.
In the following decade, however, as Mexico plunged into years of inter-
necine war, the population of refugees from Mexico was greater than that
of all other immigrant groups relocating to Los Angeles. By 1930 the flow of
Mexicans coming to the city dropped precipitously and was the lowest of
all the aforementioned groups for that decade. The 1940s saw another dra-

## Table 1. Population of Los Angeles, 1900–1940

| | 1900 | 1910 | 1920 | 1930 | 1940 |
|---|---|---|---|---|---|
| Native-born white[a] | 80,165 | 244,723 | 434,807 | 891,736 | 1,191,182 |
| Foreign-born white | 17,917 | 60,584 | 112,057 | 181,848 | 215,248 |
| Negro | 2,131 | 7,599 | 15,579 | 38,894 | 63,774 |
| Mexican | NR | NR | NR | 97,116 | NR |

*Sources*: The figures for 1900 and 1910 are from "Table II—Composition and Characteristics of the Population for Cities of 25,000 or More," *Thirteenth Census of the United States Taken in the Year 1910*, vol. 2, *Population 1910*. The figures for 1920 are from "Table 13—Composition and Characteristics of the Population, for Assembly Districts of Cities of 50,000 or More: 1920," *Fourteenth Census of the United States Taken in the Year 1920*, vol. 3, *Population 1920*. The figures for 1930 are from "Table 15 —Composition and Characteristics of the Population, for Cities of 10,000 or More: 1930," *Fifteenth Census of the United States: 1930, Population*, vol. 3, pt. 1. The figures for 1940 are from "Table B-36—Race by Nativity and Sex, for the City of Los Angeles: 1940 and 1930," *Sixteenth Census of the United States: 1940, Population*, vol. 2, pt. 1. The 1930 figure for the category "Mexican" is from "Table 17—Indians, Chinese, and Japanese, 1910 to 1930, and Mexicans, 1930, for Counties and for Cities of 25,000 or More," *Fifteenth Census of the United States: 1930, Population*, vol. 3, pt. 1.

*Note*: NR = not reported.

[a] For much of the twentieth century, Mexicans and Mexican Americans were classified as "white" for census purposes. In the 1930 census, however, Mexicans were identified as a separate racial category and grouped together in statistical information with Indians, Japanese, and Chinese. Mexican American activists successfully lobbied to have "Mexican" returned to the "native white" category of the 1940 census. For an example of this, see U.S. Department of Commerce, Bureau of the Census, *Sixteenth Census of the United States: 1940, Population*, vol. 3, *The Labor Force: Occupation, Industry, Employment, and Income*, pt.2: *Alabama-Indiana* (Washington D.C.: United States Government Printing Office, 1943), 1.

matic rise of immigrants from Mexico, far surpassing all other immigrant groups coming to Los Angeles. And although Canadians, English, and Italians remained the largest immigrant groups to settle in Los Angeles during the first half of the twentieth century, Mexicans were the largest group of *racialized* nonwhite minorities. Mexicans were classified as "white" for census purposes, but their reception in Los Angeles was closer to that of African Americans.

In addition to immigration from abroad, the internal migration to Cali-

## Table 2. Foreign-Born White Residents of Los Angeles by Country of Origin, 1900–1940

|           | 1900  | 1910   | 1920   | 1930   | 1940   |
|-----------|-------|--------|--------|--------|--------|
| Canada    | 2,888 | 15,907 | 13,741 | 30,740 | 27,896 |
| England   | 3,016 | 16,920 | 11,478 | 22,254 | 19,713 |
| Germany[a]| 4,032 | 28,591 | 10,563 | 18,094 | 17,528 |
| Ireland   | 1,720 | 12,804 | 4,932  | ·7,212 | 5,840  |
| Italy     | 763   | 6,461  | 7,930  | 12,685 | 13,256 |
| Mexico    | 816   | 8,917  | 21,598 | 2,803  | 36,840 |
| Russia[a] | 293   | 7,478  | 9,691  | 19,744 | 25,595 |
| Sweden    | 808   | 6,150  | 4,998  | 8,917  | 7,844  |

*Sources*: Figures for 1900 are from "Table II—Composition and Characteristics of the Population for Cities of 25,000 or More," *Thirteenth Census of the United States Taken in the Year 1910*, vol. 2, *Population 1910*. The figures for 1910 are from "Table 12—Foreign White Stock, by Nationality, for Cities of 100,000 or More," *Thirteenth Census of the United States Taken in the Year 1910*, vol. 2, *Population 1910*. The figures for 1920 are from "Table 12—Country of Birth of the Foreign-Born White, for Counties and for Cities of 10,000 or More: 1920," *Fourteenth Census of the United States Taken in the Year 1920*, vol. 3, *Population 1920*. The figures for 1930 are from "Table 18—Foreign-Born White by Country of Birth, for Counties and for Cities of 10,000 or More," *Fifteenth Census of the United States: 1930, Population*, vol. 3, pt. 1. The figures for 1940 are from "Table B-40—Foreign-Born White, by Country of Birth, by Sex, for the City of Los Angeles: 1940 and 1930," *Sixteenth Census of the United States: 1940, Population*, vol. 2, pt. 1.

[a] Possibly Jewish.

fornia from other parts of the country dramatically increased the population of white Los Angeles. The aggressive marketing of California real estate created large pockets of conservative midwesterners in the middle-class neighborhoods of both Los Angeles and Orange Counties during the 1920s.[3] As Becky Nicolaides reveals, the following decade, Dust Bowl migrants also made their way westward to California and settled in working-class communities such as Southgate.[4] A growing number of white working-class families began to mix with Mexican Americans in relocating to racially segregated neighborhoods, where the housing was often more affordable than in the white-only enclaves. "In almost every section of Los Angeles where Mexicans lived," George J. Sánchez observed, "they shared neighborhoods with other ethnic groups."[5]

MAKE NOISE BROKEN WINDOWS

Political and economic changes were at hand that would frustrate the best efforts of California real estate developers to create a white utopia out of southern California. Devra Weber argues that the rapid capitalist expansion of the Mexican economy from foreign investment changed the lives of hundreds of thousands of workers in Mexico toward the end of the nineteenth century, creating a large, landless, and mobile population of laborers.[6] The transformation of the Mexican workforce and economy coincided with the growth of the Mexican railroad industry and the demand for labor in the American Southwest as agribusiness expanded. These factors allowed for the international migrations of Mexican laborers into California and other southwestern states on a scale previously unknown. The upheaval of the Mexican Revolution, however, swelled populations within the historically Mexican American areas of Los Angeles as refugees fled the devastation. As Ricardo Romo and George J. Sánchez documented in their respective studies, Mexicans settled mostly in East Los Angeles but also in enclaves throughout Los Angeles County.[7] With community resources stretched to the limit, the presence of Mexican refugees complicated already existing tensions between native-born white Americans, European immigrants, and Mexican Americans living in the United States.[8]

The war profoundly altered economic patterns and social relations of Los Angeles, which had well over a million inhabitants by 1942. The wartime labor demands brought thousands of African Americans to southern California from the South during the 1940s. Although the vast majority of blacks relocated to south central Los Angeles and Watts, an appreciable number also moved into the Mexican neighborhoods of Los Angeles. While the war industry attracted civilian laborers to Los Angeles, the military sent thousands of sailors and soldiers to southern California to train for overseas duty or to staff the bases and outposts along the Los Angeles–San Diego corridor. Although military men were only temporarily assigned to the Los Angeles area before moving elsewhere, the presence of a large and transient population of young white males training for combat added further complications to an urban environment undergoing rapid expansion.

### Popular Responses

Since the turn of the century, white Californians reacted in related ways to the burgeoning population of nonwhite Mexicans. Nativism ran strong among whites in southern California, to the extent that many Angelenos openly supported the Ku Klux Klan. More than a few white Californians saw the rise of a mostly Roman Catholic, mestizo, and politically radical population as a threat to the internal security of the United States.[9] City officials debated how best to manage "the Mexican problem," which included discussion about the imagined biological proclivities of Mexicans for violence, fecundity, and crime. One sociology student at the University of Southern California published a study of Mexicans in Los Angeles in 1912 that, although sympathetic for his day, reflected many of the predominant views: "The problems presented by this race of ignorant, illiterate and non-moral people, complicated by their low plane of living, their tendency toward crime, and their bad housing conditions, are serious and extreme and urgently demand the attention of all Christian reformers and social workers."[10] There was also some controversy over whether racially mixed Mexicans fit in the tripartite division of races. Max Handman reported to the National Conference of Social Work in 1926: "Their white strain may be $\frac{1}{16}$, $\frac{1}{32}$, or $\frac{1}{64}$. The rest may be Amerind (American Indian), Negro, or a mixture of the two."[11] But wherever one placed the Mexican on the scale of racial purity, the received wisdom among nativists held that racial hybrids produced a stock "superior to the poorer strain and inferior to the better strain."[12]

Nativist sentiment and concern over the fate and preservation of the "American stock" continued to be the subject of extensive public dialogue throughout the nation during the 1920s.[13] In the Southwest the debate arose from fears that the entire region might be overrun by the Mexican "race," and some scholars argued that Mexican Americans in the Southwest, much like African Americans in the South, represented a social problem that might not end for centuries.[14]

The nativist discourse folded neatly into another popular philosophy in the early twentieth century. Just before the First World War, Joseph Pomery Widney, Madison Grant, and a host of other eugenicists promulgated au currant theories of social difference that collapsed culture into race and attributed behavior to biology.[15] In the process, eugenicists added scientific weight to popular nativism. Grant copiously studied the imagined "Alpine" and "Teutonic" races and in *The Passing of a Great Race* compiled a hierarchical list of all the races in the world. The peoples of northern Europe stood at the pinnacle of human advancement in Grant's study, and the peoples from Asia, the Americas, and Africa fell considerably lower on his list. Within such a paradigm, social behavior—particularly behavior that the laws considered inappropriate and criminal—was neither situational, conditional, nor culturally determined but was seen as an outgrowth of breeding and biology.[16]

Although as an organization the eugenics movement never came to dominate American politics, it nonetheless tapped a deep vein in national thought. It was a time when social Darwinism held the public imagination and Margaret Sanger began her pioneering work on birth control to lower the birthrate among immigrant families.[17] Books such as Thomas Dixon's *The Clansman* and films such as D. W. Griffith's *Birth of a Nation* were wildly popular. Indeed, even President Woodrow Wilson encouraged every American to watch *Birth of a Nation*, proclaiming it "history written with lightning."[18] To be sure, "common sense" notions of race were shifting during this period, as Peggy Pascoe demonstrates in her study of miscegenation law.[19] By the advent of World War II, eugenics had fallen out of fashion in the United States (while finding new life in Nazi Germany), but it is clear from the "expert witnesses" called before the Los Angeles County Grand Jury in 1942 to testify about the psychology of the Mexican that white Americans continued to struggle with the legacy of eugenics well into the twentieth century.[20] The national discourse on race and identity continued to draw from a host of perceptions, assumptions, fantasies, fears, and half-truths about the meaning of bloodlines. Perhaps not surprisingly, the belief that anatomy was destiny was a powerful argument that explained and justified the status quo of privilege in America.

The political mood of the post–World War I period, described by Alan Dawley as "restoration by repression," gave rise to the Americanization *separatist* movement.[21] The horrors of mechanized, global war so terrified Americans in the wake of World War I that the nation turned inward—and on immigrants, too. Federal activism waned in enforcing progressive legislation designed to protect wage earners. American foreign policy became markedly more isolationist than in the Progressive Era, and the 1920s saw a series of legislative actions that closed the door to immigration, which had been open since the founding of the nation. Widespread nativist sentiment made organizations such as the Ku Klux Klan popular, national, and respectable. With the blessings of the White House, the American Protective Agency conducted Americanization classes throughout the land for fear that ethnic loyalties had led to American involvement in the First World War and that cultural diversity would lead to national disunity at home.

This approach was believed to be a more benign response to cultural differences among immigrants because it looked more to conditioning and education as the cause of behavioral difference rather than breeding. In the same way that progressives looked to science and reason for intellectual authority, the popular, organized efforts to Americanize the foreign-born also drew from the best of American scholarship. A survey of a series of what could be adequately termed "problem studies" conducted in the early twentieth century reveals a remarkable degree of uniformity in how scholars conceptualized the problem and the answer (always written in the singular) to the question of racial minorities in America. Studies such as H. A. Mills's *The Japanese Problem in the United States* examined family structure, economic activity, political and social organizations, religious practices and belief structures, personal and family hygiene, clothing, and recreational activities and noted how their respective objects of study measured up to the hegemonic norms of American society. Elite whites hoped to discover through scientific inquiry why "they" did not act like "us" and what could be done to remedy the "problem." The solution these scholars derived from such studies was that immigrants must be systematically taught to conform to the dominant standards of social propriety.[22]

The result of such competing ideas was a tragic irony for racialized minorities in America. Frederick Hoxie noted in his study of American Indian policy that even if white, Anglo-Saxon Protestants succeeded in remaking American Indian children in their own image, the pervasive racism of American society would allow people of color to live only as segregated, second-class citizens no matter how assimilated they became.[23] Such were the limited possibilities for Mexicans in the American Southwest, as well. Even if they successfully Americanized themselves in dress, belief, and behavior, they could not erase the meaning of their skin within the context of their times, when segregation was the law and deference to whiteness was the custom.

### The Mexican Vogue

A number of circumstances unique to Mexican migration served as cultural counterweights that frustrated the best intentions of the Americanization reformers. The city of Los Angeles long held a complex relationship with Mexicans and Mexican culture. James Rosenau observed that the contiguity shared by Mexico and California "has substantial consequences, that the ways in which the people, communities, and structures of Mexico and California overlap, interact, or otherwise intersect along a number of dimensions are important."[24] David Gutiérrez argued that by 1910 "Mexican immigrant workers had become the backbone of the workforce in many industries," and like many cities in the Southwest, Los Angeles relied on the workforce of Mexican labor to power the economic life of the city.[25] The purchasing strength of the Mexican and Mexican American markets was also a historical and integral part of the economic matrix of Los Angeles. Many businesses in southern California relied heavily on trade between Mexico and the United States. The city of Los Angeles itself was dependent on tax revenues from Mexican vendors and businesses or on businesses that thrived on the patronage of Mexicans and Mexican Americans.[26]

Helen Delpar found an "enormous vogue of things Mexican" during the interwar period in the worlds of American art, scholarship, music, film, and even diplomatic relations between the United States and Mexico, as well as among Americans drawn to the radical politics of the Mexican Revolution. In the process of "discovering" Mexican culture, Americans encountered the works of famous Mexican muralists such as Diego Rivera and José Clemente Orozco, who in turn courted North American patronage. Even privately funded organizations such as the Carnegie Corporation and the Institute of International Education worked to formalize intercultural contact and exchange on both sides of the border.[27]

The efforts of the Americanization campaign to erase cultural differences furthermore threatened to destabilize the tourist industry in California. If Mexicans became simply a darker shade of American, to borrow from Ruben Navarrette, then Los Angeles stood to lose one of its most cherished marketing strategies.[28] To be sure, the good weather and bountiful land of the "Golden State" were mainstays in the marketing of California real estate. Yet the tourist industry depended, in part, on the creation, maintenance, and marketing of the romantic myth of southern California's glorious past, and it needed workers to play the appropriate parts. "The Missions," boasted Charles Fletcher Lummis, one of California's most energetic boosters, "are, next to our climate and its consequences, the best capital Southern California has."[29] In novels, popular histories, tourist literature, and pageants, white Californians extolled the virtues of a bygone era of pastoral simplicity, known as the "mission myth," when Spanish dons ruled over mission Indians with benign paternalism. In truth, the mission myth was, as Kevin Starr observed, "an essentially Protestant creation for an essentially Protestant Southern California." Nonetheless, entrepreneurs needed enough cultural difference in Los Angeles and enough exoticism to sell the myth of Old Mexico to tourists who wished to sample a bit of Mexico but stay north of the border. Los Angeles offered a safer, more sanitized version of Mexico.[30]

City boosters were not oblivious to the marketing potential of intercultural exchange, and entrepreneurs worked to capitalize on some of it—albeit scrubbed, cleaned, and controlled for middle-class consumption. At key locations in the city, like Olvera Street, investors such as Harry Chandler reworked historic sites to turn cultural tricks for tourists. In so doing, they played on the romanticized image of Old Mexico, hiring Mexicans and Mexican Americans to play the appropriate parts and even hosting a number of civic celebrations there.[31] City boosters, politicians, and planners then redesigned the city plan of Los Angeles to deliver incoming railway passengers directly onto Olvera Street as the official welcoming site of Los Angeles.

They furthermore encouraged the use of Spanish and Mexican architectural styles in new building projects. The transplanted Massachusetts native Myron Hunt was one of the key architects responsible for promoting Spanish Mission Revival architecture in the greater Los Angeles area during the 1920s. Developers and entrepreneurs found that maintaining a certain Mediterranean feel about town lent the rapidly expanding metropolis a sense of history and tradition, as well as providing the city with an exotic flare that was good for tourism. Thus buildings on university campuses throughout Los Angeles, from Occidental College to the University of Southern California and the University of California, Los Angeles, all bear the marks of this cultural fascination with Spanish-styled architecture.[32]

Raúl Villa advances George J. Sánchez's interpretation of the Spanish Mission Revival, that it was far from a celebration of Mexican aesthetics. Rather, it was part of the concerted and continuous erasure of Los Angeles's Mexican heritage because it drew not from Mexican architectural styles but from Anglo fantasies. Although Villa describes the revival as "ubiquitous" in the 1920s and 1930s, he concludes that as an aesthetic movement the Spanish Mission Revival never really took hold in shaping the future design of the city. By the 1930s Art Deco and other styles came into architectural vogue as the city again reinvented itself—only this time, the vision that drove urban planning was not the imagined past but the imagined future.[33]

Mike Davis offers another perspective of the meaning of urban expansion in Los Angeles. Developers and investors acted not as a cohesive and monolithic group, although the "developers' millennium" was driven in large part by an ethos of civic forgetting. Far from a decisive break with Chandler's revisioning of Los Angeles, which lasted until the 1940s, the appearance of different architectural styles during this period was an indicator of competing interests in the real estate market. The erasure of the Mexican American presence from certain areas was part of a relentless urban reinvention that swept up everyone and everything in its path. Although Mexican areas were often the first targeted for renewal, Anglo homes that still stand from the early days of Anglo settlement are also rare.[34]

The efforts to construct the city as a romanticized Old Mexico testify to the investment that city investors, designers, and builders had in things Mexican—both fantasized and real—in the decades before the riot. Such an investment was by no means uncomplicated or intended to be mutually beneficial to Mexicans and Anglos. Through segregation the economic elite strove hard both to control and to remain removed from the source of its dependence, but it was dependent in the abstract on Mexican heritage and culture in building the tourist industry, as well as more concretely on the labor, tax revenues, and trade that Mexicans provided. Although the Los Angeles of the 1940s was a vastly different place than Nuestra Señora de Los Angeles in the 1840s, enough remained in 1943 for Mexican poet Octavio Paz to note "a vaguely Mexican atmosphere, which cannot be captured in words, or concept," in Los Angeles.

In looking at the production and consumption of information in Los Angeles, there is strong evidence that the reading public was equally invested in embracing and celebrating various aspects of Mexican culture. Mexican and Latin American actors shared equal billing with white actors in the arts section of major Los Angeles newspapers. One area that is beginning to receive scholarly attention in the study of mainstream representations of race and sexuality is the use of the imagined Latino in film, and California played a large role.[35] Movies were one of the media that were more accessible to the general public in the 1940s, and moviegoers consumed a healthy dose of generic "Latino" elements in motion picture story lines and in lead characters. In movies as diverse as *Flying Down to Rio* (1933), *South of the Border* (1939), *The Gay Caballero* (1940), *Anchors Aweigh* (1941), and *The Gang's All Here* (1943), imagined "Latin" characters served as instigators of romance and sexual overture, or "Latin" settings, costumes, and music served as backdrops for romance. Indeed, the term "Latin lover" is so common a trope today that it hardly needs explanation.

Perhaps it is no surprise, then, that the city of Los Angeles was deeply invested in regularly performing ritual and symbolic celebrations of California's Mexican heritage. A commonly used symbol of Los Angeles during this period was a cartoon drawing of "La Reina," a dark-haired, white-skinned Spanish maiden dressed in the traditional clothing of Andalusia. And in any number of public festivals leading Anglo citizens could be seen dressed in the colorful garb of Spanish señores and señoras, proudly riding atop Arabian steeds in their annual parades. Of course, Mexican Americans were usually present, too, working the end of the parades scooping up droppings and cleaning the streets of confetti.[36]

Los Angeles was no haven of diversity, but between the competing demands of Americanization and the economic need for exoticism, the city allowed a particular kind of diversity to exist that fit within the paradigm of white power and privilege. It was a kind of symbolic diversity that came not from the culture Angelenos ostensibly celebrated but from the imagination and needs of the white entrepreneurs and city boosters who created the myth. Although civic leaders tended to embrace publicly the historically distant and "Spanish" influences in Mexican culture, at the same time they maintained a wary and often condescending attitude toward Mexicans who defied such imaginations.[37] The architecture utilized during this period drew not from the artistry of indigenous Mexico, or even of creole Mexico, but from the Mediterranean basin. La Reina, the symbol of Los Angeles, was not an indigenous Mexican but a re-created European woman.

The coming of World War II offered new incentives for developing stronger ties to Mexico, and government officials turned to the celebration of Mexican culture to bridge the divide between both nations. As part of the Good Neighbor Policy, President Franklin D. Roosevelt established the Office of the Coordinator of Inter-American Affairs (CIAA) and appointed Nelson Rockefeller as its director. Far from being concerned with the plight of Mexicans or Mexican Americans in California, the CIAA used much of its budget to host receptions at Los Angeles art galleries for Mexican painters, Pan-American celebrations, and cocktail parties for the Latin American consular corps.[38]

Although the romantic myth of Old Mexico existed in tension with the lives of Mexicans and Mexican Americans in California, the investment that Los Angeles had in maintaining the myth created enough ambiguity that Mexican American activists found room to push for greater participation and representation. Those who learned how to manipulate public perception within this arena of public symbols gained access to political participation and even political office, albeit on the periphery of the city's infrastructure. Those who defied the myth were judged harshly.

### Cultura Pan-Americana, Inc.

Although Mexicans found life in the United States alien and sometimes hostile, the *colonia* in Los Angeles was alive with civic activity to address a variety of conditions and concerns. *Sociedades mutualistas* (mutual-aid societies) such as the Alianza Hispano-Americana and the Superior de la Union Patriotica y Beneficia Mexicana were the oldest organizations in the Mexican *colonia*, dating from the turn of the century. They functioned in a manner similar to the fraternal aid societies popular among many ethnic communities, offering low-cost life insurance for their members, providing social activities, promoting the preservation of their culture, and teaching members civic virtues such as altruism, thrift, hard work, and moral cleanliness.[39] The proximity of Mexico and frequent transnational migration made these organizations unique, however, in the degree to which they were able to maintain close ties with their homeland. As the Mexican population increased in Los Angeles, clubs with a decidedly social and cultural purpose, such as Club Amity, Club Alegría, Club Sociál Superba, and Club

Iris, proliferated throughout the county.[40] Mexicans also engaged in community outreach through church-sponsored organizations such as the Santa Maria Center, the Catholic Welfare Bureau, and the Catholic Youth Organization and community service organizations such as the Foreign Origins Council, the Latin American Youth Project, and the Los Angeles County Coordinating Councils. The Coordinating Councils were particularly active in Belvedere and in Watts, bringing parents together with volunteers from social service agencies, schools, and law enforcement agencies to promote social welfare, morale, wholesome recreation, and character-building activities for youths. Perhaps it was no surprise, then, that student groups of the period such as the Mexican American Movement reflected a similar emphasis on character building and civic participation in their motto, "Progress through Education." El Congreso del Pueblo de Habla Española (Congress of Spanish-Speaking People) and the Federation of Spanish-American Voters organized with a particular emphasis on interacting with city, county, and state officials, addressing civil rights issues, and developing a community-based agenda within the framework of the U.S. political system.

One organization that came to play a key role during this period was the Coordinating Council for Latin American Youth (CCLAY). In an effort to expand its network into the *colonia* and better connect county resources and agencies with the needy, the Los Angeles County Board of Supervisors turned to middle-class Mexican Americans for leadership in the new organization—not so much because of their constituency but because of their socioeconomic attainments.[41] "The historical significance of the CCLAY," Edward Escobar argued, "cannot be overemphasized." Prior to the formation of the CCLAY, government leaders usually turned to the Mexican consulate, which had different objectives and interests than those of Mexican Americans in Los Angeles.[42] Given the mandate to unite and channel the activities of social clubs, community organizations, and county agencies, the CCLAY succeeded in bringing together key city officials, prominent Mexican citizens, and members of the Mexican American bourgeoisie. The group was given the primary charge to study and improve the living and working conditions of Mexican American youth and to develop a program of rehabilitation and benefit in cooperation with the Los Angeles Police Department and probation officers.[43] The real value for city authorities, however, came during the escalating social tensions of the early 1940s. The lateral coordination of community organizations and agencies proved to be an effective means of contact and communication between key community leaders. According to CCLAY founder Manuel Ruíz Jr., during this volatile period the

CCLAY "was the principal factor in maintaining community cooperation and involvement" in the issues that affected both the Mexican American *colonia* and the Los Angeles community at large.[44]

In many ways, the personal and public activities of Manuel Ruíz Jr. reflected the ideals of his cohort and generation. Born to parents who migrated to southern California from Mazatlán, Mexico, Ruíz grew up in the Belvedere Gardens section of East Los Angeles. He graduated in 1923 from Manual Arts High School, where he distinguished himself as captain of the track and debate teams, concertmaster of the school orchestra, and class valedictorian. Ruíz went on to attend the University of Southern California, where he continued his participation in track and debate. While an undergraduate he was also active in the Greek life of USC, joining Sigma Phi Epsilon, a social fraternity, and Gamma Eta Gamma, a legal fraternity. He received his A.B. in law in 1927 and an LL.B. in 1930. That same year Ruíz was admitted to the practice of law in California.

Ruíz graduated with a strong academic record, but the racial predispositions of the day effectively precluded him from joining any of the established Los Angeles firms. "Fortunately for me I was not acceptable in a regular law firm although I had good grades," he later recalled. "I had to start a law practice of my own."[45] He began his practice in a rented two-room, forty-dollar-a-month office in downtown Los Angeles and did his own secretarial work. Ruíz pursued a specialty in international private law and was admitted to the bar in Chihuahua, Mexico, in 1932. Later his brother Alexander also became a member of the firm. With the coming of World War II, Ruíz sought to join the Federal Bureau of Investigation to do undercover war work in Latin America, but instead he spent the war years in Los Angeles as a community organizer and activist.

Although he spent much of his professional life shuttling between Mexico and the United States and remained fundamentally rooted to the Los Angeles *colonia*, Ruíz's interest in the whole of Latin America was a fundamental part of his political identity and strategically important to his sense of purpose. He was part of the México Lindo generation, whose members constructed their sense of the lost homeland (at a time when Mexico itself was rapidly changing). Yet rather than remain exclusively "Mexican" in his public persona, Ruíz took the romanticization of Mexico to the next level and self-consciously identified himself as a "Latin American" man to his contemporaries. His skill in doing so allowed Ruíz to put his own spin on the Mexican vogue in Los Angeles and play on the commonalities of cultural attainment that he believed the United States shared with the southern republics.[46] Keenly aware that preconceived ideas strongly influence social behavior, Ruíz sought to reconstruct the public discourse by organizing a wide-ranging public campaign to recognize and celebrate the histories, heritage, and cultural attainments of Latin American countries through public lectures, presentations, and programs. Ruíz also led the effort, in his position as a designated community leader, to alter the public discourse in Los Angeles on Mexicans by changing the accepted terminology. He was indefatigable in urging civic leaders, political officials, and the press to use the more cumbersome phrase "of Mexican extraction," or better still, "of Latin American extraction," rather than "Mexican" or "Mexican American."

Subtle and important distinctions in Ruíz's approach distinguished his activities and basic orientation from those of other Mexican American organizations of the period, such as the Texas-based League of Latin American Citizens. Although he strenuously insisted that white community leaders rethink their indiscriminate use of the word "Mexican," he never sought to deny his own heritage or ethnicity. Indeed, his position among white civic leaders depended on their recognizing him as a citizen of the United States of Mexican origin, and he hoped to lead them toward a more nuanced appreciation of citizenship, race, and rights. He was less interested in convincing his peers that Mexicans were Caucasian, and he never sought to Americanize himself to the extent of Pedro Ochoa, a contemporary in Dallas, Texas, who penned assimilationist editorials under the name "Pedro el Gringo" in his weekly newspaper *Dallas Americano*.[47] Rather, Ruíz and a group of educated Mexican American professionals in Los Angeles attempted to strike a middle ground between what Neil Foley described as a Faustian bargain for whiteness and the desire to remain steadfastly "Mexican."[48] They hoped to bridge the divide by promoting an "appreciation for the esthetic sensibility, idealism, genius and courtesy of Spanish America and respect for the enterprise, perseverance, and energy of North America" through "the interchange of cultural relations between the peoples of the Western Hemisphere." Although such appreciation and interchange was decidedly Western in orientation, Ruíz's view of cultural attainment was not exclusively driven by class and race. A public event typical of the Pan-American celebrations Ruíz organized throughout Los Angeles during this period usually included lofty speeches from Latin American dignitaries and local political officials, with Mexican folk dances of indigenous origin strategically placed between performed selections from popular European operas and ballets.

In proselytizing a Pan-Americanism founded on a common Western heritage, Ruíz struck on a cultural lingua franca that, he believed, could unite the English- and Spanish-speaking worlds. He feared the onslaught of communism in Latin America and determined that a stronger link between the

United States and the southern republics had to be forged in the interests of national security. Moreover, he reasoned that domestic harmony in Los Angeles could be better served by building cultural bridges across communities based on the notion of a shared Western heritage. Ruíz believed that domestic harmony would be vital to the war effort, and he also hoped that ultimately a new era of friendship and solidarity among the American republics would dawn. Despite the organizational successes of the CCLAY, Ruíz concluded that a new association was needed to foster Pan-American unity. In 1940 Ruíz, along with his close friend Eduardo Quevedo, founded Cultura Pan-Americana, Inc.[49]

He found a ready audience in Los Angeles. The new coalition quickly numbered among its members Latin American consular representatives and a variety of U.S. citizens who were also interested in cultural exchange between their respective countries. Among the goals of the one-thousand-member group were promoting interest in inter-American culture and cultural exchange, supporting bicultural conferences and programs, and establishing a Pan-American cultural center and library in Los Angeles. In an effort to sell the public on "Latin American" contributions to the United States, Cultura Pan-Americana petitioned the Office of War Information to intensify its work among Spanish-speaking people to increase their understanding and support of the war effort. At the same time, he called for an information campaign to familiarize the English-speaking population with the important role that Latin America played in forwarding the Allied cause.[50] Under the auspices of the CCLAY, adult and teenage representatives from many groups came together to deal with matters such as defense employment, job training, recreational facilities and housing for minorities, police-community relations, and plans for community organizing in the postwar period.

The escalating social tensions in the early 1940s thrust Ruíz into a new level of prominence among civic leaders in his role as a representative Latin American man. Social anxieties unleashed by the war with Japan precipitated the rising tide of racism and xenophobia on the home front, despite the domestic propaganda effort to promote national unity and distance the United States from the theories of racial superiority embraced by Axis powers.[51] Such hostilities in the Los Angeles area increasingly focused on working-class youths who strutted in flamboyant "drapes" (incorrectly labeled "zoot suits" by the press), defying the unwritten codes of social propriety in the age of segregation. They soon became highly visible targets for violence by members of the military and blatant prejudice by the public at large.

MAKE NOISE BROKEN WINDOWS

Attorney Manuel Ruíz Jr. chairs a meeting of the Coordinating Council for Latin American Youth. (Herald Examiner Collection, Los Angeles Public Library)

Escalating street confrontations between military men and civilian youths in 1942, and the negative images of Mexican American youths generated by tabloid journals, threatened to destabilize the efforts of Mexican American activists to achieve racial uplift and interracial unity. Glaring headlines of Mexican criminality and daily photographs of jailed Mexican American youths directly contradicted the message Ruíz had worked hard to sell to the public about the ennobling qualities, intrinsic dignity, and fundamental respectability of Latin American cultures. Ruíz had indeed found a large audience among numerous civic organizations and met with some success in altering the public discourse among city officials by making "of Latin-American extraction" part of the official nomenclature. Yet he simply could not compete with the revival of nativist sentiment and the echo of eugenics theory that saw a budding gangster in every Mexican American teenager who did not conform to the dominant ideals of propriety. Ruíz and other middle-class Mexican Americans continued to insist at every forum that not all Mexican American youths were Pachucos, but the press as well as the police, determined to uncover the enemy within, continued to have trouble distinguishing between the two. Much of the problem arose because there was no clear consensus of precisely what made one a Pachuco. The cumulative perception of the Pachuco from press accounts, however, held that Pachucos were Mexican youths ensnared in a web of crime, illicit sex, and drugs. Such behavior was hardly unique to Mexican Americans or to immigrants, but this definition of the Pachuco found a ready audience, and soon any young Mexican American who deviated from social norms was indiscriminately labeled "Pachuco."

### Pachucos in Los Angeles

Contrary to the popular image, both then and now, not every Pachuco wore a "zoot suit." And not every Mexican American who combed his hair in the Argentinean style (also known as "duck's ass") or who wore "drapes" was a Pachuco. A close reading of the historical record reveals far greater nuances to the term that defy easy categorization. Beatrice Griffith, for example, observed in *American Me* that Pachucos were not as easily identifiable with one ethnic group as the public discourse made them out to be. "Youths of Scotch-Irish Protestant, Jewish or Italian, Russian or Negro backgrounds," she wrote, "have learned to speak Spanish with a Pachuco emphasis, wear the traditional Pachuco clothes and haircuts, and otherwise become lost in the group."[52] The historical evidence supports her view, and the magnitude of the Pachuco threat to Los Angeles during this period was greatly exaggerated, as Ruíz and others at that time had argued.[53] So few

Mexican Americans actually fit the stereotype of the Pachuco that for all practical purposes the public discourse on the so-called Pachuco menace reveals more about public anxieties over assertive, racialized nonwhite youths than it does about an actual Mexican American subculture.

The young people who came to be called "Pachucos" defied the popular constructions of the day of what a "proper" or "self-respecting" Mexican was supposed to be. They were assertive, sharply dressed, and highly visual in their presentation, and their defiance of marginalization and segregation threatened the network of behaviors and expectations that underwrote the state of social relations. Their panache and aggressiveness were the undoing of the romanticized image of Old Mexico that entrepreneurs strove to maintain. The comportment of Pachucos also undermined the campaign launched by members of the Mexican American middle class to reinvent the public image of Mexicans.

The working-class youths caught up in the Sleepy Lagoon murder trial and the Zoot Suit Riot were not "Pachucos" as Mexicans understood the term.[54] In California, "Pachuco" was often used before World War II as slang for an uncouth native of El Paso—more or less like "hick" in modern speech. In El Paso during the same period, "Pachuco" more often referred to an Anglicized Mexican from Los Angeles—more or less like "dandy." There was, however, a particular class of Mexican laborers in El Paso more commonly known as "Tirilis," or "Tirilones," who appear to have been the inspiration of the mythic Pachuco.[55]

In social station Tirilis were to Mexican society what Mexicans were to American society: marginalized from mainstream avenues of educational and economic power. There is also suggestive evidence that Tirilis were part of the underworld operating in secrecy within the borderlands, trafficking in prostitution and drugs outside the grasp or even notice of many authorities.[56] They were reputed to live a wild life of fighting, drinking, drugs, and sex, not unlike that of the African American hipster or *la vida loca* known in barrios today. They were not the kind of people to leave behind written documents of their life and world; nor were they necessarily the kind to wax nostalgic in their later years and talk about their experiences to their children, let alone to outsiders from another cultural world.

Despite the Tirilis' guarded existence, certain aspects of their lives found their way into recorded history and allow for some tentative conclusions. Some observers of border life suspected that Tirilis, who were at times called Pachucos, were devout followers of a kind of theology that appeared to mix aspects of Roman Catholicism with native beliefs on the supernatural, material wealth, and power. Rather than wearing the conspicuous "zoot suit" that came to be associated with them in Los Angeles, they adopted more ritualized means of identification, beginning with their initiation into the group. Extensive and elaborate tattoos outwardly marked initiates, and the radiant cross was a dominant, if not primary, symbol. Evidence suggests that the tattooed cross first appeared on Tirili foreheads in a manner reminiscent of the practice on Ash Wednesday. Permanently tattooing the cross on the body, however, may have derived from a lay practice of inscribing the body with religious symbols as an expression of profound devotion. The symbol of the cross as a permanent marking of the body, representing both salvation and suffering, may have had a particular appeal to those who lived or worked in hazardous conditions. Tattooing the cross on the hand or leg may have been a way of invoking divine aid or protection from the items with which one could come in contact. Other symbols suggest that suffering was another dominant motif in the ways they marked their bodies. Tirili women were reported to tattoo teardrops from the corner of an eye to represent the number of years they were separated from a partner because of work, imprisonment, or death.[57]

Such customs may have entered the United States in the early twentieth century by way of the Otomí Indians recruited to work the mines in El Paso from Pachuca, a town in central Mexico located in the rich mining district of the Sierra Madre Oriental.[58]

The passage of the Volstead Act altered the nature of trade along both northern and southern borders, and it may have been the catalyst that brought Tirilis into the trade in vice. From 1919 to the end of Prohibition, the Border Patrol and the El Paso Police reported a rise in rum running between Mexico and the United States.[59] Smuggling was not without its risks, as lamented in corridos such as "Los bandidos de El Paso," "El contrabando del Paso," and "Corrido de los Bootleggers," but Prohibition created opportunities to escape the danger and drudgery of working in the mines in El Paso and realize profits more quickly.[60] Speaking Caló, which was already an arcane language among Mexicans, may have also facilitated the Tirilis' success in coordinating activities and avoiding capture. Bootlegging rings operating along the border no doubt used the trade routes already established from the opium market among Chinese immigrants, and bootleggers in turn helped smuggle Chinese immigrants into the United States after Congress completely excluded immigrants from Asia with the passage of the Emergency Immigration Act of 1921.[61]

The word "Pachuco" appears to have derived from Tirili slang for El Paso. Lurline Coltharp found in her study of Tirilis that her informants frequently used the phrase *del Pachuco* to mean "from El Paso."[62] The word may have evolved into a term of identity, referring to natives of El Paso, as Tirilis expanded to other border cities. Popular usage of the term likely spread to Los Angeles along the railways as Tirilis expanded their areas of operation or as they simply became part of the migration westward as Mexican immigrants searched for better employment. In the process, "Pachuco" became a term of derision among California-born Mexican Americans, who commonly used "Pachuco" in reference to émigrés from El Paso or in characterizing someone as rude or vulgar.

When jazz first caught the ear of Tirilis was not a matter that aroused much public interest and cannot, therefore, be pinpointed with documented certainty.[63] What is clear is that the zoot suit did not originate in El Paso or Mexico, as some observers speculated, but among African American jazz enthusiasts and artists. Etymological and biographical evidence suggests the ways in which the two worlds intersected. The terms "hip" and "hipster," which were common to the jazz world, originally referred to someone who spent the day lying on his or her hip smoking opium, and Tirilis likely came into contact with jazz through the opium and marijuana trade.[64] Jazz artists whose drug of choice was opium tended not to associate with those who instead preferred marijuana or alcohol, but Milton "Mezz" Mezzrow, who was probably the largest marijuana distributor in Harlem, provides evidence that jazz artists interacted with Tirilis. "Most of us were getting out tea from some Spanish boys," he wrote in his memoir, *Really the Blues*, "who kept coming up from Mexico with real golden-leaf, the best that could be had."[65]

Signs of jazz style appeared among working-class youths in Los Angeles no earlier than the late 1930s, and for a number of prohibitive reasons the zoot suit was not a widespread fashion in Los Angeles even by the mid-1940s. Even during the height of the zoot suit craze relatively few teenagers actually wore zoot suits, and Tirilis were no exception.[66] Local observers sympathetic to the plight of Mexican American youth estimated that no more than 3 to 5 percent of the entire Mexican American population wore a zoot suit. Yet that number seems high when compared with the low number of zoot-suited young men who were arrested during the police dragnet in the summer of 1943 or the number of reported casualties of the Zoot Suit Riot.[67] Besides the scarcity of material due to rationing, the zoot suit, more appropriately called the "drape" in Los Angeles, was an expensive proposition. Prices ran as high as $125.00, and many young men and women could simply not afford such a luxury.

## Pearl Harbor

The attack on the Hawaiian Islands rocked the California coast like a tectonic shift. In rapid succession many of the cultural alignments of the 1930s fell, reversed direction, or stood out in stark relief, to the extent that the nation was a very different place at the close of 1942 than what it had been before Pearl Harbor one year earlier. The impact of war production on the national economy, the gender shift in the workforce, and the impact of such change on American society and culture are topics well studied by Ruth Milkman in *Gender at Work* and Susan Hartmann in *The Homefront and Beyond*. Some of the cherished fads and fascinations of earlier generations also underwent dramatic conversion. Jazz music, although it is the most authentically American musical expression ever produced in this country, went from being wildly embraced by the "lost generation" of the 1920s to being the marker of hoodlums, delinquents, and subversives in the 1940s. "Orientalism," once the fascination of elite Americans in the nineteenth century, became the conceptual antithesis of Americanism in the wake of Pearl Harbor.[68]

The American reaction to Japan, though well studied by John Dower in *War without Mercy*, bears further mention here because of the unique ways in which "Orientalism" became fixed in the minds of some Californians as the antithesis of civilization, decency, and American security. Although the American reaction to Japanese immigrants was often rocky, for the most part it was specific to the nineteenth century and contained within the local labor economies of California towns and cities. After Pearl Harbor, however, Japanese-hating became a national obsession. American artists and graphic designers in the popular media uniformly produced grotesque images of the Japanese as if evolution had long passed them by. In California, where the white reception of Japanese immigrants and their American-born children had cooled to a civil condescension, open hostility flared anew and ignited other combustible passions not directly related to things "Oriental" but close enough.

Within forty-eight hours after the attack, President Roosevelt sent Frank Knox, secretary of the navy, to assess the damage wreaked by the bombing of Pearl Harbor. The following week Knox filed one report for public consumption, praising the heroism of American servicemen and minimizing the damage inflicted on the U.S. Navy. The other, more frank and detailed report on the damage was classified "top secret" and urged the president to order a commission to investigate more completely why the U.S. Navy had been so vulnerable. Among Knox's charges in the classified report was the assertion that "the activities of Japanese fifth columnists [spies and sympathizers] immediately following the attack, took the form of spreading on the air by radio dozens of confusing and contradictory rumors concerning the direction in which the attacking planes had departed, as well as the presence in every direction of enemy ships."[69] On 16 December 1941 President Roosevelt appointed Associate Justice Owen D. Roberts of the U.S. Supreme Court to head the commission, which was staffed by several high-ranking military officers.[70]

Although Knox's public report made no mention of Japanese espionage, the belief that a Japanese "fifth column" played a key role in coordinating the attack on Pearl Harbor was already common currency by the time Knox filed his report. In less than a month after the attack, the Western Defense Command in San Francisco ordered all "enemy aliens" to surrender their radio transmitters, shortwave receivers, and precision cameras. There seems to have been little question who the "enemy aliens" were, and the belief that both foreign-born and American-born Japanese should be removed from areas of strategic importance quickly gained support among top military and civilian leaders. The Roberts Commission completed its investigation in late January 1942 and concluded that "Japanese spies on the island of Oahu . . . collected and, through various channels transmitted, information to the Japanese Empire respecting the military and naval establishments and dispositions on the island."[71] In short order, Lieutenant General John L. DeWitt, commander of the Western Defense Command and Fourth Army, met with Governor Culbert Olson to win support for the relocation of Japanese citizens and their relations. Even Attorney General Earl Warren and Los Angeles mayor Fletcher Bowron urged the governor to support the relocation plan. Olson equivocated, however, not so much because of the troubling ethical and legal questions that arose from such a scheme but because he feared that black and Mexican laborers would have to be imported into California in order to fill the labor shortage caused by the evacuation of Japanese Americans.

While civil and military authorities in California deliberated over the security procedures, the Justice Department moved ahead with its own announcement that strategic locations were to be cleared of "enemy aliens" by 24 February 1942. American citizens of Japanese ancestry were excluded from the evacuation order, but they would still feel its impact. The Japanese American communities of California were small and fairly tight-knit, and the removal of Japanese citizens directly affected many families. Within twenty-four hours after the evacuation began, the Justice Department gathered 1,266 people for removal from the West Coast.

Still, for many Californians these security precautions did not go far enough in protecting California shipyards and defense plants from a possible attack by Japan. The California congressional delegation gathered in Washington, D.C., to press the administration to evacuate "enemy aliens" from the entire West Coast. Secretary of War Henry Lewis Stimson then met with the president and urged him to authorize the evacuation of *all* Japanese from the West Coast. In one of the most lamentable acts of the war, President Roosevelt signed the infamous Executive Order 9066, authorizing military commanders to remove "persons of Japanese ancestry" from the West Coast.

The executive order drew its legal authority from an American law almost as old as the nation itself. When the United States in its infancy stood at the brink of war with France, Congress passed the Alien and Sedition Acts of 1798, authorizing the president to order the apprehension and restraint of "all natives, citizens, denizens, or subjects of the hostile nation or government" that had even threatened hostile action against the United States. And although the Japanese in World War II bore the brunt of "apprehension and restraint," they were not alone among citizens of the Axis living in the United States. Italians and Germans were also arrested and detained by the Federal Bureau of Investigation, and in some cases placed in internment camps, for subversive activities. More than a thousand Italian nationals were interned in Fort Missoula, Montana, until Italy surrendered to the Allied powers in 1943.

American citizens of Japanese ancestry were placed in a difficult position. If they protested the label "enemy alien" and the actions taken against them as such, they would face further charges of disloyalty to the nation. On the other hand, if they acquiesced to their being removed from their homes to unknown locations, they would be able to prove their loyalty but at tremendous cost to their freedoms. George Ishida was one Californian who was well aware of the tensions at work. "The reason for this racial prejudice," he wrote to the *San Francisco News*, "is the unthinking, intolerant majority of Americans stirred up by individuals . . . who have had to compete against the hard-working, earnest Japanese farmers and nurserymen." And still he was moved to conclude, with a tone of bitterness, that "for ultimate victory and greater America," "Japanese will gladly leave their homes, businesses and careers, and, having the utmost faith in America, will place their lives in the hands of the United States Government."[72]

With unfortunate timing Japanese submarines shelled West Coast facilities within a few days of the evacuation, confirming in the minds of many Californians that they had taken the correct course of action. In the evening hours of 23 February 1942, a Japanese submarine surfaced off the coast of

Goleta, 7 miles west of Santa Barbara, and fired thirteen shells at the Bank-line Refinery, damaging one oil well. The following night the U.S. Navy received intelligence that an air raid over southern California was imminent, and at 2:15 A.M. coastal radar picked up unidentified targets 120 miles off the Los Angeles coastline. At 2:21 A.M. the regional defense controller ordered a blackout, and within minutes the command center was flooded with reports of "enemy planes" spotted over Los Angeles. Four batteries of antiaircraft artillery blasted 1,440 rounds of ammunition into the air, commencing the "Battle of Los Angeles." Initially four enemy planes were reported to have been shot down during the firefight, but as dawn broke over the city, no planes could be found, and the only damage inflicted on Los Angeles was from traffic accidents caused by the blackout and by shell fragments falling to the ground (at least one individual died of a heart attack). The secretary of war dismissed the incident as a false alarm, and it was learned after the war that Japan had no planes flying over southern California at that time. But the "battle" was significant in that it revealed the heightened state of alert all along the western coastline. Between Japan and the western coast lay a crippled American naval fleet, and Californians well knew that the battlefront could be at their doorstep.[73]

## Conclusion

Multiple tensions would collide during the social crisis of the Sleepy Lagoon murder trial and the Zoot Suit Riot. Mexican immigration to Los Angeles skyrocketed in the 1940s after a lull in the previous decade, and both nativism and Americanization, the former emphasizing expulsion of the alien and the latter emphasizing assimilation of the alien, rose once again in California. The bombing of Pearl Harbor intensified reactions to the changing demographics on the West Coast. Although white Californians focused their wrath on the Japanese after Pearl Harbor, the impetus to purify their cities and towns from the enemy's presence spilled over to other groups deemed equally subversive of cherished American customs.[74] Racialized peoples have often served as signifiers of social and behavioral characteristics deemed antithetical to elite ideals in the imagination of whites, and some Angelenos readily brushed Mexicans with the taint of "Oriental behavior" in trying to explain social tensions.[75]

At the same time, it is important to note that such popular responses threatened to destabilize economic relations in Los Angeles that depended on a working level of amicability between the white and Mexican populations. Key businesspeople and city officials therefore turned to Mexican American professionals for assistance in ways they had never before attempted. This newfound access to power would severely test the loyalties of middle-class Mexican Americans as they simultaneously worked to protect and distance themselves from the very young people who undermined their work for racial uplift.

The growing popularity of jazz among Pachucos might not have attracted attention outside the barrios and ghettos of Los Angeles if the coming of war had not complicated the social dynamics. The city became a playground of booze and debauchery for military men stationed in and around Los Angeles before shipping off to combat duty. Military men roaming through the segregated neighborhoods of Los Angeles increasingly came into conflict with young people who aggressively defended the integrity of their territory.

It is significant that both the Mexican American middle class and the Pachucos embraced terms of identification that distanced themselves from their social identities as "Mexicans." Ruíz chose the more ephemeral and socially acceptable terms "Latin American" or "of Mexican extraction." Like Ruíz, the young people who came to be called "Pachucos" also sought to distance themselves from the dominant views of Mexican identity. As Douglas Monroy observed, this generation chose alternative identities for themselves that were neither fully "Mexican" nor fully "American."[76] Unlike Ruíz, however, they openly flaunted their differences as badges of identity, and many Angelenos across the color line found such audacity threatening to the social order.

# 3 : The Life & Times of José Díaz

The death of José Díaz thrust the "Pachuco problem" into the fore of home front concerns about public safety in wartime Los Angeles. José was certainly not a Pachuco, but even with the publicity surrounding his "gang-related" death, few Angelenos knew this or anything else about him. Nor was there much demand to know anything, for in life José Díaz was simply one of the thousands of young people born to the world of the working poor in Los Angeles, who frequently moved from one rented space to another in search of employment, the last hired and first fired, with little to offer a demanding labor force but the strength of their backs and the agility of their hands. No doubt he shared the aspirations of his generation, too young to be immediately involved in the war but old enough to be frightened by it, anxiously looking toward an uncertain future, ever hopeful that he, too, would be able to taste a bit of America's bounty. He was far more interesting to the public in death as a victim of gang violence than he was as the son of Mexican refugees struggling to make a place for themselves within the narrow confines prescribed by American society. Thus, newspapers and court dockets dutifully noted when he was born, when he died, the medical complications that choked off his young life, but little else.

The life and death of José Díaz frame the story of the young men and women of 38th Street who were implicated in his murder by the police and the press of Los Angeles. In life he shared many of the social ties and tensions they encountered in coming of age when the world was at war. As children of Mexican refugees they also shared a complicated relationship with mainstream society, valued for the labor they would provide but scorned for their social identities as "Mexicans." Within such a context they fashioned the horizons of their young lives, situated within the cultural resources at hand in the working-class neighborhoods of Los Angeles. In death José Díaz would continue to shadow the 38th Street youths. Were it not for that fateful night in early August 1942 when their lives entangled during a confrontation in rural Los Angeles County, they would have likely passed the remainder of their days in the relative obscurity of the working poor. Instead, José emerged a tragic symbol of gang violence, and the young people of 38th Street found their world turned upside down by the harsh glare of public scrutiny during the Sleepy Lagoon murder trial.

In a curious way José Díaz continued to live on in the lives of young men and women he barely knew, in imperceptible ways he could not have imagined or would have surely wanted. His death was the trigger of a series of events that forever imprinted themselves on the young men who stood accused of his murder, the young women who were jailed for having knowledge useful to the state, and the political activists who lobbied the public on their behalf. Although the campaign to appeal the convictions of the young men of 38th Street eventually succeeded, their lives were permanently disrupted. To this day the mystery of his death endures, and José still haunts the unanswered questions that grew out of his life and death.

### Un Vato de Atolle

The darkest hours of the revolution had passed when José came into the world in 1919, but the road to recovery for Mexico would be long after almost ten years of bloody conflict. It was a road fraught with difficulties that would prove too great for the Díaz family to endure. In 1923 the family joined the millions of refugees fleeing northward from the aftermath of war.[1]

Whole regions of Mexico lay flattened by the successive waves of ruthless political struggle that swept back and forth over the nation since 1910. As a bitter peace settled over the land at the end of the decade, the federal coffers were in no condition to lend aid to the distressed regions of the country. Particularly in the state of Durango, where the Díaz family lived, famine and fear ruled the land as the retreating Villistas stripped the outlying districts of what food and provisions they could and local strongmen battled for position in the power vacuum.[2] Since 1916 prices for basic foodstuffs had skyrocketed as battles scarred the countryside. Drought compounded want with cruel timing: up to three-fourths of the already stunted crops withered in the parched ground.[3]

In the midst of these bleak conditions, however, Durango's economy temporarily stabilized between 1918 to 1921.[4] For a brief moment the region seemed on the road to recovery. In this window of hope Panfila Gallardo gave light to José Gallardo Díaz in her bed early in the month of December 1919.[5]

Beyond these basic vital statistics, the historical record provides no more information about the life the Díaz family led in Mexico. Were they people who worked the land, part of the fledgling middle class who lost their holdings as a result of the ravages of war, or members of the elite who fled the country because their politics were on the wrong side of the revolution? The answers may never be fully known, and only hints of their lives in Mexico flicker across the panorama of national events.

By 1923 Mexico seemed on the brink of again plunging headlong into the nightmare of civil war. Pancho Villa, beloved by the field workers, laborers, and the downtrodden of Mexico, threatened to come out of retirement to champion their cause once again. In late spring of that year, however, his voice was to be heard no more after a spatter of bullets riddled his Dodge touring car on a dusty road in Parral, Chihuahua. His assassination, both mourned and celebrated throughout Mexico, signaled the severity of the growing national crisis. Ardent nationalists were already in an uproar over the Bucareli Agreement negotiated with the United States, accusing President Alvaro Obregón of capitulating to American oilmen and selling away Mexico's vital resources. When Obregón selected his secretary of the interior, Plutarco Calles, as his successor, wealthy *hacendados* and Catholic leaders wary of Calles's left-leaning record on social reform threatened revolt. Aging military men, embittered by Obregón's reduction of the national army, joined in the growing coalition of anti-Obregón forces. Before the year's end some seven thousand rebels were killed by the forces loyal to the government, and peace once again attempted its sojourn in Mexico.[6]

The sweep of national events may have had little impact on the Díaz family's decision to leave the country. Socorro Díaz Blanchard remembers that her father was a butcher before he turned to farming, and certainly the daily grind of finding food for the family during times of desperation and want was at the forefront of his concerns, regardless of the national struggles for stability.[7] Whatever the cause for their decision, the members of the Díaz family joined the thousands of Mexicans who migrated northward in search of peace and stability in the strange land across the Río Bravo.[8]

The opportunities they found in the United States, on an absolute scale, surely outweighed those they left behind. Yet Texas, observed novelist José Antonio Villareal, "welcomed them as a blessing because there were miles of cotton to be harvested, [but] had never really forgotten the Alamo."[9] Indeed, there were few avenues of employment open for the masses of refugees from Mexico, except in the growing fields in the Southwest. No records exist to document the movement and activities of the Díaz family's first years in the United States. Quite likely José and his family, like so many of their compatriots, entered the country through El Paso and eventually migrated to California.[10] There they joined in what José Villareal described as "the nomadic harvest of California's crops": lettuce in Salinas, grapes in Parlier, oranges in Ontario, cotton in Firebaugh, and plums in Santa Clara.[11]

Five years after entering the country, the Díaz family settled outside Los Angeles in 1928, just beyond the municipal line in what is now the city of Bell.[12] It was a long way from the "automobile suburbs" that arose during the interwar period—the Díaz family was too poor and too dark to meet the restrictive covenants designed to keep the suburbs of Los Angeles white and middle class.[13] What the family found, instead, was a modest bunkhouse amid a small cluster of housing units built on the Williams Ranch for the ranch hands.

Located about a mile and a half below the reservoir dubbed the "Sleepy Lagoon," these bunkhouses constituted a small village for the immigrant laborers who made the area their home.[14] Most of the ranch hands, such as the Delgadillo family, María Albino, and Remedios Parra, were either Mexican or Mexican American, many of whom spoke just enough English to fulfill their labor obligations. Others, such as Dominic and Joe Manfredi, were Italian, and at least one Japanese and one Chinese family lived in the compound.[15] Together they celebrated birthdays, weddings, and funerals in the community rituals of life that tied them to one another and to the other Mexican expatriates living in Los Angeles County.

Through these kinds of community gatherings José no doubt came into contact with Angel Padilla, Joseph "Joey" Carpio, and Eugene "Geney" Carpio, who would later stand accused of his murder with other boys from 38th Street. Just how closely they knew one another is not a matter that can be established through the extant documents. Clearly José was not part of the immediate circle of friends that prosecutors characterized as "the 38th Street gang" during the Sleepy Lagoon trial. Yet it is certain that José met many of them at least in passing through the overlapping activities of the various social nodes they shared in common, for like José, most of the 38th Street boys were children of parents who fled from the violence and deprivation that overtook many parts of Mexico during the revolution. Some even came from his home state of Durango.

Many of the teenagers living around the area of 38th Street, like José, came from large families, circulated among the same employers in East Los Angeles, belonged to the same youth groups, and attended the same Catholic school. Their school records attest to the mobility of their young lives as their parents moved from job to job: two years here, another year there. Many did not finish high school.

As these youths matured, their lives were shaped by the strict discipline imposed by family and church and the freedom to explore their own rules on the playgrounds and alleyways of East Los Angeles. There, as they formed social networks and explored the meaning of their young lives through clothes, sex, cars, and beer, they learned the harsh realities of being born poor and deemed "Mexican" in Los Angeles. Where they were lucky enough to find a restaurant that would serve them, people of color often encountered rude service and dirty utensils or tableware.[16] And in the name of law and order, members of the Los Angeles police routinely raided parties in East Los Angeles, broke up outdoor games and gatherings, and chased young people out of the parks after sundown.[17] It was common for young people growing up in the area to be arrested for loitering and then be beaten while in custody until they confessed their guilt.[18]

## Counter-Cultures U.S.A.

Denied access to the social and recreational outlets of the city, José, like most young people of color, no doubt had a complicated relationship with mainstream society. The geographical diversity and good weather of the area offered a wide variety of recreational options for the socially privileged, ranging from tennis to golf, from horseback riding to swimming. For the underprivileged, however—chief among them the children of Mexican refugees—access to private sports clubs was closed, and their use of public swimming pools was severely circumscribed. These young people adopted any body of water they could find as their place to swim and relax.[19] For recreational facilities, pool halls tended to be the favorite haunts of boys, malt shops for girls, and street corners served as informal youth centers where teenagers would spontaneously gather.[20] Weekly dances and movies sponsored by neighborhood associations at times filled the gap, as did "home parties" for young people and adults.[21]

Home parties served an important social function in the life of the community. Although young men and women of 38th Street tended to experience such gatherings largely on a recreational level common to most young people, home parties nonetheless served far-reaching purposes in maintaining social cohesion and developing community ties. Home parties and neighborhood gatherings were largely attended by people of the same social stratum, such as co-workers, relatives, and friends who were predominantly Mexican American, but would include at times African American, Italian American, or Irish American youths. Los Angeles was a segregated city, and the sections of town that were predominantly nonwhite offered the most affordable housing. Thus some poor whites such as Bobby Thompson, who came to Los Angeles as part of the "Oakie" migration to California, lived on 38th Street and grew up with Mexican American neighbors. Indeed, he was not alone. The family surnames among the young people of 38th Street reflect a rich ethnic diversity: Grandpre (French), Schneider, Zeiss (both Jewish), Kalustian (Armenian), and Matuz (Hungarian).[22]

This kind of interracial and intercultural mixing, though certainly not a citywide phenomenon, characterized the social references of the wartime generation of the 38th Street youths who lived in the cultural borderlands of Los Angeles. One could have easily found at such gatherings young men and women straining to hear one another over the excited chatter of the party punctuated by English and *pocho* as they danced the lindy hop and the jitterbug to the African American rhythms of jump blues and swing, recorded by Jewish musicians, all the while trying to stay within the social expectations set by their Mexican parents.[23]

On one level such interlingual and intercultural exchanges were part of the process of experimentation, transformation, and adaptation common to first- and second-generation American youth. On another level, however, they constituted a conduct that defied the norms of segregation. Race mixing was considered to be a social danger because it threatened to undermine the mythology of white supremacy, especially so if the different drummer to whom young people chose to march was a zoot-suited, black jazz artist.

The circumstances of both time and place played a unique role in shaping the contours of this phenomenon. The war touched almost every corner of American society, and within the Mexican American community it served to hasten the transformation of social norms. Mary Helen Ponce remembered that, as young girl growing up north of Los Angeles in "Pacas" (Pachuco slang for Pacoima), she looked with envy upon the new freedoms her older sisters enjoyed as a result of the war. Contrary to traditional Mexican mores, Ronnie, Elizabet, and Nora Ponce were all permitted to attend patriotic dances sponsored by El Salón Parra as part of the war effort. And encouraged by their new progressive priest, the Ponce sisters were allowed unprecedented social advances by inviting military men to the church bazaars. Soon these social functions teemed with men in uniform who openly flirted with the young Mexican American women there.[24]

There was also something unique about the spatial confines in which these social transformations occurred. The city of Los Angeles, more than any other urban center in the nation, played the reluctant host to a convergence of diverse cultures and peoples. More by accident than by design, the separatist aspirations of the white middle class created zones of cultural exchange where the social energy and color of compressed humanity erupted in sometimes clashing and sometimes complementary plumes of cultural expression. Mexican Americans and Russian Jews lived side by side in the area of Little Tokyo and Chinatown. African Americans congregated along the corridor of Central Avenue stretching south toward Watts, but they also spread out among the low-cost subdivisions such as Dogtown, Aliso Village, and Ramona Gardens that commonly attracted working-class people of different shades. Added to such a social mix were the middle-class college students from the University of California, Los Angeles, and the University of Southern California and military men who went slumming in these zones in search of excitement and entertainment.

To be sure, the level of cultural exchange varied greatly from neighborhood to neighborhood, and the nature of social interaction was far from utopian. Lloyd H. Fisher concluded in a 1945 study of Los Angeles sponsored by the American Council on Race Relations that "conflict, tension and interracial combat are well marked characteristics of the life of . . . Hollenbeck, Watts, and West Jefferson."[25] Yet the shared living space in the low-cost subdivisions that dotted Los Angeles also facilitated a certain level of creative exchange among the working-class youths who lived there. It was a dialogue that was spoken with their tastes and habits, their clothes and their speech.

Children of the war generation furthermore had to negotiate conflicting cultural tensions. The only way that fifteen-year-old Lupe Leyvas could leave the house, for example, was in the presence of an older brother who served as her escort. Both brother and sister closely observed traditional mores as long as they were in sight of their parents. Once they left the watchful eyes of the neighborhood, however, they headed straight for the malt shop next to the Vernon Theater, met their respective friends, and went their separate ways. At an appointed hour Lupe and her brother would meet at the malt shop and return home together, thus observing the letter of their parent's strict instructions that they leave and return home together. "Back then you had to lie or invent a story so we could go out," she later confessed. "We were the first generation that was able to go out."[26]

What Lupe and her friends decided to do with their time, once they were freed from traditional obligations, reveals the important signposts that the youth of her generation observed in exploring their new cultural terrain. Like many of their peers, Lupe and her friends would take the Red Line downtown to one of their favorite haunts, the Orpheum Theater on 9th and Broadway. There at the Orpheum, or at the Million Dollar Theater at 3rd and Broadway or the All Nations Club on 1st and Main, they could catch Glenn Miller or Cab Calloway when they were in town.[27]

Since the 1930s Central Avenue had been steadily growing with the African American migration to southern California, when waves of black laborers left the South and migrated to the North and the West in the great southern diaspora. Los Angeles quickly became a mecca for jazz artists such as Coleman Hawkins, T-Bone Walker, and Zoot Sims, and West Coast jazz began to take form there.[28] Young aficionados would gravitate toward the clubs where these artists would play, among them white teenagers such as Art Pepper, Johnny Martizia, and Jimmy Henson, listening religiously for hours and hoping to get the chance to sit in on an after-hours jam session.

Central Avenue was more than a practicing ground for aspiring musicians. It was a curious place that attracted all kinds of wandering souls in search of entertainment or spiritual release and renewal. Surely the intensity of jazz performances, the artistry of musical expression, and the seemingly effortless freedom with which the musicians' souls found release in the mournful and celebratory sounds of jazz stood out in marked contrast to the social conformity celebrated by wartime society. Moreover, jazz musicians seemed to enjoy a special kind of camaraderie among themselves that defied the racial perimeters of the day. "Music has always been the same to me," recalled Lee Young. "It never had any color to me."[29] Thus, while black working folk were the life blood of Central Avenue, one would also find Filipinos, white middle-class rebels, or Mexican American teenagers like Henry and Lupe Leyvas hoping to catch sight of Louis Armstrong, Artie Shaw, or Glenn Miller.

The appeal that jazz music and life held for young people rippled through the community, for although jazz was primarily an African American art form, there was a growing market of devotees among young people of every shade. The clothing styles, linguistic inventions, and behavior, loosely known as jazz culture, framed the nascent youth culture.

Of all the points of social energy in Los Angeles that attracted young people as diverse as Lupe Leyvas, Johnny Veliotis, and Art Pepper to the same area, none was as significant as Central Avenue.[30] During the war Central Avenue was described as a West Coast 42nd Street. It was a place with its own creative and furtive air of artistic ferment that rode the music spilling out of the clubs and onto the street, mixing with the chatter of socializing couples and the ebb and flow of traffic. Within a two-block radius of 42nd and Central, musicians would float among the clustering of clubs, listening to one another play during long intermissions. The Club Alabam lay right off 42nd Street, across from Ivy Anderson's Chicken Shack. Next door to the Alabam was a small Mexican restaurant that was the favorite retreat for musicians to relax on the keyboard. The next door down was the Downbeat, and around the corner was the Ritz Club on Central and Vernon. Farther down the avenue was Jack's Basket, and the Hi-De-Ho was on 50th. To the west was the Crystal Tea Room over on Vernon, and on San Pedro were the

Avalon, the Zanzibar, the Twin Bells, the Barrelhouse, and the Last Word.[31] Even on their days off, many of the jazz musicians employed on Central would gravitate toward the area to relax in an impromptu jam session and enjoy the sights. "It was a sea of opulence, big hats and white fluffy fur," Art Pepper fondly remembered, "and the cars out front were real long Cadillacs with little mudguards, little flappy little things, shiny things."[32]

Such moments fed into the particular fascination that some middle-class whites had with these sites of black working life that were tantalizingly untethered from bourgeois mores. In compiling a tourist's guide to the city, the Federal Writer's Project gave a passing nod to the social areas frequented by people of color, a surprising inclusion for a day when the proper thing to do was to maintain a polite disregard for such goings-on. Describing the nightlife of Los Angeles, the guide book dutifully skips over the numerous nightclubs that catered to a predominantly minority clientele but tantalizingly acknowledges that "there is the honky-tonk area of Main Street and East 5th Street where semi-nude 'B-girls' have brought Los Angeles nationwide notoriety by way of national magazine articles."[33]

Although Central Avenue served as an important source of cultural ferment for many young people of Los Angeles, technology played an even greater role in carrying the musical influence of Central far beyond the confines of its geography. Many houses in the outlying districts of incorporated Los Angeles enjoyed few of the amenities of urban life, but virtually every home in Los Angeles had a radio, and it was through this medium that the syncopated melodies of jazz flowed into the living rooms, clubs, pool halls, and sweet shops of East Los Angeles. Most of the radio stations had yet to discover the youth market and therefore targeted their musical programs at an older audience. Yet some of the smaller stations carried radio programs featuring what was then known as "race music": the rhythms and sounds of African American artists. Los Angeles disc jockeys like Al Jarvis, Hunter Hancock ("Ol' H. H."), and "Huggy Boy" played the music of Central Avenue artists such as Eartha Kitt, Billy Eckstine, Dinah Washington, and Herb Jeffreys, along with the nationally known musicians such as Count Basie, Duke Ellington, Artie Shaw, and Charlie Barnet.[34]

Local disc jockeys served as emissaries of popular culture in hosting dances and dance contests throughout Los Angeles. Dances at El Monte Legion Stadium were popular gatherings where white, brown, and black teenagers engaged in a bodily dialogue of dance, molding, transforming, and reinventing popular dance styles in dance competitions. Out of these exchanges grew a dance step popular in East Los Angeles known as the Pachuco hop.[35]

The development of the Pachuco hop illustrates some of the important markers that Mexican American youths erected in mapping out their own cultural terrain.[36] The Pachuco hop found partial inspiration from the lindy hop, so named in the 1930s both in honor of Charles Lindbergh's "hop" across the Atlantic and because of the energetic dance steps that looked like a rapid succession of rhythmic hops. But from there the Pachuco hop deviated significantly from its point of origin among African Americans in the East. The energetic steps of the lindy, through which Malcolm X found emotional release during his zoot-suited days as "Detroit Red," were too much for adolescent Mexican American males.[37] Indeed, it was considered unmanly. Thus for Mexican Americans, the emphasis on improvisation was not equally shared by male and female partners, as it was among African American youths, but was separated along gender lines. Dance movement for the male partner was drastically reduced, and the emphasis was placed on his maintaining a cool and smooth demeanor while his partner demonstrated her dancing creativity and talent.[38] "Hobo was seen Booging [*sic*] at Happy Valley's weekly dance," reported a gossip sheet circulated for a nickel in the Alpine neighborhood of Los Angeles. "I might add that he had everybody amazed with his new fascinating steps that had everybody on edge . . . never knew [he] could dance so much like a girl."[39]

## La 38 St

The social life for the young people of "La 38 St" grew out of the relationships that they brought with them to the neighborhood, and weekly dances were one of the many activities that reinforced their ties to the community at large.[40] Given the similar background that José Díaz shared with many of the young people of 38th Street, it is no surprise that he had some interaction with the youths who lived there. José and Angel Padilla were both guests at Eleanor Coronado's birthday party the fateful night of his death.[41] Díaz furthermore worked with Joseph "Joey" Carpio and Eugene "Geney" Carpio, both of 38th Street, at the Sunny Sally Packing Plant.[42] Yet the five miles that separated the semirural home life of José Díaz from the working-class suburb of 38th Street was likely enough to keep him out of the immediate circle of young people associated with that neighborhood.

The physical and social geography of the city worked in close relationship with each other to influence the social composition of 38th Street. Freeways were yet to alter the physical landscape, and working people tended to settle the residential areas surrounding the factories and plants situated to the east and southeast of downtown Los Angeles where they were employed. If employment pulled working people into these areas, the social geography certainly pushed them there. Restrictive covenants designed to create "bourgeois utopias" formed all-white neighborhoods that fanned out largely to the west and southwest of Los Angeles, leaving parts of the city toward the center and the east to people of color and working-class whites.[43]

These low-cost areas, with homes squeezed onto small tracts of land, were designed to provide working families with at least a modest residential comfort. Developers in the 1920s, spurred by an antiurban ethos, built out rather than up and turned the outlying farms and orchards of the Los Angeles valley into neatly laid out parcels of low-income homes (remnants of the area's agricultural past can still be found in the orange and palm trees peeking over the tiled roofs of unassuming stuccoed homes on 38th Street).[44] These neighborhoods, far from the southern California idyll marketed by the Chamber of Commerce, were designed to house laborers. Just a few blocks to the east of 38th Street, smokestacks still tower over fruit-packing plants, factories, and stockyards, filling the air with the smells and sounds of factory work.

It was a residential comfort that was furthermore circumscribed by the limits of geography and society, especially for the young. Most homes had yards just large enough to park a car, and the streets served as better playgrounds by default. What few public recreational facilities that existed in the area were hardly adequate alternatives because "Mexicans" and African Americans were seldom considered full members of the public. The Los Angeles Police Department regularly patrolled public parks and broke up gatherings of minority youths, arresting those who defied them for loitering.[45]

Bus transportation provided an important means of escape for young people looking for places to relax unmolested by the white public. On weekends the Red Line gave to those who could afford it access to the downtown area. When they could get a ride by car, the reservoir at the Williams Ranch about five miles down Bandini Boulevard was a favorite place to swim. Most of the time, however, the young people of 38th Street tended to gather near the intersection of Vernon and Long Beach Boulevard, where the Dorkel movie theater, a malt shop, and the "Los Amigos" pool hall (also known as "Max's Social Club") were located.[46]

What held the young people of 38th Street together lies at the heart of the controversy over the death of José Díaz. Were these young women and men "baby gangsters" who organized for nefarious purposes, as the state of California later contended, or were they merely a casual grouping of acquaintances joined by circumstance? The answer is complicated because there was no consensus on what differentiated a gang from a group of friends, especially when the friends in question were working-class people of color. Yet law enforcement officials operated on the assumption that youth gangs could indeed be identified by their tattoos or uniforms, leadership hierarchies, gender-segregated organizations, and illicit activities. Following these guidelines, the LAPD estimated that upwards of fifty gangs of "Pachuco" delinquents existed during 1942.[47]

Measured against these standards, the young men and women of 38th Street were clearly not a gang. Rather than being members of all-male and all-female groups with distinct identities, the young women and men of 38th Street interacted freely with one another. They had no leadership hierarchy to speak of, no cash-flow operations, no initiation rites, uniforms, hand signs, or any other public displays of group membership.[48] Instead of the tightly organized gang of thugs the state tried to uncover in prosecuting the Sleepy Lagoon case, the kids of 38th Street were little more than a loose confederation of young people bound together by overlapping social networks developed at work and at school. Leadership, if it existed at all, was informal and circumstantial. At best there was a central core of young men and women around which other networks of friends and relatives interacted.

Indeed, many different threads tied the social fabric of their neighborhood together. School, for some, was one of the activities they shared in common. Angel Padilla and Henry Ynostroza both attended Jacob Riis High School with Henry Leyvas, Lupe's older brother and accused "ringleader" of the so-called 38th Street Gang. Henry regularly returned to 38th Street to visit his girlfriend, Dora Baca, after his family moved out of the neighborhood to Clearwater, just north of Long Beach. John Matuz and Robert "Bobby" Telles also held on to the friendships they made on 38th Street after having lived there for only a year. Jack Melendez, Ysmael "Smiles" Parra, and José "Chepe" Vasquez Ruíz were also outlanders of the group, but they nonetheless worked at Gillespie Furniture together with Gus Zamora, Joe Valenzuela, Angel Padilla, and Gene Carpio, all of whom lived in the 38th Street neighborhood. Each of these young men spent enough of their time at the Los Amigos Club, the theater, or the malt shop to be considered regular members of the social life of the neighborhood.

As a group they were really little different from many other young people of their day. Many of the young women of 38th Street grew up in traditional Mexican homes and were closely supervised. Some of the young women, like Lupe, found ways around these customs and would go downtown or hang out at the local malt shop. At times parents would allow a daughter to sit on the porch and visit with friends, listen to rhythm and blues on the radio, and practice the latest dance step.[49] Most of the young men volunteered for armed service or anticipated doing so with the eagerness of many young men their age. On their days off from work they spent the afternoons working on cars, perhaps catching a movie with their girlfriends, or playing pool with the other members of Los Amigos Club. Some of them, like Chepe, dreamed of taking their talent on the baseball field to the Major League, and Manny Reyes hoped to dance professionally and sing on the radio.[50]

The one characteristic they shared in common was their loyalty to one another, their neighborhood, and their community. Almost all the young women and men called as material witnesses steadfastly refused to implicate their friends, even after being rounded up by the police department and grilled by the Los Angeles County Grand Jury and the district attorneys. Sixteen-year-old Josephine Gonzales, for example, repeatedly refused to answer the prosecution's questions and frequently utilized her Fifth Amendment rights to do so.[51] Her younger sister Jennie further undermined the proceedings on the witness stand through her subtle refusal to assist the proceedings in any way. Despite repeated admonitions from the court and the prosecution to speak into the microphone, her answers were often inaudible. This failure to cooperate slowed the proceedings almost to a standstill while the prosecution and even the court were forced to repeat both the question and the answer to the court transcriber. When the younger Gonzales did use the microphone, her answers tended to be evasive, and she often blamed her poor memory. As the prosecution struggled for days to elicit usable responses from her, District Attorney Clyde Shoemaker resorted to having Gonzales read her earlier statements made to the grand jury. But she refused to pick up the transcript placed in front of her. "Why won't you answer?" Shoemaker finally shouted in frustration. "On the grounds that you may charge me for the murder of Joe Díaz like you done the boys," she yelled back.[52] Such resolve, however, did not earn the admiration of the state or the press, which took such behavior as evidence of a gang mentality.

The juvenile records of the 38th Street youths reveal none of the vile criminality that would later characterize their young lives in tabloids of Los Angeles. Although it is true that many of them would never find their face on the cover of the *Saturday Evening Post*, there is no evidence that they were involved in any level of organized criminal activity. What their records do reveal is that many of 38th Street youths — primarily males — were caught up in a cycle of petty criminality and supposed criminality that forever marked their lives.

Almost all the young men had police records. But six of the seventeen boys, about a third of the group, had records simply for being *suspected* of criminal activity. Twice, for example, eighteen-year-old Bennie Alvarez was picked up on suspicion of having stolen a car. The first time he was held for five hours and the second time for eighteen weeks—all this despite the fact that he owned the car in question. During one of these arrests, the officers slapped and pistol-whipped him with the butt of a gun. Another of the boys charged in the Sleepy Lagoon trial, Joseph Valenzuela, was once arrested for rioting and held in jail for seventy-two hours before being released, despite the fact that he was nowhere near the scene of the brawl. "That's what happens always," his mother reported. "There's a fight on the other side of town and they pick up all the boys and hold them and then let them go. The cops won't ever let the boys keep a job."[53] Being young and deemed a "Mexican" in Los Angeles was enough to be held on suspicion of criminal activity.

Some of the young men simply had records with the police as the result of domestic quarrels. When Manuel Reyes was twelve years old, his mother had him taken by a Catholic welfare agency for a year and a half for playing hooky from school. The same thing happened to Joseph Valenzuela when he was fifteen: his mother had him sent to a juvenile road camp for refusing to go to school. Later, when he was seventeen, he was arrested for driving without a license and had to serve ten days because his mother could not raise the money to pay his fine.

Standing up for their rights only added to their record and endangered their physical safety while in custody. Both Henry Leyvas and Henry Ynostroza earned reputations among the police for being obstinate, and members of the LAPD rewarded the resolve of these young men by regularly picking them up for crimes committed by an "unknown Mexican male." At times they were beaten by the arresting officers in order to obtain a confession or at least a lead on who the offender might be. As if this were not enough, the young men were usually released from custody late at night and forced to make their way back home through rival neighborhoods, miles away from where they lived.

This is not to suggest that all the young men of 38th Street lived lives unblemished by the commission of criminal acts. Some of them grew up in difficult circumstances and learned early in life about theft and battery. About a fourth of the group committed acts of robbery, assault with a deadly weapon, grand theft auto, or a combination of the three by the time they were eighteen. Henry Ynostroza ran away from home at the age of fifteen and, together with Angel Padilla, Seferino "Sef" Leyvas Jr., and Joe Carpio, was arrested for stealing the car they were driving. Three years later Ynostroza served eight days in jail for hitching a ride on a freight car. José "Chepe" Ruíz was also arrested at the age of fifteen for joyriding in a stolen car and served two weeks in a road camp. He was picked up four more times over the next three years for assault with a deadly weapon.

Thus theirs was a complicated relationship with society. The tragic reality of their young lives was that repeated confrontations with the LAPD simply became one of the strands woven into their adolescent experience. For many of the young men of 38th Street, doing time in juvenile hall for acts committed or allegedly committed was simply one of the rites of passage for young people growing up in Los Angeles. Banding together with their peers was one of the ways that they created for themselves "something out of the threads of nothing," to borrow from the words of Luís Rodríguez, but their means of survival became their damnation when the glare of public scrutiny turned upon them.[54] Their friendships would be turned into something ugly and criminal during the Sleepy Lagoon trial, and the court of public opinion would quickly brand them "hoodlums" and "gangsters."

### The Shadow of Death

The first of August 1942 began as most Saturdays did in the California summer, with little hint of the tragedy that would forever alter the lives of many families in the Mexican neighborhoods of Los Angeles. José Díaz, although quite lean for his age and height, had been recently certified for military duty, and he spent his last weekend before induction with his family in rural Los Angeles County.[55] Eleanor's parents, Amelio and Angela Delgadillo, who lived in the bunkhouse directly to the north of the Díaz family, spent that same Saturday cooking and preparing their modest home for a gathering of friends and family to celebrate their daughter Eleanor's twentieth birthday.[56] A few miles away in the working-class neighborhoods of Vernon, a group of friends from 38th Street gathered at Ross Snyder Park for a game of touch football.[57]

The birthday celebration that evening got off to a slow start. The Delgadillos had invited about thirty families to the party, but the four-piece band had to wait for nearly an hour before there were enough couples to play dance music.[58] Around nine o'clock neighbors and relatives began to trickle in, and most of the single young men like José spent their time drinking beer, socializing in small groups, and taking turns dancing with the Delgadillo sisters on the patio. Most of these single men, including some of the young men who lived a few miles away on 38th Street, were friends, coworkers, and neighbors of the Delgadillos.[59] By the time the party got under way, even at peak attendance men still outnumbered women two to one. The only incident that threatened to mar the celebration came during the band's intermission, around eleven o'clock. A group of about twenty unin-

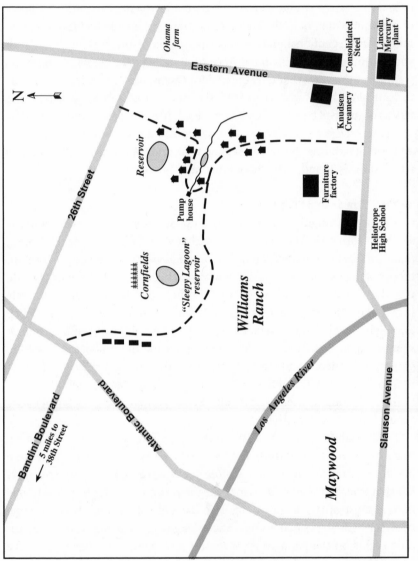

**Map 1. The Williams Ranch and the "Sleepy Lagoon" reservoir**

vited young Anglos from the neighboring town of Downey turned quarrel-some when the beer ran out.[60] They demanded that the hosts provide more beer, and the men of the party responded by promptly expelling the Downey boys from the party.[61]

The Downey boys angrily left the area, some swearing out threats of re-venge against the partygoers. About that same time, a mile and a half west of the Delgadillo home, two cars with young men and women from 38th Street pulled off Bandini Boulevard and turned onto a dirt road lit only by the full moon.[62] These cars did not continue along the rutted path that even-tually led to the Delgadillo home, however. Instead, they pulled off to the side of the winding road and parked around the small reservoir on the Wil-liams Ranch that by day served as a swimming hole and by night became the "Sleepy Lagoon" for lovers (see map 1).[63] Henry Leyvas was already there at the lagoon, sitting in his Ford with his girlfriend, Dora Baca, and with their friend Bobby Telles, all of whom knew one another through the overlapping social networks of the 38th Street neighborhood.[64]

This area of the Williams Ranch was well known to the young people of 38th Street, who dubbed it the "Sleepy Lagoon" after the song released in the early summer of 1942. For a simple watering hole the Sleepy Lagoon had an almost parklike feel to it. From the dirt road that wandered past the reservoir, a grassy area of about sixty feet gradually sloped upward to the earthen banks. A cement dike five feet high ringed the reservoir, providing water deep enough for swimming. To the northeast lay the field of corn that fed off the reservoir, and a grove of poplar and castor trees surrounding the circular pond provided shade from the sun. The natural shrubs and bushes of the area hid the clustering of homes that lay about a quarter of a mile to the east of the pond where the Delgadillos celebrated into the night.[65]

The young men and women who gathered at the lagoon that Saturday night sat in their cars talking, drinking, or necking.[66] Sixteen-year-old Jose-phine Gonzales sat with Jack Melendez and her fifteen year-old sister, Jen-nie, in the car closest to the dirt road. Henry remained in his green Ford with Dora. In the third car sat Johnny Matuz, Manny Delgado, Gilbert Mendoza, and Gus Zamora.[67] Bobby Telles stood nearby stretching his legs.[68]

Shortly after the last car from 38th Street arrived at the Sleepy Lagoon, three men in a Model A Ford came driving toward them from the direc-tion of the Delgadillos' party.[69] The car slowed as it neared the parked cars, long enough for the occupants to lean out and hurl drunken epithets in both Spanish and English.[70] Henry Leyvas, who could not turn down such a chal-lenge, leaned out of his car and responded in kind. When the car continued driving along the dirt path, Melendez, the Gonzales sisters, Matuz, Zamora, and Delgado paired off and strolled to various corners of the Sleepy Lagoon. Henry stayed behind in his car with Dora.

After about a half hour, the couples that had scattered into the dark recesses around the reservoir were startled by shouting and other noises that sounded like a fight in progress coming from where they had left their parked cars.[71] The tall poplar trees blocked out the full moon, so in the chiaroscuro lighting they were unable to see clearly what was going on.[72] Telling the girls to stay behind, the boys ran toward their cars and could see what looked to them to be about sixteen young men beating Henry and Dora as they tried to protect themselves.[73] "We will take you guys on any time you want to," one of them shouted in Henry's face, who was backed up against his car.[74] "Stop hitting him!" Dora screamed as she held on to Henry, trying to protect him with her body.[75]

The attack on Henry and Dora broke as their friends came running up from behind, but their intervention did little more than momentarily divert the fury of the mob.[76] About half a dozen young men seized Gilbert Mendoza, knocked him to the ground with clubs, kicked him several times, and then threw him in the water.[77] Bobby Telles also fell to the ground badly beaten with a beer bottle.[78] With half the group chasing after Manny Delgado and Gus Zamora, about five young men again returned to Henry and Dora, who had by now crawled into their car for protection. It did little good. Their assailants crawled in after them and continued to strike and kick the couple until one of their group pulled them off.[79]

Manny sprinted toward the cornfield to lose the three who were on his heels.[80] He ran for about twenty yards when one of them grabbed him by the foot and caused him to stumble into an irrigation ditch.[81] Muddied and wet, he picked himself up and continued running until he was well into the cornstalks.[82] "You guys think you're so tough!" one of the boys shouted as they threw a beer bottle and a tire iron after him.[83] Gus, who had also taken refuge in the cornfield, crawled over to where Manny was crouching, and they waited for their attackers to leave. After fifteen minutes they could hear someone calling after them but could not recognize the voice, so they remained in hiding for a few minutes longer. When they returned to their cars, they found that the young men who attacked them, whom Henry identified as the Downey gang, had already left the immediate area.[84]

For these friends from 38th Street, the gauntlet had been thrown, and there was little question what they would do next: they drove straight back to their neighborhood. They did not consider the assault on Henry and Dora to be Henry's problem alone but a problem that affected the entire group of young people associated with 38th Street. Why? The state of California later interpreted such a reaction as the product of gang mentality and believed that the youths' return to the Sleepy Lagoon en masse amounted to a conspiracy to commit murder. Yet there is no evidence that any of the 38th Street youths drove to the lagoon for that purpose. What is clear from their later testimonies, instead, is that they understood that the assault on Henry and Dora by a group required a group response. Clearly they could not let an assault on their peers go unpunished, but they were more likely outraged by the nature of the attack. Badly outnumbered, none of the boys stood a chance of defending themselves. Henry, furthermore, was convalescing from serious injuries he sustained in an automobile accident the previous week.[85] To make matters worse, in these boys' eyes, the young men who beat Leyvas also repeatedly struck Dora Baca on her arms, face, and back when she threw herself over Henry to protect him. Such an assault was an egregious violation of their fundamental sense of morality, and there was little debate or discussion about what had to be done next.[86]

More than a dozen young women and men were socializing in front of Bertha Aguilar's house on 42nd Street when Bobby Telles drove up with Henry and Dora beside him.[87] Few words needed to be said; all three of them were bruised and bloodied, and Dora was still sobbing on Henry's chest.[88] Henry told the group that crowded around the car that they had been beaten up by the boys from Downey, a neighboring suburb. "Right off the bat," Bertha later testified, "the boys said 'Let's go out there.'"[89] News of the assault traveled quickly around the neighborhood through the teenage grapevine. In a short time a convoy of six cars crammed with angry young people met two blocks away in the parking lot of Los Amigos Club, where Jenny and Josephine Gonzales, Jack Melendez, Johnny Matuz, Gus Zamora, and Manny Delgado were waiting in their two cars.[90] Most of the young people who gathered that night lived on or around 38th Street, but a significant number consisted of friends or relatives who were visiting in the area. Only a few were specifically recruited to fight. In all, about twenty-two young men and thirteen young women, six of them African American friends of Henry Leyvas's, gathered to drive out to the Williams Ranch.[91]

What they would do once they arrived at the Sleepy Lagoon was hardly premeditated. There was little deliberation, no threats breathed against the young men from Downey; nor did anyone give thought to articulating a plan of action once they arrived at the reservoir. Their only topic of discussion, if it was even a discussion, was the retelling of what had happened at the

Sleepy Lagoon from one person to the next. What unfolded next at the Williams Ranch was, for the most part, the result of spontaneous actions by different clusters of young people within the group.

The impending tragedy that would forever alter their young lives almost never occurred at all. Eight cars with close to forty young people left the parking lot of Los Amigos Club at 12:30 A.M., paused momentarily at a gas station, and then drove straight to the Sleepy Lagoon.[92] When they arrived, there was no one in sight. The night would have ended without further incident if someone had not suggested that the Downey boys might be found at the party going on in the cluster of bunkhouses farther down the road.[93] With that suggestion several of the boys climbed on the running boards of the three lead cars, leaving about half the group behind at the reservoir. As they proceeded to drive up the road to the Delgadillo home, Henry called out: "Turn off all your lights, except mine, so they will think there is just one car coming."[94]

By one o'clock in the morning almost all the guests had gone home or were in the process of going home, including José Díaz. The night was still young for the Delgadillo girls, who wanted to continue dancing, so they moved their Victrola radio onto the patio and turned up some dance music.[95] Victoria Delgadillo began dancing with a neighbor, Dominic Manfredi, and Josephine "Lola" Delgadillo Reyes danced with her husband, Cruz.[96] The parents turned their attention toward cleaning up the house, and a small cluster of young men gathered outside the fence, smoking cigarettes.

Just as one of the songs ended, two young women who were standing farther down the road waiting for their rides came running back up to the house. "Here come a lot of boys," one of them shouted. "They have sticks!" warned the other.[97] Several cars full of young men and women from 38th Street drove up to the Delgadillo home, and some of the boys began throwing bottles and bricks at the partygoers standing outside the fence, scattering them up toward the house.[98] Henry Leyvas and six young men from 38th Street purposefully strode up to the fence and stopped at the gate.[99] "Where are the boys that said they were going to beat us up?" he demanded to no one in particular. "There is nobody here," responded a puzzled Eleanor Coronado. "Everybody gone home."[100]

Something about Cruz Reyes, Coronado's brother-in-law, who stood behind her, caught Leyvas's gaze. Reyes may have resembled one of the boys from Downey who had attacked Leyvas earlier that night, he may have reached for something to use as a weapon in case of a fight, or he may have simply looked too menacingly at Leyvas. Whatever the reason, Leyvas brushed passed Coronado with his eyes locked on Reyes while Ysmael

"Smiles" Parra and others from 38th Street moved in behind Leyvas as backup. "Vicky, get into the house!" Dominic Manfredi shouted to Victoria Delgadillo as he stumbled over a chair trying to run for protection.[101]

Bedlam erupted. Leyvas swung at Cruz Reyes, and Lola Reyes rushed toward her husband to defend him. One of Henry's punches sent Lola sprawling backward on the ground, unconscious.[102] Delia Parra, Smiles's wife, rushed through the gate as Eleanor Coronado grabbed a beer bottle and raised it to strike Smiles Parra from behind. "You can't hit my old man like that!" she shouted and grabbed Coronado. Smiles turned around and saw the two women grappling with the bottle. "My wife!" he cried out and knocked Coronado to the ground with a blow to her face.[103] Delia's friends from 38th Street piled on top of Coronado as she slashed the bottle wildly with one hand and pulled clumps of hair with the other. Eleanor's sisters also rushed to her aid, and one of the girls from 38th Street was slashed on her leg during the frenzy.[104] The other boys and girls from 38th Street began to vandalize the cars belonging to the partygoers outside the Delgadillo home, smashing windows or shooting at the tires with a .22 rifle.[105]

Dominic Manfredi confronted Manny Delgado, who arrived with the young people from 38th Street, and demanded to know what they wanted. "What [are you] going to do about it?" Delgado snapped as he slugged Manfredi in the stomach.[106] Manfredi stumbled back and ran toward the house, with Smiles, Henry, and Manny close after him.[107]

Others were not as quick to get away. Remedios Parra (no relationship to Smiles) broke from the fight and tried to run up the road to safety.[108] Gus Zamora chased after him and caught Parra after he collapsed to the ground near some power poles. Chepe Ruíz ran up, called Henry Ynostroza over to help, and began to pummel Parra relentlessly, first with his fists and then with a rock. "Don't hit me anymore!" Remedios pleaded in Spanish. "Please, God in Heaven, I didn't have anything to do with it!"[109] Henry Ynostroza and Genie Carpio were the last to come running up, and the four took turns holding Parra up and knocking him to the ground.[110] Finally, when they grew tired of pulling Parra to his feet, Ruíz began to jump on top of him.[111] Still not sated by this merciless violence, Ruíz then picked up a three-foot-long two-by-four and began to beat the unconscious Parra. Bobby Thompson finally ran up to stop Ruíz. "Let him alone!" Thompson shouted in Ruíz's face. "Can't you see he's on the ground?" "Let me at him!" Ruíz shouted back and shoved Thompson aside. Gus Zamora wrenched the club out of Ruíz's hands, however, and threw it into the weeds.[112]

Just as the fighting exploded with screams and shouts, Amelio Delgadillo rushed out of the bathroom and to the doorway with his wife, Angela, to see what was the matter. "Coward!" he shouted out as he witnessed Smiles Parra striking his daughter Eleanor. Delgadillo rushed toward Parra, who swung around and knocked the elder man back through the kitchen door with a blow to the face.[113] Dominic Manfredi scrambled into the bedroom for fear that the boys would enter the house, and as he turned at the doorway, he saw the Delgadillo sisters, Josephine and Eleanor, grappling with three or four boys.[114]

The violence ended almost as quickly as it began. Someone yelled out that the police were coming, and the crowd of young people from 38th Street retreated to their cars and drove away in haste.[115] Dominic Manfredi came out of the bedroom when the noise died down and found Amelio Delgadillo lying on the kitchen floor with blood streaming down the sides of his face. The Delgadillo sisters staggered into the house, and when they saw their father on the floor, they crowded around him in tears, fearing the worst. Fortunately he revived after Dominic threw water on his face.[116] Eleanor then turned to Manfredi to tell him that his older brother Joe had been hurt. When Dominic ran outside the bunkhouse, he encountered Cruz Reyes, who was already half-carrying Joe Manfredi through the gate.[117] "Joe, you are— you look pretty bad," he exclaimed to his wounded brother.[118]

It was around that time, as the Delgadillos and the remaining guests began to search the grounds for others who may also have been hurt, that they found José Díaz lying face up in the middle of a rutted dirt road with his pockets turned inside out (see map 2).[119]

The ride back to 38th Street was anything but a triumphal celebration of revenge. It was a grim and silent journey back to Los Amigos Club, one that was punctuated by the uncontrollable sobs of Betty Zeiss and a curt "shut up!" from her peers.[120] "We didn't say anything because we were scared as hell," Andrew Acosta later confided.[121] As the group milled about the parking lot of Los Amigos Club, there were some hushed whispers about the brutal beating Chepe gave some man and that Henry Leyvas "cut" a couple of guys.[122] Only Chepe Ruíz seemed in high spirits, bragging about his deeds with an eerily nervous pitch in his voice.[123] Henry Leyvas brooded beside a car while nursing a beer as Frances Silva and Ann Kalustian attended to the wounds that Bertha Aguilar and Delia Parra sustained in the fight.[124]

At the Williams Ranch, Lino Díaz anxiously stood near the main road to flag down the ambulance and then rode in the back with his brother the forty-five minutes it took to get to Los Angeles General Hospital. The entire time José was in a semiconscious state and able to answer only few questions. They arrived at the hospital just past three o'clock in the morning, and the attending physician diagnosed José with a cerebral concussion, noting

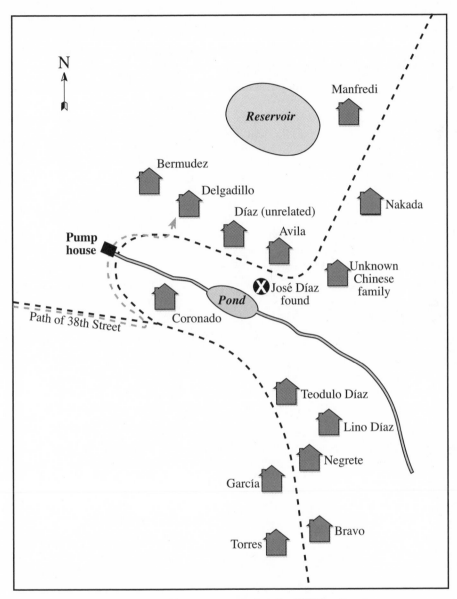

**Map 2. The bunkhouse compound at the Williams Ranch**

that on his face was an abrasion with a large swelling just above his nose and that he was still bleeding from inside his left ear. On his body were two stab wounds near his diaphragm and at the bottom of his breastbone, and a finger of his left hand was broken.[125]

An hour and a half after he entered the hospital, José Díaz quietly died.[126]

# PART II
# LA VIDA DURA

# 4 : *The People v. Zammora et al.*

he police investigation of the death of José Díaz was plagued by fundamental assumptions about race and class that ultimately skewed the evidence against the twenty-two accused young men. While personality conflicts undermined the team of defense attorneys assembled to represent the defendants, *The People v. Zammora et al.* took on political importance for law enforcement agencies in Los Angeles, and the district attorney's office became heavily invested in prosecuting the case against the 38th Street youths.[1] The death of José Díaz occurred during a particular historical moment in Los Angeles, when public confidence in the ability of the reduced wartime police force to maintain the peace was undermined by civil unrest. Especially in working-class areas of the city, respect for the wartime police force was alarmingly low, and the residents of these areas openly challenged the authority of the police.

The Los Angeles Police Department was already in the process of substantial reorganization since the 1938 election of Fletcher Bowron, who ran on a platform promising to reform corruption in the city government and police department. Edward Escobar argues that Bowron's election prompted not only widespread change in police leadership but also a recasting of the LAPD's role as a law enforcement agency. The LAPD embraced a policy that moved the Los Angeles police from being a reactive enforcer of the law to a proactive one. This move toward preventive enforcement engendered a type of racial profiling that led to newer and harsher relations with the racialized minorities of Los Angeles, the majority of whom were Mexican or of Mexican descent.[2]

If the professionalization of the LAPD led to more aggressive law enforcement in Mexican neighborhoods, a mandate from the governor to "eliminate youth gangs" wrapped the investigation into Díaz's death with newfound political significance. The Los Angeles County District Attorney's Office and law enforcement personnel seized upon the investigation as a critical moment in which to launch a public-relations offensive with a widely publicized crackdown on juvenile delinquency. Law enforcement officials assembled files on suspected gang members, coordinated men and matériel, and combed the Eastside of Los Angeles, where mostly working-class people of color lived. The combined actions of the police and sheriffs proudly netted hundreds of arrests during the summer of 1942.

As *The People v. Zammora et al.* carried over into the winter months of 1942, the trial unfolded within the larger public discourse on youth, race, and violence. Mainstream newspapers and tabloid-style magazines exploited the public fascination with juvenile delinquency, all the while feeding the growing perception that working-class youths were caught up in a zoot-suited crime wave sweeping the city. The defense attorneys clashed among themselves as they were forced to contend with growing public hostility toward their case and their defendants. Furthermore, the trial of the twenty-two defendants played out on a discursive field littered with unchallenged assumptions, words, and coded phrases that highlighted to their disadvantage their self-conscious fashioning of difference.

In the end, the seventeen young men who were convicted of murdering José Díaz were not the only ones who were made to pay the price for his death. Hundreds of innocent young men and women from central and eastern Los Angeles were rounded up during this period, fingerprinted, and booked. It was a show of force designed to reassure the white middle class that the wartime police force was indeed capable of maintaining law and order among working-class youth, who were too poor, too dark-skinned, or too aesthetically different for a mainstream Los Angeles preoccupied with wartime security and conformity to understand.

### Fundamental Assumptions

Stories of police beatings, threats, and manipulations in order to elicit "confessions" from arrested suspects were commonplace in the pre–Warren Court era of law enforcement—and even more so in East Los Angeles.[3] Eighteen-year-old Angel Padilla related that when he arrived at the Firestone substation, he was ushered into a room, seated, and then surrounded by a group of policemen who fired questions at him.[4] Padilla refused to cooperate, and the police began to slap and punch him. One blow knocked him out of the chair, and an officer reportedly snarled: "Sit down so we can hit you some more." The frightened Padilla returned to his chair, and the offending officer continued: "You Mexicans think you are smart; you guys never fight fair." "We ought to shoot every Mexican dog like you," snapped another.[5]

Such threats and epithets underscore two important things about the context of the investigation. First, some law enforcement personnel in East

Los Angeles clearly felt a racialized animosity toward those whom they were to "protect and serve." Second, the use of violence in police work was considered necessary—no doubt even "fair"—when certain police dealt with minority youths. Indeed, some of the Mexican American deputy sheriffs themselves held the arrested youth in open contempt. "You had better talk, you bastard, or we are going to fuck you up," Deputy Sheriff Miguel Gallardo snarled at Joseph Valenzuela in Spanish, while Deputy Sheriff Raymond T. Hopkinson slapped the frightened youth. "You're not so tough around here when you haven't got a gang," Hopkinson shouted, calling Valenzuela a "cholo" and a "dirty Mexican."[6]

Many law enforcement officials surely agreed with the views of Lieutenant Edward Duran Ayres of the Los Angeles County Sheriff's Department when he testified before the 1942 Los Angeles County Grand Jury.[7] Because "one cannot change the spots of a leopard," Ayres argued, Mexican American youths in 1942 shared the same "total disregard for human life" that the Aztecs displayed in performing human sacrifices. "All he knows and feels is a desire to . . . kill, or at least to let blood," Ayres said of Mexican American delinquents. He then concluded his testimony by observing that "whenever the Mexican element receives swift and sure punishment . . . he then, and only then, respects authority."[8] Captain Vernon Rasmussen of the LAPD Homicide-Subversive Bureau shared many of the same views. He expressed frustration to the grand Jury that too many Mexican American youths were being released on parole rather than doing hard time. Such leniency, Rasmussen assured the jury, only hardened delinquents and made the American judicial system look "like a joke." Rasmussen also concluded that only swift and harsh punishment for "the Mexican element" would deter youths from developing attitudes "exactly contrary to [those] adopted by the respectable Caucasian element."[9]

Thus the experiences of Angel Padilla and Joseph Valenzuela were not unique. In all, Benny Alvarez, Eugene Carpio, Manuel Reyes, Lupe Leyvas, and Henry Leyvas each came forward with corroborating accounts of harsh treatment while incarcerated.[10] So ponderous, in fact, was the collective weight of their testimony that the assistant district attorney suspended his line of questioning during the trial to put Deputy Sheriffs Gallardo and Hopkinson; Lloyd Emerson of the *Los Angeles Herald-Examiner* (said to be present during the interrogations); William L. Drumm, teletype operator for the sheriff's office; and Chief Clem Peoples on the witness stand.[11] All of them denied either having struck the boys or knowing of anyone else who did so. Frustrated by such denials, Anna Zacsek, attorney for Henry Leyvas, insisted that she be allowed to take the witness stand to testify that she found Leyvas in the room where police were questioning him, slumped forward in a semiconscious state, with his shirt dappled from the blood and saliva that fell from his swollen lips and bleeding nose. Judge Fricke overruled her request, citing that it would be improper for a defense attorney to take the witness stand in her own case.[12]

*Police Brutality*

Such were the troubled beginnings of the state's investigation into the death of José Díaz. The handling of the investigation by Los Angeles law enforcement agencies complicated matters rather than clarified them and at times skewed the justice system to the detriment of the accused. "I told [Clem Peoples] 'yes, yes' to all the questions he asked me," Angel Padilla later confessed to Judge Fricke. "I just told him 'yes' [but] they were all lies . . . everything I said to every police officer was a lie . . . except my name, address; all the rest of it were lies."[13] For those who refused to cooperate with the investigation, the police forced "confessions" out of them either through manipulations or outright coercion. Police rewarded those who continued to resist by holding them incommunicado, even from their lawyers, until they came forward with information. Some of the boys who were considered to be "problems" were booked under a different name, which effectively prolonged their time in jail because it frustrated attempts to locate them.[14]

The district attorney's initial handling of the investigation furthermore set the stage for how the case would be perceived by the public and eventually prosecuted in court. The 1942 Los Angeles County Grand Jury had already convened to investigate the problem of youth gangs, and it was there that José Díaz was officially introduced into the public discourse as the victim of gang violence.[15] The district attorney's office built its case on a fairly straightforward reading of the evidence: a group of young people were involved in what seemed to be a coordinated attack, many of the boys in that group were minority youths with police records, and a young man was found dying after the "gang" departed from the area. Only two jurors spoke out during the proceedings to challenge these fundamental assumptions—Charlotta Bass, editor of the black-owned newspaper *California Eagle* and the first African American woman to serve on a Los Angeles County Grand Jury, and Harry Braverman—but their protests failed to sway the other jurors, who resolutely supported a formal indictment along gender lines against the the young men of 38th Street.[16]

Although there was clear evidence that the girls were heavily involved in the fight at the Williams Ranch, the grand jury recommend charges only against the young men in the alleged murder of José Díaz. The use of violence is often viewed as a defining instrument of masculinity, but both young men and women appear to have shared a common view about its necessity. Young women were equal combatants with young men in the fight at the Delgadillo home, and they did not limit their responses to their respective genders. After Henry Leyvas threw the first punch at Cruz Reyes, Lola Reyes rushed Leyvas in defense of her husband, as did Delia Parra when Eleanor Coronado attempted to strike Smiles from behind with a beer bottle. Before the fight ended, most of the women from both parties were locked with one another in physical struggle. "You didn't mess with them," remembered Henry Ynostroza about several women of 38th Street; "they could fight like a man." His comment came as neither a condemnation nor a lament but respected praise. This was, perhaps, the reason that none of the 38th Street youths, both male and female, seemed particularly disturbed that Henry Leyvas and Smiles Parra struck the Delgadillo women.

Such reactions toward the use of violence suggest a larger sense of self shared by the young men and women of this generation. The young women of 38th Street were far more assertive in the public sphere than the idealized Mexican woman was expected to be, and evidence suggests that young women from other neighborhoods shared similar views about themselves. It was the familiar lament among Mexican men about the baneful effects of Americanization on Mexican women, that they became too assertive and too brazen in the United States. Yet if Tomás Almaguer is correct, that even in the United States Mexican American families remain "rigidly structured along patriarchal lines that privilege men over women and children," then how the young women of 38th Street and other neighborhoods acted outside the home reveals not simply the effects of Americanization but willful and self-conscious choices of agency in a new and different environment.[17] The encouragement and respect they received from their male counterparts also suggests that the gendered identities of the wartime generation were less rigidly "feminine" or "masculine" than those prescribed by the dominant values of Mexican and American tradition. Consistent with the *mestizaje* aesthetic revealed through street culture, they created gendered identities that were more fluid, experimental, and responsive to the needs at hand.

Although the state may not have been able to build a sufficiently compelling case against the young women of 38th Street to charge them with murder, it is also likely that the police, the court, and the jurors were unwilling to consider the women as full and equal agents in the events given the normative gender constructions of the day. Certainly such a view was consistent with the discursive construction of the Pachuca as an "unwilling neophyte" in Pachuco debauchery. Such assumptions surely underwrote the gendered ways in which the investigation and trial proceeded. Although the

Young women from 38th Street stand in a lineup after the police dragnet.
Left to right: Betty Ziess, Ann Kalustian, Frances Silva, unknown, Lorena Encinas,
Dora Barrios, Josefina "Josephine" Gonzales, and Juanita "Jennie" Gonzales.
(Herald Examiner Collection, Los Angeles Public Library)

young women of 38th Street endured untold suffering and humiliation in being held as state's evidence and in being sent to juvenile hall after the trial, they were never beaten for their confession, charged, tried, convicted, or sentenced as conspirators in the death of José Díaz. Just as members of the law enforcement agencies believed Mexicans to be biologically predisposed toward violence, it appears that they also believed that Mexican men were a greater social danger than women and that the grand jury agreed.

As the grand jury moved toward a conclusion, the parents of the arrested youths read the writing on the wall and began to secure legal representation for their children as best they could. Most of the families could not afford a lawyer, so Richard F. Bird, deputy public defender, drew the assignment to represent six of the twenty-two boys, about a fourth of the group. The rest of the families pooled their meager incomes together and hired whom they could afford. On the opening day of the trial seven lawyers gathered to defend the boys. The parents of Gus Zamora, Robert Peña, Benny Alvarez, and Jack Melendez hired Attorney Phillip Schutz; Ben Van Tress agreed to represent Chepe Ruíz, Ysmael "Smiles" Parra, Angel Padilla, and John Matuz on behalf of the Mexican consul (Ruíz was a Mexican national); Anna Zacsek defended Henry Leyvas, Victor Segobia, and Edward Grandpré; Manny Delgado's parents hired Anthony Coviello; Harry Hunt represented Joe Herrera and Lupe Orosco; and the parents of Danny Verdugo and Joe and Eugene Carpio hired David Ravin.[18]

The defense was less a coordinated team than it was a gathering of seven lawyers each hoping to prove their respective clients' innocent.[19] Harry Hunt successfully appealed to have the case against Joe Herrera and Lupe Orosco tried separately. The rest of the defense failed to come up with a joint strategy and at times disagreed so strongly among themselves that their bickering carried over into the courtroom.[20] What complicated their coordination was the differing level of courtroom skills and experience each lawyer brought to the trial.[21] Anthony Coviello was a retired policeman turned lawyer with so little courtroom experience that he rarely spoke, and only hesitantly when he did. Anna Zacsek, a Hungarian-born former silent film actress who, under the stage name Olga Grey, had a supporting role in *Birth of a Nation*, often relied on her dramatic talents and personal flair to make up for what she lacked in legal skills.[22] Other, more experienced attorneys such as Richard Bird and Ben Van Tress, on the other hand, were wary of these lawyers, and some of the men may have even resented Zacsek's assertive courtroom presence.[23]

The pretrial publicity was unsympathetic to the accused, as a number of historians have pointed out, but between news from the war front, Holly-

Dora Barrios, Frances Silva, and Lorena Encinas, dressed in prison attire, await trial. (Herald Examiner Collection, Los Angeles Public Library)

Young men from 38th Street ring the trial room for their arraignment. Seated in front of them are attorneys Anna Zacsek, Philip Schutz, and Richard Bird. (Herald Examiner Collection, Los Angeles Public Library)

wood sex scandals, and local events, the "boy wars" and weekend brawls among teenagers rarely made the front page. Instead, the reports of the grand jury investigation and subsequent trial were, for the most part, relegated to short, unassuming articles.[24] Sensational stories about love triangles, divorces, murder-suicides, and a host of other scandals that daily occupied the front pages of the major newspapers made better copy and sold more newspapers. The public was simply far more interested in the titillating details of Errol Flynn's alleged sexual trysts with underaged girls than in the fate of twenty-two working-class boys from East Los Angeles.[25]

### The Judge

*The People v. Zammora* became "the first heavy gun fired in the war on youthful gangsters" in Los Angeles when, in early October 1942, the bailiff of the Los Angeles County Superior Court called the session to order and the trial formally began.[26] Judge Charles Williams Fricke drew the assignment to preside over the case.

Small and wan, he looked prematurely old for a man of sixty years.[27] Fricke distinguished himself at an early age, despite his frail health, as a legal scholar. By the time he was twenty-one, he obtained an L.L.M., J.D., and L.L.D. from New York University and then practiced law for a short while in New York before returning home to Milwaukee. There he served as district attorney and became a municipal judge before relocating to Los Angeles as part of the generation of conservative midwesterners who flooded southern California in the early twentieth century.[28] He resumed his career as a prosecutor in the Los Angeles County District Attorney's Office and rose to the rank of chief trial deputy, aided, in large part, by a successful publishing career as a legal scholar. In 1925 Fricke wrote the *Manual of Criminal Law and Procedure for Peace Officers*, which would undergo five reprintings by the time he presided over *The People v. Zammora*. In 1926 he published *Outlines of California Criminal Procedure*, and the following year he wrote *California Criminal Law*. Governor C. C. Young appointed Fricke to the California bench in 1927, and Fricke continued to publish well-received books on California law while on the bench.[29] As a judge, Fricke continued along the same philosophical trajectory that he established as a prosecutor. Not only did he earn a reputation for favoring the prosecution during his twenty-five years as a judge in Los Angeles, but he also earned the nickname "San Quentin Fricke" for having sent more people to San Quentin State Prison than any other judge in California history.[30]

The first test between the defense and the prosecution in *The People v. Zammora* certainly seemed to uphold his reputation as a prosecutor's judge.

Seating all twenty-two boys and seven lawyers proved to be a logistical nightmare for the courtroom, and Judge Fricke finally ordered the boys to sit alphabetically in two rows of chairs at the side of the courtroom, while their lawyers remained at the defense table.[31] Fricke acknowledged the objections raised by the defense to this highly unusual arrangement, but he assured the attorneys that such an arrangement did not deprive the boys of a fair trial because they would still be able to consult with their clients during breaks and at day's end. The defense had little choice but to comply.

Yet Fricke was not entirely unsympathetic to the defense, either. Numerous times throughout the three-month-long trial he tutored some of the less experienced defense lawyers in proper courtroom procedures. On one occasion the prosecution challenged Anna Zacsek's cross-examination on the grounds that she was asking the witness for hearsay. Fricke agreed but encouraged her to reformulate her question. "I do not see how I can get at it in another way," Zacsek finally admitted. "I am sorry," Fricke responded; "I could not very well coach you from the sidelines." She posed the question again, and again the prosecution objected. Finally, Fricke intervened for the defense: "If I understand the question, perhaps I can reach it. In a number of these statements . . . did they not [testify] that Henry Leyvas had gotten into some difficulty up to the lagoon?" "Oh, yes, that is right," the witness responded.[32] Fricke also worked patiently with young witnesses hesitant to testify and even made an effort to be sympathetic to the linguistic challenges some of the witnesses faced in having to testify in English.[33] He also warned the defendants, at least once, about their flippant behavior in court. Once, after he noticed that Joe Carpio appeared to be grimacing and making faces at the jurors, Judge Fricke counseled Carpio's lawyer at the end of the day. "It doesn't do anybody any good and may unconsciously do somebody a great deal of harm," he said, urging the attorney to caution his client.[34]

### The Prosecution

Opposite the defense sat two experienced prosecutors, Assistant District Attorneys Clyde Shoemaker and John Barnes, who followed a simple strategy in quickly laying out the evidence of the case. Bert McAtee, deputy county surveyor for Los Angeles County, was the first witness called to the stand in order to establish the physical setting of the Sleepy Lagoon area with maps and graphs. Teodulo Díaz and Lino Díaz, father and brother of José, respectively, came next in order to give the jury an appreciation for the life of José Díaz. Then Frank Webb, chief autopsy surgeon for Los Angeles County, was called to establish the cause of death.

Shoemaker and Barnes expected to reconstruct the events of the fight and establish a link between the accused and the deceased by calling to the witness stand a succession of young women from the Delgadillo party and from 38th Street. Fifteen-year-old Juanita (Jennie) Gonzales, sixteen-year-old Betty Zeiss (also known as Betty Nuñez), Ann Kalustian (also known as Ann Cummings), sixteen-year-old Josephine Gonzales (sister of Juanita Gonzales), fourteen-year-old Bertha Aguilar, and eighteen-year-old Dora Barrios were all subpoenaed to tell what they saw the night of the fight at the Williams Ranch.[35] But the prosecution encountered an unexpected snag in its attempts to weave a seamless case, however, in the bonds of friendship that tied the youths of 38th Street to one another.

Most of the girls refused to implicate the boys and subverted the trial proceedings or defied the court outright.[36] Some of the girls openly contested the basic premise of the prosecution's case: that the young people of 38th Street were an organized gang. Ann Kalustian testified that the 38th Street gang was "not really a gang, as I know of," and she refuted the notion that the Los Amigos Club was any kind of gang headquarters.[37] She did concede that other kids referred to their group as the "38th Street Gang" but denied that they used it as a specific name for themselves.[38] Shoemaker continued to press her on the issue: Were the 38th Street youths a *gang*? "How am I supposed to answer as to this man?" she finally retorted. "How am I supposed to know if it is a gang? It has not been organized or anything; no one has told me 'this is a gang and I am the leader.'"[39] On cross-examination defense attorney Richard Bird asked, "Does the word '38th Street gang' mean anything to you at all?" "It means just a group of kids that are known to each other and run around with each other that live in that district," Kalustian answered. "I mean, if kids from a different neighborhood ask me where I am from, I will say '38th,' because that is the group I run around with."[40]

Undeterred, the prosecution pressed on with its basic presumption by continually referring to the "the 38th Street gang" throughout the trial. There is no evidence that the district attorney's office was aware of or informed about the current sociological research regarding gangs and juvenile delinquency. It did not really matter if it was. The state needed the 38th Street kids to be a gang in order to promote *The People v. Zammora* as a major strike against youth gangs in Los Angeles.[41] Thus the prosecution spent very little time establishing just what actually defined a juvenile gang. It was simply a given that the young people of 38th Street were gang members.

From this reading of the evidence Shoemaker and Barnes sought to prove that this so-called gang had both motive and opportunity to kill José Díaz. They made short work of establishing that many of the young people of 38th

**Eleanor Delgadillo Coronado takes the witness stand to testify in**
*People v. Zammora.* **(Herald Examiner Collection, Los Angeles Public Library)**

Street were alarmed by the attack on Henry and Dora and that they returned en masse to the lagoon to have it out with the boys from Downey. With this admission from many of the participants in the fight, the prosecution sought to prove that the subsequent actions of the 38th Street youths proved that they conspired to commit murder. "Anyone would know," the prosecution asserted, "that the reasonable result to be expected from an attack by a mob of this temper, armed as they were and seeking vengeance, would be bound in all probability to take human life."[42]

To support its case further against the 38th Street youths, the prosecution tried in vain to establish who was the leader of the gang. Few of the witnesses, however, could provide the prosecution with the answer it was looking for. The prosecutors believed that the witnesses hid this critical piece of information behind a code of silence, which was taken as further evidence of gang behavior. The fact of the matter is that the young people of 38th Street simply did not conceive of themselves as a gang.

Yet the prosecutors pushed onward, hoping to uncover in the history and dynamics of the group what they presumed was being hidden by the witnesses. There were a number of boys of 38th Street who could have easily filled the role of the leader. Smiles Parra was older, methodical, and fearless; Chepe Ruíz had a wild streak but was charming and stylish; Angel Padilla was cunning and edgy, but he was not without his own appeal. None of them, however, commanded the attention of the police and prosecution like Henry Leyvas.[43]

Henry was a fighter. The eyebrows and nose that framed a pair of intense dark eyes had been blunted by years of fighting for honor, for protection, for survival. Like his peers, only more so, Henry was not about to let slights, real or imagined, go unpunished, and for this he was on a collision course with the law. Yet still, underneath his coarsened facade, he had a certain charisma about him, a raw charm undimmed by the weight of growing up in the American underclass.[44] "He was a natural leader," Ben Margolis later recalled of Henry. "The same person, under different circumstances . . . would have moved toward leadership. He was very bright, not much education; he had great emotions. But most important was . . . that of all of them, he had the greatest sense that he was a member of a group that was being walked on, being discriminated against, and that he was going to fight against it . . . he was going to carry on the fight wherever he was . . . regardless of what would happen to him, he was totally courageous and [showed] no physical fear as far as you could tell."[45] "Henry was a powerful presence," Alice McGrath also remembered of him, "and he had a sense of pride that went into, through, and beyond *machismo* . . . he knew how Mexicans [were] viewed and . . . how *he* was viewed, [and] that made Henry angry, defensive, short-fused."[46]

Some of the boys called to the witness stand challenged the prosecution and scoffed at the notion that Henry was their leader. "Does Henry Leyvas have a reputation among the gang there as being a leader?" Shoemaker asked Gus Zamora. "A lot of guys don't pay any attention to him," Zamora responded.[47] Yet the prosecution continued to press its contention that Henry was the leader of the gang, no doubt because of his personal charisma and the role he played in leading the assault on the Delgadillo party.

The personal strengths that earned Henry a measure of respect among his peers did not translate well in the courtroom. He was wholly unprepared for the limelight suddenly thrust upon him as the trial gained publicity, and he unwittingly played into the popular perception that the 38th Street youths were little more than "mad-brained young wolves."[48] A photographer caught Henry—who was unaccustomed to the attention and notoriety that police, lawyers, and reporters were paying him—trying to cover his nervous laughter with his hand over his mouth. The resulting photograph showed a young Mexican man, with long, unwashed hair and unkempt clothing, apparently smirking at the proceedings. "Ring leader of the blood-thirsty mob," blazed the caption in *Sensation* magazine, "smirking Henry Leyvas stands accused of dealing fatal blows in murder."[49]

### George Shibley and the Defense

Despite the growing public hostility toward the accused, not everyone in the packed courtroom found the case convincing. LaRue McCormick was a seasoned labor organizer and Communist Party regular who earned high praise from her colleagues for her energy, wit, and organizing skills.[50] As an active member of the International Labor Defense, she had long hoped to find a case on the West Coast like the Scottsboro case, one that would highlight the racism and economic disfranchisement that people of color regularly faced and rally the progressive community together. She found it in abundance with *The People v. Zammora* and stepped forward to assist in organizing a defense campaign.[51]

Bert Corona remembered the founding of the defense campaign differently, and the question of who founded the Citizens' Committee for the Defense of Mexican American Youth (CCDMAY) has been a source of considerable debate among Chicano scholars.[52] According to Corona, "Josefina Fierro, as national secretary of El Congreso Nacional de los Pueblos de Habla Español, carried out two very significant actions. One was the formation of the Sleepy Lagoon Defense Committee," and the other was that she traveled all over the nation, assisted by Luisa Moreno, "to develop the broad national campaign against the racist and divisive indictments and yellow journalistic depictions of the Hearst press."[53] The evidence is clear that McCormick turned to El Congreso for support and that Bert Corona and Josefina Fierro, on behalf of El Congreso, raised money and made speeches for the defense effort. But it is also clear from the organizational records of the defense committee that Irish and Jewish activists remained in control of the campaign throughout its entire existence. Although McCormick gave of her time, energy, and effort to correct a terrible miscarriage of justice, her primary goal was to organize what seemed to her and other labor activists to be a largely unorganized Mexican American community. McCormick and those who followed in this effort reached out to a handful of Mexican American activists, but for the most part they were unable to recognize and utilize adequately the vast network of political, community, and cultural organizations that had long existed among the Mexican Americans of Los Angeles.

One of McCormick's first priorities was to contact George Shibley, a Lebanese American lawyer she knew through the Congress of Industrial Organizations and the International Labor Defense.[54] Six years out of Stanford Law School, Shibley had established himself in progressive circles as a lawyer willing to take unpopular cases.[55] He was a passionate man, funny, a bit of a free spirit, but thoroughly committed to progressive issues.[56] Although not fluent in Spanish, he nonetheless tried to communicate with the families of the accused in their native language, and they were grateful for the sensitivity and respect he showed them.[57] In replacing the court-appointed attorney Richard Bird, Shibley brought with him an edge that the defense previously lacked. He put the prosecutors on the defensive with his frequent objections and challenges to their case. The judge almost always overruled him, but Shibley injected the defense with an energy and a fighting spirit that it previously lacked.

One of McCormick's other strategies backfired terribly, however, and caused serious damage to the defense effort. In a not-so-subtle attempt to challenge the partiality of Judge Fricke, McCormick and other members of the nascent defense committee asked Judge Lester Roth to become part of the defense team. Roth was a member of the District Court of Appeals who had overturned an earlier ruling of Fricke's involving the conviction of Mexican American youths. Thus, when Roth requested a two-day continuance in order to familiarize himself with the case, Judge Fricke adroitly declined the request. Without the time to catch up, Judge Roth was forced to remove himself from the defense.[58] Fricke clearly won the challenge but seems never to have forgiven the slight to his credibility. As the trial wore on, he grew increasingly temperamental toward the defense, often focusing his ire on George Shibley.

With the arrival of George Shibley, the dynamics at the defense table also changed. Zacsek had previously assumed the lead in the defense, much to the discomfort of her male colleagues. Early in the trial, for example, Richard Bird grew exasperated with Zacsek's attempts to advise the defendants collectively without consulting their respective lawyers and appealed to Judge Fricke to remonstrate her for crossing the lines of professionalism. Zacsek readily admitted to the court that she advised the youths "as their mother would scold them" about their behavior in the courtroom.[59] Yet Fricke declined Bird's request and stated, wisely, that even though Zacsek's behavior was an unfortunate breach of professional courtesy, "everybody is basically trying to do the best they can under the circumstances."[60]

An undercurrent of tension rippled between Shibley and Zacsek as the two strongest personalities of the group vied for control. Zacsek did not relinquish the lead willingly. She possessed a quick mind and a strong presence, but her relative inexperience ultimately undermined her effectiveness in the courtroom. Throughout the trial she repeatedly started down a line of thought only to be stymied by the prosecution's objections that her questions were not properly formulated for a court of law. The judge agreed. At other times she seemed to be caught unprepared and flustered, owing, perhaps, to her involvement with other time-consuming cases.[61] Yet she refused to give up fighting for her clients to the best of her ability or to concede to the discomforts of her male colleagues. Her real strengths came through in her ability to hone in on the issue at hand, in translating legal jargon into everyday terms for both witness and jury, and in playing to the emotions of the jury.

George Shibley and the defense, on the other hand, would hardly have done better without her. Shibley was a gifted defense attorney, perhaps the only lawyer the boys unilaterally trusted and admired.[62] Yet his courtroom manner irritated the judge, who was already sensitive to the earlier challenge to his authority.[63] As the trial wore on, Judge Fricke and Shibley increasingly locked horns over an endless stream of objections and overrulings while Zacsek and others tried to run interference between the two. Both Shibley and Fricke refused to back down, and as the trial neared its conclusion in late December 1942, Judge Fricke often ignored or belittled Shibley in front of the jury. "I am getting thoroughly tired of useless and unnecessary objections being made in these proceedings," Fricke snapped at Shibley. "There is some reason back of the making of these repeated objections!" Shibley shot back. "I wish to assign these remarks of your Honor as error, and ask the court to instruct the jury to disregard them!" Turning an icy shoulder to Shibley, Judge Fricke said to the prosecution, "You may proceed, Mr. Barnes."[64]

### Judgments

Although Shibley breathed new life into the defense, the trial was clearly going badly for the accused. The jury, consisting of six women and four men, all white, noticeably disapproved of the defendants. "The hostility of the jury was almost palpable," remembered Alice McGrath, who had been hired by George Shibley to take notes at the trial. "You could see that they were looking at the defendants as though they were loathsome."[65]

The boys' behavior in the courtroom did not help, either. Some were so confident that the state could not prove its case that they were noticeably flippant about the proceedings. At times the boys threw spit wads at one another, poked at one another, or laughed to relieve the tedium of seemingly endless testimonies. A few even took to imitating the peculiar twitch of their own attorney, George Shibley, behind his back. The older boys, aware that they were constantly being observed by the judge and jury, tried to keep the others in line, but the weeks of impudence took their toll. "They were all laughing and joking," remembered Lino Díaz. "The judge would stop them and would not put up with . . . not showing any respect for the courthouse. They were actually laughing at each other!"[66]

Judge Fricke had already lost patience with the defense and bellowed at the lawyers for minor infractions, both real and perceived. Once, as Fricke instructed Anna Zacsek on the admissibility of evidence, he halted his remarks abruptly. "I am sorry," he said, glaring at Ben Van Tress sitting at the defense table; "if you want to engage in conversation at the counsel table the court won't even attempt to assist you. The objection is sustained!"— to which Van Tress protested, "I have not said a word yet!"[67] On another occasion Fricke interrupted Zacsek's cross-examination of a policeman accused of slapping the boys. "Now, just a moment," he said to Zacsek; he then looked over at Shibley, "If there is any more demonstration—and that includes counsel—the court is going to have to discipline somebody." "If your Honor please," Shibley protested, "you're looking right at me!" "I am looking right at you, Mr. Shibley," said Fricke; "I did not like that smiling attitude on your face, the minute the answer came in. It is wholly unnecessary." "If your Honor please," Shibley came back, "I wish the record to show I meant no disrespect, and I was simply smiling because someone else was smiling at me . . . I do assign your Honor's continual . . ." Fricke interrupted, "The record will show that was immediately spontaneous to the answer of the witness and the court's impression of it was that it was a demonstration, and the court so termed it!"[68]

Still, the defendants had good reason to hope. George Shibley delivered a stirring, emotional summation to a rapt courtroom.[69] Furthermore, the state simply could not produce the evidence to support the charges filed against the twenty-two young men after three long months and dozens of witnesses. The district attorney's office never produced the murder weapon—indeed, it failed to prove that Díaz had been murdered at all. At best, what the evidence could support was that many of the young people who went to the Sleepy Lagoon did so with the express purpose of confronting the Downey gang and that some of the group were seen during the ensuing fight at the Delgadillo home in the area where Díaz was later found. Thus, on the day the jury returned with its verdict after six days of deliberation, some of the boys were optimistic that the outcome would be in their favor.[70]

The defendants had all knelt in prayer in the prisoners' room before entering the courtroom that January morning in 1943, and thirty-five deputy sheriffs escorted the jurors as they filed in for the last time.[71] Jury foreman Arthur Cubbage handed the verdicts to court clerk Arthur Moore, who read the verdicts to the packed room. Joe Carpio, Richard Gastelum, Edward Grandpré, Ruben Peña, and Daniel Verdugo were found not guilty.

For the rest of the boys, however, their lives would forever be changed on that cold morning.[72] Henry Leyvas, José Ruíz, and Robert Telles were each found guilty of murder in the first degree, with two counts of assault with a deadly weapon with intent to commit murder. Manuel Delgado, John Matuz, Jack Melendez, Angel Padilla, Ysmael Parra, Manuel Reyes, Bobby Thompson, Henry Ynostroza, and Gus Zamora were convicted of murder in the second degree and two counts of assault with a deadly weapon with intent to commit murder. Finally, Andrew Acosta, Eugene Carpio, Victor Segobia, Benny Alvarez, and Joe Valenzuela were found guilty of assault. Stunned by the verdict, many of the boys wept openly.[73]

Judge Fricke complimented the jurors on their handling of "the most difficult matter which has come before me during the 25 years on the bench."[74] The following day he handed out sentences that shocked even Robert Kenney, the attorney general for the state of California.[75] Henry Leyvas, José Ruíz, and Robert Telles were all given life sentences at San Quentin. Manuel Delgado, John Matuz, Jack Melendez, Angel Padilla, Ysmael Parra, Manuel Reyes, Bobby Thompson, Henry Ynostroza, and Gus Zamora received sentences of five years to life at San Quentin. Finally, Andrew Acosta, Eugene Carpio, Victor Segobia, Benny Alvarez, and Joe Valenzuela were given one year in either the county jail, road camp, or the county farm.[76]

Delia Parra, wife of Smiles Parra, collapses after the verdict is read.
(Courtesy of the University of Southern California, on behalf of the *Los Angeles Examiner* Collection, USC Specialized Libraries and Archival Collections)

## The Discursive Context of the Trial

Not everyone who followed the case was surprised by the outcome of the trial. Before the defense and prosecution addressed the jury with their final arguments, LaRue McCormick drew on a wide network of labor and progressive organizations in creating the Citizens' Committee for the Defense of Mexican American Youth. With prominent Los Angeles attorney Clore Warne serving as chairman and McCormick as secretary, the CCDMAY sent out an appeal for funds in order to "procure full justice for the boys."[77] "We are not being unduly pessimistic," the letter began, "just factual."[78]

No doubt what colored their dire prediction for the trial was the community climate, which had gone from indifference to outrage during the three months of testimony. By midtrial, news of the proceedings moved to the front page of most Los Angeles newspapers. With the increased attention, a small but significant number of newspapers and tabloids took creative license and sensationalized their reporting of the trial. In the early stages of the grand jury investigation, many of the larger newspapers devoted no more than a few brief lines to it. Yet from the beginning, the *Los Angeles Evening Herald and Express* latched on to the term "Sleepy Lagoon" and immediately turned it on the accused youths. "Goons of Sleepy Lagoon" was a favorite moniker that skewed the brief and otherwise bland reporting of the grand jury investigation and subsequent trial.[79]

*Sensation* magazine was one of the tabloid journals that shamelessly reinvented the events of the trial in order to spice up its stories. It was hardly a bastion of responsible journalism, as the title implied, but it nonetheless boasted to its readers that it had access to the "true stories behind the news headlines."[80] What lent credibility to *Sensation*'s supposed exposé of Pachuco gangs was that one of the articles was written by none other than Clem Peoples, chief of the Criminal Division of the sheriff's office.[81] In "Smashing California's Baby Gangsters," he described the illegal activities and immoral lives of the 38th Street defendants and characterized them as "reckless madbrained [sic] young wolves" that were tracked down by the Los Angeles law enforcement agencies. "Sheriff Biscailuz, knowing he must stop the wolf-packs before they committed further murders, organized a special anti-gang squad and named me as its chief," Peoples said of the police action taken in the wake of José Díaz's death.[82]

Peoples's seemingly casual reference to youth gangs as "wolf-packs" was not incidental but in fact quite significant. "Wolf-packs" was a well-understood reference to the tactics of the feared *Unterseebooten* of Nazi Germany that silently stalked Allied ships and sunk them in coordinated surprise attacks. It was an allusion not lost on those who saw the supposed wave of juvenile delinquency through the lens of wartime fervor and interpreted the seemingly uncontrollable working-class youths as a matter of national security.[83]

The impact of the December issue of *Sensation* on the public discourse on crime, race, and youth was surely limited. Ten thousand copies of the tabloid were sold in a two-week period, but that was hardly significant relative to the 1.5 million residents living in Los Angeles.[84] Of greater significance was the apparent ease with which a larger newspaper such as the *Herald and Express* adopted such blatantly prejudicial terms as "goon," "hoodlum," and "gangsters" in reporting on the trial and that its readers all too willingly accepted the notion that Mexican youth gangs ran amok in the city.

Other Los Angeles newspapers avoided the slanted terminology of the *Herald and Express* but nonetheless picked up on the spirit of the day. Most journals liberally mixed new words such as "Pachuco" and "zoot suiter" with recognizable, emotionally charged words such as "gangster" and "delinquent" in their reporting on crime in the downtown area or on the Eastside. In actuality, the number of crimes committed by minority youths during this period *dropped*.[85] Yet public fascination with juvenile delinquency—itself a coded phrase in Los Angeles for seemingly deviant working-class youths—increased dramatically, revealing the subtle relationship in the public discourse between cultural difference and national security. During this historical moment, public concern over juvenile delinquency assumed a new sense of urgency because it tapped into the same assumptions that underlay much of the public rhetoric calling for wartime sacrifice and unity, namely, that America was in danger from foreign powers and that nothing short of a unified community could defeat the threat.[86]

### The Political Significance of the Trial

To say that the United States faced tremendous challenges at the dawning of 1942 would be something of an understatement. The Axis won a string of victories while the nation's leaders worked feverishly in Washington, D.C., to coordinate national resources, reorganize the economy, and re-create a War Department capable of conducting two distant wars overseas. In February 1942 German and Italian armies quickly overwhelmed two battalions of ill-prepared American soldiers in North Africa and almost wiped out the U.S. First Armored Division. Since the attack on Pearl Harbor, the Japanese military swept virtually unimpeded through Hong Kong, Malaya (Malaysia), the Dutch East Indies, Wake Island, and Guam. Japanese troops landed in the Philippines within weeks after crippling the American fleet in Hawaii and quickly pushed the vastly outnumbered American and Philippine forces into the mountains. In March President Franklin D. Roosevelt ordered General Douglas MacArthur to escape to Australia, and one month later Major General Edward King surrendered his starving troops in Bataan. Lieutenant General Jonathan Wainwright surrendered Corregidor the following month. An estimated ten thousand Filipino soldiers and six hundred American servicemen were shot, bayoneted, or beheaded by Japanese soldiers in the march of prisoners toward Luzon that came to be called the "Bataan Death March." By mid-1942 the American navy succeeded in halting Japanese advances with the Battle of the Coral Sea in May and the Battle of Midway in June, but the victories were costly. American forces could launch only small, shoestring counteroffenses in the Soloman Islands and New Guinea, and it took another six months of hard fighting against the Japanese, the elements, and tropical diseases before the small islands of Guadalcanal and Buna could be secured.

The forced removal of Japanese Americans from their homes in the name of public safety had already begun in the spring of 1942, and clearly the rationale for doing so was fresh in the minds of many Californians as the Sleepy Lagoon murder trial got under way. What made juvenile delinquency a particularly salient issue during that year was a number of civil disturbances that thrust public safety into the forefront of community concern. Public confidence in the LAPD weakened in the early summer when the police lost control of two civil disturbances that turned into small-scale rioting. These much publicized riots raised serious questions about the ability of the reduced wartime police force to maintain the peace.[87] Furthermore, although violence was not an unusual part of city life, such outbreaks involving a significant portion of minority youths laid the seeds for widespread public support for the military men who would later roam the streets of Los Angeles assaulting zoot-suited youths in the name of law and order.

On a clear Friday afternoon in early June 1942, throngs of spectators began to exit the Los Angeles Memorial Coliseum as the all-city high school track meet ended.[88] A small group of teenagers huddled together against the flow of people, however, carefully eyeing the departing spectators as they filtered past. They stood waiting for nineteen-year-old Frank Torres of Clanton Street to exit the coliseum. As Torres came into view walking with his girlfriend, one of the boys leveled a firearm at Torres's head and shot him. Panic rippled through the crowd with the echoing crack of gunfire, and Torres's assailants melted into the hundreds of scrambling spectators. Near riot conditions prevailed at the coliseum until fifty armed soldiers from a nearby encampment were called out to subdue the crowd.[89]

Soldiers may have been called to the scene instead of the police merely as a matter of expediency. The soldiers were at hand when a sufficient police force was not. Another riot the following month, however, may have revealed a deeper motive behind why Angelenos were more comfortable in turning to the military to maintain public safety than the police. Respect for the wartime police force in certain areas of town was embarrassingly low.

Two unmarked police cars answered a call one Sunday evening in July about a crap game in progress on the corner of Pomeroy and Mark in Boyle Heights, almost directly opposite of what was then the Los Angeles County Hospital.[90] Four plainclothes policemen rushed into the crowd surrounding the game, announced their identities, and broke up the game. Two of the spectators, a serviceman and his wife (the police were unsure whether he was wearing an army or a marine uniform), protested loudly as the officers dragged gamblers back toward their unmarked cars. Hurling epithets at the police, the man and woman urged the crowd of spectators to rescue their arrested comrades. A boisterous throng of mostly Mexican Americans charged the police, cutting them off from their one car with a radio. The overwhelmed officers tried to arrest whomever they could, but as soon as they managed to push someone into the police car, members of the crowd yanked open the door on the other side of the car and allowed the person to escape. During the melee, the rioters doused the policemen with cold water and tore at their clothing, and one officer's hand was slashed by a sharp instrument.

After these embarrassing incidents, the LAPD and the sheriff's office seized upon the investigation into the death of José Díaz to launch a major public relations offensive in conducting a much publicized crackdown on juvenile crime.[91] In early July police and sheriffs combed the entire eastern area of Los Angeles. "Not in years has there been such an extensive and well organized drive for the capture of hoodlums and other malefactors," boasted Peoples.[92] The LAPD assembled a secret "hoodlum list" and assigned one hundred officers to "apply aggressive police technique" in arresting suspected gang members.[93]

The sweep produced an impressive number of arrests, but the public relations campaign was far more problematic for the LAPD.[94] The more the police cracked down on juvenile crime, the more crime seemed to spread, if one was to judge by the amount of space devoted to juvenile delinquency in the Los Angeles newspapers.[95] In truth, the police crackdown contributed substantially to the creation of a crime wave that was far more imagined than real. The dragnets resulted in more boys and girls being processed through the judicial system, which in turn produced a significant amount of press attention devoted to crime and other stories highlighting the seemingly lurid details of life in East Los Angeles. All this gave rise to the illusion that a wave of crime was sweeping Los Angeles. Ironically for the police, the supposed crime wave only reinforced public concern that the LAPD was not doing enough to halt the spread of juvenile lawlessness.

Not all the reported crime was imagined, however, and a small number of Mexican American youths reinforced the popular perception that Pachucos as zoot suiters threatened public safety. Young people in the area just north of downtown Los Angeles bitterly resented the intrusion of unruly military men on leave trespassing through their neighborhoods and confronted them with a show of force. During the summer months of 1942, furthermore, someone—perhaps a couple of young men—stalked the streets of downtown Los Angeles sexually assaulting a number of women and robbing them of their purses and jewelry.[96] The descriptions of the assailants provided by the LAPD were vague at best, and the rape survivors could identify their attackers only by their presumed ethnicity and gender: Mexican males. The mounting publicity made these attacks appear to be coming from random groups of young men rather than what may have been a serial rapist. But accuracy is a luxury during times of unusual social unrest, and these crimes against women provided enough anecdotal evidence for those who would believe that a wave of juvenile lawlessness was sweeping Los Angeles, while at the same time feeding the press what it craved most: tales of sex, violence, and scandal on the "darker" side of town.[97]

### The Logic of Conviction

The timing of the Sleepy Lagoon trial fell within this particular discursive and political moment in Los Angeles. Two of the twenty-four boys originally indicted for murder were able to have their cases heard separately, and the charges were dismissed for lack of evidence.[98] The mass trial held a far greater significance for the district attorney's office and the law enforcement agencies, which were heavily invested in procuring a conviction. Not only did the governor send a telegram instructing them to investigate juvenile gangs thoroughly and to "take such steps as will bring about their termination," but prosecuting the remaining twenty-two boys for the murder of José Díaz would secure a much needed boost in public confidence.[99] If a trial represented a major strike against juvenile crime, a conviction would demonstrate the ability of the wartime law enforcement agencies to maintain order.

Neither judge nor jury was oblivious to the social importance of the trial; nor were they impervious to the discursive climate of the times. The terms "gang" and "gangster" that were gratuitously used during the trial had a clear and unmistakable reference in the 1940s to the violence and lawlessness created by mobsters who ruled parts of Chicago and other urban centers in the 1930s. Little wonder, then, that the prosecutors never attempted to nuance their use of the word "gang" during the Sleepy Lagoon trial, and the judge knowingly endorsed such an unquestioned assumption. For the prosecution, judge, and jury, the difference between a casual grouping of friends and an organized gang of delinquents was negligible when it came to working-class kids from East Los Angeles seemingly devoid of proper morals or parental authority.

The question of race appeared in the trial in complicated ways. At no time did anyone express the idea that what happened to Díaz and the members of the Delgadillo family was of little public concern because they were Mexican Americans. The state, furthermore, put its full weight behind the prosecution of those it considered responsible, and Mexican American law enforcement personnel readily contributed to the arrest and prosecution of the 38th Street youths.

The racial identities of the defendants remained just underneath the layer of coded words and phrases about appearance. When Anna Zacsek remonstrated the defendants for not looking more "presentable" within earshot of the prosecution, Shoemaker and Barnes quickly moved to block what they saw as a strategic attempt to alter the "distinctive appearance" of the accused. The defense protested vehemently to the judge when it learned that the district attorney's office asked the county jailer to not allow the boys to get haircuts and a change of clean clothes.[100] Shibley charged that the prosecution was "purposely trying to have these boys look like mobsters, like disreputable persons, and [was] trying to exploit the fact that they [were] foreign in appearance."[101]

Judge Fricke interrupted before the prosecution could respond to the defense's charge. For a moment he pulled back the veil on the coded dialogue: "The question of Mexican nationality was injected into this case during the examination of the jurors time and time again by defense counsel . . . [calling] attention to the fact these boys are of Mexican or Spanish extraction, and I do not see any reason for criticizing a reference to that *in that way*" (italics added).[102] Assistant District Attorney John Barnes then protested the defense's insinuation that race made any difference in the prosecution of this case and accused Shibley of hoping to blame racism for the conviction of his clients. But his partner, Clyde Shoemaker, saw things differently. "The very fact that Mr. Shibley saw fit . . . to bring in the insinuation of my endeavoring to retain their appearance as mobsters or gangsters would indicate to me that he, himself, realizes that their appearance may be distinctive."[103] After a lengthy debate filled with charges and countercharges, the judge ruled against the defense motion to allow the boys to clean themselves up. Their very appearance was a significant fact of the case, Fricke told the courtroom, and he felt obligated to block any attempt that would make the defendants look different.

Although in the end the evidence did not support the charges against the boys of 38th Street, both judge and jury clearly believed that they were nonetheless guilty. Why? Toward the close of the trial George Shibley discovered that members of the jury had been exposed to the Los Angeles newspapers and tabloids. They had clearly consumed the inflammatory constructions of juvenile delinquency, crime, and Pachucos. The jurors were subpoenaed, and Shibley was prepared to call them to the witness stand, but it was all for naught. Judge Fricke declined the motion for a mistrial, confident that the Los Angeles newspapers could not sway the opinions of the jury.[104] In the end, he may have been right. These were the times when, only months earlier, Angelenos widely supported the internment of Japanese residents of Los Angeles County, their American-born children, and even grandchildren, not because they had proved themselves disloyal but because they were merely suspected of being disloyal.[105] How perfectly logical it must have therefore seemed to convict a gang of working-class youths from the Mexican side of town who were certainly guilty of *something*. No doubt members of the jury shared many of the fundamental assumptions that produced the inflammatory reports about life on the Eastside. Like many Angelenos, they readily consumed what they already suspected about young people who self-consciously deviated from the social norm, especially those from East Los Angeles.

# 5 : Dangerous Fashion

ow did the zoot suit come to be a symbol of social danger? Because fashions have varied so widely since the 1940s, and because the drape shape has come and gone in various forms since then, it can be difficult for someone today to understand why it seemed perfectly reasonable for the Los Angeles City Council to pass an ordinance outlawing zoot suits within city limits for reasons of public safety. As material objects in themselves, neither the zoot suit nor the drape posed a particular threat to the physical safety of the public. It was the economic, political, cultural, and historical context in which the fashion operated that gave these items of clothing the power to undermine the notion of public safety. In other words, the drape shape evoked visceral reactions from many Angelenos because they ascribed meanings to the fashion and situated those meanings within their operative assumptions about social propriety and order.

The growing popularity of swing jazz among working-class youths in the era of segregation, as America moved toward another world war, was significant. Jazz was hardly new to popular culture by the 1940s, having been embraced by leisured young people of the "lost generation" during the post–World War I period as an expression of disaffection. The Great Depression of the 1930s had sobered much of the Roaring Twenties, and the Jazz Age came to an end, according to Louis Erenberg, as national tastes changed with the times. But that all changed on the night of 21 August 1935. At the end of a disappointing national tour, Benny Goodman's band electrified the audience at the Palomar Ballroom in Los Angeles by reinterpreting and energizing the arrangements of jazz great Fletcher Henderson. The era of swing jazz was born in Los Angeles that night, and by the end of the decade, dance bands flourished across the country, catering to young audiences caught up in the swing craze.[1]

The zoot suit was part of a larger complex of ideas and practices that the white middle class of Los Angeles found threatening to social order. That complex was summed up in a single word: "jazz." Jazz was to white Americans in the 1940s what rock and roll was in the 1950s and rap was in the 1980s. The very word itself was slang for sexual intercourse, and as a performative art form, it defied social conventions of the body through music, dance, and clothing. It was a powerful form of black expression and behavior that captured the frustrations and aspirations of a marginalized people. Through sound and movement, it gave power in its very ability to convey the substance of existence, however difficult or inglorious that existence might be. Although jazz originated among African Americans, it was an art form and a way of life that was not exclusively black. Race mixing on and off the stage and dance floor was common, and in the age of segregation, such a violation of white supremacy was an outrage.[2] As a behavior spreading among the youth, it was perceived as a social danger.

For the California youths that donned the drape and grooved to the sounds of jazz, blending the styles and language of the African American hipster with the Mexican Tirili was a means of celebration and transformation. It was, at the same time, a very visual and public expression that blurred the conventional boundaries that delineated gender, class, and social propriety. The creative and subtle ways in which young people refashioned these styles went unnoticed by the larger public, which conflated differences not only between jazz subcultures in the East and West but among youths in the Los Angeles area as well. Observers of this small but symbolically charged zoot suit phenomenon on the West Coast largely dismissed outright the individuality of the youths they scrutinized, seeing only a mass of undifferentiated "zoot suiters," and read public signs of difference in hairstyles and clothing as signs of juvenile delinquency on the rise.

Two men of the period, one a president and the other a popular illustrator, captured the operative definitions of wartime patriotism that framed how many Americans viewed the subculture of jazz. President Franklin D. Roosevelt's "Four Freedoms" address to the Seventy-seventh Congress on 6 January 1941 articulated a vision of a war against fascism that would create in the future days a world order founded on inalienable human rights. In calling the nation to prepare for war, he advised: "The best way of dealing with the few slackers or trouble-makers in our midst is to shame them by patriotic example. . . . Those who man our defenses and those behind them who build our defenses, must have the stamina and the courage which come from unshakeable belief in the manner of life which they are defending. The mighty action that we are calling for cannot be based on a disregard of all the things worth fighting for."[3] Wartime patriotism thus revolved around an unqualified support for the war, but it also drew on closely related concepts of what America stood for and what stood for America. Norman Rockwell's popular illustrations of the four freedoms for the *Saturday Evening Post* in 1943 illustrated "the manner of life which they are defending."[4] In each representation of American life, Rockwell's view of America—and Roosevelt's, for that matter, "translated in world terms"—was a homogeneous nation of a hardworking, church-going, white, middle-class people of middle American values. Nowhere were racialized minorities represented, much less conceptualized, as full and equal participants.

The effort to unify the nation around this particular conceptualization of patriotism faced challenges, however, from the nation's multiracial and multiethnic populations. These challenges crystallized into notions of what was "American" and "un-American," and the faith that many civil and military authorities held in the melting-pot ideal, so prominently promoted in the previous decades, quickly devolved into open suspicion and fear during the war.[5] Harmless cultural differences between Japanese Americans and white Americans led to accusations of conspiracy and subversion, and such suspicions spilled over onto working-class youths who publicly signaled their differences through their clothing and hairstyles.

Youth rebellion as an un-American activity, then, was the lens through which the swing craze was viewed. Both visually and conceptually, swing jazz represented an altogether different world, not so much in articulated pronouncements as through the voice of practice. The swing craze revealed a growing youth culture far removed from parental control. It was not about maintaining the status quo, if one was to judge by the innovative sounds, dance, and clothing of jazz. Erenberg details how parents and authorities looked upon the reactions of young audiences at swing concerts with alarm, interpreting them—the throngs of screaming youths, young women sitting on men's shoulders, young people rushing the stage, dancing in the aisles and on table tops, near and with racialized youths—as behavior bordering on mass hysteria.[6] Critics of the swing craze in Los Angeles focused inordinately on the appearance of the Pachuco as zoot suiter, making a fetish of the "long hair" and dress of hip cats as clues to the pending collapse of domestic security.

### Thick, Heavy Heads of Hair

Within the social context of the day, the "Lamar" was a strange hairstyle, made even stranger by being on the heads of young Mexican American men. At the very least, the longer hair necessary for men to wear a pompadour conveyed a disregard for the conventional. Of larger significance, however, was the meaning of an appearance deemed rebellious by the greater society. One pulp magazine writer, in attempting to describe the Sleepy Lagoon defendants, made it a particular point in his article to describe their hair. Reporter Barnaby Frame collapsed their separate identities into a singular type and wrote that "he wore his hair in a bizarre 'ducktail' cut, with a low, thick, V-shaped wedge extending far down the nape of his neck."[7] Such a description seemingly established a relationship between appearance and criminality. Indeed, in Santa Ana, California, one judge ordered six Mexican American boys charged with loitering to surrender their zoot suits to the court and to change their "Pachuco hair cuts."[8]

The ways in which hair can be arranged on one's head convey both intentional and unintentional social cues. Hair is one of the means by which social standing, gender, sexuality, race, and even politics can be publicly signaled, particularly in the degree to which one's hairstyle deviates from or conforms to the expected custom. Among the ways that men arranged their hair in the early 1940s, there was a remarkable consistency in both the length and overall appearance. Short hair symbolically differentiated men from women, and an unspoken emphasis on a neatly groomed appearance identified one's class standing and, by implication, race. Hair considered to be well groomed was almost always smoothly brushed back away from the face, and, depending on hair type and displacement, it tapered downward, was about two inches long, and finished in a tight trim around the ears and collar.[9]

The onset of war introduced a style of hair strikingly different from the prevailing trend: the uniformly cut, short hair of the military. "Everybody had the G.I. fever," recalled Manuel Cruz, and the "military cut" or "short pompadour" gained popularity among young civilian men.[10] The style called for hair to be trimmed about a half inch long around the top and sides of the head, tapering smoothly down around the ears and the back of the neck.[11] Although it was in opposition to the popular style of men's hair, the military cut was a manipulation of the body sanctioned by the state, one that represented the nation's involvement in the global conflict between totalitarian regimes and, ostensibly, democracy. Thus, in a very public and communal way, the young men who adopted the military cut signaled a certain fascination and solidarity with the wartime mobilization not uncommon among pre–draft-age men.

Some young men, however, favored a look popular among Tirilis that, if not intentionally in opposition to the military cut, was at least visually so. The Lamar required hair along the top and sides of the head to be about three inches in length, combed straight back from the face (some versions added a pompadour lift on the top of the head) and neatly trimmed around the ears and collar.[12] The cut was not terribly long by the standards of the day, except for one visible difference: hair on both sides of the head had to be long enough to be combed straight back so that it met behind the head to form a wedge or "duck tail." For the most part it was a style that did not stray significantly outside the predominant fashion standards for men's hair, except for the design of the hair at the back of the head.[13] The ducktail could have been combed downward to follow the contour of the head and, as a consequence, look as respectable as other styles. Yet the ducktail was a relatively subtle detail requiring an extra amount of attention that distinguished the wearer from the ordinary, signifying that the young man wearing the Lamar could afford to put stock in his appearance. Had Elvis been born in East Los Angeles a decade earlier, he would have been labeled a "Pachuco."

Women's fashion allowed for a wider variety of ways in which their social identities could be signaled. Hair arranged more elaborately implied a sufficient amount of leisure time to spend on one's appearance. Further, fashionably arranged hair, because it required more attention to maintain it, gave the impression that one was engaged in the kind of work environment that could sustain coiffed hair.

If there was one fashion rule that dictated popular hairstyles for women at the time, it was that hair should be arranged in a manner that was not too flashy or ostentatious.[14] Thus, because of the prevailing gender ideals, hair cut any shorter than four inches for women was quite rare, and standard women's hairstyles generally tended to consist of wavy or curly hair usually brushed back off the face or with modest bangs and cut no longer than the shoulders. Particular styles within these bounds varied widely from the wavy, shoulder-length hair parted to the side of Veronica Lake to the Betty Grable look, in which the hair was swept up and back from the front in a wave with the ends finished in a ring of curls that swung down to the shoulder. Women who deviated from the prevailing beauty standards in arranging their hair did not elicit the same degree of denunciation as the men who did so. Yet the Pachuca pompadour some women adopted, particularly popular among teenage Mexican American women, unwittingly contributed to the conflict between working-class youth and the larger Los Angeles community.[15]

In its basic form the pompadour was not altogether different from many of the popular hairstyles among young women. However, the hair was arranged in an exaggerated manner—as if in parody of prevailing trends—that, if not intentionally designed to do so, certainly aroused attention. It was a style in which hair ballooned up and back from the front of the head in a large pompadour, was tethered in back by berets or hair combs, and

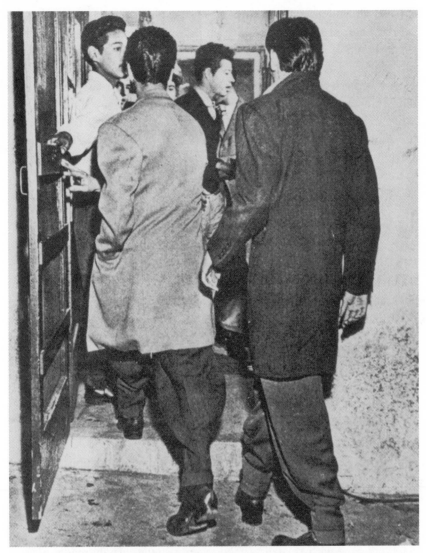

Two young men with "duck tail" hair, upturned collars, and drapes strut into a party in the Alpine neighborhood. (*Lowrider* 2, no. 4 [1979]: 12)

then fell down loosely from there about the shoulders.[16] This was not the practical hair of the previous generation, when women wove their hair in simple braids or pulled it back in a bun for work.[17] Rather, this was evidence of a generation that enjoyed changing social and economic boundaries, and the styles these women adopted suggested that they were eager to explore the perimeters.[18]

Oppositional in their creativity, such styles were some of the important ways in which working-class youths in Los Angeles delineated their presence in relation to the cultural resources from which they drew. Gone, for example, were the extensive tattoos on the face, arms, and body of Tirilis and Pachucos from El Paso.[19] Some young people continued the use of tattoos to mark their identity, but the designs became more discreet and were etched almost exclusively on the back of the hand between the thumb and index finger.[20] For the majority of Mexican American youths, however, tattooing the body was an altogether nonexistent practice. On the other hand, hairstyles reminiscent of those worn by eastern hipsters and Tirilis found favor among teenage youths. Male African American hipsters in the urban North largely preferred the "conk," and hairstyles among young men in Los Angeles reflected a similar look in the pompadoured hair popular among Tirilis.[21] Such changes and continuities in both the basic style and substance of the customs they drew from reveal that the young people of this generation were moving away from the overt and permanent method of publicly marking the body in favor of a more subtle and temporary means of establishing difference, while at the same time maintaining some symbolic ties with their stylistic roots.

However subtle these changes, they were nonetheless public means of signaling difference that contributed directly to the public discourse over juvenile delinquency in Los Angeles. Many Angelenos and visitors to Los Angeles who interpreted the fashion cues of young Mexican American women—big hair combined with a generous use of cosmetics—collapsed class and race with sexuality. "They were usually heavily made up with mascara, lipstick, and with their hair piled high into a pompadour," wrote Beatrice Griffith of the young women with whom she worked; "flowers and earrings [added] to their vivacity."[22] News reports eager to expose the scandalous behavior of Pachucos contributed to the conflict by alluding to the practices of girlfriend swapping and drunken orgies among Pachuco gangs.[23] The major Los Angeles newspapers also reported that Pachuca gangs recruited and tattooed other young women, sometimes against their will, and required them to "obey and to yield to male members of their gang in all

**"La Dora, El Paul, La Lupe, El Chubby." "La Dora"** wears a zoot suit with huarache sandals, while the other women wear hairstyles and clothes popular among young Mexican American women. (*Lowrider* 2, no. 6 [1979]: 22)

things." Furthermore, one Los Angeles newspaper reportedly discovered that the "fantastically high pompadour of the girls serves . . . to conceal both a knife and a fingernail file."[24]

The tactics utilized by Deputy District Attorneys Clyde C. Shoemaker and John Barnes in setting up their case in the Sleepy Lagoon Trial also revealed the social significance of hair deemed too long and thick during this period. As noted earlier, to support their contention that Mexican American youth gangs behaved little better than wolf packs in the wild, the prosecution ordered that the jailed boys not receive a clean change of clothing or a haircut for almost three months prior to the trial.[25] George Shibley, one of the attorneys for the defense, protested in vain to the court, but Shoemaker retorted that the appearance of the defendants, "their style of haircut, the thick heavy heads of hair, the ductail [sic] comb, the pachuco pants and things of that kind," were critical pieces of evidence in the case.[26] The connection between appearance and behavior was a relationship made particularly damning to the public during a time when the unquestioned duty of all Americans was to band together (both socially and symbolically) for the purpose of prosecuting the war.

The relationship of the boys' appearance to the charge of murder was, of course, spurious at best. Yet the perceived connection between appearance and behavior was an important component in the state's case against the boys. Many law enforcement officials, as well as civilians at large, read the length and thickness of the Lamar hairstyle as a wildness made evident through its disregard for the conventional. Even the defense attorneys, in arguing that their clients be allowed to clean up, conceded a connection between being "foreign in appearance" and a likeness to "mobsters" and "disreputable persons." The prosecution could not have agreed more.

The lines between fashion, phenotype, and behavior grew terribly thin as representatives of the state drew from eugenics theory to account for youth behavior. Lieutenant Edward Duran Ayres of the Los Angeles County Sheriff's Department, with the endorsement of Sheriff Eugene Biscailuz, argued before the 1942 grand jury that one must first understand the biological proclivities of Mexican Indians in order to comprehend adequately the nature of the "Mexican problem" in the United States. Alluding to the recent internment of Japanese Americans, Ayres justified the police crackdown on Mexican American youths by comparing Mexicans to wild cats that must be caged in order to protect society. "The Indian from Alaska to Patagonia," he concluded, "is evidently Oriental in background—at least he shows many of the Oriental characteristics, especially so in his utter disregard for the value of life."[27] Reaching into history, Ayres pulled together connections between

Aztec sacrifices and the machismo of modern Mexican American youths that, at times, led to bloodshed. Such connections between biology and youth culture, history and behavior, appearance and criminality, were the conceptual joists that held up the rationale of law enforcement policy outside the all-white enclaves in Los Angeles. Ayres's words, though extreme, reflected the fears of many of his contemporaries, who felt that repression was the only response for a people biologically programmed for "Oriental" behavior. "When are the Sheriff and the Chief of Police going to issue instructions to their men to go out and give the same rough treatment to these hoodlums that [they] give their victims?" an enraged Angeleno wrote to the *Los Angeles Times* in late 1942. "The officers might kill or seriously injure some of the young hoodlums? Well, why not?"[28]

### The Evolution of the Drape

In ways no less obvious than hairstyles, clothing can place a person within social categories, depending on not just what is worn but when, where, and by whom. Men's fashions during this period deviated remarkably little from the basic look established for nearly a century. The "business" suit in particular, which evolved from the clothing of the gentry, served to demarcate symbolically one's gender and class standing. By the mid-twentieth century, "wearing the pants in the family" was still considered the domain of men, but almost every man—regardless of his class standing—strove to wear a suit for special social events such as funerals, marriages, or a night on the town. Even then, when working men wore suits, their economic station was revealed only to the discriminating in the quality of material and fit. In the 1940s men's suits were almost always worn over a shirt and tie, and the suit coat, moderately padded in the shoulders, retained constant features such as notched or peaked lapels, flap or patch pockets, and rear or side vents. The standard length of the suit coat, either single- or double-breasted, was measured at a man's curled-up fingers, arms hanging comfortably by his side. Pleated or plain-front trousers were worn at the navel and retained a "stove pipe" appearance, with legs the same width from knee to ankle, around twelve inches, finishing at the bottom cuffed or uncuffed. Accessories always included conservative dress shoes, a belt or suspenders, and a hat.

As the nation slowly emerged from a period of want owing to the Depression to one of sacrifice imposed by war, the zoot suit was one of the few styles that threatened diversity in the otherwise staid world of men's fashion. "The zoot suit," sniffed William Davenport for *Collier's*, "is strictly Filipino houseboy on his day off."[29] It was a fad that pushed at the edges of social convention, playing on fashion mores by mixing gender styles and flaunting consumption beyond the unspoken limits of tolerance. The zoot produced a striking silhouette, exaggerating the upper male body by high-lighting wide shoulders and tapering dramatically down to what Davenport described as "a girlish waist . . . snug as a pre-war girdle."[30] From the mid-section down, the zoot utilized a more overt symbol of female fashion in the length and shape of the jacket skirt. The jacket flared out from the waist to the knees enough to allow sufficient movement and looked like something between a formal day coat and a fitted overcoat. It was a garment that could be worn by either men or women. When men wore the drape, the jacket concealed flowing, pleated pants that flared at the knees and angled dra-matically down to a tight fit around the ankles. Some women in Los Angeles took to wearing pleated skirts underneath the zoot jacket with hosiery and huarache sandals.[31]

A number of contemporary accounts traced the origins of the zoot suit to the African American community, although Chester Himes would have none of that and passed it off as a white invention.[32] Renowned sociologist Emory Bogardus offered a theory that the zoot suit was an American adaptation of a native costume in Pachuca, Mexico, but there is no evidence that the Mix-tec or any neighboring tribes wore clothing that even remotely resembled a Western-style suit.[33] The *New York Times* places the birth of the zoot suit with Clyde Duncan, an African American busboy who ordered a customized suit at Freirson-McEvere's department store in Gainesville, Georgia, in February 1940. The measurements were then sent to the Globe Tailoring Company in Chicago, and the "killer diller" style, as it was called in Georgia, caught on in Mississippi, Alabama, and Louisiana. From there the fashion found life in Harlem and spread throughout the rest of the country.[34] Duncan was report-edly inspired by Clark Gable's wardrobe in *Gone with the Wind*, according to the *Negro Digest*.[35]

*Newsweek*, however, placed the origin of the zoot suit in Harlem a decade earlier, in the 1930s.[36] Evidence from *The Autobiography of Malcolm X* cor-roborates this dating because it was a fashion already popular and readily available in retail stores in the Roxbury section of Boston when Malcolm X moved there in the summer of 1940.[37] Likewise, jazz musician Art Pepper re-called in his autobiography, *Straight Life*, that the zoot suit was popular on Central Avenue when he arrived in Los Angeles in 1940.[38] Given that, before 1943, the fashion elicited no media attention, which would have certainly facilitated the migration of the style from coast to coast, it is likely that jazz artists popularized the style in the cities they annually toured. Since the zoot suit was already popular and in production on both coasts by the summer of

1940, it likely originated not with Clyde Duncan in early 1940 but elsewhere in the mid- to late 1930s.[39]

Born of uncertain parentage, the zoot style wandered from region to region, assuming as many names as it did stylistic variations. Some of the earliest recorded names from the Northeast incorporated sounds that rhymed with "suit," suggesting, perhaps, that the zoot was a fashion twice that of ordinary suits.[40] From "root suit," "suit suit," and "zoot suit" in the Northeast, and "killer diller" in the South, the names turned more functional and descriptive in the West.[41] In addition to "zoot suit," many youth preferred to call the suit "the drape shape" or simply "the drape," names that captured the flowing look of the style. It was also called "fingertips," because the jacket skirt usually fell to where one's down-stretched fingers ended, or "*el tacuche*," which was Spanish slang for "the dress" or, more self-mockingly, "the wardrobe."[42]

In Los Angeles, young people took creative liberties with the zoot style that distinguished the drape from its eastern counterpart in important ways. "During the period from 1940–1945," Beatrice Griffith perceptively noted, "the dress of the Pachuco boys was, with little variation, a *version* of the zootsuit, though their own triple-soled shoes and ducktail haircuts were not widely adopted by zootsuiters in other areas" (italics added).[43] These and other alterations overlooked by Griffith were imprinted by the influence of these boys' material circumstance, culture, and even social restraints.

The most significant development in the evolution of the West Coast drape from the eastern zoot suit was in the color of the suit. Eastern zooters vied with one another to wear the most eye-catching suit, ranging from a conservative "sharkskin gray" to ostentatious lime greens and bright oranges or mixing overstated plaids ("glad plaids") with chalk stripes ("ripe stripes").[44] Malcolm X described his first zoot suit as "just wild": a sky-blue coat that pinched his waist and flared out below his knees.[45] Youths on the West Coast, however, eschewed the "walkin' rainbow" look of the eastern zoot suit in favor of a more conservative appearance of the drape, or *tacuche*.[46] In March 1942 the War Production Board issued Order L-85, which established the maximum measurements for men's suits and pants and restricted the availability of material for civilian use.[47] As a consequence, men's fashion in general became more conservative; gone were the double-breasted suits, wide lapels, vests, pleated pants with cuffs, and even overlapping waistbands. The drape was no exception. "No [retail] stores would sell them," "Vibora" related in *Lowrider* magazine. "We used to go down to [the tailor shop of] Young's, Murray's and Earls in downtown."[48] "There weren't that many different kinds of materials to choose from," Manuel Cruz also remembered; "the most popular was shark skin, the gabardine, [and] flannel."[49] Thus, by preference as well as because of the limited availability of materials, drape-shaped youths in Los Angeles tended to wear suits of more somber colors: black, sharkskin gray, or charcoal gray pinstripe.[50]

For the uninitiated the drape was, in the words of two Los Angeles reporters, "rather a remarkable spectacle" and the "oddest phenomenon of the new brand of California nightlife." For those familiar with the jazz world, however, the silhouette of the drape shape in Los Angeles tended to be quite conservative.[51] Whereas the skirt of the zoot suit jacket flared down below the knees, looking more like a form-fitting overcoat, the drape jacket was considerably shorter. The length ranged from the standard measurement for men's suit coats (slightly below the crotch) to the eastern version below the knees, but the more popular length in Los Angeles fell at midthigh— no doubt earning the jacket the name "fingertips." Eastern zoot suits were characterized by broad lapels and shoulders widened by up to six inches of padding, but these features on the drape were no wider than those of men's business suits in the previous decade. Indeed, many of the young men accused of being zoot suiters looked as if they were simply wearing their father's hand-me-down suits altered only so that the sleeve length, waist, and inseam would fit their smaller frames.[52] Trimming down larger-sized suits to achieve a draped silhouette was less expensive than having a suit tailor-made, but it necessarily limited the length the drape jacket could attain. The decreasing availability of material owing to war rationing at the time when the popularity of the zoot suit style was on the rise on the West Coast may have also directly contributed to the conservative length of the drape in Los Angeles. There was, perhaps, even a simpler reason. Nightclubs in Los Angeles often refused to admit young men in suit coats that extended past their fingertips, suspecting anyone wearing the outrageously long zoot suit of having a similarly outrageous personality, and young men eager to dance modified the length of their drape accordingly.[53]

The one feature from the zoot suit style that was more widely worn in Los Angeles than the suit itself, however, was the "Punjab" or "reet-pleat" pants.[54] Perhaps because of the warmer climate on the West Coast, or because, owing to war rationing, they could afford only enough material to have pants made, many young men paid up to fifty dollars for drape pants and wore them in the place of dress slacks.[55] Hipsters in the East donned pants with the rise so high that the waist came up to just a few inches below their armpits, cinched with a narrow belt or wide suspenders. On the front of the pants were two- to three-inch-wide pleats that allowed up to thirty-four inches of material to balloon out at the knees, which then dropped

Several variations of the "drape shape" were popular in Los Angeles during the war. Among them were suit jackets with shirt collars, contrasting sleeves and accents, and more conservatively cut slacks. (*Lowrider* 2, no. 2 [1979]: 42)

**The drape was popular among jazz aficionados of all colors.**
(*Collier's* 110, no. 8 [1942]: 25)

Although jazz enthusiasts favored the more outlandish zoot suit, this young man models the drape style that was popular among Mexican Americans in Los Angeles: double-breasted jacket cut to the length of the fingertips, in a conservative color and pattern, topped with a porkpie hat. (*Probation* 22, no. 3 [1944]: 83)

down toward a six-inch ankle and finished off in a cuff three to five inches deep.[56] This prompted one fashion critic to comment that the zoot pants looked like two "up-ended baby blimps."[57] When the fashion caught on in Los Angeles, however, material was less abundant, and many "reet pleats" were altered accordingly. Some young men were able to purchase pants with high waists, full pleats, and wide drops from knee to ankle, but many others could only afford pants with less extravagant features. The rise of the pants was significantly shorter so that the waistline fell slightly above the navel, the pleats were thinner, and at the knees the pants were only seventeen inches wide, tapering down to twelve-inch-wide ankles. Although not enough fabric was available to achieve the largest of the hipster's version of the pants, the goal was to make pants as narrow at the ankles as possible to achieve the same draped look. "At the ankles, the smaller the heper you were," remembered Vibora; "everyone would try 14 then 13. At 12 inches [in circumference] your foot wouldn't fit."[58]

Eastern hipsters generally looked for flamboyant accessories to complement their flashy attire, and the boys who wore the drape usually followed suit. Both eastern and western versions of the zoot were incomplete without an extremely long, thick-linked, gold-plated watch chain drooping to the knee from vest to pants pockets. From there the accessories diverged in both form and style, further differentiating the eastern from western versions of the zoot. Eastern hipsters topped their look with a felt porkpie hat, which was a perfectly respectable choice of hatwear for the day. Draped young men in the West tended not to wear hats because of their carefully stylized hair. Among those who did, however, some sported a porkpie hat whereas others preferred a more striking choice that further delineated the contrast between the *tacuche* and mainstream fashion: a low-crowned, broad-brimmed sennit made of felt.[59] Eastern hipsters wore their zoots with a shirt and string bow tie. In the West, however, young men wore pullover knit shirts or collared shirts opened at the neck or buttoned up and tied with a wide tie.[60]

None of these accessories, however, provoked as much controversy for draped youths in Los Angeles as the shoes they wore. To complement his sharkskin gray zoot, Malcolm Little purchased shoes that were dark orange with paper-thin soles and knob-style toes, "the kind that were just coming into hipster style."[61] Cab Calloway also purchased a number of thin-soled shoes to wear with his zoot suits, bragging that his shoes were so thin that he could roll them up in a ball. The rationing of material, however, prompted youths in the West to add another detail that contributed to the evolution of the zoot. Shoe leather was part of the material rationed by the War Production Board, and many civilians took to wearing double-thick soles to prolong the life of their shoes. Yet this simple act of thrift was neither understood nor appreciated by the larger public when teenagers began to wear them with their *tacuches* and rename their shoes *calcos*.[62] Carey McWilliams speculated that Pachucos adopted thick-soled shoes to serve as counterweights that would anchor them down while swinging their dance partners in the air.[63] Los Angeles police and county sheriffs attributed a more sinister motivation to the wearing of *calcos* with the drape, suspecting the boys of using them as offensive weapons during gang fighting.[64] "If you got stopped by a cop, they used to call our shoes 'deadly weapons,'" recalled Bobby García.[65] "We were trying to help the country, and they were calling us Nazis."[66]

The clothing that young working-class women wore when on the town tended not to attract the same kind of attention as young men's clothing. A female companion suit to the *tacuche* never developed in Los Angeles, most likely because there was no need. However short-lived the female "juke suit" on the East Coast, the androgyny of the *tacuche* proved a more popular style for some young women in the Los Angeles area.[67] "Some girls wear a modified 'zoot-suit,' with black skirts and hose, including the broad-shouldered and longer coat of the boy's costume," observed University of Southern California sociologist Emory Bogardus. "They are sometimes known as 'Pachucas' or 'slick chicks,' and glory in the role."[68] Beatrice Griffith further described the way Pachucas looked, wearing the *tacuche* with short skirts and flowers in their billowed hair, like "little tornadoes of sexual stimuli, swishing and flouncing down the streets."[69] For the most part, however, young women's dress habits were far more restrained and, as a consequence, more socially acceptable. "The guys dressed sharp," remembered Henry Leyvas's younger sister Lupe, "[but] the girls didn't dress as good."[70] For many young women, the rewards of social approval surely outweighed the desire to create a stylistic complement to the *tacuche*. Many dance halls and nightclubs in Los Angeles refused to admit women who were not wearing a skirt, hose, and appropriate blouse, and women hoping to gain admission to these night spots dressed accordingly.[71] Furthermore, in those few places where the dress standards were more relaxed, teenage women tended to prefer comfortable dress for dancing, such as sweaters or jerseys, "hip-loving" slacks or knee-length skirts, bobby socks, and huarache sandals.[72]

### The Social Significance of the Zoot

The retelling of the Sleepy Lagoon murder and the Zoot Suit Riot in Chicano literature has created the perception that the zoot suit phenomenon was unique to Mexican American youths. A broad reading of the historical evidence, however, reveals that many of the characteristics attributed to Pachucos were not limited to the confines of the Mexican neighborhoods of Los Angeles. Viewed from a larger perspective, working-class Mexican American, African American, Asian American, and Irish American youths in the Los Angeles area shared a kind of syncretistic fashion and manner through their music, dance, clothing, and language. Although still inchoate, the evolution of the *tacuche* from the zoot suit was but one form of creative response among the working-class youths caught between the eventuality of the draft and the immediacy of war labor demands. That largely Latino and Asian American youths chose to adopt and modify the "expressive style" of the dress and behavior of African American hipsters indicates the degree of cultural creativity and adaptation at work among second- and third-generation youths. More important, the hipster-cum-Pachuco was a new variation of Pachuco identity. For those who put on the drape and played what Robin Kelley called "the Stagolee-type rebel," the social energy behind the lindy hop and the zoot suit offered an empowering re-creation of the self.[73]

In many northern African American communities during the 1930s, where the zoot flourished before migrating westward, the hipster was layered with meaning not unlike that of the Pachuco in the Southwest. Cab Calloway, who perhaps popularized the zoot suit more than anyone in his day, recalled that the hipster style of sporting flashy clothes and lindy hopping to the creative sounds of jazz were ways of shamelessly celebrating life in spite of the difficulties African Americans faced during the 1930s. For Calloway, it was as if the "glad rags" broadcast an inaudible but profoundly resonant message to the public: "Listen, I know it's rough out there, but drop that heavy load for a while. Laugh and enjoy yourself. Life is too short for anything else."[74] Indeed, the hipster seemed to live for excitement, hovering about pool halls, dance clubs, and any hot spot where gambling, drinking, or uninhibited sex flourished in the nightlife. Where the improvisational celebration of jazz music and dance joined creative forces, the unconventional look of the zoot suit (as with its 1920s forerunner, the jazz suit) seemed to follow.

These celebrations of life in the face of difficulty promised rich possibilities for transforming cultural expression into a form of resistance. For Malcolm Little, putting on the zoot was nothing less than a rebirth of identity, transforming him from an awkward country boy who couldn't dance to the bezooted hipster who exploded on the dance floor in the rhythmic fury of the lindy hop. He wrote of one occasion:

That night, I timed myself to hit Roseland as the thick of the crowd was coming in. In the thronging lobby, I saw some real Roxbury hipsters eyeing my zoot, and some fine women were giving me that look. I sauntered up to the men's room for a short drink from the pint in my inside coat pocket. My replacement was there—a scared, narrow-faced, hungry-looking little brown-skinned fellow just in town from Kansas City. And when he recognized me, he couldn't keep down his admiration and wonder. I told him to 'keep cool,' that he'd soon catch on to the happenings. Everything felt right when I went into the ballroom—I grabbed some girl I'd never seen, and the next thing I knew we were out there lindying away and grinning at each other. I couldn't have been finer.[75]

The zoot suit was an important symbol in the transformation of Malcolm Little from an awe-struck yokel to a self-assured urbanite. His zoot was his public signal that he had gone from square to cool, from awkward to hip. He was born a new man.

The uncertainties Little faced in moving to the city, as well as the elation he experienced in transforming himself from a country boy into a cool cat hip to the happenings, recurred thousands of times as workers across the nation migrated to urban centers, eager for new employment opportunities brought on by war production. As a way of signaling to their peers that they were "in the groove," young people in the Southwest adopted the cool manner of the hipster and Tirili and in the process provided space for the reinvention of themselves. Some Tirilis scorned the popularity of the zoot as the passing fad of kids and looked on the fastidiousness of the hipsters with contempt.[76] Yet other Pachucos swept up in the popularity of the zoot suit craze adopted a style they hoped would create room for the transformation of identity and thus provide distance between them and other Pachucos whom they considered "backward, square, 'farmers.'"[77]

For Sleepy Lagoon defendant José "Chepe" Ruíz, the oldest child of eight from immigrant parents, the drape cut a suave silhouette. The broad shoulders, thin waist, and ballooned thighs of the drape shape were social assets for the nightlife because they created a dashing, if not scandalous, image, one that Chepe believed women would find irresistible and men notice. While serving time in San Quentin prison, Chepe wrote to Alice McGrath, relating verbatim an alleged conversation he had with his mother, who carefully argued for turning his zoot suit into a dress:

MOTHER: Let's take the case of Don Juan, for example. . . . The movies typify him as a distinct type of that day and age. He leaves a[n] impression of a sort. When you see him depicted you form a conclusion. That conclusion may or may not be an agreeable one. But, regardless of the conclusion you arrive at, you leave Don Juan with one thought. And . . . you arrived at a conclusion by the clothes Don Juan wore. So, for God's sake, son, give me permission to take the zoot suit of yours and have it made over into a dress.

CHEPE: (after being revived): Never, mother, never. I shall keep that suit for a keepsake. Who knows, perhaps in the 25th century someone may look at that suit, and say, WHAT DON JUAN WORE THAT?[78]

"And seriously," he concluded, "I am serving a long, long, time for wearing a suit like that." In truth he was convicted for more than his fashion sense, yet it is clear that Ruíz found something tantalizing in flirting with an image of disrepute and even criminality. He was not alone.

The edge of danger and rebellion implicit in the badass swagger of both the hipster and the Pachuco appealed to a variety of working-class youths who, though not initiated in either group, drew on elements of both icons as a way of catching on to the happenings. Jazz musician Art Pepper remembered how he looked up to his bezooted mentor Dexter Gordon through the admiring eyes of a fifteen-year-old. "Dexter Gordon was an idol around Central Avenue [in Los Angeles]," Pepper reminisced in his autobiography, *Straight Life*. "He wore a wide-brimmed hat that made him seem like he was about seven feet tall. He had a stoop to his walk and wore long zoot suits . . . he had those heavy-lidded eyes; he always looked loaded, always had a little half-smile on his face. And everybody loved him."[79] Twenty-two-year-old drummer Johnny Veliotes, who renamed himself Johnny Otis after arriving in Los Angeles, also eagerly assimilated the cultural forms of the jazzmen he admired.[80] Emulating the hipster style of his idol Cab Calloway, Otis proudly strutted around Los Angeles in his new zoot suit until his mentor, Patsy Hunter, pulled him aside and urged him to wear it only while performing on stage.[81]

Putting on the zoot suit meant different things for women than it did for men, especially at a time when women's gender roles were in significant flux. The image of the woman as vulnerable creature was a powerful ideal that serviced wartime propaganda aimed at recruiting men into military service.[82] At the same time, as Kelly Schrum argues, popular media aimed at young women strove to reinforce hegemonic ideals of normative girlhood. Magazines such as *Seventeen* attempted to shape the behavior, appearance, and thinking of adolescent girls so that they would become prim and proper young women whose sexuality was controlled and whose life's choices were "normal."[83] But such touted ideals of proper womanhood competed with both fantasized and real-world images in popular culture of independent and strong women. The cartoon heroine Wonder Woman, who debuted in 1941, came from "that enlightened land of women," wrote William Marston, the creator of the character, "to save the world from the hatred and wars of men in a man-made world." She was not alone, as Susan Hartman showed in *The Homefront and Beyond*. Other female superheroes such as Sheena, Queen of the Jungle; Mary Marvel, the long-lost twin of Captain Marvel; and Miss Fury emerged in popular cartoon magazines from the period.[84] The 1942 song "Rosie the Riveter" also acknowledged in the popular media the six million women who worked in wartime defense industries and support services such as shipyards, steel mills, foundries, lumber mills, warehouses, offices, hospitals, and day care centers. While the growing popularity of Wonder Woman and other female superheroes during the war coincided with the changing social boundaries for women at work and at leisure, clothing also reflected the changing attitudes toward women's gender roles. The sight of women wearing pants, overalls, jumpsuits, and other clothing traditionally associated with men's work became common both at work and at leisure. "Oh, aren't we cute and snappy in our cover-alls and slacks?" ran a "Maidens in Uniform" advertisement campaign for Sanforized in 1942.[85]

Vicki Ruíz reminds us that race, class, ethnicity, national identification, and generation profoundly influenced the ways in which immigrant and racialized young women negotiated multiple societal expectations. Although public attention focused on Mexican American young men during this period, Mexican American young women, Ruíz suggests, "may have experienced deeper generational tensions as they blended elements of Americanization with Mexican expectations and values." Indeed, Mexican American young women exercised a good deal of creativity and invention in carving out leisure spaces of their own between the expectations of an American work environment and a Mexican home environment.[86]

The sight of Pachucas wearing the drape on the streets of Los Angeles clearly challenged prevailing American notions of the feminized, vulnerable, or proper young woman. Their carefully composed public persona was gender-ambiguous, if not more masculine than feminine. At the same time, as Catherine Ramírez notes, a complicated relationship has long existed between working and racialized women in the United States and hegemonic notions of femininity and idealized womanhood, which were often products of bourgeois tastes and sensibilities.[87] Thus, defying hegemonic notions of idealized womanhood was not entirely unexpected of working women of color, and this may be the reason why "zooterinas," per se, did not provoke the same visceral reaction from white Los Angeles that draped young men received.[88] To be sure, some cultural critics dolefully noted the effects that wartime labor demands seemed to have on women in giving rise to a "new Amazon" who could "out-drink, out-swear, and out-swagger" men. Yet public criticism of the female zoot suiter never entirely revolved around issues of appropriated masculinity or offended femininity, perhaps because it was not entirely outside the bounds of changing societal values to see women wearing items of male clothing.[89]

To dismiss the zoot suit phenomenon as little more than a fad, as many did at the time, is to ignore the powerful implications of the fashion among teenagers. It was part of a symbolic lexicon that facilitated interaction between teens on terms of their choosing and their identification with a larger world outside the barrios. Emulating the hipsters was a way of grabbing at coolness, that mythical quality in which everything was all right and in control. Implicitly, to live "cool" was nothing short of a status rebellion perpetuated by working-class youths across the nation whose roots stretched deep into the communal experiences of the socially disenfranchised. By setting up a dichotomy between the hips and the squares, the zooters established a social hierarchy based not so much on material assets as on attitude and personal attributes. It was a way of subverting the capitalistic paradigm that material acquisition lends social status. By creating a social hierarchy based on cool, and all the social attachments that went with it, the hipsters set up a situation in which they were on top and in which social recognition and acceptance could be acquired only through adopting their mores.

### Public Readings of the Drape

The stylistic foundations of the drape were rooted in the zoot suit and can be traced back to the gentlemanly fads of earlier decades. The separate parts that made up the zoot suit look, such as frock coat, peg-top pants, and the porkpie hat, were all fashion staples of the well-dressed gentleman at the turn of the century.[90] In truth, the zoot suit differed so little in general appearance from the formal day wear popularized by England's Prince Albert that one might well argue that the drape was the direct descendant of elite fashion standards.[91] What made this incarnation of previous fashion worthy of public censure, however, was less the clothes than the man who wore them. Hipsters were self-made men, but not of the kind that Michael Kimmel argues were idealized in the dominant discourse on masculinity in the twentieth century.[92] Hipsters embraced a manhood that ran parallel to that masculine ideal, albeit on the other side of white middle-class respectability. Hipsters were not consumers of high fashion; nor did they aspire to live according to bourgeois values. Rather, the hipster carried the air of the trickster about him, of a man living by his wits, enjoying life on his own terms, existing for the constant edge of excitement and pleasure. Hookers and marijuana were rumored to be his constant companions and defiant manhood his creed.[93]

War production facilitated the introduction of working-class youths to new levels of consumption, and purchasing expensive and distinctive clothing, acquiring a used car, or affording greater access to dances, concerts, and movies signaled their entrée into the material culture of the United States.[94] These were not acquisitions based on middle-class notions of thrift and respectability but youthful indulgences framed by a popular culture, largely inspired by African American hipsters and jazz artists. Certainly young people were not completely unaware of the scandalous reputation of jazz life or of societal expectations of thrift and sacrifice, but flaunting convention was part of what gave the music, the language, and the clothing their appeal.

That flaunting of convention came at a price, however, by feeding into public concerns about juvenile delinquency. The more that drape shapes were seen on the streets of Los Angeles—not only because of the growing popularity of the style but also because of the increased ability to consume material goods—the more that zoot-suited "menace" appeared to be a growing problem. The *Los Angeles Times* reported in frustration during the rioting of 1943 that there seemed to be "no simple or complete explanation for the growth of the grotesque gangs."[95]

The public simply could not accept that working-class youths of color obtained material goods through honest means.[96] When Los Angeles police searched eighteen-year-old Johnny Matuz, who had no criminal record prior to his conviction in the Sleepy Lagoon case, they found ninety-eight dollars in his pocket and refused to believe that he had earned it. The arresting officers tried to beat a confession out of him until he passed out.[97] When Henry Leyvas was seventeen, police arrested him and his fifteen-year-old brother, Sef Jr., for driving a stolen vehicle. The police refused to believe that the car belonged to their father, and the brothers were held in jail for three days until Seferino Leyvas Sr. could prove that he owned the car.[98] Benny Alvarez was also arrested twice for suspicion of driving a stolen vehicle, pistol-whipped, and then released when he was identified as the car's owner.[99]

The latent symbolism of the drape evoked as visceral a reaction from those who saw it as did the Lamar. Perhaps because the drape required a significant outlay of money to acquire—anywhere between $50 and $125— some saw the suit as a waste of precious funds on a product of questionable merit.[100] Indeed, many questioned precisely how young men of color obtained enough money to purchase such an expensive suit. In addition, because the drape shape also required the use of material resources that patriotic citizens were forgoing for the war effort, wearing the drape suggested an unabashed disregard for community values of thrift and sacrifice.[101] Strong community reaction to conspicuous consumption during times of sacrifice was not a phenomenon unique to the twentieth century. The war profiteer in particular, usually recognized by his flamboyant garb, has been the target of irate communities in the United States during many conflicts.[102] Although it is highly unlikely that anyone in the 1940s would have confused draped young men for war profiteers, there was a perceptibly critical edge in the reporting about these young men as if their activities revealed a significant lapse in patriotism and commitment to the war effort. Such a view was not without some merit. The men who wore zoot suits in northern communities were quite vocal in their opposition to fighting a "white man's war," and the young men who adopted the zoot in Los Angeles were guilty in the minds of many Angelenos at least by association. Further, although it was never explicitly stated in the news accounts, reporting the ages of the young men suspected of criminal activity implicitly suggested not only that they enjoyed life while others were giving theirs but also that they were flagrantly abusing the privilege by endangering the quality of life in the community.

Pachucas found the greatest condemnation within their own community, which objected not so much to what they wore as to how they wore it. Whereas some young women enjoyed blurring gender distinctions in wearing the fingertip jacket, far more Pachucas seemed intent on clarifying and accentuating their bodies and their gendered identities through traditional female clothing such as blouses, sweaters, and skirts. In some ways it was a clever use of traditional items to defy tradition, as Catherine Ramírez argues, because for many members of the community the blouses that Pachucas wore showed too much bare shoulder or too much cleavage, their sweaters were too tight, or their skirts were too short.[103] Editorials in *La Opinion* excoriated Pachucas as whores and as traitors to their race ("malinches") for the brazen ways in which they defied decorum and respectability.[104] Surely these young women were not unaware of the expectations of their community or of the price of defying social norms. For some, their tight clothing or shorter skirts may have simply been the result of ill-fitting hand-me-downs. For others, pushing the boundaries of propriety may have been their specific intent. Although it may never be established with certainty how many Pachucas read normative magazines such as *Seventeen*, what is clear is that they were part of larger social and historical phenomena of young women, studied by Rachel Devlin, who increasingly explored the meaning and power of their sexuality through clothing and behavior.[105]

Ramírez also points out that a growing number of young women during World War II were arrested "for violent crime and sex delinquency."[106] Indeed, some of the Pachucas appear to have been far more comfortable with their bodies and with their sexuality than their mothers' generation. Some young women appear to have embraced group names for themselves—such as "Cherries," "Bow Legs," and "Black Widows"—that were rich in double entendre. But if names that referenced sexualized identities were of their own choosing (rather than imposed by others and readily consumed as "fact" by reporters fixated on adolescent sexuality), they were far from straightforward or uncomplicated signifiers. Whereas "cherry" was part of jazz slang for the hymen and "bow legs" implied ready availability, "black widow" referenced the potential power and autonomy of female sexuality in evoking the image of the spider that kills its male companion after copulation.[107]

At the same time, some Pachucas vigorously resisted characterizations in the English- and Spanish-language press in Los Angeles that reduced them to sexual roles.[108] A group of Mexican American women in their teens were so enraged at published reports alluding to their sexual laxity that they planned to submit themselves to medical examination to prove their chastity. It was only when older voices prevailed that the plan was dropped, and they instead appealed to Al Waxman, editor of the small newspaper *Eastside Journal*, to register a protest in their behalf with the city officials and newspaper publishers.[109] Many of the larger Los Angeles newspapers were uninterested in printing their story, including the Spanish-language press.

The *Eastside Journal* had a modest circulation, but these young women nonetheless took an unprecedented step in openly discussing and challenging public assumptions about their morality. "It is true that [articles in Los Angeles newspapers] did not say that of every girl of Mexican extraction," said one young woman. "But the general public was led to believe that such was the fact. The girls in this meeting room consist of young ladies who graduate from high school as honor students, of girls who are now working in defense plants because we want to help win the war, and of girls who have brothers, cousins, relatives and sweethearts in all branches of the American armed forces. We have not been able to have our side of the story told." The report went on to note that not one of the girls had an arrest record or had been in trouble with the law. "It is a shame," said Waxman, "that these girls have been treated in this manner by the daily newspapers of this city. They deserve a better break and we are happy to present them to the public." Although none of the girls were specifically named in the article, suggesting that they may have felt some ambivalence over the publicity, they nonetheless allowed their picture to run alongside the article. None of the young women wore clothing or hair in an identifiably Pachuca fashion, and only one young woman wore draped pants.[110]

The efforts of some young Mexican American women to exert their autonomy amid competing social constraints collided with the presumptions of white males who saw public displays of racialized female bodies in a very different light. Military men gazed at, called to, cajoled, harassed, and followed young Mexican American women on the streets with abandon, and several observers attributed the escalating tensions between military and civilian young men to the sexual harassment of Mexican American women.[111] Many military men soon learned the price of pursuing Pachucas as the objects of their sexual desires, however, when Pachucas turned their fantasies against them. Some Pachucas led stalking military men into alleys where friends and neighbors lay in ambush with chains and bats.[112]

### Conclusion

In important ways middle-class activists such as Alice McGrath, Guy Endore, and Carey McWilliams, who labored tirelessly on behalf of the beleaguered youths, were quite insightful in arguing that criminality did not necessarily follow appearance.[113] They were among the few in Los Angeles who saw something harmless—perhaps even innocent—in the popularity of the zoot suit among working-class youths. Yet in vigorously promoting their position they argued the point to extreme.[114] Reading conspiracy behind the public outcry over the Pachuco, they failed to appreciate the powerful impact of the cultural forms that young people chose to adopt, both for the youths themselves and for the public who reacted to them.

Perhaps the clearest voice for what the zoot meant to the young men who wore it comes from a drawing made by nineteen-year-old Manny Delgado, born in Los Angeles to immigrant parents from Mexico.[115] A high school dropout, Delgado was earning ten dollars a day at the Hammond Lumber Company to support his pregnant wife, Beatrice, when he was arrested in connection with the Sleepy Lagoon case. In a sketch drawn on the letterhead of the Sleepy Lagoon Defense Committee, there is a studied neatness in the lines that form the shape and details of the draped young man who is "on time." This "mad cat" looks almost clean in appearance with a buttoned-up jacket, tightly knotted tie, pocket square, and boutonniere.[116] There is a certain finesse and poise to the look that Delgado described as "terrific as the Pacific" and "frantic as the Atlantic." This was not at all a study of a working man or a "*cholo*" but that of a dandy.[117] And still there is a hardness that creeps into Delgado's idealized representation of the self. Below the phrase "38th St Mad Cats!" is the name of the nation's premier fighter plane, "P-38." It is the only phrase adorning the sketch not framed in the jive language of the jazz world. Delgado's evoking the image of a formidable fighting machine in connection with the 38th Street neighborhood reveals the relationship between fighting prowess and home turf he felt important to maintain.

Emulating the hipster and the Pachuco was a way of grabbing at a particular kind of social approval, articulated by young people in little more than the word "cool."[118] As social psychologist Fritz Redl argued in a 1943 issue of *Survey Monthly*, in some ways putting on the zoot was simply the emulation of a style associated with the fast times of jazz life, not unlike wearing the jacket of a winning sports team.[119] Yet the members of this "team" were not the cultural heroes of mainstream America but its outcasts and villains. What meaning did these antiheroes hold for the young people who were fascinated by them? In some ways these two types, the hipster and the Pachuco, were the embodiment of something profoundly American. They were underdogs who, through savvy and determination, had risen up from obscurity and attained a visible degree of success in living life on their own terms, maintaining composure, and gaining the respect of their peers. But it was a particular kind of respect gained through socially disapproved ways that earned these groups public contempt, not celebration. Hipsters and Tirilis were groups living on the edges of society whose underworlds one dared not enter undaunted. For young people to invest themselves in the visible markers of these groups was to assume the public fear they engendered, a fear made particularly acute as their influence appeared to be growing among the young.[120]

# 6 : The Significance of the Pachuco as a General Category and Conception

arey McWilliams and Guy Endore shared a visceral distrust of William Randolph Hearst, the publishing magnate who, at the peak of his fortune, owned major newspapers, magazines, radio stations, film companies, and news services across the nation. Their distrust was most clearly manifest in blaming Hearst for the hostile reaction to the zoot suit phenomenon. They were certainly not alone in their view of Hearst; nor was it undeserved. "Mr. Hearst in his long and not laudable career has inflamed Americans against Spaniards, Americans against Japanese, Americans against Filipinos, Americans against Russians," observed Ernest Meyer, former editor of the *New York Post*, "and in the pursuit of his incendiary campaign he has printed downright lies, forged documents, faked atrocity stories, inflammatory editorials, sensational cartoons and photographs and other devices by which he abetted his jingoistic ends."[1]

McWilliams and Endore used national newspapers, journals, and private publications to attack Hearst with, what seems in retrospect, a rather fantastic accusation. They argued that Hearst succeeded in convincing Los Angeles citizens that the Pachuco was every Mexican and that he had demonized the Pachuco in order to provoke anti-Mexican animosity. Hearst's motives for doing so, according to McWilliams and Endore, were many: to foment racial discord, to aid the enemy in sowing dissension, and to increase the value of his real estate holdings in southern California by causing a riot that would purge the community of Mexican immigrants.[2] The 1944 publication of Endore's *The Sleepy Lagoon Mystery* helped popularize what became one of the main arguments of causation—that the Los Angeles press was responsible for raising community tensions to the point of riot.

But how effectively did weeks of sensationalized and unflattering reports undo years of neutral or even positive coverage and direct the community to riot? In 1951, Ralph H. Turner and Samuel J. Surace published a sociological study that seemingly confirmed the basic premise of the McWilliams thesis—that press coverage of Mexicans grew increasingly negative in the weeks leading up to the riot.[3] There is no question that many of the reports in circulation during the crisis often conflated young jazz aficionados with Pachucos and that unflattering news reports implicating Spanish-surnamed youths provided an opportunity for California nativists and xenophobes to hoist their tired banner once again. But the overwhelming majority of rioters were from a highly transient and specific sector of the Los Angeles population rather than longtime white residents, and the fury of military men was focused on a particular subset of the civilian population rather than on the entire Mexican community. The answer, then, seems clear: if negative media coverage provoked the riot, it was largely ineffective on the Los Angeles reading public as a whole. The findings of Turner and Surace deserve a closer look.

It remains unclear how Turner and Surace arrived at their conclusion from the methodology they utilized. They did not specify the criteria used to determine a negative, neutral, or positive tone in newspapers or how judgment calls were normalized among the graduate students conducting the research. Thus it is unclear whether any report of an arrested Spanish-surnamed individual was deemed "negative" in itself. It is also difficult to determine if and how student researchers weighted qualitative considerations, such as the significance of the length of a news report, where that report was placed, and how that report compared in relation to the headlines, lead stories, and editorials of a given edition.

To be sure, Los Angeles newspapers served as one of the main sources of information about the zoot suit phenomenon, but a broad reading of material available at the time reveals a complex and contested community dialogue in process. Community activists, researchers, and concerned citizens engaged one another through the popular press, as well as scholarly venues, about what a Pachuco was and why the Pachuco phenomenon came into existence. Although certain constructions of the Pachuco held sway, no clear consensus evolved. The competing myths of the Pachuco were born out of the struggle to comprehend the growing popularity of jazz among working-class youths. The reading public imagined and reimagined the Pachuco in a variety of ways as different sectors struggled to identify the phenomenon, decide whether it was a problem, and, if so, propose a cure. Although the dominant representation imagined the Pachuco as a maladjusted male Mexican juvenile—a view incidentally shared by influential voices within the Mexican communities—white Angelenos could not even agree that Pachucos were a particular problem. Progressive activists such as

Guy Endore passionately argued that Pachucos were simply misunderstood youths.

It was during this time, as politicians, police, welfare workers, parents, and teachers struggled to come to terms with a creative generation of working-class youths, that the meaning of the word "Pachuco" underwent rapid metamorphosis. It was a label that conveyed different meanings depending on who applied it, to whom, and when. As "Pachuco" became part of the public discourse, it became a word in search of a definition, not because it lacked one but because those who invoked it often seemed to want it to mean more. An archaeological exploration of the term and the different purposes for which it was used reveals the nature of the political struggle between various factions in Los Angeles as they labored to influence events.[4]

## Discursive Origins of the Pachuco

The history of the original bearers of the name remains obscured by the unrecorded past. Like so many people of working-class origin, those who were called "Pachuco" prior to the 1940s left behind few written records to explain their own sense of self or how they understood their place in the world. As a consequence, much of our current understanding of the origins of the Pachuco derives from social scientists and other interested observers of the period who scrambled to come to grips with the growing popularity of jazz among working-class youths. Such observers were outsiders looking in, who, in their quest to understand a strange and fascinating group of Mexicans and Mexican Americans, relied heavily on definition by description or on the testimony of informants trying to explain the existence of a group deemed a nuisance to their own community.[5]

Prior to the 1940s Pachucos were known outside the *colonia* only through the handful of social workers, police, and youth counselors whose work brought them into regular contact with the young people in the working-class districts. Many of the early "authorities" who wrote on the "Pachuco problem" after that time were less interested in the point of origin of the Pachuco than in the sociological variables that factored into the Pachucos' notoriety. As a consequence, scant attention was paid to the alchemy of site and circumstances that gave rise to the Pachuco until 1950 when George Carpenter Barker published a significant study on Pachucos in Tucson, Arizona, in *Social Science Bulletin*. Haldeen Braddy followed in 1960 with a parallel study of Pachucos in El Paso in *Southern Folklore Quarterly*.[6]

The earliest published accounting on the origin of the "Pachuco" came from the period when the Pachuco was already larger than life in the pages of the Los Angeles newspapers. In early 1943 Carey McWilliams, who would later go on to write the seminal work in Chicano history *North from Mexico*, makes only passing reference in the *New Republic* to the origins of Pachucos, identifying them as migrants from El Paso who were responsible for the forty to fifty juvenile gangs in Los Angeles.[7] That same year Emory Bogardus, who was then one of the premier scholars in the study of ethnicity in the United States, also published an article that briefly mentioned the Pachuco connection with El Paso.[8] It was not until four years later that Beatrice Griffith published what remains one of the most detailed and sensitive attempts at understanding the life of Pachucos; the article first appeared in the journal *Pacific Spectator*, a publication of Stanford University.[9]

Drawing on her experiences as a social worker with Mexican families in Los Angeles on relief during the Depression and later as an art supervisor in the same location for the National Youth Association, Griffith had perhaps the closest contact of all the white authors with the people about whom she wrote.[10] Although it is not explicitly articulated, Griffith implicitly understood at least the evolutionary development of the name "Pachuco" and that the meanings of the term were contested. She also acknowledges El Paso as the birthplace of the Pachuco, but like other activists of her day, Griffith argued that its origin was not so much a consequence of geographical place as it was the result of social space denied. The Anglo scholars and activists who wrote about the Pachuco during the 1940s reflected the common understanding that the origins of the Pachuco pointed to El Paso. It will perhaps never be entirely clear whether El Paso served chiefly as the gateway to the United States through which Pachucos passed or whether the Pachuco grew out of the confluence of cultural exchange in the borderlands.[11]

Whatever its origin, the fact that the Pachuco was perceived by many "Californios" (Mexican American Californians) in the 1940s as having originated outside their community is an important element in understanding how the Pachuco fit within the Mexican American community at large. To be called Pachuco was not a badge of honor; it was a name that was meant to evoke shame and, more important, fear. Although it is likely that Pachucos from El Paso first began to arrive in the Los Angeles area in the 1920s, Californios in the 1940s continued to use "Pachuco" somewhat derisively to refer to the Mexicans and Mexican Americans who emigrated from El Paso in the waves of unemployed laborers searching for work.[12] The term also conveyed a specific meaning that pointed to a unique identity and lifestyle within the Mexican American community. Even before the advent of the zoot suit, Tirilis seemed to have employed other means designed to set them apart from society. Their hair was characteristically combed smooth and straight back, they wore tattooed markings on their forehead or below their eyes, and they bore tattooed designs on their forearms or tattooed crosses and initials on their hands.[13] They were known to employ an arcane language and were associated with a specific class of merchants who dealt in vice. To some authorities along the border, the Pachucos were more than mere pimps and pushers; they were members of an entire underworld network that operated in the borderlands and specialized in drugs, theft, and prostitution.[14]

### The Permutations of the Imagined Pachuco

Pachucos burst upon the public consciousness in the early 1940s when a number of sensationalized events gave bodily form to the public's fear of a resurgent juvenile delinquency. Yet the way in which reporters used the word "Pachuco" in the pages of the Los Angeles newspapers was significantly different from how it was used in the barrios of Los Angeles.[15] The front page of the *Los Angeles Times* on Tuesday, 4 August 1942, reported that a police dragnet filled the Firestone station with teenage boys and girls who were suspected of having some connection with the death of José Díaz at the Williams Ranch the previous weekend.[16] Curiously, in reporting on the police crackdown the word "Pachuco" was not used as a noun to identify a group per se but rather as an adjective to describe a common article of work attire that some teenagers adopted as their group symbol. Citing Deputy Sheriff Clem Peoples, of the Criminal Division on Youth Gangs, the news report described how teenage gangs dressed in their group uniforms "so that they can identify each other easily during a brawl." Further quoting Peoples, the report described how his investigation had uncovered the existence of "closely organized groups of youths, mostly Mexican, engaged in the rival gang fights. . . . In one of the gangs the boys wear black shirts. The girls wear green blouses. In another gang the boys wear pachuco (cowboy) hats. Still, others wear leather jackets or a certain type of sweat shirt."[17] Introducing the word "Pachuco" to the public in relationship to one aspect of gang violence implied some negative connotation. Yet at that moment the word held no more overt public significance than a nickname for a cowboy hat — an item of clothing as American as dungarees.[18]

Despite the differing attitudes among Mexican Americans toward the zoot suit, some Mexican American activists played a role in shaping the image of the Pachuco as a zoot-suited delinquent. Soon after the police began to crack down on juvenile delinquency in mid-1942, Mexican American interest groups urgently appealed to a wide variety of government officials, imploring them to use their power to curb the inflammatory news coverage of the trial. Motivated in part by the fear that overtly unfavorable news coverage could upset the state of race relations at home and provide propaganda material for the Axis information network abroad, Alan Cranston of the Office of War Information approached members of the Los Angeles press with the suggestion that they find some other means of identifying Mexican Americans accused of criminal activity.[19] In some ways Cranston's cure was worse than the illness. The zoot suit became the indelible sign of the Pachuco in the public consciousness when newsmen began searching for alternative nouns for "Mexican" in their coverage of the local crime scene.[20]

No matter how carefully the major newspapers at first tried to meet the spirit of his request, following the letter required less work and made better copy. Reporters covering the case of *The People v. Zammora* initially played off the name "Sleepy Lagoon" and referred to the accused boys as "goons" or "gooners."[21] From that point the major newspapers in Los Angeles seemed to compete with one another gleefully in creating new and more dire descriptions of Mexican Americans accused of criminal behavior. As the trial progressed through the winter of 1942 and the Los Angeles police continued to crack down on working-class youths, the newspapers featured sensational reports of "gang" activity that in effect converted all Mexican Americans accused of crime into gang members. Although by late August "Mexican" was no longer the noun of choice, the association of Mexican American youths with gang violence was nonetheless obvious. Spanish-surnamed youths were continually characterized as "hoodlums" and "gangsters." By the time the trial ended in January 1943, the transformation of the "baby gangsters" into "zoot suiters" and "Pachucos" was complete.[22] There was no inherent connection between Tirilis and the zoot suit, and the accused boys themselves were not members of a "Pachuco gang," yet these distinctions became blurred in the pages of the local news journals as the Pachuco *as a symbol* came to embody the essence of juvenile rebellion.[23]

The popular perception that an amoral and violent subculture was incubating among "foreign" youths in the Los Angeles area precipitated a storm of words both accusatory and apologetic of Pachuco life.[24] From lurid accounts of Pachuco activity in pulp magazines to reasoned articles in more sophisticated journals, the writing ranged in purpose and quality and came from authors as diverse as Clem Peoples, chief investigator for the sheriff's office, and Carey McWilliams, chief of the Division of Immigration and Housing.[25] Yet in the process of attempting to expose or clarify Pachuco life, neither side successfully demystified the image of the Pachuco—in part because neither Peoples nor McWilliams ever managed to get inside the heads of the young people they called Pachuco, and as a consequence they never understood the world underneath the "righteous sky bonnet" that hipsters wore on their head.[26] Furthermore, the enigma of the Pachuco's very existence remained a powerful argument for both authors that proved their respective views on the larger shortcomings of modern society. In the end the primary methodology employed for explaining "the Pachuco" remained a description by deficiency and an evaluation of how "the Pachuco" failed in some way to measure up to the American ideal.

The Pachuco as symbol mystified even those who sympathized with the Pachucos' plight, and both their critics and defenders encountered difficulty in dealing with an inventive and assertive generation of working-class youths. It was not the press alone that created and maintained a certain mythology about the Pachuco, as liberal activists then charged and historians have later repeated.[27] The encounters between working-class youths and the larger Los Angeles community were mediated by the particular paradigms utilized to explain "the problem" of their existence.

For many Angelenos the major newspapers in Los Angeles were the only source of information they had on life in the working-class districts. There were indeed smaller and more liberal journals, such as the labor-oriented *People's Daily World*, the black newspaper *California Eagle*, the Jewish *Eastside Journal*, and the conservative *La Opinion*, published in Spanish, but their cumulative circulation was not large enough to counteract the impact of the major newspapers.[28] Reporters for the larger newspapers seemed unable to find any other word but "gang" to describe the social networks of teenagers in the working-class districts. The choice was probably intentional because readers in the 1940s would have clearly understood the word "gang" in reference to organized criminals of the 1930s, and reporters probably used that association to illustrate the social danger of uncontrolled youths. Certainly there were youth gangs in Los Angeles as elsewhere, but not every gathering of teenagers was a gang meeting, and not every in-group custom practiced within teenage clusters was a cabalistic rite of gang membership. Indeed, there is compelling evidence to suggest that young people in many black and Mexican neighborhoods originally organized to defend themselves against white teenage groups who violently resisted black and Latino families moving in or near "their" neighborhoods.[29]

The "gang" description came naturally to reporters in part because of the a priori assumptions made by the sheriff and police in responding to the altercations between young people of color in the working-class districts. Sheriff Eugene Bizcailuz assigned Clem Peoples to the Criminal Division on Youth Gangs with the charge of supervising "the cleanup of all boy gangs" in the county, and Captain Joe Reed drew the assignment from Clemence

Horrall, chief of police, to coordinate the crackdown within the city.[30] The police crackdown on working-class youths and the general public support for it resulted in part from the long-standing tensions in the economically depressed sections of Los Angeles between the people residing there and the almost all-white police force. Minority youths taken into custody were regularly beaten by police, and they in turn retaliated by carrying on a protracted war of resistance, ranging from "pantsing" patrolmen to rescuing suspected wrongdoers from the police who were attempting to arrest them.[31] Yet there was also a more insidious element at work that permeated the larger discourse on juvenile delinquency: working-class youths were, as a matter of course, suspected of deviant behavior because of their self-conscious expressions of difference. Although there were no immediate associations between the zoot and organized crime, the "gang" association, with all the baggage the label carried, fit almost too easily on the African Americans who dressed the part of the hipster and the first- and second-generation Filipinos and Mexican Americans who put on the drape.

The image of the Pachuco as a particularly male phenomenon evolved in the public discourse during this period into three competing views: the incorrigible Pachuco, the bad-but-redeemable Pachuco, and the Pachuco as the kid next door. Certainly the constructions of the Pachuco were not static or impermeable, but as a few individuals realized during that period, the language and imagery used by reporters from the major Los Angeles newspapers were generally quite negative regarding the Pachuco. As a consequence, those who chose to defend the Pachuco responded primarily in two different ways: by admitting the errors of Pachuco youths and blaming their circumstances or by significantly downplaying their culpability and arguing that Pachucos were as normal as the mythical kid next door. The first two constructions of the Pachuco—the incorrigible and the bad-but-redeemable Pachuco—developed almost simultaneously, although the image of the incorrigible Pachuco clearly dominated the public discourse. And whereas the incorrigible Pachuco lived primarily in the pages of the major newspapers, with circulations in the thousands, more sympathetic views of the Pachuco were published by scholars and liberals in journals unread by the general public. The image of the Pachuco as the kid next door arose from the arguments constructed by the Sleepy Lagoon Defense Committee (SLDC) in mid-June 1944, when the SLDC began a nationwide fund-raising campaign by selling *The Sleepy Lagoon Mystery*, written by the well-known Hollywood screenwriter Guy Endore (with foreword by Carey McWilliams).[32]

Between the summers of 1942 and 1943, Angelenos increasingly came to believe that "juvenile gang warfare flared anew" in Los Angeles County and that zoot-suited youths were primarily responsible for the "grisly toll" of deaths, beatings, and severe injuries. Perhaps as further evidence of the depravity of the situation, the Los Angeles Times reported that even "girl hoodlums" joined in the "free-for-all fight" that resulted in the death of José Díaz at the Williams Ranch.[33] By the end of the Sleepy Lagoon trial, the problem of juvenile delinquency had a defined identity, and a range of private and public organizations devoted their time to deciphering the Pachuco problem. More than ten thousand copies of the December 1942 issue of Sensation sold in Los Angeles County over a ten-day period. The tabloid-style magazine carried eight pages on the Sleepy Lagoon murder trial, featuring as its lead article "Smashing California's Baby Gangsters," written by Clem Peoples, chief criminal investigator of the Los Angeles County Sheriff's Department. Above the bold red, white, and black headline spread across the two pages was a photograph of twenty-four bedraggled defendants at their arraignment with a quotation from a police officer describing the young men as "vicious young terrorists."[34] Even more reputable organizations followed the lead established by Sensation's pulp style. The superior court released a report in July 1944 with the purpose of exposing the lurid practices of Pachucos. According to a news report of the study, Pachucos performed "sadistic mutilations upon unwilling neophytes," carried concealed weapons at the ends of "grotesquely huge chains," fought one another, robbed for money, reveled in drunken orgies, and smoked marijuana.[35]

It was in this context of dominance and submission and violence and sexuality that the Pachuca entered into the public discourse. The overwhelming emphasis on the Pachuco as a particularly male phenomenon may have led to the dominant view of the Pachuca as an accomplice to the male delinquent, as opposed to a female phenomenon in its own right. Circulating news reports about Pachucas in Los Angeles were very few but significant in that they repeated information that appears to have been gathered from the same unnamed source, one that was likely exaggerated to conform to and confirm public prejudice.

One Los Angeles Times report is typical of the gross generalizations made about young Mexican American women during the period. A 9 June 1943 headline, complete with a sneering picture of twenty-two-year-old Amelia Venegas holding up her fist, reported: "Brass Knuckles Found on Woman 'Zoot Suiter.'" "Now comes a lady zoot suiter," the report states in apparent disbelief, but then the reporter momentarily rethinks that statement and inserts the following modifier: "or at least a sympathizer with the zoot suit fraternity."

Yet it is not clear in either the report or the picture that Venegas was a "woman zoot suiter" or necessarily a sympathizer. Venegas appears to be wearing an ordinary sack dress with little or no makeup and an unremarkable hairstyle. In other words, none of the identifying marks of the Pachuca or zooterina are present in the photograph. A careful reading of her statements furthermore reveals that Venegas held a more complicated view of zoot suiters than what the newspaper asserts. Venegas clearly denounced the aggressive police response to zoot suiters, yet it also appears that she was personally wary of zoot suiters. She carried brass knuckles with her on her way to the market, she explained, because she saw a group of zoot suiters congregating near her home. Clearly the presence of draped youths provoked Venegas to arm herself for protection. Apparently it made the story more interesting to cast Venegas as a "lady zoot suiter," however, and thereby imply that young Mexican American women critical of the police crackdown were "sympathizers" who undermined civil society.[36]

Such salacious accounts were not confined to the popular media. Anthropologist Ruth Tuck alleged in her study of Mexican Americans that, upon arrest, nine Pachucas confessed that they were part of a pact to seduce and murder sailors. In truth, had Pachuca seductresses actually murdered sailors, the response from the police, military, and public would have surpassed that which was given to the imagined Pachuco. Apparently the seduction and murder pact never came to fruition, and the complete lack of police or military response to the so-called Pachuca menace, or of further news of Pachuca-inspired violence, suggests that such "confessions" may have been less than authentic.[37]

Nonetheless, it was primarily to this end that the imagined Pachuca served, to illustrate the depths of depravity of the Pachuco menace. The discourse on Pachucas held that girls were forced to become Pachucas on threat of severe violence. Once they had submitted themselves, they were then forced to undergo a series of initiation rites that included getting drunk, having sexual experiences with one or more Pachucos at a time, and committing theft, assault, and arson.[38] The language of violated womanhood was a well-worn trope within the national discourse, one that often signaled the urgency of action, if not extralegal action, to preserve the status quo. The lack of further public outcry over violated Mexican womanhood, however, was quite revealing of public attitudes and had much to do with the racial and ethnic identities of imagined Pachucas. The belief that Mexican males were abducting white women surely would have moved Los Angeles to more immediate action, but breaching social boundaries was not entirely unexpected of working women of color, and Mexican women in particular have been historically burdened with the baggage of wanton immorality in the white imagination.[39] It may have been for these reasons that the imagined Pachuca failed to mobilize Los Angeles to the same degree as did the imagined Pachuco.

A number of scholars and liberal-minded citizens responded to the image of the incorrigible Pachuco by arguing that Mexican American youths were no more criminally inclined than other impoverished young people, and they blamed the press for whipping up the flames of racial discord through their inflammatory reporting. In January 1943, within days after twelve of the seventeen defendants in the Sleepy Lagoon Case were sentenced to jail, Carey McWilliams argued in the *New Republic* that fundamentally there was nothing wrong with young Mexican Americans, "but for want of a satisfactory adjustment to their environment, their energies have taken this form of expression." McWilliams perceptively outlined the socioeconomic conditions found in many Mexican American neighborhoods and ominously predicted that nothing short of massive "affirmative federal programs" designed to improve the living and working conditions of resident Mexicans and Mexican Americans would eliminate the social and economic discrimination that produced the Pachuco.[40] George I. Sánchez, the foremost Mexican American scholar of the 1940s, elaborated the position advanced by McWilliams that if Pachucos were guilty of criminal behavior, society was the accessory. Sánchez documented in *Common Ground*, a magazine founded to explore national unity, case after case of the discriminatory attitudes and practices of society toward Mexican Americans. The crimes of Pachucos should be appropriately punished, he conceded, yet their greatest crime was being born into an environment that made them "fair prey to the cancer of gangsterism."[41]

Other scholars were also sympathetic of the Pachuco, yet they were not as forgiving. Ruth Tuck shared McWilliams's views, but she attributed the Pachuco's existence to "economic and political impotency, discriminatory law enforcement, [and] a high ethnic visibility." Although her writing was largely sympathetic toward the plight of racial minorities in the United States, Tuck did not view Pachucos as being fundamentally normal teenagers. Not only was the political and economic powerlessness of Mexican Americans the result of their culture, Tuck argued, but they in turn contributed to their own exploitation. "The Mexican," she announced, "arrived leaderless. The *patron* system, established in labor gangs crossing the border, remained a basic organization in Mexican colonies; the prominent

Mexican is too often the exploiter of his own people." Finally, Tuck concluded that the generational struggle common to immigrant families played an important role in shaping the rise of the Pachuco. "The older Mexican has always thrown the burden of facing the Anglo-American world on his children. It is the teenage child who interprets for bill collectors, landlords, employers, relief agencies—and the police." As a consequence, the teenager caught between two conflicting cultures grows up "a tragic puzzle to his parents; their background of a rural, semi-feudal culture leaves them incapable of guiding their children in urban life."[42] Sociologist Emory Bogardus was equally harsh on both society and victim. Pachucos were the tragic result of a series of social and economic inadequacies that led to their condition of being "culturally underprivileged and starved." Their inability to speak English correctly and the inability of their parents to provide them with a quality education exacerbated their already low IQs "due to inbreeding." Thus Pachuco gangs resulted from the "terrible freedom" teenagers enjoyed in the United States, which was followed by harsh punishments by parents.[43] Gang violence in turn was "aggravated by the use of liquor, and sometimes by the smoking of marihuana cigarettes . . . which may drive their victims literally mad with hallucinations."[44]

Even members of the Sleepy Lagoon Defense Committee, which was perhaps the most organized opposition to the printed reconstruction of the Pachuco, never directly challenged the Pachuco's public image. Indeed, the predominant views of the Pachuco seem never to have been in question *within* the organization itself. Speeches and other printed matter prepared by the SLDC on the "Pachuco problem" were supported by unfiltered facts and information gathered directly from the major newspapers, and an air of benign paternalism lingered about the private and public communications coming out of the SLDC. An early internal report of the SLDC reveals its members' quandary as they struggled to understand the meaning of the very term "Pachuco":

> There are various explanations for the word "pachuco," by which term the Mexican boy gangs are known. Some say that (a) it derives from the word "pachuc," meaning that part of the duck which goes over the fence last, referring to the custom of the Mexican boys of letting their hair grow long and combing it straight back in two black wings that meet at the back of the head in a little top-knot; (b) it originated in a little town in Mexico called pachuco [*sic*]; (c) it refers to a fierce Mexican warrior by that name; (d) it is simply slang for "El Pas[o]an." Whatever the origin of

the word "pachuco," it is known that a great many of the customs of the boy gangs have been imported from an undesirable element in El Paso, Texas.[45]

Despite the tireless devotion of the SLDC to correct a terrible miscarriage of justice and free the Sleepy Lagoon boys from prison, the Pachuco was never more than a symptom of a larger societal ill. Through the SLDC's appeal to the heartstrings of the public by playing on its sense of fair play, its compassion for the less fortunate, its love of "America," the Pachuco remained as the rhetorical counterpoint that proved that something was terribly amiss in society. The Pachuco was nothing less than the living result of the failure of American society to live up to its creed.

Thus the strategy of the SLDC was to reframe the discourse by shifting public focus away from the Pachucos themselves toward the larger issue of racial intolerance and the damage that social discord caused the Allied war effort. The SLDC began the task, through a variety of media, by challenging the weaknesses of the state's case, highlighting the blatant prejudice of the judge who adjudicated the trial, and generally seeking to undermine the perception that the Sleepy Lagoon boys held any responsibility for the free-for-all that broke out before José Díaz was found dying from a blow to his head. Albee Slade, host of "Our Daily Bread," the "labor newspaper of the air" sponsored by the Congress of Industrial Organizations (CIO), remarked on one of his Friday night broadcasts that "these boys are actually clean-cut, loyal American kids who have become the innocent victims of race prejudice."[46]

Guy Endore, a renowned Hollywood screenwriter who donated his talents to writing *The Sleepy Lagoon Mystery*, also described the Sleepy Lagoon defendants as practically the boys next door.[47] They were "frolicsome kids" whose "escapades were always on Saturday night . . . for they were hard workers the rest of the week."[48] The assaults that occurred at the Delgadillo home on the Williams Ranch, resulting in several injuries requiring stitches and hospitalization, were "an evening of revelry."[49] Unlike the murderous teenagers the public had come to know through the newspapers, the Sleepy Lagoon boys were "fine youths" who were little more than "downy-cheeked youngsters" caught up in a contest of social forces that had little to do with them.[50] The real cause of this tragic miscarriage of justice, according to Endore, was the Hearst press, which stirred up racial antagonism for the purpose of selling more papers. He further reported that despite the time the boys were spending in San Quentin prison, their "hearts are warm, their minds are active," and they remained hardworking athletic heroes of cheery dispositions. Indeed, Endore's view of the boys was so optimistic that he wrote that "among these boys the Mexican community may some day find the leaders it is so badly in need of."

Alice McGrath spent more time in the barrios of Los Angeles with the families of the boys than any other member of the SLDC, yet she too saw the boys, their families, and the Mexican *colonia* at large through the lens of victimization. To McGrath, the Mexicans labored under a cloud of defeatism produced by a cycle of unfairness within American society. In articles that she published in the pro-labor newspaper the *Peoples' Daily World*, McGrath wrote with a view of the Mexicans that was common in her day. They came, according to McGrath, with the anticipation of escaping impoverishment and starvation in Mexico and participating in the American dream. But soon they met more heartbreak and were forced to perform "hard, dirty work for less money than other workers" and live in "shabby houses shabbier . . . rickety houses more rickety." Having come from Mexico before the Revolution, "they didn't bring with them the experience of having fought for themselves," and "the helpless, hopeless shrug of the shoulders is met too often." They were hobbled by the barriers of language in the United States and by leaders who bled and betrayed them. Yet McGrath was optimistic about their future, particularly if given a helping hand to realize their full political potential. "When they fully comprehend the tremendous latent power which they possess not only to better their conditions as a group, but to enrich and better the life of their entire community," she concluded, "when they realize what they can do if they organize . . . Que Maravilla!"[51]

### The Rhetorical Importance of the Pachuco

The perception of the destitute Mexican was an important element in the way middle-class reformers conceptualized the relationship between themselves and those they sought to aid. The image of the helpless immigrant engendered reactions among Angelenos that ranged from critical disdain to benign paternalism, spurring reformers to work on behalf of the needs—both real and imagined—of the communities of color. Yet at the same time the image inspired a benevolence from white, middle-class activists that also clouded their understanding of the political life in the working-class districts of Los Angeles. At times even the most well meaning reformers tended to overlook the numerous grassroots organizations already in existence that could have furthered their cause for justice and failed to notice the advances people of color were slowly making into mainstream politics.[52]

Part of the problem also lay in the sources of information reformers consulted about Mexican Americans. Emory Bogardus was a well-known scholar in the study of ethnicity, and Ruth Tuck was a trained anthropologist who had served as a case supervisor for the Federal Emergency Relief Administration for seven years in communities where a large part of the Mexican population was on relief, and she had also traveled to Mexico to study repatriated Mexicans.[53] Although these authorities were sympathetic toward the plight of the boys convicted of murder in the Sleepy Lagoon case, they nonetheless reflected many of the deeper, prevailing assumptions about race. Even prominent members of the Mexican American and African American middle class, to whom whites usually listened as spokespersons for their people, looked on working-class youths with measured disdain and apprehension.

Still, even if the middle-class activists and reformers had been able to extricate themselves from their time and place and see past the racial predispositions of their day, the Pachuco served a very useful role in being larger than life. The creation of the public Pachuco gave activists on the left, from New Dealers and union organizers to the Communist Party U.S.A., a cause to fight for, an evil to unite against, and a powerful rhetorical weapon to wield in pushing forward their own social agendas. The radio program "Our Daily Bread," sponsored by the Los Angeles CIO, featured periodic updates on the activities of the SLDC and its efforts to raise money to appeal the conviction of the Sleepy Lagoon boys.[54] These broadcasts regularly explained the anti-Pachuco hysteria within the framework of fifth-column conspiracy (a term commonly used to describe behind-the-scenes subterfuge by enemy sympathizers). One broadcast that aired on Wednesday, 5 May 1943, blamed pro-fascist Mexican Sinarquists for stirring support for the police crackdown on working-class youths in the Mexican American community because the Mexican Sinarquists viewed Pachucos as being "corrupted by American thought and habits." Noting the identical surnames of local Sinarquist leader Pedro Villaseñor, who was an outspoken critic of Pachuco youths, and Richard Villaseñor, whom the program hosts identified as the young man who "put the finger on the kids," the hosts concluded that a conspiracy was afoot that was "without a doubt Hitler inspired, Hitler organized."[55] This was not the first time Mexican Sinarquists were blamed for creating disharmony by promoting juvenile delinquency on the one hand and stirring up anti-Pachuco sentiment on the other. At one rally for the SLDC, Josefina Fierro de Bright of the Congress of Spanish-Speaking People identified "'pachuco terrorism' as the work of dupes [and] puppets of Sinarquists" and called for greater government intervention to better conditions within the *colonia*.[56]

As a rhetorical strategy, speeches and other public appeals by the SLDC also waved the banner of fifth-column conspiracy to interpret events or explain causation and appealed to patriotism to gain support for its efforts. A broadcast on Thursday, 14 October 1943, described the police crackdown as "mass arrests reminiscent of Nazi methods." In a Friday night broadcast, on 18 February 1944, one commentator remarked that the trial of the Sleepy Lagoon boys "was conducted on a basis of . . . the Nazi doctrine of Aryan supremacy as snugly as any I've ever seen."[57] Calling on the patriotism of the program's listeners, the commentator urged them to oppose the tougher police policy on Mexican American teenagers because it could damage Allied solidarity in the Western Hemisphere. "The persecution of these Mexican boys," the commentator warned, "has given the Axis radio as juicy a bit of anti-American propaganda as they have ever had—and they have used it skillfully."[58]

The charge of enemy subversion and conspiracy filled an important gap in how the SLDC tied together the events of that year. Not only did conspiracy place the events in a comprehensible framework, but it also supplied the cause with a rallying point and helped counter the charge that "the whole movement for the defense of the kids was being run by 'Reds.'"[59] The many volunteers who worked for the SLDC were convinced, as were Guy Endore and Carey McWilliams, that William Randolph Hearst was largely to blame for stirring up racial antagonism. In *The Sleepy Lagoon Mystery*, Endore relates an encounter he had with a news reporter while preparing to write the booklet; the reporter shared information that implicated Hearst in creating the anti-Pachuco hysteria in order to rid Los Angeles of the so-called Mexican problem. According to the source, whom Endore quoted extensively, Hearst had sent word to his editors in Los Angeles to gather statistics on Mexicans, African Americans, and crime and report on the findings to other Hearst editors. Endore went on to suggest strongly that Hearst was a closet fascist sympathetic with Hitler's regime in Germany and that he had acted to disrupt American unity.[60] Certainly the tabloid style of journalism some of the newspapers used did not help ease public fears of a wartime crime wave by juvenile delinquents or by fifth-column activities.[61]

To look to "the press" as the catalyst for the anti-Pachuco hysteria creates more questions than it answers, however. William Randolph Hearst and Harry Chandler may have indeed personally wanted to do something to drive the "Mexican problem" from Los Angeles. But to instigate a conspiracy for the purpose of manipulating the public would require an amazing feat of logistical coordination, corporate cooperation between rival newspapers, and employee compliance from the beat reporter all the way to the city desk. It is a story the likes of which has yet to be told.[62]

Toni Morrison's reflections about the constructions of blackness and whiteness in American literature offer a useful way to understand the rise of the imagined Pachuco: "The subject of the dream is the dreamer. The fabrication of an Africanist persona reflexive; an extraordinary mediation on the self; a powerful exploration of the fears and desires that reside in the writerly conscious. It is an astonishing revelation of longing, of terror, of perplexity, of shame, of magnanimity. It requires hard work *not* to see this."[63] The imagined Pachuco existed as an expression of public anxiety that illustrated and critiqued the problems of society from a variety of political perspectives. The discourse on Pachucos and juvenile delinquency indeed managed to capture accurately some aspects about the growing youth culture within the Los Angeles working class, such as carousing in groups, drinking, engaging in premarital sex, and occasionally fighting one another. As juvenile authorities, reporters, and civic officials struggled to identify the reasons for such behavior among youths, both real and imagined, the name "Pachuco" grew from being an in-group Spanish word to assume a place in the public terminology to describe any young person who wore the drape, fought, drank, talked back, or rebelled against social convention in some way. But these traits did not describe all working-class youths; nor were they uncommon for most young people. The public construction of the Pachuco served as a way of allowing middle-class reformers and other concerned citizens to identify and remove, in a discursive way, the sin from among them.

# PART III
# SHOUTING CURSES ON THE STREET

# 7 : Wars of Resistance

**W**ithin five months after the Sleepy Lagoon murder trial concluded, Los Angeles erupted in a week of rioting between military men, civilians, and zoot-suited youths. Although the Zoot Suit Riot and the trial were unrelated by a direct causal link, they were related by the context of the discursive moment. Many Angelenos saw the death of José Díaz as a tragedy that resulted from a larger pattern of lawlessness and rebellion among Mexican American youths, discerned through their self-conscious fashioning of difference, and increasingly called for stronger measures to crack down on juvenile delinquency. For this reason many Angelenos joined or supported the servicemen who rioted to restore social order.

The ongoing conflict over social propriety transformed into battles on the streets over social space, and military records provide compelling evidence that local civilian youths increasingly harassed and intimidated sailors stationed at the Naval Reserve Armory who entered their neighborhoods for months before the outbreak of rioting. The source material for the servicemen's claims is not without controversy because the sailors who filed grievances did so just as the rioting started in early June 1943. The startling constant in all their reports is that in more than eighty cases of harassment, not once did the sailors confess to provoking such responses from civilian youths; neither did they admit to retaliating in any way. Had they reported otherwise, they would have undermined their implicit justification for taking the law into their own hands in early June 1943.[1] Still, despite such reported restraint, critical elements of plausibility filter through these mediated accounts. Sailors were surprisingly frank in the details of the events they reported, such as the time, place, who was involved, and the language used. Other historical documents lend credibility to their accounts. Police reports; studies conducted by Mexican American community groups; sociological studies conducted by graduate students at the University of California, Los Angeles, and the University of Southern California;

census information; and oral histories all corroborate that civilian youths came into increasing confrontation with military men long before the riot broke out.[2]

What is clear about the social tensions before the riot is that city planners complicated the social geography of the low-income, mostly Mexican American neighborhoods just north of downtown Los Angeles by erecting a million-dollar training school for the all-white navy in the Chavez Ravine. Not only did this make all the more obvious the wages of racialized privilege, but it also exposed the families in this area to the widespread problem of controlling the often uncivil behavior of military men on leave. Although many white Angelenos complained bitterly about the unruly and sometimes destructive behavior of military men, they nonetheless endured these affronts in the name of patriotic duty and supporting "our boys." Conflicts between servicemen and civilians, however, became qualitatively different encounters when racial differences became part of the mix. The residents of these historically Mexican neighborhoods, where the majority of conflicts occurred, responded aggressively to white military men who transgressed the physical and social spaces of their community.

The fight waged by these predominantly Mexican American youths to enforce their sense of place earned them little sympathy and few allies outside their neighborhoods. The public at large viewed these acts of resistance through the lens of juvenile delinquency and subversion. Many civilians cheered on rioting sailors who not only acted to reassert the authority of the state in taking local law enforcement into their own hands but also sought to shore up the segregated boundaries of race that this assertive generation of young people increasingly challenged and transgressed. Although the Zoot Suit Riot initially broke out as an act of vigilantism in direct response to the confrontations between sailors and local youths, it became a more complicated conflict as thousands of military men who were stationed in bases throughout southern California poured into town in the following days. The Zoot Suit Riot was at once a contest between the military and civilians, between whites and Mexican Americans, between social conformity and individuality, between men *as* men, and between competing fictional geographies that shaped their sense of place and their responses to each other.

### Los Angeles Geopolitics

If there was a ground zero where local youths and military personnel increasingly clashed during 1942 and 1943, it was the narrow stretch of Figueroa Boulevard that ran between the armory to the north and downtown Los Angeles to the south. Along this two-laned road lay three distinct neighborhoods connected by Figueroa: Chavez Ravine, Alpine Street, and Temple Street (see map 3). Each neighborhood was defined by its own geographical setting, history, demographics, and street culture, but together these neighborhoods made up one of the many ethnic enclaves in Los Angeles that were created by the forces of imperialist expansion, industrial growth, and racialized privilege.

Sailors came to the armory to learn communications at the Naval Training School that was established there. After their training the majority of graduates went on to serve as radiomen aboard combat and support vessels in the Pacific theater. Contrary to what was later charged, they were not all white southerners, although they were certainly all white. The navy, and the armory, remained segregated institutions during World War II. The recruits that arrived at the Naval Training School came from every region in the country, from large urban centers to small hamlets. A few were from southern California, but most sailors seem to have had little experience with Mexicans or Mexican culture before coming to Los Angeles. The majority of sailors stationed at the armory had been there between eight and twelve weeks before the riot broke out. Most were between the ages of eighteen and twenty. Half of the recruits had not completed high school, and only a handful had any college experience.

The hills of Chavez Ravine that surrounded the armory had long been occupied by Mexican workers. It looked little changed in the 1940s by almost a hundred years of American domination of California. Many Angelenos thus considered the Chavez Ravine to be a provincial blemish on the face of a modern city.[3] Within sight of the granite pillars of City Hall and the Hall of Justice, children could be found playing on the hard-packed dirt roads that meandered throughout the ravine. Potted geraniums and flower gardens framed the patches of grass that lay in front of time-worn homes, occasionally interrupted by the rusting remains of an ancient automobile. Only about 40 percent of the residents owned their own homes.[4] The rest of the families rented places to live in during the winter until their hands and backs were needed again in the nearby orchards and fields to power the agricultural industry.[5] Some of these households kept goats in their backyard and penned-in chickens, and 13 percent of the homes still had outhouses on the property. Almost none had central heating, and almost a quarter of the houses were in need of major repair. Yet the residents of Chavez Ravine were not without a few amenities of modern living: more than three-fourths of the families owned a radio, and most owned a car.

Most of the residents of Chavez Ravine were native to the United States,

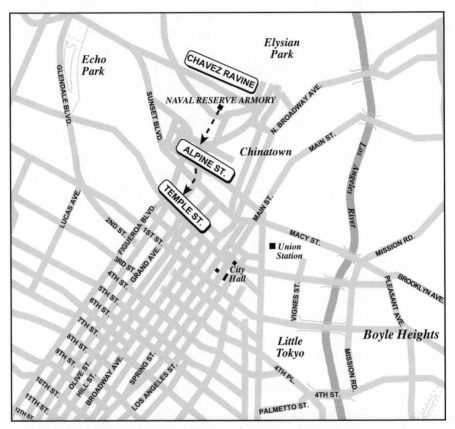

Map 3. The neighborhoods of Chavez Ravine, Alpine Street, and Temple Street in downtown Los Angeles, 1943. Arrows indicate the path along Figueroa Boulevard that sailors at the Naval Reserve Armory took to reach downtown Los Angeles.

**Table 3. Demographic Profiles of Chavez Ravine, Alpine Street, and Temple Street Neighborhoods, 1940**

| | Chavez Ravine | % | Alpine Street | % | Temple Street | % |
|---|---|---|---|---|---|---|
| Native-born[a] | 3,144 | 67.5 | 2,836 | 55.8 | 2,828 | 75 |
| Foreign-born | 1,457 | 31.3 | 1,938 | 38.1 | 746 | 20 |
| Negro | 3 | <0.1 | 6[b] | 0.1 | 0 | 0 |
| Other | 52 | 1.1 | 306[b] | 6 | 206 | 5 |
| Total | 4,656 | | 5,086 | | 3,780 | |

*Source: Sixteenth Census of the United States, 1940.* Figures for the Chavez Ravine neighborhood are based on tract 67. Figures for the Alpine Street neighborhood are based on tract 115; see Chapter 7, n. 8, regarding the statistical information on this neighborhood. Figures for the Temple Street neighborhood are based on tract 180.

[a] See Chapter 7, n. 6, for information on the ethnic composition of these neighborhoods.

[b] Drawn from housing statistics.

predominantly of Mexican origin, although close to a third of them, about fourteen hundred, were born outside the country.[6] The greatest majority of the foreign-born migrated to Los Angeles from Mexico, and there was also an appreciable number of immigrant families from Italy and central Europe.[7] Most of the residents were employed as farm laborers, domestics, craftsmen, and machine operators. Many did not finish elementary school; the average number of completed years was a little more than seven.

Although only a few blocks separated Alpine Street from Chavez Ravine, there were unmistakable differences between these two neighborhoods. The houses and apartments near Alpine were erected within the boundaries of incorporated Los Angeles. Thus residents there enjoyed the amenities of the municipal services, such as paved streets, regular trash pickup, and running water. Alpine was far from an affluent area, however.[8] Although some small businessmen and white-collar workers made their permanent homes in the Alpine area, for the most part it was a transitional place where primarily blue-collar workers and unskilled laborers came in search of better opportunities. Only one family in ten owned its own home; the other 90 percent rented apartments in structures that ranged from duplexes to large apartment buildings.[9] Only two people out of every ten finished grade school, and the average number of school years completed in the area was not quite six. More than one-third of the residents of Alpine were born outside the United

**Table 4. Foreign-Born Residents of Chavez Ravine, Alpine Street, and Temple Street Neighborhoods by Country of Origin, 1940**

| | Chavez Ravine | % | Alpine Street | % | Temple Street | % |
|---|---|---|---|---|---|---|
| Mexico | 918 | 70.3 | 721 | 41 | 220 | 48 |
| Italy | 286 | 22.0 | 282 | 16 | 41 | 9 |
| Central Europe[a] | 56 | 4.3 | 275 | 16 | 71 | 16 |
| Germany[b] | 45 | 3.4 | 86 | 5 | 77 | 17 |
| Russia[b] | — | — | 374 | 22 | 47 | 10 |
| Total | 1,305 | | 1,738 | | 456 | |

Source: *Sixteenth Census of the United States, 1940.*

[a] Including Yugoslavia, Hungary, Poland, Romania, and Czechoslovakia.

[b] Possibly Jewish.

States, many of whom were single men from Italy and central Europe. Of the foreign-born, Mexicans made up the largest group at 37 percent, with Russian Jews making up the next largest group at 19 percent.

Farther south of Alpine, along Figueroa Boulevard, was the transitional zone of Temple Street where downtown Los Angeles began. The relative affluence of the downtown area reflected the demographics. The architectural extravagance that adorned the Victorian buildings along Main Street, which ran parallel to Figueroa, was by the 1940s only a fading reminder of the boom days before the economic elite began their exodus to the suburbs in the 1870s. Yet Main Street, from Temple south to 6th Street, known since the days of Mexican occupation as *calle principal*, still retained a degree of economic importance for the city. By the Second World War the businesses occupying the street-level floors were a serviceman's delight, being a mixture of small shops, makeshift bars, honky-tonks, barber colleges, tattoo shops, pawn shops, flophouses, and all-night movie houses where homeless audiences tried to sleep through the blaring sound tracks of continuous movie reels.[10] The navy did its best to steer sailors clear of places deemed "troublesome," declaring some thirty bars and taverns in the downtown area off-limits for "sanitary reasons" and posting the shore patrol along the business streets of Los Angeles to enforce the sanction.[11]

Above these streets some thirty thousand people crammed into the apartments reaching up into the California sky. Although most were American-born, there was still an appreciable number of Mexican, Russian Jew, Italian, and some Asian immigrants living there, all drawn toward Los Angeles by the hope of finding better employment and a better fate in the Golden State.[12] The blocks most populated by people of color lay between Temple Street and 1st Street. The majority of the residents there were Mexican American, with Mexican-born residents making up only 5 percent of the immigrant population.[13] Most of these residents owned the small businesses along Main Street or were employed in white-collar work as clerks, salespeople, managers, and the like. The farther south one traveled in the downtown area, the more affluent the neighborhoods were, in proportion to the whiteness of the residents. Germans, English, and Canadians were the largest groups of immigrants living in the blocks from 1st Street down to 9th.[14]

## Competing Geographies

The young women and men of these neighborhoods came of age within a complicated nexus of local and global forces that shaped their sense of who they were. Segregation cut a deep swath through Los Angeles, negatively affecting residents' interactions with one another, and divided areas of town, employment, recreational sites, cultural production, and even material consumption along racialized lines. Conversely, as Robin D. G. Kelley argued in exploring black bars and dance halls, local clubs, cafés, restaurants, dance halls, and movie houses owned and operated by Mexican or African Americans became important loci of communal interaction, where social ties could be reaffirmed and renewed in private by people otherwise disfranchised from "public" Los Angeles.[15] Global migrations of working people also shaped the cultural orientations of the young people in these neighborhoods, creating through residential patterns a sense of "belonging" for the children of immigrants that combined the global with the local in the ethnic enclaves of metropolitan Los Angeles. Many of these young people were children of refugees from the Mexican Revolution who struggled to raise their families in a foreign land according to strict Mexican mores, while their children learned English in school and danced the jitterbug to the swing music of black and Jewish musicians.

Young men (and some women) in all three neighborhoods situated their sense of place and negotiated their identities by participating in an economy of social relations in which status and honor were earned through episodic violence within and between neighborhood groups. Although the phenomenon of street violence in Los Angeles was nowhere near the level that it is today, the Los Angeles Police Department considered the area between Alpine and Temple to be a locus of considerable juvenile delinquency. Thus social workers, community activists, and the LAPD, in trying to establish more socially approved outlets for youths, concentrated their efforts in this area.[16] In one study of inner-city crime, however, Susan J. Smith suggests another way of seeing how street violence between young people of rival neighborhoods served to shape and construct their social identities around their sense of place. Although crime clearly has a negative impact on a community, in some important ways it also serves as a "positive social interaction." "The short geographical distances between offenders and private victims," writes Smith, "could be interpreted as reflecting small social distances."[17] Indeed, these neighborhoods where young people were identified by the names of their streets constituted one of the ways in which they anchored their sense of place and created their identities within the geographical and social boundaries of Los Angeles. Although deservedly criticized and much denounced during this period, "gang wars" served as one of the socializing agents through which mostly young males marked and measured themselves.

The complicated social networks of these three neighborhoods were deeply affected in different ways by the aggressive expansion of public space in Los Angeles. Since the 1920s city planners and politicians envisioned a modern city connected by extensive roadways, with a civic center in the heart of the downtown surrounded by cultural sites that celebrated the diversity of the populace and the advancements of the arts. Yet that vision of modernity projected into the future the racialized realities of the day. The envisioned citizens who staffed and utilized that civic space, the patrons of the arts, and the consumers of local "culture" were, without question, white. City planners, furthermore, were not considering unused and unpopulated lands or even neighborhoods of the white middle class as sites for this growth of public space. Much of the reconstruction of Los Angeles would pave over neighborhoods long occupied by predominantly Mexican American families.

To be sure, the reconstruction of Los Angeles that began in the early twentieth century and continued into the postwar period altered the shopping habits and pedestrian traffic of the local citizens. But for many families who invested important meaning in the physical and social geographies of their community, the expansion of public space in Los Angeles was more than an inconvenience. It disrupted and dislocated communal sites, family sites, and familiar patterns of social interaction. American Indian and mestizo families had lived on the sites cleared in the 1930s for the twin towers of City Hall and the Hall of Justice, for example, since before the days of Mexican occupation.[18] In 1940 the city exercised the right of eminent domain to claim part of the Chavez Ravine in order to build a million-dollar training school for the navy, the Naval Reserve Armory. Asian families were also directly affected by these changes. In 1939 the city razed the neighborhoods that made up Chinatown in order to make way for the new Los Angeles Union Passenger Terminal. And although it was not part of the expansion of public space, it is no less significant that during the same period the Little Tokyo community also disappeared almost overnight as Japanese Americans were physically removed from Los Angeles in 1942 in the name of "public" safety and forced to sell their homes and businesses at below-market prices.[19] Each of these sites were erased or significantly altered in the name of greater public interests, either in the expansion of public spaces or in the exercise of state power that racialized the rights of citizens and defined who was part of "the public" and who was not accordingly.

In the process of altering the physical geography of Los Angeles, civic leaders complicated the social geographies of these neighborhoods in either downplaying or disregarding the investment that families living there had in maintaining the integrity of their communities. Thus the Naval Reserve Armory, which served as a training facility for the navy, stood out like an island amid a sea of time-worn homes in Chavez Ravine. In keeping with the architectural impulse of the day, the armory was constructed with California granite and complemented with a Mediterranean architectural style that suggested a tie to the romantic Spanish past, but the facility could not have clashed more with its immediate surrounding.[20] The mostly Mexican American, working-class residents of Chavez Ravine lived separately in a very different cultural and economic world than the white, middle-class officers who staffed the training school. The armory, furthermore, looked every bit the frontier outpost standing watch over the surrounding enclaves of the local population. Although by the 1940s Los Angeles was hardly a frontier town, a palpable tension nonetheless existed between the locals and the military. In the months prior to the outbreak of mob violence in June 1943, sailors, their wives, and their friends all reported a growing number of hostile encounters with civilian youths in the area surrounding the armory. It was not an entirely new phenomenon in the region; nor were the sailors stationed at the armory the first to feel the resentment of the native residents who chafed under the presence of the military in their land. The sailors who left the protection of the armory and headed into town down Figueroa also walked into a social economy between young males in rival neighborhoods in which maintaining the integrity of place through street violence served as an important agent of socialization.

## Border Crossings

"Different societies," wrote Anne Godlewska and Neil Smith, "practise different kinds of geography," and the conflicts between local youths and military men grew, in part, out of competing fictional geographies of Los Angeles.[21] In expanding public space, the city of Los Angeles imposed its own vision of geography on the land in erasing the past and erecting a "modern" city over the "condemned" Mexican American neighborhoods that once stood there. White naval officers stationed in the Chavez Ravine, and the sailors who trained there, saw the streets as public venues and acted on the assumption that they were entitled to free and open access to all of Los Angeles by virtue of their citizenship, race, class, gender, and military service. However, the local youths who patronized these same clubs, cafés, and movie theaters saw that same space very differently. Their places of socialization had yet to become "public" regardless of the changes around them, and they actively resisted the unwelcome presence of outsiders, particularly those who tried to exercise assumed privileges of whiteness. In August 1942, for example, four young men wearing zoot suits confronted a sailor and his girlfriend near the Chinatown area.[22] Standing shoulder to shoulder, the young civilians blocked the sidewalk and refused to yield passage to the couple. The sailor dropped back in order for his girlfriend to pass, and when he came abreast with the zoot-suited phalanx, the boy nearest him shoved him off the sidewalk into the street. The sailor and the civilian squared off with each other, silently standing their ground. Tense moments passed until the sailor finally backed away.[23] This was not an isolated incident.

Uncomfortable moments of contact were perhaps to be expected as some fifty thousand military men on leave poured into Los Angeles each week. In the process of sightseeing and wandering around town, they no doubt transgressed the unspoken mores of the predominantly Mexican, African American, Italian, and Jewish neighborhoods that lined the downtown district.[24] Most Angelenos tended to dismiss the abusive behavior of military men as simply "blowing off steam."[25] But the meaning of abusive behavior took on a different significance when racial dynamics became a part of the exchange, and the ways in which many Mexican American men responded to military men reveal important clues about how they viewed themselves, their identities as men, and their obligations to community and nation. One Mexican American man reportedly told a white sailor who walked into the Tip Toe Inn in East Los Angeles that it was unhealthy for him to eat there. The sailor hesitated, and the civilian responded: "If you don't leave now you will be in one fucking mess when you get in town—if you are able to get there after we are through with you."[26] As Electrician's Mate Third Class Domenick Valleta walked along Alpine near Broadway in late May 1943, a carload of young men, some reportedly dressed in zoot suits, drove close to the curb and spat on him. "Son of a bitch!" "Bastard!" they yelled as they drove off.[27] That same afternoon Seaman Second Class James Jerome Granner walked along Figueroa Boulevard and encountered a group of young men dressed in zoot suits at the corner of Temple and Figueroa. "There's another one of those sons of bitches," someone called out, and someone spat on the sailor as he turned around and headed back to the armory.[28]

Many of the physical challenges and verbal retorts from minority males defied the unwritten but often violently enforced codes of white privilege. Although there are some reports that Mexican American women also verbally harassed sailors, the overwhelming number of aggressive responses to military men came from Mexican American men who, regardless of the threat of white violence, refused to back down to the exercise of white privilege. Sailors often reported that for months prior to the Zoot Suit Riot young civilian men, mostly Mexican American, often blocked their access to dance halls, theaters, or restaurants or chased after them as they walked in the "public" areas of town. These street-level responses suggest a more complicated picture of how men within the Mexican American communities of Los Angeles responded to a systematic practice of segregation that socially undermined their identity as males. Rather than conforming to the image of the docile and deferential campesino-as-victim, held even by sympathetic white activists and social workers of the period, a number of young Mexican American men fought back with both words and deeds.[29] Although many of these sailors chose to retreat rather than respond, the verbal and physical challenges of minority youths were transgressions of white privilege that both sailor and civilian understood well.

The systematic denial of autonomy to racialized nonwhite males in the era of segregation positioned them in conflict with normative definitions of masculinity as they strove to assert themselves as men within that social context. Rosa Linda Fregoso offers an insightful observation about the context in which Latino males have operated, particularly the context of these street confrontations.

This positioning of the Chicano subject as a "problem" in dominant culture derives from the more general historical re-construction of the identities of non-Europeans as the negative or pathological manifestation of the Western male subject. While a heterogeneous range of masculine identities is emphasized for the dominant culture, the representation of the identity of non-Western males stands out for its singular and homogeneous economy, resting entirely within the negative side of the masculine equation.[30]

Robert Staples offers a similar argument about black manhood, that it has always existed in conflict with normative definitions of masculinity; such definitions "implied a certain autonomy and mastery of one's own environment" that were denied to black men.[31] Although nonwhite civilian and white military men acted with differing notions of masculinity, shaped by their experiences with class, race, and heritage, the contests also took place within the context of a hegemonic masculinity, in which both parties understood that personal and collective autonomy was the prize sought from the contest.[32] White masculinity, in large part, defined itself through the subjugation of racialized and gendered others, and nonwhite civilian youths challenged white military men through a masculinist language understood by both camps—that of of taunts, feints, and affronts—as a contender would challenge the acknowledged champion in anticipation of a showdown.

What is remarkable about such direct taunts and challenges is that these nonwhite civilian youths acted in defiance of the past and present. As survivors of the repatriation efforts in the previous decade, and as witnesses to the increasingly violent opposition to black homeownership in the West Adams district, the Van Ness–Cimarron district, West Slauson, Watts, and Maywood, they were certainly aware of the power of the state to enforce or at least acquiesce to popular will.[33] Their willingness to act irrespective of the violence that underwrote the practice of segregation suggests critical ways in which they viewed themselves in relation to the larger society. They were not sojourners in a foreign land, like their parents, and they were not content to play the roles assigned them by racial privilege. Their vision of American society was more complex, one that included them as full and equal participants, and they understood well the value of self-assertion. Whether it was a lesson learned through history books, hard knocks, or desperation, they viewed the neighborhoods of Los Angeles as their ground to defend in the face of assault, and they rose to the challenges.

Both military and police reports attributed these localized contests of social space to the imagined unpatriotic or un-American sympathies of juvenile delinquents. Although neither police nor sailors demonstrated much critical insight or understanding of the issues confronting the young people of these neighborhoods, much less their political loyalties, their interpretation has some merit in the abstract. As Gail Bederman argues in exploring an earlier generation of Americans, male power and racial dominance were intimately connected to the discourse of "civilization," and certainly the myth of the white man's burden of civilizing the imagined savage continued to shape how the majority of Americans saw themselves in relation to racialized minorities.[34] Thus the myriad acts of resistance to white prerogative challenged some of the fundamental assumptions that underwrote American society.

At the same time, however, Mexican Americans did not oppose the national war effort or encourage disrespect for national symbols. Indeed, in some ways they contributed to the war effort with even greater sacrifice than other populations within Los Angeles: according to Raul Morín, Mexican Americans earned a disproportionate number of combat decorations for valor.[35] The war in some way had touched the lives of almost every family in the area, and many had sons, brothers, or cousins fighting abroad. Many of the younger brothers and sisters, furthermore, worked in war-related industries and participated in scrap metal drives and USO dances and carnivals, and the majority of the young men expressed their willingness to join the war effort when their time came. Yet their general support for the nation at war and their investment in patriotism did not include deferring to the written and unwritten codes of white privilege, and they opposed it in a variety of venues and with a variety of methods.

In June 1943, Seaman Second Class Francis Harold Lloyd Jr. transgressed one boundary as he edged his car in front of a group of zoot-suited young men crossing a downtown intersection. "You god-damned sailors think you own the streets," they shouted at him.[36] Such a remark was (and still is) a common criticism of aggressive drivers, but it is important to remember that for the boys who shouted at Lloyd the streets of the city often served as the landmarks that shaped their identities: they delineated the boundaries of their neighborhoods, defined their social units and networks, and were sites of social interactions. Lloyd's encounter with civilian youths at a busy intersection was more than a matter of the pedestrian's right of way. It was a confrontation between the uses of physical space and the maintenance of social boundaries. The civilian youths' protestations of the sailor's behavior were as much a reassertion of proprietorship as they were a reminder to the sailor that he was merely a visitor in their territory.[37]

There was perhaps no other issue more incendiary between military and civilian men than transgressing the imagined boundaries of male responsibilities toward, competition for, and prerogatives with women. Both white and Mexican American men repeatedly challenged each other's manhood in challenging the other's ability to protect "their" women, while reserving for themselves the prerogative to harass and abuse women of their own racial group. The wife of a white navy officer stationed abroad, for example, anonymously wrote to the admiral in command of the Eleventh Naval District, headquartered in San Diego, to complain about the sexual harassment she faced nightly from sailors. "Every time I leave my work I am approached by some Navy men wanting to date me," she wrote. "I tell them NO, then they call me the most vulgar names." She received little support or sympathy from the white military police or the San Diego Police Department. "Where I am living the women don't have a good word for the Navy," she concluded.[38] Another civilian anonymously wrote the admiral with a similar complaint about sailors harassing women on the streets of San Diego, the worst occurring after nine o'clock at night. "The servicemen seem to hide and wait for ladies passing on their way home annoying them by remarks and following them—which makes it very unpleasant and unsafe," reported the concerned civilian; "these men seem to disregard a person's age and make the same advances to both young and old."[39]

The noted writer Chester B. Himes witnessed an incident involving military men and a civilian man and woman shortly before the rioting in June 1943. Publishing his account in *The Crisis*, Himes wrote in a style that captured the sound of the white sailors' words as he sat riding in a street car going up Central Avenue. Three drunken white sailors bragged about their prowess as fighting men as they boarded the car. "Ah'm tellin' yuh, Ah fought lak a white man!" bellowed one of the sailors. "Did Ah fight lak a white man, boy?" At the next stop a young Mexican couple boarded the car and took the empty seats opposite the sailors. "Boy, did those native gals go fuh us," the sailor said, as he eyed the attractive Mexican girl. The other passengers began to shift uncomfortably as the sailor's bragging turned to his sexual prowess. "Boy, uh white man can git any gal he wants," he continued. "Can't he, boy, can't he git 'em if he wants 'em?" Hearing enough, the young Mexican man stood up and said to his girlfriend, "Let's move down front." "Oh, why do you want to move?" she protested; "we're going to get off in a few minutes." The sailors burst out laughing as the young man sat back down. A few moments later he reached up, yanked the cord to stop the car, and dashed out. On other occasions, Himes noted, white servicemen trying to "pick up" a Mexican girl were properly disciplined by Mexican boys. "We hate to think of what might have happened to a darker-skinned Mexican in a white bar in a white district, trying to pick up . . . a white girl," he wryly observed.[40]

Yet white sailors certainly held no monopoly when it came to the sexual harassment of women. Some young Mexican American men cruised Los Angeles looking for casual sex with white women and harassed those who refused. In the process, they unwittingly provided enough anecdotal evidence to stir the wrath of all of white Los Angeles over an imagined assault on white womanhood. One sailor reported that his wife had a disturbing encounter with two young men wearing zoot suits one Saturday night in early May 1943. As she walked home from visiting her husband at the armory, she noticed a car driven by two young men in zoot suits cruising up and down Chavez Ravine. After driving by a few times, they pulled up next to her and asked her to get in the car. "How about a fuck?" one of them shouted out.[41] The report does not include what happened afterward, but such encounters no doubt stoked the climate of hostility between whites and local minority youths. As scholars from Ida B. Wells-Barnett to Joel Williamson have ably illustrated, the protection of white womanhood from the black rapist (in this case, brown) was a familiar trope that both male and female whites evoked to justify violence against a racialized individual or an entire community of racialized men.[42] And, as Gail Bederman further adds, white womanhood often served as a metaphor for civilization.[43] Thus, for white military men the harassment of white women challenged not only their identity as men but also their heightened sense of responsibility as men who were in military service to defend the nation from assault.[44]

### Articulated Signs of Resistance

The young people living and working in the areas surrounding the armory were quite savvy in the way they harassed sailors and other military men. The great majority of comments and epithets that sailors reported from civilian youths revolved around three central themes. Some young people ridiculed patriotism by suggesting that servicemen were fools because there were so many ways to avoid military service. Others questioned the bravery of sailors by asking if they had joined the navy to avoid facing combat duty. Finally, a number of young men hurled sexually explicit taunts at sailors that called into question their status as heterosexual men. Seaman Second Class Benny Claire Boatright had an encounter that was typical of the many incidents servicemen reported in May 1943. Around 10:30 P.M., two young men started to follow Boatright as he passed through Pershing Square. They spoke to each other, loud enough for the sailor to overhear, commenting on how "rotten" the navy was and referring to it as "a bunch of dirty-looking sons of bitches." When Boatright wisely chose not to acknowledge their taunts, they called out to him directly and told him that he was a sucker to be in the navy when there were so "damn many ways to get out of it."[45]

Remarks that questioned patriotic duty or challenged the respect of the navy rang with a particular dissonance in the ears of sailors who heard them.

Belittling the navy and ridiculing patriotism were considered fighting words in themselves by many a sailor, but these comments were made especially biting because they came out of the mouths of those who should have been the last to complain. Civilian youths were the direct beneficiaries of the sacrifices sailors made in the name of country and flag. What complicated the matter further was that such overt opprobrium came from young people of color. The United States in 1943 — the Armed Forces especially — was still the domain of the white man. To question openly the rightness of patriotic duty or the prowess of the navy was to ultimately challenge white, heterosexual masculinity itself.

Among the most common epithets hurled at sailors were remarks ridiculing and denigrating same-sex activity between sailors, intended to challenge the military men's status as heterosexuals. In late March 1943, for example, J. C. P. Miller walked along Broadway on his way home from the Hollywood Canteen around one o'clock in the morning. As the sailor neared 2nd Street, a group of men dressed in zoot suits shouted out: "Fucking Navy bastard!" and "Cock-sucker!"[46] Such epithets suggest that at least part of the conflict between military men and civilian youths may have been linked to gay-bashing. A small but relatively open homosexual civilian community lived in the area surrounding Pershing Square, and gay men reportedly frequented the park as a popular place for socializing and for sexual encounters. However, Gregory Lehne's argument that "homophobia is only incidentally used against actual homosexuals — its more common use is against heterosexual males" suggests another way of understanding such epithets. Accusations of homophobia are common among heterosexual males as a way of policing the boundaries of "appropriate" heterosexual masculine behavior, and young civilians of color who assumed the role of policing the masculinity of military men constituted yet another subversion of racialized privilege. Although the word "cocksucker" was by far the most common epithet sailors reported hearing from civilian youths, it cannot be determined whether it was the favorite denunciation of civilian youths or whether sailors simply found it to be the most egregious epithet worth reporting. In either case, such words had a powerful effect, festering in the minds of the military men as challenges to their status as heterosexual men and as white men.[47]

The nature of confrontation between military personnel and civilian youths shifted markedly in the spring of 1943. During the winter of 1942–43, sailors collided with civilian youths, on the average, no more than once a week. Yet by May 1943 such confrontations had become a daily event — sometimes two and three times a day. Young men also became more brazen in their attacks on sailors. Prior to the spring of that year they came no closer to their adversaries than the width of a street, but now they engaged in acts of aggression that brought them into face-to-face contact with sailors.[48]

Was there a Rubicon crossed that season, some border transgressed by servicemen that elevated verbal harassment into physical confrontation? If such a pivotal moment occurred, it has escaped the recorded past. There were other flash points between sailors and civilian youths that could have ignited mass reprisals at some point. Some young men in the inner city regularly engaged in the sport of "rolling" drunks as an easy way to obtain money.[49] With the completion of the Naval Reserve Armory near downtown Los Angeles in 1940, the targets of inner-city boys certainly expanded to include drunken sailors and other military personnel who had the misfortune of staggering into their areas of operation.[50] Such attacks on drunken sailors would clearly have generated resentment among military personnel. They were, after all, putting their lives on the line to protect the very civilians who beat and robbed them. But this resentment would probably not have precipitated a riot in itself. Relations between civilian and sailor would likely have remained strained but free of mass reprisals were it not for the escalating street theater of power and aggression that led both groups down a slippery path of increasing confrontation.[51]

As the days grew warmer after the winter chill, so too did the climate of confrontation. Shouted insults from passing cars had become commonplace by the midspring of 1943, and standing toe to toe with the interlopers may have earned more respect among the groups of boys who routinely lashed out at the servicemen. Seamen Second Class Robert Lafayette Calkins, Wallace Stetich, and Benny Claire Boatright, each of whom had previous encounters with civilian youths, were all walking down Figueroa one Tuesday in May.[52] As they reached the area just north of Sunset Boulevard, four young men dressed in zoot suits crossed from the opposite side of the street and approached them from straight ahead. As the civilian youths came nearer, some of them picked up beer bottles and broke them over the edge of a nearby garbage can, holding the jagged edges in front of them like knives. The two groups faced off as they slowly walked passed each other in tense silence.[53] Such confrontations spun out webs of meaning for those ensnared by escalating violence in the summer of 1943.

### Portents of Storm

At first, few Angelenos felt the ominous wind rising from the tensions between local youths and military men. As the clashes became more frequent, however, each collision thundered warnings to the community that something was terribly amiss. Soon after the founding of the Citizens' Committee for the Defense of Mexican American Youth in October 1942, Director of Immigration and Housing Carey McWilliams began warning all within earshot that the growing violence among working-class youths would soon result in the murder of a policeman. Worse, McWilliams feared that Los Angeles would consequently experience a wave of police terrorism rivaling the work of Hitler's black shirts.

The events that unfolded during the period leading up to the rioting in the summer of 1943 did not follow his dire predictions to the letter, but McWilliams was right on many counts. On New Year's Eve, 1942, a policeman was indeed shot to death at a North Main Street café by an inebriated patron—"a drunken Pachuco," Officer Vance Brasher bitterly recalled.[54] But the death of a Los Angeles policeman did not precipitate the wave of state terrorism that McWilliams foresaw. Since the time of José Díaz's death four months earlier, the Los Angeles Police Department had already been engaged in a protracted war on youth "gangs" by conducting dragnets, enforcing curfews, searching cars and homes, erecting road blocks, and arresting young people by the hundreds.

The war on juvenile delinquency was fraught with unchallenged assumptions about race and behavior. Deputy Sheriff Edward Duran Ayres, head of the Foreign Relations Bureau of the Los Angeles County Sheriff's Department, framed the police response in his testimony before the 1942 Los Angeles County Grand Jury investigating juvenile delinquency. Antisocial behavior was as much the product of social conditioning as it was biology, he conceded to the jury, yet he clearly favored the latter as a causal explanation for the perceived rise in juvenile delinquency among Mexican American youths. Comparing Mexicans to a wild cat and whites to a domesticated cat, Ayres concluded that caging the wild cat was the only way it could be kept safely within society. In case any of the jurors missed the point, Ayres pushed the argument further in comparing the human sacrifices of the Aztecs to the fighting habits of Mexican youths in Los Angeles. "All he knows and feels is a desire to use a knife or some lethal weapon," he concluded. "In other words, his desire is to kill, or at least let blood."[55] Certainly Ayres could not speak for the entire law enforcement community of Los Angeles, yet his words rang with approval from the heads of the LAPD and the Los Angeles County Sheriff's Department. Chief of police C. B. Horrall called Ayres's testimony an "intelligent statement of the psychology of the Mexican people," and Sheriff Eugene Biscailuz commented that Ayres's report to the grand jury "fully covered the situation."[56]

Police repression stoked the level of hostility among inner-city youths rather than cooling down the underlying flames. Thus the widescale rioting in June 1943 came as little surprise to the observant, but the leaders of the uprising were altogether unanticipated. Instead of a pitched battle between the imagined zoot-suited gangs and police over state terrorism, members of the military took to the streets of Los Angeles over the perceived impotence of the LAPD in going far enough to control civil disorder.

In May 1943 two confrontations between large groups of servicemen and civilian youths signaled the impending violence that would come to be known as the "Zoot Suit Riot." Tension had been mounting in the Venice area for months over the brazen behavior of young men dressed in their equally brazen clothes. At times these bezooted young men walked down the board-walk four abreast, arm in arm, much to the consternation of the local citi-zens. "Everybody else would have to scram out of their way," an informant told Beatrice Griffith, "and all concerned would make dirty cracks."[57] The residents of Venice did not take the intrusions lightly, and both civilian and sailor bitterly protested the presence of the zoot-suited young men who adopted Lick Pier as a favorite hangout.

Around sunset on a Sunday in the middle of the month, a police sergeant working security at the Aaragon ballroom overheard a group of high school boys outside near the entrance. "It's talk the zoot suiters have taken over the beachfront," they reportedly said; "we're going to straighten things out." At that moment some excited sailors arrived with the news that a sailor had been stabbed. "Let's get the zooters!" they urged the high school boys. The sergeant stepped in to assure them that the things were under control, at least in the Aaragon ballroom. "The troublemakers have been kept out," he told the growing crowd of sailors and civilians; "no sailor has been stabbed." But his words offered little reassurance for the crowd. As one eyewitness later said, "They didn't care whether the Mexican kids wore zoot suits or not, and for that matter most of the kids dancing were not in drapes—they just wanted Mexicans." When the dance ended and the Mexican American teen-agers started to leave the ballroom, a crowd of about five hundred sailors and civilians began to chase them down the boardwalk. "Let's get 'em!" the mob shouted as they ran past the bingo parlors and concession stands. "Let's get the chili-eating bastards!"[58]

Not all the pursued youths ran, however. Sometime after nightfall, plain-clothes policemen Layman and Trout responded to a radio dispatch about a civil disturbance in Venice. As they pulled up to the pier darkened by a coastwide blackout, a Mexican-looking young man ran up to the car and asked if they were policemen.[59] When they affirmed their identity, the young man informed them that there was a fight in progress at the end of the pier.

Layman and Trout got out of their patrol car and walked into the darkened pier. Immediately they found themselves caught in a maelstrom of brass-knuckled fists and flailing blackjacks. About half a dozen young men, all wearing tight-legged trousers and long jackets, except one who was dressed in a military uniform, converged on the hapless officers with the fury of their age. Layman was knocked to his knees by a blow to his left eye. As he staggered about the pier trying to stand up, his eye filling with blood, he was again struck on the face with a blow that drove his front teeth through his upper lip. The youth continued to pound the struggling policeman, who lay virtually prostrate on the ground, several more times on his back with leadened pipes. Layman's partner, Trout, was shoved against the rail of the pier and drew his weapon to avoid being pushed over. Amazingly, the young men involved somehow managed to escape arrest.

The general mayhem in Venice continued until two o'clock in the morning and then spilled over into Santa Monica. The shore patrol, together with the military police and the Los Angeles Police Department, finally managed to scatter the rioters. At daybreak a number of Mexican American boys were badly beaten, and others had been jailed for their own "protection."

An important precedent had been set in controlling crowd behavior. "The sailors and high-school kids got hold of rumors," a police officer later explained; "everybody was upset with jittery emotions wanting to let off steam . . . and the zoot-suiters were the safety valve. You'll admit the only thing we could do to break it up was to arrest the Mexican kids."[60] Since servicemen had little regard for civilian police officers, he further reasoned, "Our actions are limited, by what the public thinks." Mexican Americans far outnumbered the military population in Los Angeles, and by virtue of the majority they should have been "the public" that the police listened to the most. But it is clear that what defined "the public" had more to do with the political and economic power of the whites involved in the rioting than it did with population figures or residency. The rights of privilege thus held greater sway than the rights of citizenship.

An act of retaliation on Monday night, 31 May 1943, would allow the LAPD the opportunity to put into practice its philosophy of riot control learned in Venice. Although the ensuing riot in Los Angeles was, in the words of Patricia Adler, "a brief episode in a long conflict," the attack on a group of military men that Monday night was the spark that ultimately touched off an explosion of rage.[61] Around 8:00 P.M. a dozen sailors and soldiers strolled down Main Street, and among them was Seaman Second Class Joe Dacy Coleman. Near Chinatown the military men spotted a group of young women on the opposite sidewalk, and most of the men—with the exception of Coleman and a soldier—crossed the street to talk to the women.[62] Coleman continued ahead, and as he passed a small grouping of zoot-suited boys, he saw, out of the corner of his eye, one of the boys raising his arm in a manner that looked threatening. The sailor quickly spun around and seized the young man's arm. Something struck Coleman on the head from behind, and he fell to the ground unconscious, breaking his jaw in two places.

Whether the young civilian acted in a threatening manner or not, Coleman clearly made the first aggressive contact in seizing the young man by the arm, and the other civilian boys responded in kind. On the other side of the street young civilian men pounced on the servicemen from all directions, seemingly out of nowhere, swinging rocks and bottles and fists and feet with fury. In the midst of this fusillade the military men managed to fight their way over to where Coleman lay and drag him off to safety.[63] The triumph of the civilian youths would be short-lived, however, for it would ultimately provide the sailors at the armory with all the justification they would need to take the law into their own hands.

It was by then too late to turn back from the course dictated by both the sailors' and local youths' sense of manhood. Most civilian boys who defended the integrity of their social and geographical homeland for almost a year initially engaged military personnel and their families in acts of harassment designed to do little more than frighten away these outsiders from a different class, culture, and color. The group of boys who held broken beer bottles in front of them would probably have run away, like so many did, if the older sailors actually challenged them. Yet the level of hostility grew exponentially with each public act of bravado as both groups lashed out blindly at anyone who wore the uniform of the sailor or the zoot suit of the hep cat. The Monday night fracas on the last day in May 1943 lasted little more than a few minutes, but the shock waves reverberated for days. Rather than settling the score between civilian youths and sailors, the details of the fight only grew larger and more distorted in each retelling from sailor to soldier. Thus the following Thursday night, when a number of the sailors walked past the armory gates to go into town, they were spoiling for a fight with any teenage boy who got in their way.

### Conclusion

Military men largely saw themselves as the innocent parties in these confrontations, responding only defensively to the aggressive behavior of the other. Indeed, in more than eighty cases of harassment reported by navy personnel, not once did the sailors confess to provoking such responses from civilian youths. Neither did they admit to retaliating in any way against the youths who harassed them. For them to have reported otherwise would have undermined their justification for taking the law into their own hands in early June 1943 in order to make tolerable what seemed in their minds to be an intolerable situation. As impressive as their testimonies are in demonstrating the remarkable restraint of navy men, the records tell a different story.

The Eleventh Naval District Headquarters in San Diego, which included Los Angeles, logged numerous complaints from civilians about the disorderly and destructive behavior of naval personnel. At times these complaints centered on relatively harmless problems, such as the traffic hazards caused by large groups of service men wandering through town on leave. Other times, however, military men were far more abusive, pilfering shops, assaulting civilians, and damaging property.[64] "You will find that the papers don't write up half what's going on," an anonymous civilian wrote to the admiral in command, urging him to investigate the baneful behavior of military men.[65] Indeed, most Angelenos tended to tolerate such behavior considering that the young men carousing through town were vitally needed to prosecute the war.

Yet the young people living in the residential areas between the Naval Reserve Armory and downtown Los Angeles saw things differently. The coming of war was only part of a larger trend of geographical and a cultural encumbrances on the social spaces that made up their community. For young people coming of age, the often intrusive presence of white military men swaggering through their neighborhoods was not a sacrifice to be tolerated, particularly when servicemen displayed a lack of respect for the established social boundaries of the community. And in their myriad acts of resistance and affirmation, the young people of Chavez Ravine and Alpine Street helped create the storm that would rain destruction upon them in the summer of 1943.

In the end, many of those who reported or recorded their violent encounters may have been innocent parties at first. Yet in the recorded cases of harassment and assault on both sides there is a remarkably consistent blurring of the other, so that a strike against one "Mexican" was a strike against all "zooters" or that one sailor was like any other. In truth, both sailor and civilian were guilty of engaging each other in an escalating theater of street violence that led from one dehumanized, violent act to another, each time drawing more and more people into the fray.

# 8 : Days of Riot

n early June 1943, military men swept through Los Angeles to strip
drapes off boys and club those who resisted. Not satisfied with that,
they generally assaulted anyone who even remotely looked the part
of the imagined Pachuco.[1] The smaller riot that broke out in Venice
the week before the Zoot Suit Riot established an important precedent for how the Los Angeles Police Department would respond to
the mob of military men. Rather than attempting to arrest the rioting servicemen, members of the police department found it more expedient to jail
the mostly Mexican American and African American victims. It was an expediency wrapped in the racial paradigms of who constituted the "public"
in public safety. As a matter of policy the police response to young people
of color was remarkably the same, whether they were suspected of acting
in a criminal manner or were clearly the victims of crime: jail.

The ineffectual responses of the LAPD, shaped by personnel reductions
due to the draft and by dominant assumptions of race and class, played a significant role in perpetuating the riot in Los Angeles. Alert authorities could
certainly have stopped the relatively small mob the first night. Yet the meager attempts of both civilian and military authorities to halt the rioters only
emboldened the servicemen to carry on. In the days that followed, military
men divided their growing forces and launched punitive strikes into East
Los Angeles and Watts. It was not until senior military officials declared Los
Angeles out of bounds to military personnel on leave that the riot effectively
shut down.

Progressive activists of the period saw conspiracy behind the events and
blamed the riot on the pro-fascist machinations of William Randolph Hearst
and the sensationalized press coverage of the so-called Pachuco problem in
the *Los Angeles Herald and Express* and the *Los Angeles Examiner*.[2] In 1984
Mauricio Mazón shifted the origins of the riot in arguing that the outbreak
of violence was a by-product of published fears of an imminent enemy invasion of the West Coast.[3] Another look at the riot reveals that complacency
and the lack of coordination among high-ranking civil and military authori-

ties were more responsible for the spread of rioting than conspiracy. While junior police and military officers haggled with each other over jurisdiction, high-ranking police and military authorities simply failed to appreciate the seriousness of the nightly rioting—no doubt because of where the riot occurred and who was being attacked—until the fifth and final day. Hearst's Los Angeles newspapers were, furthermore, not alone in dramatizing the so-called Pachuco problem; nor was public fear of an invasion immediately responsible for the Zoot Suit Riot.[4] Long-standing tensions between military men and civilian youths played a far greater role in the outbreak of mob violence. Many military men, and civilians too, believed that the Los Angeles Police Department was simply incapable of controlling the seemingly rebellious population of minority youths. Thus it was, ironically, in the name of law and order that servicemen rioted throughout Los Angeles.[5]

Mazón theorized in *The Zoot Suit Riots* that for servicemen the act of destroying zoot suits was a symbolic annihilation of the other. In subjecting civilian boys to rituals of humiliation, servicemen were using the same attacks on individuality and difference that they had faced in the military. Yet my research has uncovered that *civilians* engaged in stripping zoot suits off young men well before the riot broke out. In light of this discovery, I add the dimensions of class and race to Mazón's analysis. By mid-1943 the zoot suit had become a powerful symbol of deviance in the public discourse about juvenile delinquency because it was a visual means of dissent from the social mores of the day. Thus stripping the zoot suits off the dark bodies of working-class youths was as much the destruction of their public symbols of affluence as it was an act of humiliation designed to remind an assertive and seemingly rebellious generation of minority youths of their place in segregated Los Angeles.

### The Zoot Suit Riot: The First Day

As dusk settled over the city darkened by a dimout on Thursday evening, 3 June 1943, Chief Carpenter's Mate George King reported back to armory officials that he saw several groups of young men in zoot suits congregating near the area of Euclid and Whittier.[6] Such a sighting was not unusual for that time of the day or the location. Young men dressed in zoot suits were most commonly seen on the streets of Los Angeles toward the weekend and after hours, precisely the same time when military men were themselves most likely to head into town in search of entertainment. Yet by June 1943, the presence of zoot-suited young men in any number, however innocent the purpose of their gathering, was all the evidence servicemen needed to confirm that "zoot suiters" were also looking for a showdown.

A little after 6:00 P.M., about sixteen navy men exited a bus on Sunset Boulevard and began to walk northward along Figueroa Boulevard toward the armory. As the sailors came to the corner of Alpine and Figueroa, two young men dressed in zoot suits reportedly shouted across the intersection: "Sons of bitches and bastards!"[7] The pair of young civilians shook their fists at the sailors, the group later reported, and called the sailors "mother fuckers."[8] About the time these sailors arrived at the armory gates, a couple of other sailors left the compound and headed toward town on Adobe Street. Not far from the armory they ran into two Mexican girls and four boys dressed in zoot suits, who reportedly accosted the sailors with a tirade of foul language that reportedly made even the sailors blush. During the verbal assault on the sailors some of the young people reportedly raised their hands in the Nazi salute and shouted out: "Heil Hitler!"[9]

This was not the first time that civilian youths had evoked Nazi symbolism, and a facile reading of such complex interchanges led many observers, military and civilian alike, to fear that fascism had somehow taken hold of minority civilian youths. Early one morning in 1942, a swastika and a "puzzling" series of letters were found chalked in the middle of a residential street of East Los Angeles.[10] The police and reporters who investigated the incident took the lettering to be a kind of secret code, suggesting that covert enemy agents were operating in the barrios of Los Angeles. The puzzling series of letters were likely the initials of the young people who tagged the street, as is the common practice today. But why would they invoke a swastika or, at other times, the Nazi salute? They scarcely understood the depths of Nazi ideology, much less embraced it. They knew what frightened the police and the military men who roamed their neighborhoods, however. Although some civilian youths may have used Nazi symbolism for a prank, it was an act that nonetheless undermined the shaky confidence that many Angelenos had in home front security. That may have been the intent of other civilian youths who stood in the faces of military men and shouted "Heil Hitler." Saluting white American military men as if they were Nazis was a bold accusation that Nazi Germany and the segregated U.S. military, if not race-conscious American society in general, looked remarkably similar from the vantage point of racialized minorities.

At 8:00 P.M. on 3 June 1943, a few hours after military men were greeted with a Nazi salute from civilian youths, a group of about fifty sailors burst past the armory gates and started toward the downtown area with hastily made weapons concealed from the sentries and shore patrol.[11] Some of the sailors followed the mob in cars as it swept along Figueroa Boulevard until it reached Alpine Street, where young people had earlier greeted a group of sailors with the Nazi salute.[12] Swarming around the cafés, beer joints, and restaurants sprawled along Alpine Street, the sailors searched in vain for "zoot suiters." Finding little initial success, they continued on to the Carmen Theater, where they turned on the house lights and roamed the aisles looking for young men in zoot suits. There they found their first victims, most of them twelve- and thirteen-year-old boys who were probably guilty of little more than wearing the wrong clothes at the wrong time. Ignoring the protesting patrons, the sailors clubbed the boys and the adults who tried to stop them, tore the zoot suits off their victims, and burned the tattered clothing in a pile. Their work being done at the theater—their superiority of force established over the naked teenage boys—the mob moved on to search the rest of the neighborhood for more zoot suiters.

At what moment the sailors at the armory decided to mount a collective assault on "zoot suiters" that night has been an important point in how liberal activists in Los Angeles reconstructed the riot. In *North from Mexico* Carey McWilliams was the first of many scholars who argued that sailors were acting as part of a larger conspiracy orchestrated by the press, the police, and the navy to rid Los Angeles of the Pachuco problem.[13] However, another look at what is known about the riot—namely, the weapons the sailors carried with them and the timing of the event itself—places in question the notion of conspiracy as an adequate causal explanation.

It is significant that the rioting sailors utilized makeshift weapons fashioned out of broom handles, dumbbells, and whatever else they could sneak past the sentries rather than taking any number of arms or matériel stored at the Naval Reserve Armory. To have secured the use of naval armaments would have required the authorization of armory officials, which the rioting sailors clearly did not have.[14] Without the cooperation of naval authorities, the sailors who marched into the Alpine district were forced to rely on common articles immediately at hand for weapons, such as their belts or rocks, sticks, and palm saps picked up along the way.[15]

Quite likely the plan to search for "zoot suiters" en masse was a spontaneous decision by the sailors who were accosted by civilian youths earlier in the evening. After the busload of sailors reported the harassing remarks of zoot-suited boys to their watch commander, they returned to their barracks and began to compare stories of insult and injury with one another. In the process of rehearsing past injustices and venting their anger at the state of affairs with civilian youths, they hatched a plan to settle the score against young civilian men.

Although there is evidence that young civilian women were either present or participants in the campaign of harassment, it is clear that the violence between the military, civilians, and police remained exclusively male on male. No civilian women were reported injured or jailed during the course of the riot. Why the riot proceeded on clearly marked gender lines remains another curiosity of the conflict. For some military men, the code of masculinity requiring a man to refrain from striking a woman may have shifted the focus of their fury exclusively on young men, although clearly such a masculine ideal was more often honored in the breach. Keenly protective parents may have played a greater role in keeping young Mexican American and other women off the streets during the weeks of escalating tensions, and certainly during the riot, characteristically reigning in the activities of their daughters while allowing their sons freer passage.

Had fate not intervened and removed the majority of boys from the Alpine district that night, no doubt the rioting sailors would have met stronger resistance. For a month prior to the riot police officers García, Chapman, and Burgoyne sponsored weekly activities at the Alpine Street School for the neighborhood boys, but because they were unable to secure the use of the building for that particular night, the officers instead arranged for the boys to meet them at the Los Angeles Central Jail on 1st and Broadway.[16] About twenty-five boys attended the Thursday night meeting, according to Beatrice Griffith, "some dressed up, draped out in their zootsuits. Others wore their work jeans and black leather jackets."[17] The agenda for the meeting that night was to discuss the formal organization of a neighborhood club sponsored by the Los Angeles Police Department. Rudy Sánchez, one of the boys in attendance, later wrote that they were making "some progress, to keep us out of the street, and we were all for it."[18]

The meeting ended on a promising note, and the boys began to make their way home when a sailor, himself from the Alpine neighborhood, came to warn the boys about the mob.[19] The Alpine boys arrived in their neighborhood only to find the aftermath of sailors' work.[20] A crowd of patrons stood outside the Carmen Theater angrily discussing what had just taken place. It appeared to Sánchez that the bloodied boys emerging from the theater were beaten worse than when the boys from different neighborhoods fought each other. Some of them had to be taken to the Georgia Street Hospital. "This is supposed to be a free country," he was moved to write. "We don't go around beating up people just because we don't like the clothes they wear. . . . On who's side is the Navy on anyway, Uncle Sam or Hitler?"[21] Such a question would hang in the air as the mob swept through Alpine Street and headed south on Main Street to downtown.

A boisterous mob of military men is a difficult thing to miss, and Carey McWilliams cited the failure of the police or the shore patrol to stop the rioting as further evidence of a conspiracy. Yet inattention and indifference were far better conspirators than the military and the police that night. Watch commanders at the armory offices and police stations failed to take seriously rumors of riot, and the mobs surged through the streets of Los Angeles unabated.[22] Furthermore, the majority of the Alpine Street boys were not even in the neighborhood when the sailors swept through the Alpine district; they were attending the meeting at the downtown station. Had the press, the navy, and the police department actively conspired to orchestrate an extralegal assault on the so-called Pachuco problem, they could not have picked a more ineffective time and means to do it.

Rumors trickled back to the watch commander at the armory as early as 9:00 P.M. that something was amiss. Sailors returning from leave reported that they had seen a group of zoot suiters amassing at the corner of Alpine and Figueroa. Quite likely the crowd was simply the Alpine boys arriving from downtown, but because that area was known to be particularly troublesome for sailors, executive officer Lieutenant Charles Bacon decided to investigate. Driving to the intersection of Alpine and Figueroa, he found the Shore Patrol already on the scene. The area looked to him as if some sort of confrontation had occurred, and one sailor was being treated for a laceration wound that he claimed he received when a large crowd of sailors accidentally pushed him into a showroom window. Apparently satisfied by this explanation, Bacon did not press the sailor any further. He also picked up on a rumor that zoot suiters and military men were fighting on Main Street, but he could find no one who would admit to having direct knowledge of the event. Bacon therefore chose *not* investigate the matter and returned to the armory, satisfied that the situation was under control.[23]

When liberty expired at 11:00 P.M., an unusually large number of men were still out. Bacon again drove to area of Alpine and Figueroa and again found everything quiet.[24] While en route to the shore patrol headquarters, he stumbled upon a scene that surely startled him: the shore patrol and military police had rounded up the mob of military men on Main Street and 2nd. In the glare of the flashing red police lights, the shore patrol was marching a group of sailors to the Central Police Station, where they were to be put in jail. Bacon discovered that sixty of the arrested sailors were stationed at the armory and requested that senior patrol officer Commander C. H. Fogg release the men into his custody. The sailors appeared to Bacon to be a sober group, orderly and manageable, and he saw to it that no charges were recorded by the shore patrol. At 12:52 A.M. the lieutenant returned to the armory with the men.[25] Their night of revelry had finished, but the riot was far from over.

## Offensive Maneuvers

Underestimating the significance of the previous night's activities, civilian and military authorities took few, if any, steps to prevent the riot from spreading. Hence, servicemen continued their rampage on the following night, Friday, 4 June 1943, but with a new twist. Rather than continuing to terrorize the territory that lay between the armory and downtown Los Angeles, they curiously shifted their attack to two areas of the city far away from where the vast majority of confrontations had taken place over the previous year. Driving deep into East Los Angeles, where few, if any, confrontations occurred, sailors turned their assaults on zoot-suited youths into a punitive strike against the Mexican American population itself.

That night began like the previous ones, with young civilian men defiantly shouting at sailors whenever they encountered them. Some of the young men took the offensive to the gates of the armory itself, shouting "Fuck you!" and giving the finger to the sentinel as they drove by for about two hours after sunset.[26] None of these challenges, however, amounted to more than verbal affronts. No sailor was physically attacked.

Later that night, around nine o'clock, sailors, soldiers, marines, and civilians nonetheless heard a rumor that zoot suiters were holding a group of sailors captive somewhere on Main Street. A mob of servicemen and civilians gathered there to rescue the supposedly captive sailors, but the absence of zoot-suited gangs or sailors in distress failed to sober their lust for vengeance.[27] Leaders of the mob decided to take the battle into East Los Angeles and called the Yellow Taxi Company for a fleet of twenty taxis.[28] Part of the fleet split from the main group and headed a few miles north to Lincoln Heights, where some of the hapless civilian youths along the way had only beer bottles thrown at them from the slow-moving caravan.[29] Others were not so lucky. The rest of the strike force arrived in Boyle Heights and began to terrorize the area near the post office at 1st Street and Rowan Avenue. The sailors plunged into bars, cafés, and theaters searching out zoot-suited young men, pummeling those few who were unable to escape and destroying their *tacuches* (see map 4).[30]

Alert authorities surely could have anticipated the continuation of rioting that night, but complacency ruled. About the time that the mob of military men began to terrorize Boyle Heights, a dispatcher from the Los Angeles Police Department telephoned the armory. Lieutenant Carl T. Cobbs was on watch that night and followed the appropriate line of authority in relaying to his commanding officer that a large group of servicemen had gathered at 1st and Rowan Streets. Martin Dickinson, the commanding officer, in turn ordered Cobbs to bring them back, and Cobbs contacted Executive Officer

Looking for zoot suiters, rioting military men and civilians stop a rail car on Main Street and 3rd in downtown Los Angeles in front of Murray's, a popular men's store that sold zoot suits. (Los Angeles Times Photo)

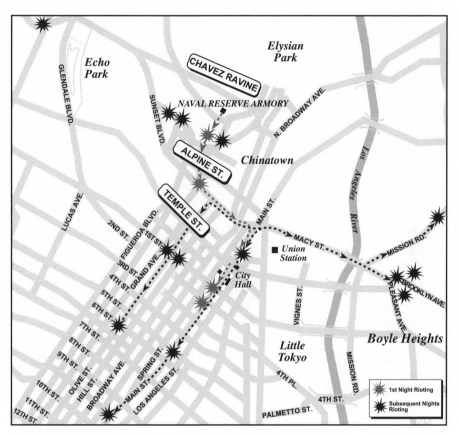

**Map 4. The progress of rioting**

Glen Litten. Little else happened for half an hour.[31] At 9:15 P.M., fifteen minutes after the first call, Lieutenant Clark of the LAPD was on the phone asking what Cobbs was doing to alleviate the situation in Boyle Heights and Lincoln Heights. Cobbs assured the police officer that he had consulted with his commanding officer and that he was sending someone out to handle the matter.[32] Five minutes later Cobbs received another telephone call from the dispatcher of the Yellow Cab Company, wanting to know who had called for twenty cabs and why they were all congregating in East Los Angeles. Apparently indifferent to this odd news, Cobbs simply informed the dispatcher that no official call had gone out from his station and that he did not know who placed the call.[33] Finally, at 9:30 P.M. Executive Officer Litten, Chief Gunner's Mate Leonard, and four men left for East Los Angeles, thirty minutes after the LAPD first notified the watch commander about the disturbance.[34]

Prompt action may not have improved the sight of the armory officers, however. Neither the executive officer nor the chief gunner's mate could find anyone as they separately patrolled the streets of Boyle Heights.[35] The LAPD and the shore patrol, it seems, had better luck in finding the large crowd of unruly men. The police arrested nine sailors whom they believed to be the instigators, and the shore patrol took another seventeen into custody. At 10:40 P.M. the LAPD called Cobbs for the third time that night, this time to inform him where he could find his men.[36]

The next morning, Saturday, 5 June 1943, the commanding officer of the Naval Training School took the first tentative steps to alleviate the tension. Commander Martin Dickinson called the men to quarters and warned them that the navy did not condone attacks on civilians. He then announced that he would post a night patrol along the streets leading to the armory for two consecutive nights in order to protect sailors returning from liberty.[37] But these measures fell far short of stopping the riot. Pachuco hysteria spread like a communicable disease among the other military men stationed in and around Los Angeles, and marines, soldiers, and sailors from other encampments filled in where the sailors from the armory left off.

Rumors about zoot-suited gangs continued to run rampant among the armory personnel, despite the protective measures taken. Continued encounters with civilian youths, however casual, were consequently blown out of proportion by sailors fearing reprisals.[38] And of the hostile encounters sailors reported during this period, most appear to have been little more than demonstrations of power designed to reassert the authority of civilian youths in their own neighborhoods. When Seaman Second Class Bobby Gene Crosland was returning to the armory about 2:30 in the morning, four boys in zoot suits at the corner of Whittier Boulevard and 4th forced him against a showroom window.[39] All of them displayed their knives and flicked their switchblades open and closed in the face of the terrified sailor. This piece of street theater came to an abrupt end, however, when two soldiers came upon the scene and chased the boys away. Clearly the young men could have caused Crosland serious damage and even killed him if they desired. But they did not. Instead, they seem to have purposefully set out to demonstrate their ability to strike fear in the sailor and little more.[40]

Despite the lack of actual reprisals from civilian youths, military men continued to riot throughout Los Angeles for the third night, bringing violence to anyone who even remotely looked the part of the imagined Pachuco. When a group of Mexican and Mexican American musicians came out of the Aztec Recording Company on 3rd and Main, they were attacked by a gang of sailors. None of the musicians wore a zoot suit; nor did they much look the part of a juvenile gang. Rather, they were a group of composers, writers, and singers newly arrived from El Paso, Texas, and Mexico.[41] Even white teenagers were swept up in the upheaval and were thrown in jail for their own protection from the riot.[42]

Scores of servicemen marched arm in arm down the streets of downtown Los Angeles, accosting everyone in a zoot suit. The Los Angeles police came out in full force that night, having called out every available officer for riot detail, but they did little to stop the military men. Instead, they concentrated their power on arresting civilian boys—purportedly for their own protection. The majority of them were, coincidentally, Mexican American, and the arrests were made despite the lack of actual reprisals or counterattacks by civilian youths.[43]

### Last Days: The Worst of the Rioting

Sporadic confrontations flickered throughout greater Los Angeles on Sunday, but none of them amounted to more than threats and aggressive displays of power on the part of civilian youths.[44] The animosity and fear engendered by three days of battle spilled over to both military and civilian residents who were not directly involved in confrontations. Sailors reported negative remarks from civilian adults, such as an elderly Mexican American woman who leaned over her fence and said, as sailors passed in front of her house, "There goes some of those yellow sailors." One sailor even feared Pachucos so much that he sent his family north to Sacramento during the rioting.[45]

The worst of the violence flared on the fifth and final night of rioting when sailors, soldiers, and marines poured into the city, reportedly by the

**Black and Mexican American youths from Watts jailed during the
Zoot Suit Riot for allegedly throwing stones at Pacific Electric cars.
(Herald Examiner Collection, Los Angeles Public Library)**

thousands.[46] On Monday, 7 June 1943, Martin Dickinson canceled liberty for the men stationed at the Naval Training School, but his action extended only to the men under his immediate command at the armory. Word had already spread to other encampments of soldiers, sailors, and marines stationed in southern California, and they came spoiling for a fight.[47] As darkness overtook the city, a crowd of military men, mostly from San Diego and El Toro, began congregating on 1st Street between Main and Central. They swelled in numbers as civilians who were equally eager to rid Los Angeles of Pachucos joined in. Before long the mob divided into two groups. The first pushed southward along Central toward the predominantly African American neighborhoods in Watts, and the second drove eastward into the predominantly Mexican neighborhoods in East Los Angeles.

Al Waxman, editor of the small Jewish newspaper *Eastside Journal*, had sent out a general call for young people on the Eastside to meet that night and discuss the events of the past few days. About 250 young men, most of them Mexican American, showed up at the designated location and were escorted in by policemen guarding the auditorium. After Waxman pleaded with the youths to forget their differences with the military men and end the confrontations, one of them stood and asked some difficult and sobering questions. "Isn't this a free country?" the boy asked. "Can't we wear the kind of clothes that we like? Must we be disrobed at the order of other men?" The ensuing discussion was tense and difficult, but Waxman felt sure that they were making headway toward deescalating the conflict—until news of rioting servicemen interrupted the meeting. "Come quick," someone shouted out. "Soldiers and sailors are beating us up on Central Avenue and Main Street!" "The results," Waxman recalled, "were electrifying." Talk of battle-readiness filled the air as grim-faced boys began to make plans for retaliation. Waxman called out to the young men in the audience, reminding them of their promise to set aside their differences with the military men. After more discussion the majority of the boys agreed to return home and let the situation on Central Avenue cool down. About fifty of the boys, however, elected to go downtown to protect their friends and relatives living there.

When Waxman arrived with the boys at the corner of 12th and Central, he saw an unforgettable scene. Before him was a mass of humanity, shrieking with anger and locked in violent struggle with arms swinging and legs kicking. The police were making dozens of arrests, not of the rioting servicemen but of the zoot-suited young men. "Why am I being arrested?" one of them defiantly asked, and an officer clubbed him savagely with a nightstick. Someone else kicked the unconscious boy in the face as he lay sprawled in his own blood on the sidewalk. A mother clutching a baby rushed toward the police and cried out: "Don't take my boy, he did nothing. He's only 15 years old—don't take him!" An officer turned around and slapped the woman across the jaw with his nightstick, sending her reeling backward. Elsewhere servicemen forced two boys to undress and watch as their *tacuches* burned in front of their eyes. Rushing over to the Eastside, Waxman found the second mob of rioters stopping streetcars on East 1st Street and crashing through bars, shops, and penny arcades as they searched for Pachucos.[48] All the while three police cars silently watched the mob. It was not until 11:30 that night, when Captain Joseph Reed came to East Los Angeles, that the mob began to break up.[49]

For all practical purposes the riot ended by Tuesday morning, 8 June 1943.[50] Senior military officials, fearing the negative publicity in the morning newspapers, declared Los Angeles out of bounds to all navy, marine, coast guard, and army personnel in the early morning hours.[51] The shore patrol, furthermore, was concentrated in the downtown area and given orders to arrest any disorderly personnel. The LAPD responded by calling in all off-duty men and auxiliary police for riot detail.[52] Hot spots of confrontation continued to flare sporadically between civilians and military men for another week, but the coordinated efforts of military and civilian authorities ended the most concentrated violence. In the end, an estimated ninety-four civilians and eighteen servicemen were treated for serious injuries from the riot. The LAPD arrested all ninety-four civilians and only two servicemen.[53]

The number of casualties is suggestive of the nature of the riot. The small number of wounded relative to the total number of military men and civilian youths in Los Angeles suggests that young civilians made difficult prey. They well knew the streets and alleyways, far better than military men temporarily stationed in town, and many civilian youths may have easily outrun and outwitted the military men determined to "search and destroy." Certainly other civilian youths chose to stand their ground and fight back, and the unofficial count averages sixteen serious casualties a night over a one-week period. Five civilian youths were injured for every one military man, and it is likely that many more casualties of a less serious nature went unreported by both sides. The total number of young civilians and military men involved in shouting, shoving, and other forms of confrontation that bruised more egos than bodies was possibly even higher.

In all the official communications about the riot, both for public consumption and for internal use only, none of the civilian or military officials endeavored to address the nagging question posed by Rudy Sánchez: Who's side was the navy on—Hitler's or Uncle Sam's? At the time, such a question no doubt seemed too preposterous to be taken seriously. But Sánchez under-

Colonel Levi Ankeny, Mayor Fletcher Bowron, Commander C. H. Fogg, and Deputy Police Chief Clarence B. Horall meet during the Zoot Suit Riot and pledge, according to the *Herald-Examiner*, "'two-fisted action' and not 'slaps on the wrist'" to stop the rioting. After military leave was canceled, the riot ended. (Courtesy of the University of Southern California, on behalf of the *Los Angeles Examiner* Collection, USC Specialized Libraries and Archival Collections)

stood the central issue behind the riots. In reasserting control over juvenile delinquency and shoring up the transgressed walls of segregation in the process, the men of the military were blinded to the reality that they utilized fascist means in order to achieve nominally democratic ends. To the military men and civilians who rioted to "clean up the situation" that threatened society, difference and dissent were clearly problems to be eliminated—or at least swept under the rug, hidden from the view of the white public.

Despite their young age, some of the working-class youths implicitly understood the contradictions. For them, the war was less about upholding the traditions and customs of the nation than about realizing the measure of its creed. A week after the rioting broke out, Dan G. Acosta wrote to the *People's Daily World* on behalf of the "so called 'pachucos.'" "We are hoping, praying and fighting for a beautiful FREE world minus Nazism, fascism, aggression and most of all racial discrimination," he wrote. But the recent riot, he said, severely undermined their commitment to the nation. "'Zoot suiter' brothers, cousins, [and] friends" were dying in the battlefields abroad for the cause of freedom, he noted, but the actions of the servicemen and the police who tacitly encouraged the riot gave Mexican Americans and zoot suiters reason to pause in answering the call to duty and made all the more real the rumor that the internment of Mexican Americans was at hand.[54] And although canceling liberty in the greater Los Angeles area ended the riot, the underlying tensions that erupted into violence remained unresolved, and civilian youths continued to chafe under the presence of the war machine in Los Angeles. Later that night, as a number of officers sat with their wives on the terrace of the armory in the cool of the evening, a black Plymouth coupe slowly pulled up along the curb. Some zoot-suited boys leaned out the window and lifted a defiant cry into the night: "Fuck you, you bastards!"[55]

### Dezooting Los Angeles

What did the sailors ultimately hope to accomplish through rioting? Those who were interviewed by the Los Angeles newspapers revealed little introspection regarding their behavior or concern for their actions. Members of mobs seldom do. It would be easy to dismiss the riot as simply the work of disorderly military men "blowing off steam" or to conclude that military men were acting out their anxieties over military service, as psychohistorian Mauricio Mazón theorized. Surely there were elements of both in the complex set of motivations and perceptions that fueled the rioting in June 1943.

The way the rioters viewed their activities, however, is particularly significant. Los Angeles attorney Manuel Ruíz Jr. received an exasperated letter from a young friend who was stationed at the Victorville Army Flying School during this period:

> Say what the hell is being done about these god-damn Mexican punks, I think the city officials and police are scared of them. . . . They are certainly raising hell in L.A. raping women and knifing lone soldiers, one of our men came back to the outfit all cut up and its really getting us hot. This will naturally lead to a bunch of our men going into L.A. and there will be a lot of sorry Mexicans. . . . I for one would kill any of them that hurt anybody I know in L.A. I don't see why the army doesn't just go in and take the situation over, because the police can't handle it. We have wives and sweethearts there, and the soldiers won't stand for much more of this s——.[56]

The soldier clearly spoke for many of his peers who believed that only the military was capable of restoring order in Los Angeles. One of the petty officers who led an "expedition" into town the following week during the rioting voiced a similar view. "We're out to do what the police have failed to do," he told a reporter. "We're going to clean up this situation."[57]

Just how they were going to "clean up" the situation provides another insight into the assumptions that justified rioting in the minds of servicemen. In *War without Mercy*, John Dower explores how World War II became invested with a moral purpose as the United States entered the worldwide conflict. Furthermore, as a moral drama was being created out of industrialized warfare, entire populations were reduced to simple characterizations and demonized in popular images. The people of Japan became "Nips" and "Japs" and were portrayed in almost every public forum with monkey faces or as subhumans in order to represent them as a barbarous race and the antithesis of American civilization.[58]

In the year before the riot, the imagined Pachuco tapped into similar assumptions about "Oriental" behavior and subversion. Edward Duran Ayres of the sheriff's department took great pains to establish the predominance of Indian blood in the Mexican, which, as he coolly reasoned, "is evidently Oriental in background—at least he shows many of the Oriental characteristics, especially so in his utter disregard for the value of life."[59] Driving his biological theory of behavior to its logical conclusion, Ayres made a veiled reference to the recent internment of Japanese Americans as the answer for the Pachuco problem: "Although a wild cat and a domestic cat are of the same family, they have certain biological characteristics so different that while one may be domesticated, the other would have to be caged to be kept in captivity, and there is practically as much difference between the races of man as so aptly recognized by Rudyard Kipling when he said when writing of the Oriental: 'East is East and West is West, and never the twain shall meet,' which gives us insight into the present problem."[60] If other public officials were loath to embrace the overt racism of Ayres's analysis, many nonetheless suspected that minority youths had fallen under the influence of subversive powers. Even Los Angeles mayor Fletcher Bowron publicly speculated that agents provocateurs were behind the seeming proliferation of juvenile gangs and announced the establishment of a commission to investigate the matter.[61]

Because of social tensions exacerbated by war, Pachucos had been invested with a power far beyond their capabilities or intent. For the many sailors, soldiers, and civilians who rioted in Los Angeles, the imagined Pachuco represented a threat to the war effort and perhaps even the foundations of American society in Los Angeles. Thus they were little troubled by the questions of where they would find the actual young men who accosted them or how they would determine the guilty from the innocent. Indeed, they were less concerned with who was responsible for juvenile delinquency in general—or the attacks on their buddies in particular—than they were with exercising control over civilian youths through violence. But the problem with such a grand show of force, the police would later discover with their own dragnets, is that such operations often sweep up the innocent along with the guilty. In effect, anyone resembling the imagined Pachuco, regardless of his actual culpability in assaulting sailors, was attacked because he was seen as part of the so-called Pachuco problem.

Much of the mob violence revolved around a curious practice, laden with meaning, started by Angelenos almost from the moment zoot suits first appeared on the streets of Los Angeles. William Davenport, political correspondent for *Collier's*, was the first to chronicle an incidence of it almost a year before the riot. In the parking lot of the Casa Mañana near Culver City, Davenport met a young man wearing a flamboyant, custom-made zoot suit around one o'clock in the morning. "I had it made special," the youth proudly told the group from *Collier's* as they made their way to the Skyline Club. Skyline was, in the words of Davenport, "a nice place," popular among the swing-shift workers from the airplane plants of Vega and Lockheed.[62] Yet just as Davenport and his newfound friend were entering, a fight was about to break out between the Vega and Lockheed crews. The appearance of a zoot-suited young man was apparently enough to shift the tide of hostility. "Look," roared one of the workers, pointing at the zoot-suited patron, "a character!"[63] The unruly crowd turned on the young man and vigorously seized his clothing. The women in the group pulled off his buttons for souvenirs, and the men pulled apart what was left.[64]

Davenport's unfortunate companion was not the only one to suffer the peculiar wrath of Angelenos. Several more times that warm night in August 1942, Davenport reported seeing young men in zoot suits expelled from nightclubs or denied entrance altogether. And not long after Davenport's foray into the Los Angeles club scene, Los Angeles policemen reportedly gathered outside a popular dance hall on 2nd and Spring and ordered the young people out into the street. Standing at the exits with razors attached to the end of long sticks, the police ripped the peg-top trousers and *tacuche* jackets of the Mexican American boys as they came out of the New Mexico–Arizona club.[65]

By the summer of 1943, the zoot suit itself had clearly become a convenient and powerful symbol of subversion, and it was this symbol, more than anything else, that suffered the brunt of the damage during the riot. The rioters were otherwise a remarkably disciplined mob, perhaps even focused in their rampage through the city. No murders, rapes, or deaths were reported in connection with the riot, no serious damage had been done to property, and in only a few cases were there reports of severe injuries. Rather, the energy of the mob was, for the most part, engaged in the work of seeking out and destroying zoot suits.

The totality of the destruction caused by rioting may have been tempered because the ostensible objects of violence were adolescent boys. Yet in many cases the wearer seemed rather secondary to the ritual of humiliation and was given the choice to disrobe or suffer the consequences.[66] It was as if destroying the fashion itself had the power to substantially alter the complicated dynamics between servicemen and civilian youths.

In truth, William Davenport's dismissive description of the zoot suit as "strictly Filipino houseboy on his day off" spoke volumes about how most Americans tended to view the *tacuche*.[67] At best it was considered to be garish and inappropriate; at worst it was an affront to the social mores of the day. It was in this latter context that many of the rioters stripped zoot suits off the bodies of working-class boys. On the surface the zoot suit was simply a convenient symbol of supposed criminality and subversion, but it was also one of the symbols that many young people embraced as they experimented with material culture, blurring the lines of race, gender, and class along the way. Thus destroying the zoot suit ultimately amounted to the destruction of the public symbols of newfound wealth for working-class kids. It was a focused show of power designed to reassert the social norms of privilege and behavior and to remind young people of color of their place in segregated

A motorcycle policeman holds back a crowd of shocked onlookers as they gather
around two young men, disrobed and beaten during the Zoot Suit Riot.
(Associated Press)

Los Angeles. It was an act that sought to erase their self-determined signs of difference and dissent from mainstream American society.

Los Angeles police actually speculated during this period whether putting on the zoot suit inspired crime.[68] In some ways, they were not far off—not in that the young people who wore zoot suits were any more inclined toward criminality because of their clothes but in that many Angelenos *perceived* them to be criminal and reacted accordingly. Indeed, many Angelenos still considered it criminal in 1943 for people of color to stand out in their own ways and on their own terms in the public arenas in town and to refuse to remain within the social norms of segregated Los Angeles. The zoot suit cast a striking silhouette that pushed at the limits of tolerance for many white Angelenos, particularly at a time when war was changing the world and people of color were vigorously lobbying for greater social and economic rights at home.[69]

# PART IV
# THE VIOLENT POETRY
# OF THE TIMES

# 9 : Uneasy Truce

**C**ommunity leaders and city politicians responded in a variety of ways to the Zoot Suit Riot. This social crisis brought a new sense of urgency to the work of Manuel Ruíz and the Citizens' Committee for the Defense of Mexican American Youth (CCDMAY). The week of rioting made the reality of anti-Mexican sentiment more than apparent, they argued, calling on civic-minded citizens everywhere to fight against racism by rallying to their cause. Civic leaders interpreted the events differently, however. They were loath to call the events of early June a "riot," much less a "race riot." The damage to property was minor, they pointed out, and Mexican American boys were not the only casualties of the brawl.

Behind the public spin, however, city officials readily conceded that they were ill prepared for another outbreak of rioting and drew up plans with military authorities to coordinate their resources better. In addition, they turned to leading citizens within the Mexican American and African American communities to participate in various panels and committees to better understand the issues in the barrios. Yet the Mexican American community was as deeply divided on the meaning or significance of the riot as the rest of Los Angeles. Mexican American professionals, in particular, largely sided with civic authorities in condemning Pachucos for inciting the riot. Despite their reservations about Pachucos, however, the Mexican Americans called on to serve on commissions and committees took their positions seriously and actively lobbied for greater social and economic reforms in Los Angeles.

The reversal of *The People v. Zammora et al.* in early October 1944, after the national publicity campaign mounted by the Sleepy Lagoon Defense Committee, was a triumph of grassroots politics. Yet the larger issues of social and economic injustice raised during the two-year effort were never adequately addressed on a substantive level, and the lives of the young people directly affected by these events remained little improved once they were freed from prison. Progressive activists continued to encounter frustration in trying to organize community activism among minorities in Los Angeles along the models of progressive politics, and middle-class Mexican Americans faced setbacks in the postwar period as city politicians turned their attention to other issues. While working-class youths discovered new modes of expression and experimentation, the Pachuco found new life in mythical status, inspiring a new generation of Mexican American youths to political action.

### Conspiracies of Interest

The riot quickly took on a social significance independent of the events that initially spawned it. In grappling with the underlying causes of the riot, most Angelenos turned not to the abuse of civilians by the military but instead to the problem of juvenile delinquency. A range of existing county and state agencies, as well as newly created organizations, all sprang into action to investigate the barrios of East Los Angeles, hoping to discover among the casualties of violence the cause of the riot.[1] It was, in effect, the riot policy of the Los Angeles Police Department taken to another extreme: the Mexican American community was being blamed for the riot, and the resources of the state were turned on the victims of riot, not the rioters themselves.

Part of this reaction grew out of the spirit of the times. The worldwide conflict had invested the military with deep reserves of social and political capital, and many Americans were reluctant to question the motives or actions of "our boys" who were fighting the war.[2] The deeper and far more insidious issue was the question of race, and it would take someone thousands of miles away to see it clearly. Eleanor Roosevelt appalled many Angelenos by suggesting that the Zoot Suit Riot had all the markings of a race riot. City boosters and officials launched a round of denunciations of Roosevelt, claiming that her remark "shows ignorance . . . and an amazing similarity to the Communist Party line propaganda." Editors of the *Los Angeles Times* proudly pointed to Olvera Street and to the city's celebrations of California's mission past as proof that "we like Mexicans, and we think they like us."[3] Yet had sailors and soldiers rioted in Beverly Hills or Hollywood, there would have been no end to the public outcry over the abuses of military men in Los Angeles. As it was, the public at large could muster no such outrage, for the victims of the riot were primarily boys of color from working-class neighborhoods. Eleanor Roosevelt was right, after all.

Even the "Sleepy Lagoon boys," after all they had endured, were shocked by news of the riot. Manny Reyes was perhaps more so than the others, because he recognized two friends whose battered faces were featured on the front pages of newspapers. "I never dream [sic] that things like that would happen in the U.S.A., a land of freedom," he wrote to Alice McGrath. "I thought it alone happen in Germany and Japan."[4] Sadly, the news of the riot surpassed even the boys' understanding of how difficult the times really were.

Not everyone in the Mexican American *colonia* saw the riot in the same light, however. For Manuel Ruíz and other middle-class professionals, the riot was less the result of color prejudice than it was the conduct of social misfits. He consequently felt little remorse for aiding the investigations into the cause of the riot and turning in those Mexican American youth he believed to be guilty of instigating the violence. "[We] pitched ball and we were able to bring a lot of guys to task for the part they took," he related to a friend stationed in a nearby army base. "A few Mexican Zooters have gotten all the rest in a dutch. There are just as many Mexicans mad at them as other people . . . there were hot heads on both sides. . . . You can bet your sweet life that we're getting after the trouble makers. . . . In the meantime tell your [army] buddies that most of the Mexican kids are doing O.K. in the service, and that they feel like you do about the trouble makers."[5] Ruíz was not alone in blaming the cause of riot solely on behavior. "I was sorry to hear by letter and read a few clippings on the rumpus a few bums kicked up a month or two ago," Alphonso Rendón wrote Ruíz. "From what I gathered the police *are* permitted to rough them up a bit. . . . Has the demeanor of the youth improved any, lately?" (italics added).[6]

Richard Griswold del Castillo found that citizens in Mexico equally displayed mixed reactions toward Pachucos and the riot. Although the Mexican government expressed concern for the fate of its citizens living in Los Angeles and sent officials to meet with city and state authorities over the riot, it was also wary of the charge that "anti-Mexican hysteria" was the cause of the riot. In mid-June 1943, the first article to report on the riot appeared in Mexico City's *La Prensa*, and it was critical of Pachucos. "Without being truly Mexicans," the article headline read, "they are an affront to our Republic." In denouncing Pachucos (also called "Tarzanes"), *La Prensa* also raised the specter of race mixing by characterizing them as "almost always mestizos of Mexican and Negro, or Mexican and Chinese or Filipino; the great majority of them are not by birth or nationality Mexicans."[7] The prizewinning Mexican poet Octavio Paz, living in Los Angeles during the riot, also saw Pachucos as "sinister clowns" caught between the "labyrinth of solitude" in Mexican culture and the materialism of American culture.[8]

Ironically, two days before a planned student protest in Mexico against American racism, two young Mexicans were beaten and stripped of their zoot suits as they passed the Faculty of Medicine in downtown Mexico City.

Nonetheless, the protesters went forth, "booing, jeering, and hissing every store that displayed American signs." An American-owned pharmacy and restaurant named Sanborn was the target of particular violence, and some students attacked an American patron who was eating there. The protest ended with the establishment of the Comité de Defensa de los Mexicanos de Afuera (Committee for the Defense of Mexicanos Abroad) to continue protesting American racism and the lack of more forceful response from the Mexican government in protesting the riot.[9]

Paul Coronel of the student-run Mexican American Movement interpreted the events in California in a manner similar to that of the Mexican students. Pachucos were responsible for the violence that was directed at them, he conceded, but he saw juvenile delinquency in the barrios as only the symptom of racism in America. As editor of the small newsletter the *Mexican Voice*, he seized upon the moment to call on government leaders to encourage community self-help and educational programs that would assist all people in understanding and appreciating "each other's contributions . . . and background."[10]

Coronel's view that underlying racial tension had profound social consequences for Los Angeles found greater support among many progressive groups in California. Yet many activists of the period also understood that Americans were little disposed to attack racism on the merits of ethics alone. Taking a page from those who argued for a stronger police state in the name of national security, they turned the discourse around and couched racism in terms of the present national crisis.

LaRue McCormick stood before the first meeting of the Citizens' Committee for the Defense of Mexican American Youth and gave the group the main theme that would dominate the organization's existence. "Fifth column elements are egging Mexican youths on," she told the audience. "The only way to solve this problem is by . . . doing away with discrimination and unequal opportunities where the Mexican people are concerned."[11] Philip Connelly, president of the California chapter of the Congress of Industrial Organizations, elaborated on the message: "[Mexican American youths] are being tried in order to allow the fifth columnists to go forth and say to the Mexican people, 'This is your justice, this is your equality, this is the kind of break you get here!'"[12] Indeed, Connelly's prediction was largely correct. The Axis propaganda campaign picked up on news of the riot and beamed its message toward Latin America about American hypocrisy: "The concentration camps of Los Angeles are said to be overflowing with members of this persecuted minority. This is justice for you, as practiced by the Good Neighbor Uncle Sam, a justice that demands seventeen victims for one crime."[13]

But had organizers of the CCDMAY really stumbled on a conspiracy? Did the progressive activists who rallied to the CCDMAY truly believe that enemy agents were fomenting rebellion among minority youths while at the same time actively encouraging a stronger police state? Quite the contrary, they conducted no investigations or discovered any evidence to support their claims, and well they knew it. Crying conspiracy was an important way to rally the resources of the community in fighting a larger injustice: racism in America.[14]

To this end they used language strategically to frame the larger social issues of race and class in the most immediately recognizable terms for their audience. By characterizing racial and economic injustice as the work of the imagined "fifth column," they placed the trial within the language of crisis that dominated national priorities. If fascism produced intolerance and inequality, then democracy should be about tolerance and equality. Despite this use of language, it was far from crass manipulation. Progressive activists adopted the language of crisis to present a competitive vision of American society, one that included a more expansive notion of "liberty and justice for all."[15] Thus the public communications of the CCDMAY regularly sought to inspire sympathy for its cause by waving the flag of patriotism.[16]

Public officials were no more cautious in their use of rhetoric, for they, too, seized upon the convenience of crying conspiracy for their own purposes. For the sake of political expediency they largely sought to steer to the middle ground between McCormick's denunciation of racial and economic injustice on the one hand and Ayres's biological theory of criminality on the other. To acknowledge that the Zoot Suit Riot was the result of racism would have required that community leaders publicly admit that racism was indeed a serious problem in Los Angeles, which was something they were not about to do. On the other hand, to publicly endorse Ayres's assessment of juvenile delinquency, although many political officials may have privately shared his views, would have been a serious breach of social etiquette. Waving the flag of conspiracy therefore provided an attractive way out of the rhetorical straits before them because blaming the riot on outside agitators was a way of removing the cause of the riot from among them. Thus, while law enforcement officials secretly met with the military to draw up plans of cooperation in the event of another riot, they publicly fell behind Mayor Fletcher Bowron in neutralizing the worst of McCormick's charge while saving the best of it. Los Angeles law enforcement officials claimed that Mexican American youths were being treated no differently than anyone else and blamed the riot on foreign influence—usually fifth-column agents or white southerners newly immigrated to Los Angeles.

## Manuel Ruíz as Cultural Interpreter

Such allegations of subversion from foreign powers opened up fissures within the segregated walls of Los Angeles politics, large enough to allow some Mexican American activists room to maneuver. The County Board of Supervisors desperately needed help in understanding the perceived rise in juvenile delinquency and turned to members of the Mexican American middle class for leadership. It was primarily for this reason that Manuel Ruíz increasingly found favor with many elected officials as the spokesman for the "Mexican" people of Los Angeles. Certainly there were others who could have equally filled such an auspicious role: Josefina Fierro de Bright, Luisa Moreno, perhaps even Bert Corona at his young age.[17] But they were all too far to the left for Bowron's purposes. What counted more in Ruíz's favor was that he fit the middle-class notion of minority leadership. He graduated as a star athlete and as valedictorian from his high school, earned a law degree from the University of Southern California, and distinguished himself as a gifted orator and a skilled administrator. More important, he had developed the right connections with law enforcement agencies, and many city politicians considered him to be level headed. In other words, he appeared to be nonthreatening.[18]

City and county officials tapped Ruíz to head or participate in numerous committees, all of which revolved around trying to understand what "the Mexican" wanted. In some ways they received more than they bargained for. Ruíz was not blind to the political circumstances behind the newfound attention he received from city leaders; nor was he flattered into playing the apologist for the white middle-class. He was an astute man who well understood the lashes of racial prejudice, as well as the power of symbol and language. Thus he seized upon the opportunity presented to him by the moment of crisis to represent the interests of his people as faithfully as he knew how.[19]

Ruíz used his position as cultural interpreter to appeal for greater understanding between racial groups and to forward a progressive agenda he believed would bring about a postwar society of greater tolerance. In the name of the city and county organizations to which he belonged, he toured widely throughout Los Angeles and southern California speaking to white service clubs, teachers, merchant associations, veterans organizations, school superintendents, government officials, and politicians.[20] He was an accomplished orator and used these opportunities to call boldly for the desegregation of Los Angeles.[21] He argued that more and better schools in the barrios, coupled with greater economic opportunities, would stem the rising tide of Mexican American youth gangs. He called upon white community leaders and businesspeople to pressure the Los Angeles newspapers to put an end to denigrating portrayals of Mexican Americans in the press. And finally, he urged that the government adopt language and terminologies that would recognize the difference between cultural identity and national citizenship. Rather than indiscriminately using the term "Mexican," as was the common practice, he advocated that terms such as "Americans of Mexican extraction" or "Americans of Latin background" be adopted in order to remind Californians that Mexican Americans were indeed citizens of the United States.[22]

Ruíz published a widely read analysis of juvenile delinquency in *Crime Prevention Digest* that harshly criticized city officials for the roles they played prior to the outbreak of riot.[23] He faulted police officials for reacting too hastily to solve "the Pachuco problem" by indiscriminately arresting working-class youths. Such tactics only served to fuel the perceived rise in juvenile delinquency, which the press further fanned with its lurid accounts of Pachuco life. Perhaps the biggest problem, he argued, was that instead of stopping juvenile delinquency, the police crackdown only provided more grist for the Axis propaganda mill. Ruíz also chastised the civic authorities for failing to integrate Mexican Americans more fully into American society. If Pachuco activity was on the rise, according to Ruíz, it was because California law forbade public instruction in any language except English—even for the purpose of Americanizing recent migrants from Mexico. Thus he maintained that the only effective way to achieve "affirmative active parental cooperation" in the raising of good citizens was through a kind of bilingual education as a means to achieving Americanization. Anything less served to exclude Spanish-speaking citizens from a full cooperation and participation in American life.

Although Ruíz was an indefatigable lobbyist on behalf of the Mexican American community, he simply was unable to represent *all* members of the community. Throughout the period he continually cast a wary eye toward the young people called "Pachuco," not only because they threatened to undermine his work for racial uplift but because they defied the very way he constructed "the Mexican problem" that he was called on to resolve.[24] They were not in need of English-language instruction; nor did they need to be schooled in American ways. Rather, they were fluent enough in English and in American popular culture to determine on their own how they would engage with the U.S. society. It was perhaps no surprise, then, that Ruíz marshaled the resources at hand to aid the police in ferreting out those believed to be responsible for instigating the rioting in the weeks that followed. He did this not out of malice or for Machiavellian reasons, for he took very seriously the opportunity before him to lobby public officials for desperately needed social changes. Rather, he acted in cooperation with law enforcement agencies because he believed that public safety had no color and that all people should be responsible members of society. In the end, despite his best intentions, he became part of the problem in his quest to find a greater solution.

Another consequence of the contradictory roles he was forced to play as cultural mediator was that Ruíz, like many of his peers, never fully understood the work of the CCDMAY. This was due, in part, to the limited range of political organizations from which McCormick drew to organize the defense committee. Ruíz's politics were considerably more toward the center than that of the Communist Party U.S.A. (CPUSA), and it appears that McCormick never considered working with men such as Ruíz. The CCDMAY furthermore had a complicated relationship with the Mexican American community in general. These were not people who well understood conditions in the barrio or the complexities of life for Mexican Americans. They were largely outsiders in relation to the community, and their motives were constantly under suspicion. The involvement of people such as Josefina Fierro de Bright and Bert Corona in some ways further complicated the relationship because many church leaders who worked in the Mexican American neighborhoods of Los Angeles questioned the motives of progressive activists. "They would sign their name to anything," remarked Father Arthur of the Franciscan friary.[25] The local parish priest for the 38th Street neighborhood even red-baited the CCDMAY in his weekly homilies.[26] The CCDMAY could never quite overcome the stigma of communism, no matter how relevant the issue or how just the cause.

### The Sleepy Lagoon Defense Committee

Ironically, what greatly aided Ruíz in his role was the work of some of the very activists he distrusted. Carey McWilliams had taken an early interest in the "Sleepy Lagoon" trial and was among the first to organize the defense campaign with McCormick. Although McWilliams had never formally participated in CPUSA functions, he was a broad-minded, socially conscious individual who cared less for political persuasion than for justice.[27] Indeed, he had already distinguished himself early in his law career as a writer and a social activist. *Factories in the Field*, his widely read exposé of agribusiness and the exploitation of migrant workers, earned him the tag "California's number one agricultural pest."[28] He also brought to the CCDMAY important political connections he had made while serving as the state commissioner for immigration and housing.[29] These connections would prove vital to the improvement of race relations during the outbreak of rioting.

While Ruíz and other Mexican American professionals met with city officials during the third night of rioting, McWilliams placed an important phone call to his friend Robert Kenny, the California attorney general. Kenny agreed to talk to Governor Earl Warren that night about appointing a commission of inquiry to investigate the riot. In the early morning hours of the following day Kenny flew down from Sacramento to meet with McWilliams and discuss strategies. Out of that meeting came the McGucken committee, headed by the Catholic auxiliary bishop of Los Angeles, Joseph T. McGucken.[30]

In astonishing time (especially for a committee), the three-member panel came up with a remarkable document, one that largely supported the agenda that Ruíz pushed. Although the committee members reaffirmed the need to arrest lawbreakers, they largely faulted the press for its irresponsible tone of journalism and the police for overreacting to the situation. Race was indeed a critical matter in the riot, they argued, and the committee urged that police be trained not only in the Spanish language but also in the "psychology of Spanish-Speaking groups in Los Angeles." It furthermore called on city leaders to marshal the resources of the city and provide better housing, employment, and recreation facilities for working-class youths. The committee closed its assessment of the riot by acknowledging the work of previous bodies, among them the Coordinating Council for Latin American Youth, headed by Manuel Ruíz.[31] No doubt this was one of the reasons that Ruíz was later moved to boast that the CCLAY "was the principal factor in maintaining community cooperation and involvement" during that volatile period and in keeping the situation from becoming even worse for the Mexican American community.

In truth, Carey McWilliams had a far greater role in determining how the state would respond to the crisis, more than most people realized. It was McWilliams himself who drew up the list of "acceptable" members of the community to staff the fact-finding committee, and while Governor Warren deliberated over the appointments, McWilliams composed the draft that would eventually become, with minor alterations, the final report of the committee.[32] Carey McWilliams also came to the aid of the CCDMAY at a time when the organization was undergoing substantial reorganization. A number of the founding members of the group had moved on to other causes, and although the fund-raising campaign was successful, it was far from raising the kind of money they needed in order to launch an aggressive campaign to appeal the convictions. Thus, at the request of LaRue McCormick, Carey McWilliams became national chairman of the CCDMAY.[33]

McWilliams brought important changes to the organization. The new name of the the group, "The Sleepy Lagoon Defense Committee," reflected its sharper focus on winning an appeal for the convicted youths rather than the larger issues the CCDMAY tried to address.[34] McWilliams launched a concerted effort to broaden the spectrum of people recruited to help, particularly those of the political center and right. But perhaps one of the most important changes was that Alice McGrath became the executive secretary.[35]

Barely twenty-five years old, Alice McGrath was a dynamic woman.[36] So moved was she by outrage over the trial that she was thoroughly committed to the appeal effort, often without regard to personal expense or concern.[37] She was a person of such innate intelligence and perspective that, despite her lack of advanced schooling, she held her own as she moved about the circles of lawyers, intellectuals, politicians, and dignitaries with whom she would come to work.[38] "Alice was very effective," remembered McWilliams years later. "She knew how to get these people into action."[39] As executive secretary, she worked with a core of regular volunteers who busily kept meetings organized, presentations booked, and contributions coming in.[40]

McGrath first started out as an assistant to Bella Joseph, the executive secretary, but soon moved into positions of greater responsibility as she learned new skills and discovered new talents for activist work. Because McGrath was primarily responsible for how the CCDMAY promoted itself to the public through press releases, articles, and campaign literature, she became, as a consequence, one of the key figures in the life of the organization.[41] Although leadership of the organization would change substantially over its two-year existence and McGrath would assume other positions of responsibility, no one seemed to embody the organization more than she. Moreover, McGrath brought a greater sensitivity and intimacy with the community that the defense committee was ostensibly serving. She was responsible for hiring a bilingual office assistant, and together with Carey McWilliams she enlisted the aid of Coronel Vicente Peralta, consul general of Mexico in Los Angeles.[42] Peralta contacted prominent members of the Mexican American community to introduce Alice McGrath, and she would follow up with visits to win their support. With this tactic the SLDC soon could count on the aid of middle-class professionals who had previously maintained a distant and wary relationship with the organization.[43] In time, the Spanish-language newspapers of the city also grew more supportive of the defense committee and critical of the policies adopted by the LAPD.[44] McGrath also regularly worked with the families involved in the "Sleepy Lagoon" case and made regular visits to the incarcerated youths, often at her own expense.[45] As a consequence, she brought to the life of the organization tangible ties with the Mexican American community that it previously lacked.

Through letters and packages Alice (née Greenfield) McGrath became the adopted older sister of the incarcerated youths, their sweetheart, their confessor, and their political coach. "Dear Miss Greenfield," many of their early letters began, but as the months turned into years, their relationship with Alice warmed. Although the tone of their letters to Alice always remained respectful, grateful, perhaps even bashful, in time she became "Querida Alicia" to some or "Grandmother" and even "sweet chick" to others. The boys would enjoy visits from other volunteers and well-wishers from time to time, but Alice was the one constant person they could count on for news, advice, and words of encouragement.[46]

Such qualitative changes in the organization had much to do with Carey McWilliams, who brought a leadership style that encouraged the creativity and talents of those who worked with him. He was a warm and witty man of great personal strength; although he brought a greater sense of focus to the organization, he refused to impede the various fund-raising efforts by volunteers despite his personal disagreements with their approach. Thus, the period under his leadership saw the greatest strengths and weaknesses of the appeal effort, and *The Sleepy Lagoon Mystery* was a prime example.[47]

The Sleepy Lagoon Defense Committee enjoyed a growing support at home and abroad, owing in large part to the work of Hollywood screenwriter Guy Endore.[48] Endore was an accomplished biographer, novelist, and linguist well before coming to Hollywood and was no stranger to volunteering his talent to write political tracts for progressive causes.[49] He therefore wrote *The Sleepy Lagoon Mystery* in a lively and engaging manner that captured the salient themes of the cause, such as racism being anathema to the American creed, fifth-column conspiracy, and patriotism. Yet he did so at the expense of fairness and accuracy, for he took creative license in restructuring many of principals of the story in order to fit his larger critique of money and power unfettered. The young men of 38th Street were considered too problematic for public consumption, so they were scrubbed clean and sanitized almost beyond recognition. With the innocence of the 38th Street youths implied after their whitewash, he went on to vilify the judge and the district attorney in quasi-melodramatic tones. In order to establish causation he distorted the significance of the press and the influence of the fifth column.

In truth, *The Sleepy Lagoon Mystery* was never meant to be a dry, scholarly monograph about the trial. It was a political tract designed to raise sympathy for the cause, and in that regard it was a brilliant piece of advocacy. He used conspiracy to fill in the gaps of the story and to explain the events in a way that would stir the wrath of his readers. It was a conspiracy that was fundamentally anathema to the open democracy that Americans at least rhetorically cherished, for it originated with a wealthy and powerful man who sought to manipulate the public through the media into marching in lockstep with fascist doctrine. Thus he solved the mystery of Sleepy Lagoon with a stirring call to arms. "[The trial] was not directed against zoot-suited Mexican youth," he concluded. "It was an attack upon your nation. It was a conspiracy against you. It was an attempt to assassinate your future."[50]

Within the logic of his paradigm he did not overstate his case, but he accurately represented the significance of the volunteers' work as many of them understood it.[51] What happened to the "Sleepy Lagoon" boys could happen to anyone if democracy perished in the worldwide conflict with fascism. The fact that these boys were working-class Mexican Americans was important only in that fifth-column agents attempted to make it an issue to divide the public. Moreover, the work of the Sleepy Lagoon Defense Committee represented a working experiment in interracial cooperation in the defense of cherished liberties.

The Sleepy Lagoon Mystery was also an important resource in helping the boys to reconceptualize the events that led to their imprisonment. At the beginning of their ordeal, some of the boys ascribed their fate to simple misfortune because facing arrest or serving time for crimes they did not commit was simply part of the social terrain they had to negotiate in growing up. "I am sorry that things turn out the way they did," Henry Leyvas wrote to Alice shortly after his sentencing, "as I had very rozy expectations for the future. Did you ever make a castle out of sand or mud when you was a very small girl in pigtails and took much pains and trouble to create it, and all of a sudden a bigger kid came over and destroyed it for you? Well my feelings are somewhat similar. It seems like the whole world just folded up on me, and their [sic] is nothing I can do about it."[52] Others blamed themselves for their bad luck and stoically resolved to endure their fate. "I got in this and I might as well take it like a man," Chepe Ruíz also wrote to Alice. "That's the way I look at it . . . we all make mistakes."[53] Yet The Sleepy Lagoon Mystery helped the boys to understand that there were larger social forces at work in the events that shaped their lives, forces that played a significant role in their arrest and imprisonment. They learned to perceive and articulate more accurately the pattern of discrimination in the events they had to endure. Perhaps most important, they learned that they were not alone. They responded less to Endore's conspiracy theory than to the affirming power that came from discovering that others also believed their imprisonment to be a gross miscarriage of justice. "I had lost all faith before," Henry Leyvas was moved to write when even the prison warden responded favorably to the booklet. "And now there is plenty of nice people . . . that are really trying their best to see us get a fair trial. And that's really all I ask, to get a fair trial."[54]

There was a price to be paid, however, for the SLDC's exclusive focus on appealing the conviction of the boys. Some of the young women detained as witnesses for the state during the trial were forgotten, and zealous social workers trying to rescue the young women from the baneful effects of gang life found reasons to extend their detention. According to Elizabeth Escobedo, Dora Barrios, Betty Zeiss, Jenny Gonzales, and Lorena Encinas were processed through the California Youth Authority and sent to the newly founded Ventura School for Girls. On average the girls stayed at the "school" (which was run like a military camp) for sixteen months, depending on the girl's behavior. Upon release to the custody of a parent, guardian, or work home, they remained wards of the state until the age of twenty-one and had an acceptable parole record. Although Alice and the other Sleepy Lagoon volunteers were sympathetic to their plight and visited them as often as they could, there simply was no legal recourse to fight for their release. Many of the girls' parents, believing that they were getting their daughters off the streets by sending them to receive vocational training, gave permission to the California Youth Authority to place their daughters in the Ventura School for Girls.[55] The lack of a larger public outcry over the fate of the Sleepy Lagoon girls suggests that the public was willing to overlook a certain amount of violence as an acceptable part of masculinity but not female violence. The community silence over the fate of the Sleepy Lagoon girls may have resulted from the belief that these women who defied normative gender constructions got precisely what they deserved.

And despite the efforts and enthusiasm of the volunteers in rallying to right a terrible wrong, their beneficence only extended so far. The larger problems of underemployment, exploitation, and inadequate health care that daily confronted the friends and families of the imprisoned youths went unheeded. Delia Parra wrote a letter to Alice in September 1944 that illustrates the desperation she faced while her husband "Smiles" was in prison. She began the letter by apologizing for not having been by the SLDC office to continue her volunteer work. Her mother had been hospitalized for two weeks and was in need of an operation, she explained. To make matters worse, she was being evicted from her apartment. As if her burdens were not enough, she worried that her husband's feelings were hurt because she could afford to take the train up to San Quentin only once a month. "I am sick and tired," she confessed. "My only way out [is] if I can find a dam [*sic*] place where to move and then I can go to work."[56] In fairness, many of those who responded to the work of the SLDC were indeed aware of the larger problems that confronted the families of East Los Angeles, and some of them did participate in fact-finding committees and in issuing reports calling for greater attention to the social needs of the working-class communities. But filing reports fell far short of actually addressing the problems of inequality, and many, like Delia Parra, could only press forward as best they could, largely unaided by the work of these committees.

### Turning the Tide

In 1944 the work of the SLDC entered its most important phase. The Los Angeles newspapers, responding to the SLDC campaign, haltingly started to rethink their earlier coverage of the Sleepy Lagoon trial. The *Los Angeles Daily News* was the first to do so when Alice McGrath won over columnist Matt Weinstock.[57] He devoted the major part of his daily column to the appeal effort and commented on the exceptionally clean records the boys had while at San Quentin penitentiary. "The irony is somewhat heavy," he noted one day, "when a dozen boys, pushed around outside, find democracy inside prison walls."[58] Before the Weinstock column the only sympathetic coverage the appeal could count on came from ethnic-oriented newspapers with relatively small circulations such as the Jewish *Eastside Journal*, the African American *California Eagle*, or labor newspapers.[59] Most of the other Los Angeles newspapers simply considered the subject to be passé and rarely commented on news of the appeal work, even when hundreds of Hollywood stars gathered for a benefit to raise money for the cause.[60]

The work of the volunteers also gained momentum that year, and for a moment it seemed as if the SLDC actually succeeded in creating the progressive community it envisioned. McWilliams's efforts to broaden the constituency base of the organization paid off handsomely as hundreds of people rallied to the cause in donating time, talents, or money.[61] In time the SLDC could proudly count among its sponsors labor leaders, professors, Hollywood stars, religious leaders, and national politicians from many political perspectives. Even modest donations came pouring in from marines, soldiers, and sailors as news of its work reached the troops stationed abroad.[62] "I should like to go on record as vigorously opposing the unjust conviction of the Mexican prisoners in the 'Sleepy Lagoon' case," one white wrote from the Fiji Islands. An African American soldier in Hawaii also wrote: "We members of the colored race are sympathetic to your worthwhile and moral fight to free the Mexican boys."[63]

Hollywood stars, furthermore, proved to be among the best fund-raisers on which the SLDC could draw.[64] The appeal effort long enjoyed a strong connection to Hollywood, largely through the efforts of Josefina Fierro de Bright. She was a striking and vivacious woman who was well known among progressive circles in her own right and in the Hollywood community through her marriage to John Bright, a celebrated screenwriter.[65] Because of her the fledgling CCDMAY was able to count on the star power of some of its early supporters, such as Rita Hayworth (born Margarita Cancinos), Orson Welles, Canada Lee, and Anthony Quinn. Through parties, buffets, and benefit concerts, the SLDC raised thousands of dollars to underwrite the legal costs of the appeal and counted among its supporters the likes of Elia Kazan, Vincent Price, Gene Kelly, Lena Horne, and Nat "King" Cole.[66]

McWilliams's connections also found the attorney who would represent the SLDC's cause in the courts. With George Shibley drafted by the army, Ben Margolis assumed the lead in directing the legal aspects of the appeal. Margolis was long active in the National Lawyers' Guild, and it was through this organization that he came to know Clore Warne, who was also a close friend of Carey McWilliams's.[67]

Margolis was, by all accounts, the perfect lawyer to take the lead in appealing the conviction. Margolis was a gifted attorney who was in the process of moving to Los Angeles. While in San Francisco, he had established a strong record among labor and professional circles for tackling difficult and unpopular cases. Indeed, so committed to progressive issues were he and his law partners that they almost faced bankruptcy for taking on low-paying, unpopular cases. Warne and McWilliams could offer him little better, with only a promise that they would continue to raise the necessary funds to underwrite his expenses. With his acceptance Margolis stepped into a case that would cost him close to five thousand dollars of his own money.[68]

Together with a team of researchers, Margolis pored over the six-thousand-page transcript of the trial. They found a consistent pattern of bias that unfairly influenced the outcome of the trial. Not only had the community climate and judicial favoritism tainted the proceedings, but Judge Fricke had effectively denied the defendants their constitutional right to consult with their lawyer in ordering them to sit as a group away from the defense table. Worse, although the evidence did not support the initial charges of conspiracy and murder, the jury nonetheless found almost half of the accused guilty.[69]

The long-awaited opportunity to argue the case before the appellate court was in some ways anticlimactic and the work itself tedious. It was hardly the stuff that had sustained the life of the SLDC in its campaign to raise community awareness and support. There was no place in this arena of legal briefs and motions for the impassioned speeches of patriotism or the theories of conspiracy that had rallied people together. It was instead a place of deliberation and exactitude, and Margolis would not be able to argue the case before the panel of judges until May 1944, even though his team had been ready since November 1943.[70]

Waiting, however, did not dull Margolis's edge. When the moment finally came to argue the case, he was at his best. He was eloquent and cogent, arguing in his conclusion, "It was not just these boys who were on trial. The Mexican people were tried. . . . Neither is guilty."[71] Indeed, so effective was his oral argument that one of the judges was moved to exclaim: "The appellants are well-represented here today!"[72]

The state, on the other hand, seemed to lack the same intensity of purpose. The arguments presented by John Barnes for Los Angeles County and Eugene Elson, who represented the attorney general, simply lacked luster, and they presented little more than a summary of the case argued previously in the lower court.[73] Whether the two prosecutors were so confident in the power of their case or whether they had by that time lost the stimulus for winning a conviction, their point had been made about the young people they believed to be criminal. After all the arguments had been proffered and all the briefs filed, the judicial panel began its long deliberation in July 1944.[74]

Even with the legal work securely under way, the life of the Sleepy Lagoon Defense Committee was far from over. Although not uncooperative with the appeal effort, the boys themselves posed a potential threat to the cause. The prison environment offered the young men unique opportunities to complicate further the public's support for their appeal effort. Much of the rhetorical value of the case, represented in the speeches, press releases, and pamphlets produced by the SLDC, rested on a strategy that steered away from questions about the character of the convicted youths and focused, instead, on the injustice perpetrated by the state. Any incident in prison could undermine the sympathy of a fickle public, which had already/feasted on the rhetorical flesh of the Pachuco, so Alice McGrath took it upon herself to coach the young men regularly in proper behavior.[75] In retrospect, she had little to worry about.

In an environment dominated by hardened criminals, the boys from 38th Street were simply out of place. Although some of the young men had records for theft and assault, the boys were a far cry from the reputations that preceded them. They worked themselves up the prison reward system with relative quickness and won the trust and sympathy of prison officials who took a particular interest in their case.[76] For the most part, many of the boys attended mass regularly, enrolled in school when permitted, and were among the first to volunteer for war work. Almost all of the group actively joined in the prison sports program, and those who did soon dominated the baseball and boxing teams.[77]

The irony of their newfound status in prison was not lost on them. At home they were considered misfits and delinquents, but in prison they were role models of good behavior and given opportunities that were denied them on the outside. They also observed a prison ethos of social integration that was dramatically at odds with the segregated norms of society. "Mexican, Jews, Negroes—we all mix and are friendly," Bobby Telles noted. "Why *can't* we do that on the outside?"[78]

There were still some social boundaries that some of the boys would defend, even at the price of their freedom. Out of desperation Delia Parra approached the SLDC for financial assistance, and McGrath was able to offer her a meager gift. But somehow in the exchange Delia thought that she would be required to solicit funds on Central Avenue. This was simply an unacceptable situation for Smiles, and he asked Alice to drop him from the appeal if his wife would have to "go through any embarrassment just on account of me."[79] For Henry Leyvas, who enjoyed none of the privileges of his peers, no amount of coaching or coaxing could dissuade him from his fundamental sense of self. Even in prison he could not let slights or offenses go unchallenged, and he paid the price.[80] McGrath was able to correct quickly the misunderstanding with Parra, but she had no such luck with Henry. While the rest of the boys of 38th Street were earning parole for good behavior, Henry earned a transfer to Folsom, a higher-security prison.[81]

Ironically, the good prison record of the boys almost worked against their collective best interests. Freedom was their foremost concern, whether it was obtained through parole or an appeal. When four of the twelve boys were released on parole in August and September 1944, some of them never quite fully appreciated the continued work to be done on their behalf. They were not ungrateful; they were simply unaccustomed to the world of legal technicalities. Despite Alice McGrath's best efforts to keep them actively engaged in clearing their records, the details of the appeal ceased to be a top priority for some of them once they were free.[82]

The long struggle for justice ended in early October when the judges announced their decision.[83] They agreed with most of the contentions Margolis brought before the appellate court. Perhaps most egregious to the panel was the tone of judicial bias that prejudiced the case against the defendants. The judges declared that the state lacked sufficient evidence to convict the young men of either conspiracy or murder and remanded the case. It was hardly a sweeping victory for the SLDC, however. The panel of judges unanimously agreed that race played no role in the outcome of the trial. They argued that because the victim was Mexican American and the witnesses for the prosecution were largely Mexican American, the case had been an example that all were treated fairly before the law. They furthermore upheld the correctness and propriety of the district attorney's handling of the investigation and prosecution of the case.

Two weeks after the court's decision, the SLDC won a surprising victory that exceeded its expectations. The state conceded defeat in announcing that it would formally make a motion to drop all the charges against the young men of 38th Street. On 28 October 1944, Judge Clement Nye dismissed the case against the boys and ordered them to be released from prison and their records cleared.[84] Within two hours a jubilant throng of friends, relatives, and volunteers mobbed the halls of the county jail, to which the boys had been transferred, and greeted them on their release with a celebration of tears and laughter that lasted for more than an hour.[85]

### Victory's Aftermath

Although the Sleepy Lagoon Defense Committee could justly claim a major victory, it was a limited victory in retrospect. The damage that had been done to the young men and their families was in many ways irreparable. An apology from the state, though meaningless in any legal sense, would certainly have gone a long way in healing the wounds inflicted, but one was not forthcoming. The appellate court ruled in favor of the boys and censured Judge Fricke for prejudicing the outcome of the trial, but little changed in actuality. Fricke remained on the bench until his retirement. The Los Angeles Police Department continued to raid the neighborhoods of East Los Angeles as public anxieties over juvenile delinquency rose and fell over time. No doubt many in the Los Angeles Police Department and the district attorney's office shared the views of one prison guard who smirked on the release of the 38th Street boys: "They'll be back."[86]

Sadly, some of them did return to prison. For Henry Leyvas the two years in San Quentin and Folsom were but a small portion of the time that he would spend in prison over the course of his life. Soon enough, Chepe Ruíz, Angel Padilla, and Manny Delgado also returned to prison. Of the four, only Manny Delgado escaped the hard and tragic cycle of prison and parole. After his second incarceration Delgado settled down with his wife, never again to return to jail. The rest of the group traveled down the various avenues that were open to them as working people from East Los Angeles. Smiles Parra found employment as a metalworker, but in time he separated from Delia and his children and moved out of state. Bobby Thompson left Los Angeles immediately after being released from prison and never reunited with his friends. Bobby Telles died at a relatively young age, and Gus Zamora never escaped the ignominy of having the case bear his name. Because his father never forgave him for the dishonor, Gus died estranged from his family and embittered.[87] Hank Ynostroza, Manny Reyes, John Matuz, and Jack Melendez settled down in the Los Angeles area. The last three became small-time entrepreneurs. The forgotten girls of 38th Street were also released from juvenile hall, most of them paroled before their eighteenth birthday.

The Díaz family did not experience the events that unfolded since the death of their son and brother as "anti-Mexican," if anti-Mexican meant harsher treatment toward their people. The sentences Judge Fricke gave to most of the 38th Street boys for the death of José were so lenient that to the Díaz family the outcome of the trial was an affront to José's life and memory. Although three of the 38th Street boys were given life sentences for murder in the first degree and nine were given five years to life for murder in the second degree, all of them would be free within two years. The success of the appeal effort for the 38th Street boys was a bitter turn of events. The communitywide effort to win an appeal had not corrected a miscarriage of justice but perpetuated one. To the Díaz family, it was as if the boys of 38th Street had become minor celebrities in Los Angeles while the memory of José quickly faded from view. Even in the retelling of the story within the Mexican American community itself, José's name was soon forgotten.[88]

The work of progressive activists and members of the Mexican American community to aid the families of the 38th Street boys never included the members of José Díaz's family, and they were left to grieve for their loss unaided. Teodulo Díaz suffered a mental breakdown and never fully recovered. Before his son's death he entertained his children by playing the violin, and he regularly performed at neighborhood parties with his own small orchestra. After José's death he never picked up his violin again. Lino named his son after his departed brother, but the elder Díaz could never bring himself to embrace his grandson.[89]

Winning the release of the 38th Street boys on appeal was far from the social corrective that progressive activists argued it would be. The trial was only one branch of the larger social ills of racism and economic injustice faced by many working families, and few took on the task of striking at the roots. Although a number of activists who rallied with the SLDC may have wanted to, they were kept busy with other concerns. The following year state senator Jack Tenney brought the hearings of the Un-American Activities Committee to Los Angeles and gave the progressive community a taste of the McCarthyism to come in the postwar period. He subpoenaed a number of members of the SLDC in order to determine whether Communists fronted the defense committee or inspired the Zoot Suit Riot as part of a master plot to disrupt American society.[90]

Despite the social limits of the victory, it was a remarkable triumph in collective action and coalition politics. For a moment the SLDC succeeded in bridging the divides of race, class, and politics in the quest for justice and brought together the rich and famous and the poor and obscure.[91] Because enough people along the way stood up to be counted, one small consequence of social evil was defeated. The events could have easily turned out another way had it not been for the intervention of key individuals who had it within their power to make a small difference. Had LaRue McCormick not stepped forward to organize a defense committee, George Shibley would not have become involved in the case. Had Shibley not laid down a pattern of objections and assignments throughout the proceedings, Ben Margolis would not have been able to argue for an appeal according to the rules of law. Had Margolis been unable to appeal the conviction, the boys would surely have spent their youth in prison, alone and largely abandoned to the correctional system of California. Individually McCormick, Shibley, and Margolis were powerless to stay the power of the state, but collectively they changed the lives of twelve young men.

The Sleepy Lagoon Defense Committee officially disbanded on New Year's Day, 1945. It was a bittersweet moment for the corps of volunteers who were the lifeblood of the organization. They, too, had changed immeasurably during this period. Both Ben Margolis and George Shibley went on to distinguished careers in law, all the while fighting for the progressive causes they believed in and defending the rights of the accused no matter how unpopular they were. Indeed, one of George Shibley's most notorious clients was Sirhan Sirhan, who was accused of assassinating Robert F. Kennedy and convicted.[92] Carey McWilliams went on to publish numerous works of critical achievement, among them the seminal work in Chicano historiography *North from Mexico*. He continued to play a prominent part in progressive politics in southern California until he moved to New York City and eventually became editor of *The Nation* for close to twenty years. After the SLDC disbanded, Alice McGrath and her husband, Max Schechter, began their family with the birth of Laura, but Alice never left the arena of grassroots poli-

THE VIOLENT POETRY OF THE TIMES

tics. Putting her newborn child into a stroller, she quickly became involved in the petition campaign to improve city services to Chavez Ravine. Today she is still active in the fight for human rights and spends much of her time shuttling between California and Nicaragua.

The interracial conflict that followed in the wake of the Sleepy Lagoon trial severely tested the loyalties of the Mexican American middle class and challenged its sense of representation to the larger Los Angeles community. Mexican American community leaders were initially conflicted over how to respond appropriately to the interracial violence and cautiously supported the authorities in their handling of the "juvenile delinquents." It was not until they began to fear indiscriminate reprisals on the *colonia* as a whole, however, that, instead of falling behind the embattled Pachucos, the Mexican American bourgeoisie rallied together and threw its fortune in with the city officials. During the height of rioting, Tomás Chacon appealed to Manuel Ruíz and other politically visible members of the *colonia* to unite against the danger that threatened the community. "Please understand that I do not advocate the adoption of extremist, racial viewpoints on the matter," he cautioned. "I am not attempting to defend, or to apologize for the deplorable acts of gangsterism perpetrated by so-called Pachucos . . . [I] seek the cooperation, through unity, of the many English speaking Americans who profess and demonstrate to be our friends effectively to uproot racial discrimination in every walk of life—the driving evil behind the present wave of Pachuco lawlessness."[93]

During this period of volatile race relations in Los Angeles, Ruíz maintained a curious relationship with the young people in the *colonia*. His work with Cultura Pan-Americana and the CCLAY brought him face to face with the awful realities of daily desperation and want in the poorer parts of town, but he never quite understood "delinquency" as the product of economic, political, or social marginalization. For him, young people's frustration with and hostility toward the social norms of segregation lay in their failure to understand how the system worked.

Ruíz was fundamentally a political being whose faith in American society and democracy was never in question. He could not afford it to be. His access to power and his vision of a postwar pluralistic society ultimately rested on the essential maintenance of the body politic, modified only enough to be more accessible to those who could merit participation in it. Certainly Ruíz realized the relationship between racism and economic power, and he devoted much of his energies to reinventing the Mexican image in the minds of the politically dominant. Yet the programs he outlined for the eradication of juvenile delinquency among Mexican American youths more closely resembled the leadership-development programs of the Boys Scouts than a program for community renewal.[94] For Ruíz and other "Latin" reformers, their main objective was to provide "positive" avenues of expression and development through teaching Pachucos and other Mexican American youths the kinds of social behavior necessary to gain acceptance within the larger community.

There is a measure of irony in his approach to racial uplift. During a period of intense hostility directed at Mexican Americans, Ruíz embraced a vision of Pan-Americanism and "Latin" pride and identity in the name of self-preservation for his people. Ultimately, however, his agenda to increase access to power for Mexican Americans proposed to accomplish what the Americanization campaign of the 1920s could not: make good "Americans" out of the Spanish-speaking population.

As time passed, the problem of juvenile delinquency in the *colonia* grew too large for Cultura Pan-Americana and the CCLAY to handle, and Ruíz turned his attention to other pursuits. A new generation of middle-class Mexican American activists in the 1960s turned their back on the "Latin American" identity of their parents, embraced "Chicano" as their identity, and idolized the Pachuco as their political and cultural predecessor. No longer were they content to learn the ways of the politically dominant. The new generation of *colonia* activists questioned the very foundations of the system and called for a new political order altogether. Some even advocated armed insurrection. Ruíz lived to see the image of the Pachuco grow to mythical proportions among Mexican American youths and overshadow his earlier contributions to better the conditions within the *colonia*.

Despite their reservations about Pachucos, Mexican American community activists stepped into the breach of social relations to lobby for progressive reforms. Although their success was limited in a quantitative sense, their qualitative impact was profound. For a time Cultura Pan-Americana and the CCLAY spanned a communicational gap that existed between the political establishment, the Mexican American middle class, the Mexican government, and the restless youths of the *colonia*.

The activism of Ruíz and his companions was not without significance. One year after the SLDC succeeded in overturning the convictions in *The People v. Zammora*, Manuel Ruíz led the fight to desegregate public schools in Los Angeles. In 1945 Ruíz, together with House representative William H. Rosenthal, drafted a proposal that would overturn portions of the State Educational Code that sanctioned segregated schools. The proposed bill passed the House but stalled in the Senate for two years. It was not until 1947 that the Senate took a renewed interest in the bill when Gonzalo Méndez won his suit against the all-white Westminster School District, and people of color across California began to join together to demand an end to segregation.[95] Later that same year Governor Earl Warren signed the bill desegregating California's public schools, seven years before he would make a similar ruling in *Brown v. Board of Education* as chief justice of the Supreme Court. With the victories of *The People v. Zammora* and *Westminster* cases, Mexican Americans joined in the growing legal and political challenges to segregation from people of color that found greater fruition in the decades to follow.

The work of the SLDC also continued to reverberate for decades after the group disbanded. *The People v. Zammora* became a landmark ruling protecting the right to fair trial. The interpretive paradigm that progressive activists used to rally community support for the appeal effort helped cultivate one of the main branches of political thought growing out of the Mexican American community of Los Angeles. The nascent ideology of Chicanismo in the 1960s, with its affinity for progressive politics, was largely shaped by a paradigm that saw the collective experiences of Mexican Americans as the struggle for cultural resistance in the face of oppression and victimization. It is no wonder that many Chicanos appropriated the image of the Pachuco in rediscovering *The Sleepy Lagoon Mystery* and in the process reinvented the Pachuco as the cultural forebear of the movement. For many students of the "Pachuco era," the papers of the Sleepy Lagoon Defense Committee at the University of California, Los Angeles, continue to serve as the main source for understanding the events of the period.

### The Enduring Significance of the Pachuco

One cannot help but note a sense of irony in viewing the attacks on the imagined Pachuco of the 1940s from the vantage point of history. The many Angelenos who labored to rid Los Angeles of the Pachuco presence ultimately guaranteed its longevity. Although in time the zoot suit fell out of fashion as the jazz world moved from swing to be-bop, the Pachuco lived on in barrio lore and in time rose immortalized in the dramatic and scholarly works of Chicano artists and intellectuals. Arturo Madrid first explored the permutations of the Pachuco myth in his 1973 article "In Search of the Authentic Pachuco." Beginning with the critical observations of Mexican poet Octavio Paz during the 1940s and ending with José Montoya's classic poem "El Louie" in 1970, Madrid found that the Pachuco had become larger than life. The many words in condemnation or praise of the Pachuco over the years revealed more about the respective political lenses of the authors, he perceptively argued, than they did about the Pachuco "in human terms."[96]

Each generation envisions the past according to the needs of the present, and the myth of the Pachuco as zoot suiter continued to evolve in popular representations despite Madrid's insightful criticism. The Pachuco emerged as a central figure in the symbolic history of Chicano nationalism on stage and screen, pioneered by Chicano playwright Luís Valdez. Valdez first began to explore his notion of the Pachuco as the spiritual ancestor of the Chicano movement in one of the early productions of El Teatro Campesino, *Los Vendidos* (1972). Although the Pachuco character was only part of a larger ensemble of Mexican stereotypes, the direction that Valdez would take with the Pachuco is signaled in one of the lines of the play: "Inside every Chicano is a little bit of the Pachuco."

Valdez's reinvention of the Pachuco as the predecessor of the Chicano movement found its fullest expression in *Zoot Suit* (1981), the condensed film version of the production that played for packed houses at the Mark Taper Forum in Los Angeles and had a brief run on Broadway.[97] Drawing inspiration from the narrative in Guy Endore's *The Sleepy Lagoon Mystery*, Valdez cast the events of the period as an epic struggle. But rather than follow Endore's story line, which portrayed the historical moment as a contest between community activism and concentrated power, Valdez recast the story as both an existential struggle and a Pachuco passion play.

Although Valdez modeled the protagonist Henry Reyna after Henry Leyvas, he elevated the Pachuco as the central figure in the Chicano drama by creating the character "El Pachuco" and moving him to center stage as the narrator and as Henry's alter ego. Valdez also historicized the represented present in the play by invoking pre-Columbian references, thereby placing El Pachuco firmly within the continuum of Chicano symbolic history. He appears adorned in a red shirt and black zoot suit, rather than the more conservative drape favored by Los Angeles youths. Valdez chose those specific colors, Yolanda Broyles-González explains, in reference to the Aztec deity Tezcatlipoca.[98] In another scene he superimposed the image of El Pachuco on a victim of the riot to signify, as Rosa Linda Fregoso points out, "the symbolic convergence of two historical events: the sailor's attack on pachucos (1943) and the Spanish conquest of the Aztec nation (1519)." In that climactic moment, El Pachuco allows himself to be sacrificed for Henry, and when the spirit arises from the dead body of El Pachuco, he is no longer a zoot suiter but an Aztec warrior. Valdez's meaning is clear—the Pachuco is an incarnation of the revolutionary from the time of the Aztecs to the modern-day Chicano.[99] In communicating this meaning, Fregoso argues, Valdez confirms "the central problematic of cultural nationalist discourse, namely that Chicano brotherhood, existing to time immemorial, involves the symbolic elevation of the Pachuco desire."[100] Indeed, it was Valdez who speculated that "it was the secret fantasy of every *bato* in or out of the *Chicanada* to put on a Zoot Suit and play the Myth *más chucote que la chingada*" [the baddest Pachuco around].[101]

Valdez's observation of the Chicano desire signaled the ways that many of his contemporaries looked to the past, and he was hardly alone in favoring myth and symbol over the personalities and particulars of the historical actors. Social critics, artists, and scholars since the 1960s have attributed to the wartime generation a cultural nationalist intention far beyond the worldview of the young people who donned the drape and grooved to swing jazz.[102] "The Pachuco movement was one of the few truly separatist movements in American history," Octavio Romano speculated in *El Grito*. "The Pachuco indulged in a self-separation from history, created his own reality as he went along even to the extent of creating his own language."[103] Jazz poet Larry Neal also saw the zoot suit as the symbol of African American cultural resistance, and Chicano artist José Montoya explained in *Lowrider* magazine that he considered Pachucos "to be the first Chicano freedom-fighters of the Chicano movement."[104] Recent scholarship resonates with a similar impulse. From Rodolfo Acuña to Stuart Cosgrove, Steve Chibnall, and Robin Kelley, a number of scholars have argued that "the zoot suit looms large in the tradition of Chicano and Afro-American cultural resistance."[105]

A decade after *Zoot Suit*, Chicano actor and producer Edward James Olmos illustrated the powerful place the Zoot Suit Riot continues to occupy in the prison epic *American Me* (1992). Olmos, who played the part of El Pachuco in *Zoot Suit*, reimagined the riot not as crucifixion of the Pachuco but as a rape of the entire community. The opening sequence of the film begins with a rape of a Pachuca by sailors during the Zoot Suit Riot while her Pachuco boyfriend struggles to protect her but is savagely beaten into submission. Although no rape was ever reported in connection with the riot, the scene was probably distilled from an account in Beatrice Griffith's book of the same title. Griffith charged that sailors not only invaded Mexican American neighborhoods during the Zoot Suit Riot but also violated the sanctity of their homes in the search for zoot suiters.

Olmos employs rape as one of the central metaphors of the film, and reimagining the riot as rape allows him to explore several key themes of Chicano nationalism. Drawing from a paradigm of history as trauma, which holds that the history of a group is framed by the circumstances of its creation, Olmos grounds his work within the interpretive framework of Mexican intellectuals such as Samuel Ramos and Octavio Paz. The framework of traumatic conception allows Olmos to signal parallels with the Chicano experience through the film's protagonist, Santana. Santana's life begins with the rape of his Pachuca mother by American sailors, echoing the view that the history of Chicanos began with the rape of Mexico by the American military. And although the Pachuco boyfriend marries his violated girlfriend, he can never bring himself to accept a son born of rape. Reminiscent of Paz's notion of the "hijos de la chingada," Santana thus enters the world alienated from a disdainful father and unwanted by a society that can never accept his dual heritage. Even though the trauma of violence is both his history and his inheritance, there is a particular kind of nobility found in stoic endurance, reminiscent of the defiant refrain in Corky Gonzales's epic poem *Yo Soy Joaquín*: "I will endure, I shall endure!" And just as Joaquín withdraws to "the safety within the circle of life—MY OWN PEOPLE," shedding tears of sorrow and sowing seeds of hate, Santana is not entirely alone.[106] He has himself, his raw courage and determination, and he has his compadres.

The paradigm of Chicano nationalism continues to provide a meaningful way for many students of the period to understand the social tensions in wartime Los Angeles. The zoot suit revival inspired by Valdez continues in popular venues, and productions of *Zoot Suit* draw large audiences in the Southwest. Some Internet businesses cater exclusively to customers interested in zoot suits, and zoot-suited youths striking the Pachuco pose invented by Olmos, leaning back on one leg in an impossible stride, are a staple at some Lowrider car shows.[107]

The Internet has facilitated the evolution of the narrative about the Pachuco, one that ultimately succeeds, in a strange way, where Hearst's newspapers failed. The cyber narrative utilizes characterizations of the Pachuco drawn largely from the Hearst newspapers in retelling the story of the Sleepy Lagoon murder trial and Zoot Suit Riot. José Díaz, who was in many ways the antithesis of a Pachuco, is reimagined as a Pachuco and the events leading to his death a "gang rumble" between Pachucos. Popular Web sites also envision the entire war generation of Mexican American youths in a singular style and lifestyle that draw more from the zoot-suited creation of Luís Valdez, popularized in the artwork of José Montoya, than from historical images of the drape and its variations. The cyber narrative also tends to read the Hearst press as the most significant social barometer of wartime Los Angeles. Rather than reflecting moderate voices of the time and McWilliams's view that the Hearst press alone sensationalized the so-called Pachuco problem, the cyber narrative describes the entire period as an "environment of ethnic and racial paranoia."[108]

Through various media the imagined Pachuco has evolved as an expression of a profound desire. To be sure, its modern incarnation, as Fregoso rightly concludes, is a masculinist desire, as it has largely been in the past. Critics, scholars, and concerned citizens during the war years, who gave birth to the imagined Pachuco and collectively nurtured the image through print, viewed the Pachuco as the offspring of some systemic social flaw. What that flaw was depended on the political view of the author, but such fears over uncontrolled youths could not have been far removed from related fears about the unseen future and that the nation might very well fail from within in its war with the Axis forces. The imagined Pachuca, in contrast, never developed as fully as the imagined Pachuco in the 1940s or later. She enjoyed the longest life in the Spanish-language press during the war, existing largely as a smear on the respectability of the Mexican *colonia* and as an indictment of Mexican parents failing to instill a proper appreciation of Mexican traditions and customs in their American-born children. The imagined Pachuca lived a shorter life in the English-language press quite likely because the unseen future that provoked such anxiety, embedded within the discourse over youth, was always envisioned as a masculinist future. Despite the fundamental need for women to leave traditional roles and places during the war and the obvious contributions they made in doing so, few people considered such changes long term. As Sara Evans and Elaine Tyler May argue in their respective works, the Roosevelt administration, employers, recruiters, and even Hollywood went to great lengths to assure the nation that such changes were only temporary, that women in the wartime workforce remained feminine, and that cherished American values about womanhood and domesticity would be preserved in the postwar period.[109]

The reappropriation of the maligned Pachuco that began with Chicano nationalists, who viewed the Pachuco as the proto-Chicano, signaled an important shift in the myth. The evolution of the Pachuco as cultural warrior in zoot suit occurred in response to not so much a national problem as a nationalistic one. Through print, poetry, art, and drama, Chicano nationalists strove to locate themselves within a historical continuum of resistance and affirmation that provided both meaning and context to the Chicano movement. Chicano intellectuals explored the Nahuatl origins of Caló words such as "tacuche" and "pachuco" and speculated on the Mexican origins of the zoot suit.[110] Poets and artists found in the essence of *Pachuquismo* a will to be that was defined not from the outside but within, and they celebrated the Pachuco for staying true to his own vision of himself and his world. The reappropriation of the Pachuco that Valdez initiated, Fregoso insightfully argues, marked the creation of an alternative Chicano identity that "reversed the negative ways Chicanos have been positioned within the dominant regimes of representation."[111]

This process of appropriation continues. The Pachuco celebrated by young people in the barrio continues to provide a sense of place, in both a historical and contemporary sense. Putting on the zoot suit and playing the myth of the Pachuco "más chucote que la chingada" serves as a way for young people to connect with a past that was self-assertive and stylish, pay homage to community elders, and assume a place in the continuum of cultural resistance and affirmation. To be sure, the conditions that evoked such strong reactions to the zoot suit during the war no longer exist, and wearing the zoot suit today is more of a nostalgic act. At the same time, however, the desire to affirm one's presence, on one's own terms, joins the generations, and young men in zoot suits still draw public attention. As the desire to exert one's presence with a bit of style, and in defiance of convention, it is not that far removed from the ways in which young men and women of color proudly wore the drape and strutted down the walkways in the era of segregation.

## Conclusion

This study recasts the Sleepy Lagoon murder trial and the Zoot Suit Riot as conflicts that arose not from the resistance to American culture per se but over competing ways of engaging *with* American culture. Clearly young people across the color line acted against the practice of segregation in finding common ground through self-expressions of their own design, drawn from the symbolic lexicon of jazz culture. In so doing they violated notions of proper social values and behaviors found in both American and Mexican cultures. But what was perhaps even more incendiary for many was their challenge to the assumptions of white privilege that relegated their social position to the periphery of public space. Through clothing, movement, articulations, and action, they created a public persona that asserted their presence in public spaces in their own ways and on their own terms. Along with the ongoing integrationist efforts of Mexican American professionals, Mexican Americans of the war years challenged the walls of segregation and white prerogative through complex and sophisticated negotiations of place at multiple locations.

*The People v. Zammora* was a gross miscarriage of justice that resulted from systemic, multifaceted community bias, if not outright hostility, against the wartime generation of barrio youth. The community backlash to this inventive and assertive generation engaged almost every organ of community power in the press, the police, and mobs—most of whom were military men. At the same time, the community backlash created new opportunities for progressive whites to establish more direct linkages with black and

Mexican American activists and tap into a common vision of a more tolerant and equitable postwar society. It also informed the context of social friction *among* Mexican Americans during the period.

Manuel Ruíz emerged as a central figure among the cadre of Mexican American professionals who were thrust into new prominence with the Sleepy Lagoon murder trial. Ruíz never met Díaz and likely never would have, but the events that spun out of Díaz's death shaped Manuel Ruíz's activism on behalf of the Mexican American communities. The experiences of Manuel Ruíz and José Díaz serve as counterpoints that illustrate the limits and possibilities for Mexican Americans during a relatively fluid moment in Los Angeles. Ruíz became a key resource to Los Angeles officials as a "spokesman" for the Mexican American communities in part because of his ability to assimilate structurally and negotiate public perceptions of social propriety. Díaz and the youths within his social networks traveled down dramatically different paths, partly because of their individual choices within the limited opportunities available to them as the children of working-class Mexican immigrants.

Although the trial may have been "local" in origin and impact, the riot was far more national in scope. Military men from across the county, temporarily stationed in the Los Angeles area on their way to overseas duty, with little or no connection to local issues or communities, brought to the mix their own passions and prejudices about white privilege. Changing demographics in Los Angeles led to tensions over changing social spaces and increased confrontations between military men and civilian youths, most of whom were Mexican American. The Sleepy Lagoon murder trial fed perceptions of lawless juveniles and impotent civil authorities that eventually erupted into vigilante justice. Through street violence mobs of military men sought to reinscribe the prerogatives of whiteness, quite literally over the bodies of those who challenged them. Although civil and military authorities struggled to downplay the significance of the riot or redirect the discourse away from racial tensions as a precipitating factor, the trial and riot revealed the precarious balance of wartime unity on the home front and the assumptions on which American "unity" rested.

# ✝ Epilogue : Who Killed José Díaz?

*Requiem aeternam, dona eis, Domine,*
*et lux perpetua luceat eis.*

Grant them eternal rest, O Lord,
and let everlasting light shine upon them.

**T**he trees that were saplings when José was buried now thickly shade his gravesite at Calvary Cemetery in East Los Angeles. For more than fifty years his murder has remained unsolved. Many of the defense lawyers believed that they could never come to a reasonable understanding of what happened that fateful night at the Williams Ranch because the evidence was riddled with complications.[1] Some of the testimonies were confused, contradictory, or recanted on the witness stand. Neither did the progressive alliance of activists and intellectuals who rallied behind the appeal effort seek the answer to what happened at the Delgadillo home. Their efforts to appeal the conviction were based on the irregularities of the trial that led to a prejudicial outcome, such as the judicial bias and the unusually hostile climate of the community. The fundamental question of José Díaz's death, the circumstance for which the young men and women of 38th Street lost their youth in prison, has remained unanswered.

Ysmael "Smiles" Parra was hopeful that the truth would one day be found "between the links of the transcript." "If the jury or the judge had been at the scene of the crime to witness what really happened," he wrote to a friend while at San Quentin prison, "we would have never been convicted. I say this because I know."[2] Remarkably, despite the ostensibly complicated nature of the evidence, enough corroborating information indeed remains to allow for a plausible reconstruction of the events the night José Díaz died. The truth may not be buried as deeply as Parra thought.

The question of opportunity is a critical element in reconstructing the events of that night. Timing is a crucial factor in determining how José Díaz died and what role the 38th Street boys had in his death, if any. Establishing the amount of time the 38th Street kids spent at the Delgadillo home has important implications for the nature of the damage they caused, whether they had time to do considerable bodily harm to those they fought with or whether they had but a few minutes. This is especially important in considering the extent of the wounds José Díaz received that night. Henry Leyvas, Josephine Gonzales, and Lorena Encinas all separately estimated that from the moment they pulled up to the bunkhouse compound to the time they left, their entire stay lasted no more than ten minutes. Using this estimate as a base point of reference, the actual time spent fighting was probably closer to nine minutes, considering the time it took for them to travel the distance from their parked cars to the Delgadillo home and back and for the fighting to begin.[3]

With this basic time frame established, the next important part of the puzzle is to establish the sequence of events. At what point did members of the 38th Street group have contact with José Díaz and in what manner? Two young women of 38th Street, Betty Zeiss and Dora Barrios, were the first to find Díaz, just moments after the group arrived at the bunkhouse compound. Zeiss and Barrios had been riding in Benny Alvarez's car when, as they drove up to the bunkhouses with their headlights off, Alvarez ran into a shallow irrigation ditch alongside the road.[4] Betty and Dora left the car as Alvarez and the others began to push the stranded automobile out of the ditch. Just when the two started walking up the inclined road in search of the rest of their group, they heard the sounds of screams and breaking glass from up ahead.[5] However, as they hurried toward the noise, something on a darkened patch of ground just before the rise caught Dora's eye, and she and Betty went over to see what it was. There, about twenty feet before the courtyard gate just to the side of the road, they found a bruised and bloodied young man, groaning lowly and lying facedown in the dirt. Betty fell to her knees and turned him over on his back, cradled his bloody face in her lap, and tried to wake him.[6] It was José Díaz.

Manny Reyes corroborated Betty Zeiss's account.[7] Reyes was with Henry Leyvas and the group of young men and women who walked up toward the Delgadillo house just minutes before Zeiss discovered Díaz lying on the ground. Reyes split off from the main group, however, and swung around toward the darkened back of the Delgadillo house as Henry made his way into the lighted courtyard to confront the partygoers. His view of what happened next on the patio was cut off, so when screams, shouts, and the sounds of broken windows shattered the night, Reyes ran back toward to the front of the house, following the fence that enclosed the courtyard. There, to the side of the road, he encountered Zeiss cradling Díaz's head in her lap. Farther up the road he could make out what looked to be José "Chepe" Ruíz and Gus Zamora beating a man who was lying on the ground and pleading for mercy.[8]

Ruíz was acting drunk that night.[9] When the group walked up to the Delgadillo courtyard with Henry Leyvas, Ruíz remained behind close to the cars parked along the picket fence. When the fighting broke out inside the courtyard, however, Ruíz was among the young men who bolted after the fleeing partygoers. The first one he cornered was Remedios Parra, the same man Manny Reyes saw on the ground. Despite Parra's pleas, Ruíz beat him maliciously with a club.

As Zeiss tried to nurse the unconscious boy in her lap, wiping his face and talking to him, two boys ran over to where she knelt.[10] One of them ordered Zeiss to leave the boy alone, lifted her up by the arm, and pulled her down the inclined road back toward the parked cars.[11] As she looked back to where the wounded boy lay, she saw the other boy, Chepe Ruíz, standing over him and striking his body with a large stick.[12]

Bobby Thompson came upon the scene just as Ruíz began to swing at Díaz with a club.[13] Díaz was not making any motion to defend himself and did not make a sound. Thompson stood there as Ruíz took four or five swings at the leg and chest area of the motionless boy until his conscience got the better of him, and Thompson intervened to stop the beating.[14] Unsatiated with the assault on Díaz, Ruíz ran back to where Parra was lying on the ground and struck him with another three or four blows. At that point someone yelled out "Run!" and the young people fled back to their cars.[15]

With these testimonies the prosecution believed that it had found direct evidence that linked the death of José Díaz to the 38th Street youths. Before their arrival, the prosecution pointed out, Díaz was last seen socializing with friends and drinking beer. Furthermore, three of the young people who went with the 38th Street group implicated their peers in the beating of Díaz and Parra with clubs. And after the 38th Street kids left the scene, José Díaz was found dying of severe trauma.

As reprehensible as Ruíz's conduct was, the significance of these testimonies lies in establishing not that Ruíz struck a downed man but that the man was down when Ruíz struck him. The testimonies indicate that Díaz was unconscious and probably already in shock before the 38th Street youths arrived at the Delgadillo home.[16] However he sustained his injuries, the greatest damage occurred before Ruíz struck him, between the time he was seen leaving the party and the moment Dora Barrios and Betty Zeiss found him.[17]

The forensic evidence indicates that José put up a strong defense during a violent and protracted struggle. His skinned and swollen knuckles on both hands indicate that he landed a number of solid punches on a hard surface, probably the head or face of his assailant. The damage he sustained also suggests that he withstood a lengthy and brutal beating. Under normal circumstances the coroner would have been able to trace the hemorrhaging back to the point of impact, but the damage to his brain was too severe. Although there was a three-inch fracture running from his left eye back to the top of his left ear, the coroner was unable to establish the point of impact because of the profuse hemorrhaging over the entire brain, much like the damage that a boxer would sustain over multiple rounds.[18] The nature of this damage, along with the stab wounds on his left side and a contusion that stretched across the left side of his swollen lips, reveals the brutality of the last moments of José's young life. He was first beaten with fists, stabbed twice, and then struck on his head several times with a blunt instrument by a right-handed assailant or assailants.

The evidence also indicates that the injuries Díaz received from Ruíz were not the blows that killed him. The cerebral contusion, swollen cheekbones, puncture wounds in the middle chest and upper stomach, swollen knuckles, and broken finger all suggest an extensive pattern of damage localized about his face, upper body, and hands. The injuries that likely resulted from the four or five blows Ruíz gave to the legs and body of Díaz as he lay on the ground are inconsistent with that pattern of damage.[19]

José Díaz was not the victim of gang violence that the Los Angeles authorities made him out to be. As he lay mortally wounded, he certainly suffered injury at the hands of some of the young men from 38th Street, but they were not his murderers. Who, then, was?

There are two theories. One has the virtue of a confession, but it comes thirdhand without corroboration. The other is based on circumstantial evidence without a confession.

During the filming of "Zoot-Suit Riot" for the PBS series *The American Experience*, Lorena Encinas's son Ted spoke of the heavy burden that his mother carried all her life. Lorena Encinas's own brother Louie confessed to her that he had killed José Díaz. According to Ted Encinas, his uncle was among the young men from Downey who crashed the Delgadillo party and were thrown out for their unruly behavior. In a senseless act of retaliation, some of the Downey boys stayed behind at the Williams Ranch and attacked a guest at the party to avenge the insult. Although Lorena was fiercely loyal to her friends and suffered alongside them, she could never betray her brother. Lorena kept her brother's secret until shortly before her death in 1991.[20]

Critical elements of the Encinas account, however, are difficult to corroborate with the extant evidence (Louie took his own life during a failed bank robbery in 1971). None of the witnesses at the Delgadillo party testi-fied to seeing or hearing any further disturbance after the Downey gang was expelled from the party. It is certainly possible that Louie Encinas and a few others broke away from the main group and hid in the shadows to attack partygoers. However, if the beating took place where José was found, be-tween forty and sixty feet from the Delgadillos' patio, then surely the many partygoers present would have seen or heard something from a vicious and sustained beating in progress. Furthermore, Louie reportedly confessed "that upon leaving, he and his friends encountered a boy who had just left the party and 'jumped him.'"[21] Witnesses testified that José left the party in the company of two men, but Encinas encountered only one. It is possible that José parted company with the two men immediately after the party, but again, if Díaz fell where he was found, either Encinas would have encoun-tered three men or eyewitnesses would have seen Díaz splitting away from his companions. Finally, Encinas and others attacked a lone boy no sooner than 11:00 P.M. and no later than 11:30, which was the latest time frame for Louie and friends to have encountered a boy "upon leaving" the party. Yet according to two separate testimonies, José was last seen alive about fif-teen to twenty minutes before the 38th Street group arrived, around 1:00 A.M. In other words, José was alive and accounted for at least one hour *after* Encinas and others attacked someone.

Given the difficulty in corroborating the Encinas theory, another look at the physical evidence and testimonies allows for the construction of a sec-ond theory. Three important details about the last hours of Díaz's life can be established with a reasonable degree of certainty. First, forensic evidence revealed that José had been drinking heavily at the party. He had an alcohol blood count between 0.12 and 0.15 at the time of his autopsy several hours later. Second, two witnesses testified to seeing José leave the party in the company of two men about 12:40 A.M.[22] Third, he suffered an extensive beat-ing by blunt force and was stabbed between the time he was seen leaving the party and the time two young women from 38th Street found him lying facedown.

Díaz's clothing may provide important clues for the motive of the assault. When Betty Zeiss and Dora Barrios found him, his pockets were turned out. Someone appears to have gone through his clothing looking for something after he fell mortally wounded. What they were looking for can only be speculated on, but the day of Eleanor Coronado's birthday party was also the day after payday at the Sunny Sally Packing Plant.[23] He may have been carrying the wages for his final week of work on the night of the party. The brutality of the beating also suggests the lengths José went to in refusing to yield what was in his pockets, as well as the lengths his assailants went to in order to retrieve what was in them. He may have withstood such a violent beating because he was too drunk to feel the punishing blows, but in his drunken state he also made an inviting target for robbery.

Evidence suggests that the motive for the attack was a mugging, and the two men with whom he was last seen alive had both the means and the opportunity to attack him. Sometime between 12:40 and 1:10 A.M., when José was far enough away from the handful of remaining guests who had turned up the radio to dance, his companions turned on him, beating him first with fists, then with a discarded piece of lumber, and then stabbing him until he finally collapsed. As they plundered José's pockets, the approaching headlights of the 38th Street group's cars may have scared them off into the darkness. Although the Los Angeles law enforcement agencies arrested hundreds of young people in their investigation, they never questioned Luís "Cito" Vargas and Andrew Torres for information they might have in the death of José Díaz.[24]

Whether the motive was revenge or robbery, the police investigation should have started with the two men who were seen leaving the party with José. They could have provided vital information about the half-hour window between the time José was last seen leaving the party and the time he was found dying from a beating. That information could have implicated Encinas or at least taken the investigation in a different direction and exonerated the young men of 38th Street.

To be sure, several factors coalesced to limit the outcome of the trial. Foregone conclusions and racial assumptions shaped the way in which investigators looked at the evidence and constrained the kinds of conclusions they could draw. Political pressure on the Los Angeles County District Attorney's Office placed a higher premium on convicting the young men of 38th Street as a group than trying them individually (two of the accused who had their cases heard separately were found innocent of all charges).[25] The district attorney's office drew a judge to preside over the trial known for siding with the prosecution and for his harsh prison sentences. He did not disappoint, and during the trial he authorized a courtroom seating arrangement that effectively denied the accused access to their attorneys.

But a closer scrutiny of an article that Clem Peoples penned for *Sensation*, dismissed by the defense at the time as a piece of shameless self-promotion by the lead investigator, suggests a more insidious reason for the outcome of the trial. The article contained so much information not previously made public that it actually revealed a good deal of what the Los Angeles County

Sheriff's Department knew about the murder. Although Peoples attempted to spice his prose in describing the Sleepy Lagoon defendants as "young thugs" and "swarthy, evil looking youth," the article was, for the most part, a rather straightforward description of who was where at what time during the night in question. The timeline of events presented in the article was clearly dependent on a wealth of information gathered from the interrogations, and Peoples knew the nature of José's personality, who lived in the area, who attended the party, what time the party started to wane, when the orchestra left, and what time the 38th Street youths arrived on the scene. He even knew what kind of food was served at the party.

Despite such detail, however, Peoples's account contained serious leaps of logic and omissions that reflected the problematic nature of the case against the 38th Street youths. Peoples alleged that the 38th Street "gang" was single-handedly responsible for several incidents of violent crime in East Los Angeles that weekend. He also glossed over a critical detail recalled during the trial by two witnesses that was surely discovered during the investigation: José Díaz and the young people of 38th Street were never at the same place at the same time. Although it cannot be established how clearly the district attorney's office understood this information, it did not seem surprised by this disclosure during the trial, and it is highly curious that amid the charts, photographs, and maps prepared for the trial and presented to the jury, the prosecution never provided a timeline to link the accused clearly with the victim. And among the dozens of neighbors, party guests, and witnesses called to testify during the trial, the last two people seen with José Díaz were never included on the list.

At best, the state simply overlooked evidence in the rush to prosecute. At worst, the state knowingly underplayed evidence it had that would have weakened its case and cast a reasonable doubt on the charge. Either way, the defense entirely missed the significance of the two witnesses who placed José Díaz away from the scene of the fight. Although some of the attorneys hired to defend the young men of 38th Street doggedly defended their individual clients, the collective group ultimately proved it was not up to the task in failing to cohere as a team, and not even the best of them challenged the fundamental flaws of the investigation. Despite the weakness of the case, the prosecution had little trouble in convincing the jurors that the young men of 38th Street were guilty of murder.

What was hailed as "the opening salvo in the war on juvenile delinquency," which inflicted a punishing blow to the young men and women of 38th Street and to their families, was, in truth, an appalling systemwide failure of justice.

# APPENDIX

## A NOTE ON TERMINOLOGY AND METHODOLOGY

Perhaps no other group in American history can lay claim to so many terms of identity as Mexican Americans. It is therefore usually customary in Chicano scholarship to include a section that explains the use of terminology. It is especially appropriate here because this study goes beyond questions of identity to explore the maze of contested words, terms, meanings, and interpretations that have layered both popular and scholarly understanding of the people and events of this period.

Ethnic and racial categories are infused with particular meaning depending on who uses them and when. Born in the 1960s and coming of age in the 1970s, I remember when the term "Chicano" was an identity that one self-consciously embraced through political involvement. It was not an identity one obtained simply by birth. Hence, I am still reluctant to fall into the current fashion of using "Chicano" transhistorically or as an interchangeable term for "Mexican American." It was not a term of identity that the people of my grandparents' generation—or even my parents' generation—publicly used; nor would they have necessarily embraced it within the context of their times. Out of respect for their lives and memories, I have utilized the terms they adopted for themselves, namely, "Mexican," "Mexicanos," or "Mexican American," and reserve the use of "Chicano" for referring to the generation of Mexican American activists who self-consciously embraced the term. As part of that generation, I understand "Chicano" to be a term that carries specific meanings of identity and commitment to certain political and ideological ideals. These ideals are lost when "Chicano" becomes merely another way of saying "Mexican American."

In the 1940s, the difference between "Mexican" and "Mexican American" was negligible, both to those living within the Mexican American community and to those living within metropolitan Los Angeles. The terms were used interchangeably. However, important distinctions exist between the lived experiences of first- and second-generation families from Mexico. Thus, I have used "Mexican American" primarily to signal specific reference to the experiences of the American-born children of Mexican descent.

The term "Mexican" also meant different things depending on who used it. For first- and second-generation migrants from Mexico, embracing the term "Mexican" or "Mexicano" had clear implications of cultural affinity and identity. Yet to many Angelenos of the period (and in some parts of the Southwest today) "Mexican" was a specific social category of both race and class, independent of one's citizenship status. Many of those who were identified during this period as "Mexican" were not, in fact, citizens of Mexico but citizens of the United States. Regardless of their national status, however, many were considered "Mexican" and bore the social weight of that category.

Pachuco identity in Los Angeles during this period was a far more problematic proposition because "pachuco" was a term in profound flux. As discussed earlier, the received wisdom has been based on a circular line of reasoning that began during the period when the public discourse over Pachucos was unusually charged; Pachucos wore zoot suits, and Mexican Americans who wore zoot suits were Pachucos.[1] Another layer was added to the meaning when, in the late 1970s and early 1980s, a new generation of Chicano activists reappropriated the image of the Pachuco and celebrated the notion of *Pachuquismo* as the ideological and cultural progenitor of the Chicano movement.[2] A close reading of the historical record, however, reveals far greater nuances to the term that defy easy categorization. Beatrice Griffith was one of the first to observe that Pachucos were not as easily identifiable with a single ethnic group as the public discourse made them out to be, and the historical evidence supports her view. Not all Pachucos wore zoot suits, and not everyone who wore a zoot suit was a Pachuco. Furthermore, although many Pachucos were Mexican American, not all Mexican Americans were Pachucos; nor did those who were called Pachucos necessarily identify themselves as such. Indeed, much of the public discourse on juvenile delinquency defined the term "Pachuco" in a qualitatively different sense than the way it was used in the barrios of Los Angeles. Thus, in recognition of the contested meanings of the Pachuco identity, I have put the term "Pachuco" in quotation marks or refer to the "imagined Pachuco" in an attempt to differentiate those who were called Pachuco by others from those who identified themselves as Pachuco.

The story of the Sleepy Lagoon murder and the Zoot Suit Riot has evolved from the literature of that period as a social crisis involving only Mexican Americans. In conducting interviews and in researching newspapers, military reports, reports by community groups, photographs, and music, it became clear to me that the conflict over delinquency concerned so many racial communities in Los Angeles that to characterize the moment as particularly "anti-Mexican" is to lose the context of the crisis. Since jazz music and style were social phenomena that were more class-specific than race-specific—that is to say that working-class African American, Mexican American, Filipino, and white youths embraced the jazz "lifeworld"—I have utilized terms such as "working-class youths," "racialized youths," or even "civilian youths," not to downplay the role of Mexican Americans but to recognize the breadth of the phenomenon. At the same time, I have striven to make clear that Mexican Americans, as the largest racialized minority community in Los Angeles, played the largest role in the conflict, and when it was fitting to do so, I have identified Mexican Americans specifically.

This study relies on archival documents, the bedrock of the historian's craft, supplemented with oral histories of key actors. Although every historical document must be carefully examined for accuracy and authenticity, both archival materials and oral histories from this volatile period are especially complex for scholars, and interpretations drawn from these sources must be made with care. Every document reflects the lens and bias of its author, and court testimonies, letters, news reports, and official reports from the trial and riot were at times contradictory, impressionistic, or *intentionally* misleading and evasive for reasons that I discuss in the main body of this work. In order to establish a reasonable level of confidence in reconstructing the events, I therefore utilized information that can be corroborated by other sources or that is at least plausible and consistent with the context of the times.

Such a methodology is standard to the profession and hardly needs explanation, but what is left out of the story as a consequence are some accounts that will be familiar to students of the period. Carey McWilliams and Beatrice Griffith respectively describe an assault on the boys from Alpine Street after a meeting with police to organize a youth club. For McWilliams, this was direct evidence that the Los Angeles Police Department had coordinated the attack with the military, and for Griffith, it was evidence that the young men were law-abiding citizens unjustly targeted by white sailors. However, a letter published after the riot by Rudy Sánchez, who was among the group of boys from Alpine Street, contradicts their account.[3] Solomon Jones makes extensive use of the minutes from the 7 June 1943 meeting of the Coordinating Council for Latin American Youth to reconstruct the Zoot Suit Riot in *The Government Riots in Los Angeles, June 1943*, but I have been unable to locate the information cited in the Manuel Ruíz Papers.[4] There are also published accounts by lay and professional scholars about overlooked contributors to the Sleepy Lagoon Defense Committee that would significantly shift understanding of the events if substantiated.[5]

Oral histories have been a rich source for recovering information long excluded from scholarly works, but they are also far from straightforward sources. I am indebted to Alice McGrath and to members of the Díaz, Leyvas, Ynostroza, Zamora, and Encinas families who openly shared their stories with me. During some of these interviews, it was clear that the passing of time has shaped both memory and perspective in a way that has made it difficult to corroborate evidence or information gathered at the time of the trial and riot with what could be recalled more fifty years later. In those situations, especially when such information was critical in reconstructing events in this narrative, I drew on evidence that could be corroborated by other sources and noted the differences in the endnotes. At the same time, the issue of privacy remains an ethically delicate and sensitive issue for researchers who utilize oral histories. For very good reason, several of the surviving women and men who experienced these events firsthand have been protective of their life stories. Having lived through a time when they became objects of derision and distortion in the Los Angeles media, some of the survivors have never told their children or grandchildren of their role in these events and do not wish to revisit the events. Tensions about privacy and the media again arose within the group over Luís Valdez's *Zoot Suit*, when some of the families from 38th Street filed a lawsuit against the production company.[6] I have attempted to recover and retell with care the stories of the families affected by these events, but I have also tried to respect those wishing to keep their life stories private, and I utilize only information that was already in the public record.

Finally, in an effort to reconstruct a more complete picture of the nature of the tensions preceding the riot, I drew from some materials produced by observers, historical actors, and researchers who saw the social crisis through perspectives unflattering to Mexican American youth in particular and to racialized minorities in general. In using such documents I have employed a method utilized by scholars in American Indian studies, such as Ramón Gutiérrez, Calvin Martin, and Greg Dowd, who regularly work with such problematic documents produced by European and American colonists about American Indians. Gutiérrez contends that it is possible to "[bore] down through the numerous layers of historical artifacts" to read beyond the bias in language and the perspective of the observer to reconstruct events from the perspective of the observed, utilizing corroborating evidence to support such a reconstruction.[7]

# NOTES

## Source Abbreviations

AGM Papers
   Alice Greenfield McGrath Papers 1490, University of California at Los Angeles, Special Collections, University Research Library
Court Transcript
   In the Superior Court of the State of California, in and for the County of Los Angeles, Department 4, Hon. Charles W. Fricke, Judge. *The People of the State of California vs. Gus Zammora, et al.*
EQ Papers
   Eduardo Quevedo Papers M349, Stanford University, Special Collections, Green Library
MR Papers
   Manuel Ruíz Jr. Papers M295, Stanford University, Special Collections, Green Library
Records of Eleventh Naval District
   U.S. Navy Shore Patrol Headquarters, RG 181, Records of Naval Districts and Shore Establishments, Eleventh Naval District Headquarters, San Diego, National Archives, Pacific Southwest Region, Laguna Niguel, Calif.
RL Papers
   Ron López Papers, University of California at Los Angeles, Chicano Studies Resource Library, Sleepy Lagoon Material Collection
SLDC Papers
   Sleepy Lagoon Defense Committee Papers 107, University of California at Los Angeles, Special Collections, University Research Library
WPA
   Workers of the Writers' Program of the Works Projects Administration in southern California

## Prologue

1. Some part and chapter titles and subheads in this book have been quoted from other works. The title of this prologue is borrowed from Endore, *Sleepy Lagoon Mystery*. "Make Noise Broken Windows" is from Alurista, "The man say we making noise," in Candelaria, *Chicano Poetry*, 89. "Un Vato de Atolle" is from Montoya, "El Louie." "Counter-Cultures U.S.A." is from Villanueva, "Pachuco Remembered." "La Vida Dura" is from Fregoso, "Hanging Out with the Homegirls?," 36. "Shouting Curses on the Street" is from Delgado, "Stupid America." "Wars of Resistance" and "Articulated Signs of Resistance"

are from Sorell, "Articulate Signs of Resistance and Affirmation in Chicano Public Art." "Portent of Storm" is from *Christian Century* (23 June 1943). "The Violent Poetry of the Times" is from Linda Marquez, in Rodríguez, *Always Running*, 108.

2. Testimony of Dominic Manfredi, Court Transcript, 2128. Eleanor Delgadillo Coronado was married to Frank Coronado, had two daughters, and lived next door to her parents; Court Transcript, 2128–29, 2053.

3. Testimony of Teodulo Díaz, Court Transcript, 89–91, 94, 97–98, 100, 103. Testimony of Frank R. Webb, ibid., 143.

4. Both Socorro Díaz Blanchard and Lino Díaz remember José as "quiet" and "conservative." Socorro believes that her brother was drafted. Socorro Díaz Blanchard, interview, and Lino Díaz, oral history.

5. Lino insisted that José never drank, but forensic evidence showed a high alcohol count in José's blood. See Frank R. Webb, chief autopsy surgeon for Los Angeles County, Court Transcript, 143–69.

6. Coronado last saw Díaz leaving with two of the partygoers about five to ten minutes before the group from 38th Street arrived. Remedios Parra, however, placed Díaz leaving the party closer to twenty minutes before the 38th Street group arrived. See the following testimonies from the Court Transcript: Eleanor Coronado, 2134–36, 2244–45; Remedios Parra, 2489, 2528, 2530; Dominic Manfredi, 2049, 2074, 2078, 2050; and Joseph Manfredi, 2552.

7. Testimony of Dominic Manfredi, Court Transcript, 2049, 2074, 2050.

8. Testimony of Dr. Henry Cuneo, admitting physician and surgeon at the General Hospital, Court Transcript, 4256–63.

9. Testimony of Lino Díaz, Court Transcript, 103–9, 128.

10. Testimony of Dr. Henry Cuneo, Court Transcript, 4256. Testimony of Frank R. Webb, ibid., 169.

11. Gutiérrez, *Walls and Mirrors*, 72–74.

**Chapter One**

1. Terkel, *Good War*.

2. I use an uncomplicated definition of "power" (from vernacular Latin *potere*, "to be able") as the possession of control, authority, or influence over others.

3. United States War Relocation Authority, *Segregation of Persons of Japanese Ancestry in Relocation Centers*. See also Hansen, *Demon Dogs*; Grodzins, *Americans Betrayed*; Daniels, *Decision to Relocate the Japanese Americans*; Smith, *Democracy on Trial*; James, *Exile Within*; Irons, *Justice at War*; Yatsushiro, *Politics and Cultural Values*.

4. For more information about racial tensions in the United States during the war years, see Brandt, *Harlem at War*; Capeci and Wilkerson, *Layered Violence*; Lee and Humphrey, *Race Riot, Detroit 1943*.

5. Throughout much of this manuscript I use the term "jazz" in a broad sense, inclusive of different styles and sounds popular in the 1940s, from the Chicago to the New Orleans sound and from jump blues to swing jazz.

6. Jiménez, *Mexican American Heritage*, 199. See also Luckenbill, *Pachuco Era*. Examples of the Pachuco in popular art can be found in Griswold del Castillo, McKenna, and Yarbro-Bejarano, *Chicano Art*. José Montoya's collection of work featuring the Pa-

chuco has appeared in a number of places, both in print and on display, among them *Lowrider*; see Montoya, "José Montoya, Pachuco Artist." Luís Valdez's musical *Zoot Suit* originally debuted at the Mark Taper Forum in Los Angeles; it went on to a Broadway run and was made into the motion picture by the same name (MCA Home Video, Universal City, Calif., 1991). Another popular representation of the Pachuco as zoot suiter is Sanchez, *Zoot-Suit Murders*.

7. Other unpublished dissertations include Ramírez, "Pachuca in Chicana/o Art, Literature and History"; Green, "Zoot Suiters"; Leonard, "Years of Hope, Days of Fear"; Gonzalez, "Mexicano/Chicano Gangs in Los Angeles"; Dieppa, "Zoot-Suit Riots Revisited"; Gomes, "Violence on the Home Front."

8. Endore, *Sleepy Lagoon Mystery*, and McWilliams, "The Zoot-Suit Riots."

9. For an example of the interpretation that anti-Mexican hysteria was deep-seated and widespread among whites in Los Angeles, see Acuña, *Anything but Mexican*, 124.

10. Many of the reports filed by navy personnel failed to include the racial identity of their attackers. Rather, servicemen reported on the clothing of the young men who accosted them. Such omissions are not conclusive but suggestive. One clear example is found in the report logged by Seamen Second Class Richard Lewis Eakin and Kenneth Joseph Bielk, who stated that "both suspects appeared to be Negroes, although one of them could have been Mexican." "Statement of Eakin, Richard Lewis, SM 2/c—U.S.S. Tallulah," and "Statement of Bielk, Kenneth Joseph—SM 2/c—U.S.S. Tallulah," both dated 14 October 1943, Records of Eleventh Naval District.

11. Almaguer, *Racial Fault Lines*, 7.

12. Records from the Sleepy Lagoon Defense Committee indicate that John Matuz's father, Joe, was born in Mexico, but they do not include the birthplace or nationality of his deceased mother. However, Matuz's close friend Henry "Hank" Ynostroza insists that Matuz was Hungarian and did not speak Spanish or identify himself as either Mexican or Mexican American. It is possible that Matuz's parents or grandparents immigrated to Mexico from Hungary before coming to the United States. Notes from discussions with Hank Ynostroza in possession of the author.

13. See comments from Manny Delgado and George Shibley in Trombetta, "'Zoot Suit' and Its Real Defendants," 4. I am indebted to Mary Jane Zamora, who donated a copy to me.

14. Bakan, "Way out West on Central," 27; Kelley, "'We Are Not What We Seem'"; Peretti, *Creation of Jazz*.

15. Villa, *Barrio-Logos*, 1.

16. Cosgrove, "Zoot-Suit and Style Warfare."

17. R. T. Van Ettisch to Ruíz, 4 August 1942, and Ruíz to *Los Angeles Examiner*, 6 August 1942, MR Papers, box 2, file 15. See also Ruíz to *Los Angeles Times*, 10 August 1942 and 18 July 1944, MR Papers, box 1, file 3.

18. Foley, *White Scourge*. Almaguer, *Racial Fault Lines*. Gutiérrez, *Walls and Mirrors*.

19. Acuña, *Anything but Mexican*, 2. See also Guerin-Gonzales, *Mexican Workers and American Dreams*, 47.

20. Paz, *Labyrinth of Solitude*, 5–6; Cosgrove, "Zoot-Suit and Style Warfare," 77–79.

21. I owe much of my thinking on this topic to Berkhofer's *The White Man's Indian*.

22. Nelson, *Negro Character in American Literature*. Brown, *Negro in American Fiction*.

For monographs, see also Warren, *Black and White Strangers*; MacCann and Woodard, *Black American in Books for Children*; Cooley, *Savages and Naturals*; and Starke, *Black Portraiture in American Fiction*. For articles, see Ward, "Black Woman as Character"; Adams, "Black Images in Nineteenth-Century American Painting and Literature"; Carlson, "Comparison of the Treatment of the Negro in Children's Literature in the Periods 1929–1938 and 1959–1968"; Böger, "Content Analysis of Selected Children's Books on the Negro and on Japan"; and Johnson, "Treatment of the Negro Woman as a Major Character in American Novels, 1900–1950." For monographs on blackface minstrelsy, see Lhamon, *Raising Cain*; Toll, *Blacking Up*; Leonard, *Masquerade in Black*; and Engle, *This Grotesque Essence*.

23. Anthony Quiroz, "Whiteness Lost/Whiteness Regained: *The White Scourge: Mexicans, Blacks, and Poor Whites in Texas Cotton Culture*," H-Texas, H-Net Reviews in the Humanities and Social Sciences, www2.h-net.msu.edu, May 1998.

24. Escobar, *Race, Police, and the Making of a Political Identity*.

25. Donaldson, "What Is Hegemonic Masculinity?," 645–46.

26. Rosales, *Pobre Raza!*

27. Bakan, "Way out West on Central," 27.

28. Green, "Zoot Suiters," 11. See also Ramírez, "Crimes of Fashion," 4, and Sánchez-Tranquilino and Tagg, "Pachuco's Flayed Hide," 560.

29. Villanueva, "Pachuco Remembered," 40.

### Chapter Two

1. Camarillo documented that fewer than 7 percent of those applying for naturalization in California during the 1920s were from Mexico. See Camarillo, *Chicanos in a Changing Society*, 161, 226–27. Sánchez, *Becoming Mexican American*, 87–107.

2. For a good overview of these multifaceted efforts, see Takaki, *Double Victory*.

3. Sánchez, *Becoming Mexican American*, 88–91. Starr, *Material Dreams*, 65. Davis, *City of Quartz*, 25, 35.

4. Nicolaides, *My Blue Heaven*.

5. Sánchez, *Becoming Mexican American*, 74.

6. Weber indicates that 96 percent of Mexican families were landless by 1910; Weber, *Dark Sweat, White Gold*, 50. See also Sánchez, *Becoming Mexican American*, 77. Collins, *Black Los Angeles*, 28. DeGraff, "Negro Migration to Los Angeles," 281.

7. Romo, *East Los Angeles*. Sánchez, *Becoming Mexican American*, 63–83.

8. Gutiérrez, *Walls and Mirrors*, 69, 72. Almaguer, *Racial Fault Lines*, 4–5. Camarillo, *Chicanos in a Changing Society*, 142–64.

9. Davis, "Sunshine and the Open Shop," 116–18; Flamming, "Star of Ethiopia and the NAACP," 154–58; Engh, "Practically Every Religion Being Represented," 207.

10. Quoted in Guzmán, *Political Socialization of the Mexican American People*, 64.

11. Quoted in ibid., 68.

12. Ibid., 65. See also Guerin-Gonzales, *Mexican Workers and American Dreams*, 75.

13. See Higham, *Strangers in the Land*, 19–263; Bennett, *Party of Fear*, 171–237; Knobel, *America for the Americans*, 1–39, 235–79; Dawley, *Struggles for Justice*, 255–94.

14. Handman also reported to the National Conference of Social Work that the ambiguity concerning the scientific classification of Mexicans would eventually prove to be

a problem for white Americans: "The Negro-white situation is difficult enough, but it is simple. The Negro has his place in the scheme of things. He is disfranchised and he accepts it—for how long I do not know—but he accepts it. He is limited in his educational opportunities and in his occupational field, and he accepts that also. But the Mexican is theoretically limited neither in his educational opportunities nor in his occupational field. Neither is he disfranchised." Guzmán, *Political Socialization of the Mexican American People*, 67.

15. Widney, *Race Life of the Aryan People* and *Three Americas*. Grant, *Passing of the Great Race* and *Conquest of a Continent*. See also Huntington, *Tomorrow's Children*, *Problems in Eugenics*, *Scientific Papers of the Second International Congress of Eugenics*, *Second International Exhibition of Eugenics*, and *Decade of Progress in Eugenics*. For a good overview of eugenicist theory, see Doyle, "Of Race and Woman," 10–34.

16. Pascoe, "Miscegenation Law, Court Cases, and Ideologies of 'Race' in Twentieth-Century America," 48.

17. Kennedy, *Birth Control in America*, 115–22. Chesler, *Woman of Valor*, 216–17.

18. Quoted in Carter, "Cultural History Written with Lightning," 9–19.

19. Pascoe, "Miscegenation Law, Court Cases, and Ideologies of 'Race' in Twentieth-Century America," 44–69.

20. Kuhl, *Nazi Connection*, 53–63. Selden, *Inheriting Shame*, 74–75. For a broader discussion of eugenics in history, see Hasian, *Rhetoric of Eugenics in Anglo-American Thought*, and Lewontin, Rose, and Kamin, *Not in Our Genes*.

21. Dawley, *Struggles for Justice*, 254. See also Sánchez, *Becoming Mexican American*, 87–107.

22. For studies of Japanese Americans, see Gulick, *American Japanese Problem*; Kawakami, *Real Japanese Question*; Mills, *Japanese Problem in the United States*; and Strong, *Second-Generation Japanese Problem*. Other, similar works include Barron, *Mexican Problem*; Lee, *Negro Problem*; Riley, *White Man's Burden*; Smith, *Racist Southern Paternalism* and *Racial Determinism and the Fear of Miscegenation, Post 1900*; and Newby, *Development of Segregationist Thought*.

23. Hoxie, *Final Promise*, 239–44. See also Sánchez, *Becoming Mexican American*, 105–6.

24. Rosenau, "Coherent Connection or Commonplace Contiguity?," 3. See also Castañeda, "Mexico and California," and Sánchez, *Becoming Mexican American*, 98.

25. Gutiérrez, *Walls and Mirrors*, 45.

26. Sánchez notes that business interests in Los Angeles were in opposition to restrictionist nativists; *Becoming Mexican American*, 96–97. See also Montejano, "Anglos and Mexicans in the Twenty First Century," 8.

27. Delpar, *Enormous Vogue of Things Mexican*.

28. Navarrette, *Darker Shade of Crimson*.

29. Quoted in Starr, *Inventing the Dream*, 84–87.

30. Starr, *Material Dreams*, 95, 101, 114–15, 392.

31. Ibid., 204–5.

32. Fogelson, *Fragmented Metropolis*, 157–58. Starr, *Material Dreams*, 191–201.

33. Villa, *Barrio-Logos*, 55–57.

34. Davis, *City of Quartz*, 101–20.

35. Ríos-Bustamante, "Latino Participation in the Hollywood Film Industry, 1911–1945," 21–32. See also List, *Chicano Images*, and Keller, *Chicano Cinema*.

36. For pictorial representations of this, see Ríos-Bustamante and Castillo, *Illustrated History of Mexican Los Angeles*; Dash, *Yesterday's Los Angeles*; Yavno and Shippey, *Los Angeles Book*; Weaver, *Los Angeles*; and Hill, *La Reina*.

37. For a contemporary example, see Oles, *South of the Border*. See also Delpar, *Enormous Vogue of Things Mexican*.

38. McWilliams, *North from Mexico*, 275, 277–79.

39. Gutiérrez, *Walls and Mirrors*, 95–99. Sánchez, *Becoming Mexican American*, 108–25.

40. Letter dated 15 March 1946 to Ruíz. Leaders of Club Iris described the organization as a "Latin version of the Lions or Kiwanis Clubs." Composed mainly of college students from the University of Southern California, Woodbury College, and City College, the club was exclusively "Latin American" but maintained a keen interest in demonstrating its patriotism to the United States while elevating the "social standards" of its peers. Little is known about Club Social Superba except that it was a social organization that regularly sponsored dances for its members. MR Papers, box 2, file 18. See also Manuel Ruíz to Club Social Superba, 7 October 1942, "attn. Raul Theire," MR Papers, box 2, file 13, and Manuel Ruíz to José Garduño, 10 August 1942, box 2, file 13.

41. Escobar, *Race, Police, and the Making of a Political Identity*, 203–53.

42. Ibid., 204.

43. "Résumé," MR Papers, box 1, file 1.

44. Undated letterhead of the Coordinating Council for Latin American Youth lists the executive committee as Manuel Ruíz Jr., president; Manuel Avila, vice president; Joseph Zazuela, secretary; Beatriz Castillo, assistant secretary; Dr. José Díaz, treasurer; and Stephen J. Keating, assistant treasurer. Members of the board of directors are listed as Manuel Avila, Foreign Origins Council [illegible]; Captain Robert Bowling, Los Angeles Police Department; Dr. Reynaldo Carreon, Southern California Council of Inter-American Affairs; Arturo Casas, Mexican American Movement; Beatriz Castillo, Watts Coordinating Council; Reverend Richard Cotter, Catholic Welfare Bureau; Dr. José Díaz, Beneficia Mexicana; Guillermo Galindo, Cooperativa de Commerciantes Mexicanos; Tonias D. [illegible]; Julio Guerrero, Alianza Hispano-Americana; Mauricio Hazan, coordinator of Inter-American Affairs; [illegible], executive secretary, Los Angeles County Coordinating Councils; Carmen Lucero, Santa Maria Center; Henry Marín, CYO; Gabriel [illegible], publisher, *El Pueblo*; Ernesto Orfila, State Veterans Administration; J. David Orozco, Alianza Hispano Americana; [illegible], Religious Conference, UCLA; Eduardo Quevedo, Federation of Spanish-American Voters; Fred Rubio, publisher [illegible]; Manuel Ruíz Jr., Board of Latin American Youth Project; Peter Salas, Belvedere Coordinating Council; Dr. Camilo Servin, Sociedad [illegible] Mexicano; Helen [illegible], CYO; Joseph Zazueta, president, Mexican Chamber of Commerce. MR Papers, box 1, file 1.

45. Transcript of interview, 1972. MR Papers, box 1, folder 9.

46. Document signed by Dr. Victor M. Egas, Manuel Ruíz Jr., Atty., and Dr. Reynaldo J. Carreon, 1 March 1940, Los Angeles. MR Papers, box 2, file 11.

47. Foley, "Becoming Hispanic," 63.

48. Ibid.

49. The name of the organization was originally Club Cultural Pan-Americana but was changed when it applied for incorporation with the state and discovered that the name was already used by another organization. See Ruíz to Paul Peek, secretary of the state of California, 27 June 1940, MR Papers, box 2, file 11. "Comment by Manuel Ruíz, Jr. to be added to the files on 'Cultura Pan-Americana,'" 25 January 1977, MR Papers, box 1, file 1.

50. Draft, "Latin-American Juvenile Delinquency in Los Angeles: Bomb or Bubble!" MR Papers, box 1, file 6.

51. See Dower, *War without Mercy*.

52. Griffith, *American Me*, 51. Griffith was one of the first to acknowledge the widespread influence of the zoot suit among working-class youths in Los Angeles. Himes, however, would have none of it, writing in the *Crisis* that "Negro Youths in Los Angeles county are not organized into gangs, nor do they belong to the Mexican pachuo [*sic*] gangs." Mazón also questioned Griffith's claim by suggesting that she, as well as other progressive activists of the period, downplayed the particularly "Mexican" connection to the zoot suit or to Pachucos. Yet I find that her views are consistent with the historical evidence. The McGucken Report in 1943 also argued that "the problem was a problem of American youth generally, not that of the Mexican Americans alone. Zoot suits were worn by youths of many races." Bogardus, a contemporary ethnographer, also noted the existence of mixed Mexican American and African American groups. Placéncia echoed a similar argument in his exploration of Chicano mythology and symbolism in popular magazines during the 1980s: "The zoot suit was a widespread fashion not unique to or created by Mexicanos, but was instead a widely imitated fashion found among Blacks, middle-class and working-class whites, Italians, Filipinos, and Japanese in the United States and Japan." See Griffith, "Who Are the *Pachucos*?," 355, and *American Me*, 51; Himes, "Zoot Riots Are Race Riots," 200–201, 222; Mazón, *Zoot Suit Riots*, 4; Bogardus, "Gangs of Mexican American Youth," 58; Placencia, "Low Riding in the Southwest," 149–53.

53. The McGucken Report in 1943 originally proposed this thesis; see McGucken et al., "Report and Recommendations of the Citizens Committee." Summarizing the McGucken committee's findings, Barrett noted in *The Tenney Committee* that "the problem was a problem of American youth generally, not that of the Mexican Americans alone. Zoot suits were worn by youths of many races." See also Placéncia, "Low Riding in the Southwest," 149–53.

54. There has been some scholarly discussion on the meaning and origins of the term, but none are convincing. For the best summary of the literature, see Madrid-Barela, "In Search of the Authentic Pachuco."

55. Coltharp, *Tongue of the Tirilones*, 74–78, 230.

56. Braddy, "Narcotic Argot along the Mexican Border," 84–90. See also Braddy, "Smugglers' Argot in the Southwest," 96–101; Coltharp, *Tongue of the Tirilones*, 19–34; and Barker, "Pachuco," 190.

57. Melendez describes a tattooed cross on the foreheads of Pachucos in Arizona, a

half inch long, as well as on their hand between their index finger and thumb. Pachucas tattooed radiant crosses on the same place on their hands or on their inner leg between the knee and ankle. *Pachuco Mark*, 5. This description is consistent with Coltharp's fieldwork describing tattooed dots on the foreheads and hands of Tirili women and a radiating cross or the letters "E.P.T." (for El Paso, Texas) tattooed on Tirili men and women in *Tongue of the Tirilones*, 23–24. Braddy cites a finding in 1957 by military officials at Chanute Field, Illinois; Sheppard Field, Texas; and Lackland Air Force Base, Texas, that many of the servicemen from El Paso bore the familiar Pachuco markings on their bodies, namely, the tattooed initials "E.P.T." Braddy concurs with the conclusion of the military officials that these initials were the abbreviation for El Paso, Texas. "Pachucos and Their Argot," 257–58. See also Griffith, *American Me*, 47; "Youthful Gang Secrets Exposed: Young Hoodlums Smoke 'Reefers,' Tattoo Girls, and Plot Robberies," 16 July 1944 news clipping (identified as a *Los Angeles Times* article in the 17 July 1943 minutes of the Coordinating Council for Latin-American Youth), MR Papers, box 3, file 10.

58. Gayne et al., *Geology and Mineral Deposits of the Pachuca.*

59. Martínez, *Border Boom Town*, 57–87.

60. The Corrido Web Project, directed by Jaime Nicolopulos at the University of Texas at Austin, lists several corridos known as "Los Tequileros" relating the difficult and often violent clashes between bootleggers and *rinches* (Texas Rangers), at www.sp .utexas.edu/jrn/webproj.html.

61. See Joyner, "Immigration Border Patrol," 23–25; Frost, *Gentlemen's Club*, 30; Perkins, *Border Patrol*; Rak, *Border Patrol*. The marijuana trade appears to have played a part in bringing African Americans into contact with Mexicans. A Treasury Department official reported in 1917, after touring eleven Texas cities, that smoking marijuana was widespread among Mexicans and "some times by Negroes and lower class whites." R. J. Bonnie and Ch. H. Whitebread II, *The Marihuana Conviction: A History of Marihuana Prohibition in the United States* (Charlottesville: University Press of Virginia, 1974), 54, as quoted in Jonnes, *Hep-Cats, Narcs, and Pipe Dreams*, 128.

62. Coltharp, *Tongue of the Tirilones*, 230.

63. Jones pinpoints the arrival of the zoot suit in Los Angeles at 1941 in *The Government Riots of Los Angeles, June 1943*, 11. Placéncia gives the best summary of the various theories on the origin of the zoot suit in "Low Riding in the Southwest," 150.

64. Braddy, "Narcotic Argot along the Mexican Border," 85. See also Nelson, "Addenda to 'Junker Lingo,'" 34, and Maurer, "Argot of the Underworld Narcotic Addict," 123, and "Teen-age Hophead Jargon," 23–31. Jonnes notes that Texas served as one of the entry points of the marijuana trade, in *Hep-Cats, Narcs, and Pipe Dreams*, 127–28.

65. Mezzrow, *Really the Blues*, 214–15.

66. Griffith estimates the total Mexican American population in Los Angeles County during the 1940s to be no more than four hundred thousand. Although she does not provide numbers broken down by age, she estimates that fewer than 5 percent of the youths were classified as delinquent. She also estimates that fully two-thirds of the Mexican American youths wore a zoot suit between 1940 and 1945. Of every ten boys who belonged to a gang, three girls were associated with them. *American Me*, 44–45, 52. See also Murray and Murray, oral history; McWilliams, *North from Mexico*, 243; and Moore,

*Homeboys, Gangs, Drugs and Prison in the Barrios of Los Angeles*, 64, 70–71. On 9 June 1943, the *Los Angeles Times* reported that after the police rounded up some two hundred Mexican Americans, only a very few were wearing zoot suits.

67. Bogardus, "Gangs of Mexican American Youth," 55–66. See also McWilliams, "Los Angeles' Pachuco Gangs," 76–77, and "Pachuco Troubles," 5–6; and Redl, "Zoot Suits."

68. For a history of American fascination with the Far East, see Fields, *How the Swans Came to the Lake*.

69. U.S. Congress, Joint Committee on Pearl Harbor Attack: Hearings, 9–14 December 1941, pt. 24, pp. 1749–56. Page 1749, Exhibit no. 49 (Navy Packet no. 2), Roberts Commission.

70. Along with Associate Justice Owen D. Roberts of the U.S. Supreme Court, the commission's members were Admiral William H. Standley, a former fleet commander and chief of naval operations; Rear Admiral J. M. Reeves, a former commander of the U.S. fleet; Major General Frank R. McCoy, retired, president of the Foreign Policy Association; and Brigadier General Joseph T. McNarney of the Army Air.

71. "Attack on Pearl Harbor by Japanese Forces, Report of the Commission Appointed by the President of the United States to Investigate and Report the Facts Relating to the Attack Made by Japanese Armed Forces upon Pearl Harbor in the Territory of Hawaii on December 7, 1941," 77th Cong., 2nd sess., no. 159, S. Doc., 77–2, Vol. 8–8, p. 12.

72. George Ishida, Letter to the Editor, *San Francisco News*, 13 April 1942.

73. For an example of this, see Dos Passos, "San Francisco Looks West."

74. See Matthews, "Southern Rite of Human Sacrifice."

75. Toni Morrison argued in *Playing in the Dark* that throughout much of the nation's history white Americans have defined themselves in opposition to blacks. Morrison's thesis holds up well in extending the argument further: white Americans defined themselves against other racialized minorities in America, as well.

76. Monroy, *Rebirth*, 182.

### Chapter Three

1. Testimony of Teodulo Díaz, Court Transcript, 91.

2. Knight, *Mexican Revolution*, 332, 438. Lino Díaz remembered that the family lived in Piedras Negras, Coahuila, but Teodulo Díaz testified that the family lived in Durango and indicated the same on José's death certificate. Lino Díaz, oral history. Testimony of Teodulo Díaz, Court Transcript, 91. José G. Díaz Certificate of Death, County of Los Angeles, 12309. I am indebted to Mylène Moreno for locating José's death certificate.

3. Knight notes that only 10 percent of the usual crops raised in Durango could be planted in 1916; *Mexican Revolution*, 414–15.

4. Ibid., 418.

5. Testimony of Lino Díaz, Court Transcript, 103.

6. Meyer and Sherman, *Course of Mexican History*, 579–81.

7. Socorro Díaz Blanchard, interview.

8. Testimony of Teodulo Díaz, Court Transcript, 91. Lino Díaz later remembered that his family left Mexico "for the same reason as many Mexicans did—better opportunity in the US"; Lino Díaz, oral history. On the U.S. side of the border the Río Bravo is known as the Rio Grande.

9. Villareal, *Pocho*, 16.

10. Gómez-Quiñones, "Mexican Immigration to the United States," 56–78. See also García, *Desert Immigrants*; Montejano, *Anglos and Mexicans in the Making of Texas*; and Sánchez, *Becoming Mexican American*, 52–53, 65.

11. Villareal, *Pocho*, 31. Socorro Díaz Blanchard remembered that some of the Díaz children were "up north picking prunes" when José was killed; Socorro Díaz Blanchard, interview.

12. Testimony of Lino Díaz, Court Transcript, 103. Socorro Díaz remembered that the family moved to the Williams Ranch in 1932; Socorro Díaz Blanchard, interview.

13. Jackson, *Crabgrass Frontier*, 181. Testimony of Teodulo Díaz, Court Transcript, 89.

14. Testimony of Josephine Delgadillo Reyes, Court Transcript, 2346.

15. Lino Díaz, oral history.

16. Murray and Murray, oral history, and McGrath, "Education of Alice McGrath," 55–56.

17. Murray and Murray, oral history.

18. Ibid.

19. See, for example, Youth Committee for the Defense of Mexican American Youth [Reginald García, Dora Baca, Frank Hermosillo, and Roger Cardona] to Vice President Henry A. Wallace [October, 1942], RL Papers.

20. Leyvas, "Interview," 22.

21. Murray and Murray, oral history. MR Papers. "Alpine Weekly Gossip"; I am indebted to Alice McGrath, who shared the original copy with me.

22. Grandpre is alternatively spelled Grandpré, Grandprè, or simply Grandpre as an Anglicized form of Grandprix. I am indebted to my colleague Elaine Beretz for guiding me through the straits of Parisian pronunciation.

23. McGrath, oral history.

24. Ponce, *Hoyt Street*, 28.

25. Fisher, *Problem of Violence*, 8.

26. Leyvas, "Interview," 23.

27. Ibid.

28. Jazz artist Lee Young contested the existence of a unique West Coast jazz, attributing the concept to the creative minds of the writers of *Metronome* and *Downbeat* magazines, in Pepper and Pepper, *Straight Life*, 46.

29. Ibid., 45.

30. Manuel Delgado testified that Henry and Lupe Leyvas would regularly go down to Central Avenue; testimony of Manuel Delgado to the Los Angeles County Grand Jury, Court Transcript, 4149.

31. "Boppin' on Central," 3. For good overviews of Los Angeles jazz clubs, see George, *No Crystal Stair*; Otis, *Upside Your Head!*; and Porter and Keller, *There and Back*.

32. Pepper and Pepper, *Straight Life*, 42.

33. WPA, *Los Angeles*, xxxi.

34. Guevara, "View from the Sixth Street Bridge," 116; Murray and Murray, oral history; Ted Encinas, correspondence with author, 7 February 1999; Pepper and Pepper, *Straight Life*, 40; and Lee Young, as quoted in Pepper and Pepper, *Straight Life*, 46.

35. Murray and Murray, oral history.

36. In 1948 the Los Angeles–based Don Totsi Band recorded "Pachuco Boogie," which sold more than two million copies, and Chuck Higgins recorded "Pachuko Hop" in 1952. Lipsitz, "Land of a Thousand Dances," 217–72.

37. Malcolm X, *Autobiography of Malcolm X*, 142–43.

38. Murray and Murray, oral history, 15.

39. "Alpine Weekly Gossip."

40. "La 38 St" is the tag for the 38th Street neighborhood, commonly spray-painted on buildings and walls in the area today.

41. Testimony of Dominic Manfredi, Court Transcript, 2131, 2078.

42. Testimony of Lino Díaz, Court Transcript, 134.

43. González, "Factors Relating to the Property Ownership of Chicanos in Lincoln Heights, Los Angeles," 111–14; Romo, "Urbanization of Southwestern Chicanos in the Early Twentieth Century," 183–208; Lipsitz, "Land of a Thousand Dances," 269–70; and Starr, *Material Dreams*, 147–48.

44. Fogelson, *Fragmented Metropolis*, 137–54.

45. Murray and Murray, oral history.

46. See the following testimonies from the Court Transcript: Juanita (Jennie) Gonzales, 393; Ann Kalustian (aka Ann Cummings), 524–25, 5064; and Henry Leyvas, 5064.

47. Cullen, "Mexican Boy Gangs," SLDC Papers, box 7, file 8. Testimony of José "Chepe" Ruíz, Court Transcript, 3704. McGrath, "Education of Alice McGrath," 132–33.

48. McGrath, "Education of Alice McGrath," 132–34. Testimony of Henry Leyvas to the Los Angeles County Grand Jury, Court Transcript, 4415. Photographs from the period, furthermore, reveal no tattoos on the hands of Henry Leyvas, the so-called ringleader of the group.

49. Moore, *Going Down to the Barrio*, 27–31, and Ruíz, *Cannery Women, Cannery Lives*, 10–15. For a general history of female gangs, see Harris, *Cholas*.

50. Biographical sketch: "Joe Ruiz," SLDC Papers, box 4, file 4. Biographical sketch: "Manuel Reyes," SLDC Papers, box 4, file 4.

51. Testimony of Josephine Gonzales, Court Transcript, 787. See also testimony of Betty Ziess (aka Nuñez), ibid., 1201–2. Bertha Aguilar was found in contempt of court for refusing to answer a question; Court Transcript, 1202.

52. Testimony of Juanita "Jennie" Gonzales, Court Transcript, 207. See also Valida Dávila to Tom Cullen, 29 October 1942, SLDC Papers, box 4, file 4.

53. Biographical sketch: "Joseph Valenzuela," SLDC Papers, box 4, file 4.

54. Rodríguez, *Always Running*, 41.

55. Testimony of Teodulo Díaz, Court Transcript, 143.

56. Testimony of Dominic Manfredi, Court Transcript, 2128.

57. Located at the present-day Ross Snyder Recreation Center at Ascot and Martin Luther King Jr. Boulevard, Los Angeles. Testimony of Manuel Delgado, Court Transcript, 4764. Testimony of Dominic Manfredi, ibid., 2131.

58. Testimony of Eleanor Delgadillo Coronado, Court Transcript, 2255.

59. Lino Díaz recognized two co-workers, Eugene and Joe Carpio, among the 38th Street defendants. Dominic Manfredi also testified that he saw Angel Padilla, one of the 38th Street defendants, at the Delgadillo party before the orchestra left about 1:00 A.M.. However, Angel Padilla denied being present at the party. See the following testimonies

from the Court Transcript: Lino Díaz, 134; Domenic Manfredi, 2131; and Angel Padillia, 3669.

60. Testimony of Josephine Delgadillo Reyes, Court Transcript, 2321–24, 2327. Eleanor Coronado testified that she had heard that the crowd of uninvited boys were from Downey, and that she had seen at least some of them a week earlier at a party at their home in Downey. Testimony of Eleanor Delgadillo Coronado, ibid., 2258, 2260–61.

61. Testimony of Dominic Manfredi, Court Transcript, 2105–9.

62. H. W. Douglas of the U.S. Weather Bureau testified that the moon was between its full and last quarter on 1 August 1943, rising at 10:20 P.M. that night; testimony of H. W. Douglas, Court Transcript, 4481. Manny Reyes established the time of arrival as close to 11:20 P.M. because one of the girls asked Johnny Matuz, who was wearing a wristwatch, what time it was. Testimony of Manuel Reyes, ibid., 4145.

63. Testimony of Manuel Delgado, Court Transcript, 4671–72, 4677–4774. Testimony of Henry Leyvas, ibid., 5038.

64. Testimony of Dora Baca, Court Transcript, 4490.

65. See the following testimonies from the Court Transcript: Bert McAtee, 26, 81; Ann Kalustian (aka Cummings), 634; María Albino, 2450; and Manuel Delgado, 4672, 4770.

66. Henry Leyvas testified that both Matuz and Melendez were drunk; testimony of Henry Leyvas, Court Transcript, 5570. See also the following testimonies from the Court Transcript: Gus Zamora, 3720; Manuel Delgado, 4731; and Manuel Reyes, 4139.

67. Testimony of Juanita (Jennie) Gonzales, Court Transcript, 221–23, 264. Testimony of Gus Zamora, ibid., 3714.

68. Testimony of Dora Baca, Court Transcript, 4490.

69. Jennie Gonzales estimated that they spent about two hours total at the lagoon, from 8:00 to 10:00 P.M. Manny Deldago and Henry Leyvas offered a different chronology, placing their arrival at the reservoir between 10:30 and 11:20 P.M.; testimony of Manuel Delgado to the Los Angeles County Grand Jury, Court Transcript, 4144–55, 4677.

70. Testimony of Manuel Delgado, Court Transcript, 3524.

71. Ibid.

72. Dora Baca estimated that there was only enough light to see about ten feet in front of her. This may have been due to periodic clouds that passed in front of the moon. Testimony of Dora Baca, Court Transcript, 4502–3.

73. Testimony of Manuel Reyes, Court Transcript, 4139. Leyvas estimated that the number was closer to eighteen; Manny Delgado testified at one point in the trial that there were only sixteen but later put the number at eighteen; testimony of Manuel Delgado, ibid., 3524, 4695.

74. Ibid., 4695.

75. Ibid., 4720. Testimony of Dora Baca, Court Transcript, 4493.

76. Testimony of Manuel Delgado, Court Transcript, 4680–81.

77. See the following testimonies from the Court Transcript: Dora Baca, 4497; Henry Leyvas, 5072; and Manuel Reyes, 4139.

78. Testimony of Dora Baca, Court Transcript, 4504. Testimony of Robert Michael Telles, ibid., 3762.

79. Testimony of Henry Leyvas, 5073.

80. Testimony of Manuel Delgado, Court Transcript, 4681–82.

81. Ibid., 4722.

82. Ibid., 4683.

83. Ibid., 4687.

84. Ibid., 3525, 4684. Bobby Telles confirmed that at least one of their assailants was from Downey. Testimony of Manuel Reyes, Court Transcript, 4141. See also testimony of Gus Zamora, ibid., 3517. Testimony of Robert Michael Telles, ibid., 3762.

85. Testimony of Henry Leyvas to the Los Angeles County Grand Jury, Court Transcript, 4413–14.

86. Bobby Telles testified, "We were going to teach them a lesson about bothering couples." He also explained that it was the custom of the neighborhood boys to come to the aid of one of their friends who was unfairly matched in a fight. Testimony of Robert Michael Telles, Court Transcript, 3762, 4039.

87. Testimony of Betty Zeiss (aka Betty Nuñez), Court Transcript, 448, 539–40. Testimony of Bertha Aguilar, ibid., 1216.

88. Testimony of Henry Leyvas, Court Transcript, 5074–77. Henry Ynostroza later remembered that "everyone was at the [Vernon] malt shop" when Henry drove up after the fight at the Sleepy Lagoon. However, Ynostroza testified during the Sleepy Lagoon Trial that he was at Joe Carpio's house with several young men and women when Henry Leyvas, Manny Delgado, and Gus Zamora drove up in a car and informed them of the fight at the Sleepy Lagoon. Bobby Thompson's testimony corroborates Ynostroza's earlier accounting. Henry Ynostroza, interviews. Testimony of Henry Ynostroza, Court Transcript, 3103–3808.

89. Testimony of Bertha Aguilar, Court Transcript, 547.

90. Testimony of Josephine Gonzales, Court Transcript, 1117–18.

91. See the following testimonies from the Court Transcript: Benny Alvarez, 3246–47; Robert Michael Telles, 3771–75; Manuel Delgado, 4685; and Andrew Peralta Acosta, 3563.

92. Manny Reyes testified that he looked at the clock inside Los Amigos Club to establish the time before the group departed for the Williams Ranch. Testimony of Manuel Reyes to the Los Angeles County Grand Jury, Court Transcript, 4144–45. Historian Ricardo Romo establishes the size of the group at twenty-five, but the exact number of cars and the passengers in them was never settled. Remedios Parra, who was at the Delgadillo party when the 38th Street youths drove up, testified that he saw only six cars with about twenty people in them. Manny Delgado estimated that there were six to seven cars with about twenty-five people divided among them, Gus Zamora testified that there were seven cars and thirty people, Josephine Gonzales estimated that the number was between six to seven cars with twenty-five to thirty people, Andrew Perales Acosta put the number of cars at eight with about eight people per car, and Jenny Gonzales estimated that there were ten cars. Manny Reyes's testimony agreed with Acosta's, that the number of cars was eight. Vernon Rasmussen, captain of the LAPD Homicide-Subversive Bureau, estimated that the group ranged from forty to sixty young adults. See Romo, "Southern California and the Origins of Latino Civil Rights Activism," 386. See the following testimonies from the Court Transcript: Remedios Parra, 2475; Manuel

Delgado, 3527; Gus Zamora, 3716; Josephine Gonzales to the Los Angeles County Grand Jury, 1122; Josephine Gonzales, 1180; Andrew Perales Acosta, 3552; Manuel Reyes, 4150; and Juanita (Jenny) Gonzales, 321. Vernon Rasmussen to Ernest W. Oliver, Foreman, Los Angeles County 1942 Grand Jury, 12 August 1942, RL Papers.

93. Testimony of Lorena Encinas, Court Transcript, 5467. Angel Padilla probably made the suggestion given that he was at the party earlier in the evening, although Henry Ynostroza later remembered that they went to the cluster of bunkhouses because they heard the music; interviews with Henry Ynostroza.

94. Manny Delgado, Remedios Parra, and Joseph Manfredi testified that only three cars drove up to the Delgadillo home, but Manuel "Manny" Reyes Schnieder stated that there were four. See their testimonies in the Court Transcript: Manuel Delgado, 3530; Remedios Parra, 2475; Joseph Manfredi, 2552; and Manuel Reyes Schnieder, 4152–4153. Joey Carpio and Bobby Telles drove in the two other cars. Testimony of Manuel Delgado, Court Transcript, 3530.

95. Coronado last saw Díaz standing with Luís "Cito" Vargas and Andrew Torres, who then left about five to ten minutes before the group from 38th Street arrived. Remedios Parra, however, placed Díaz as leaving the party closer to twenty minutes before the 38th Street group arrived. See the following testimonies in the Court Transcript: Eleanor Coronado, 2134–36, 2244–45; Remedios Parra, 2489, 2528, 2530; Dominic Manfredi, 2049, 2074, 2078, 2050; and Joseph Manfredi, 2552.

96. Testimony of Dominic Manfredi, Court Transcript, 2049, 2074, 2050.

97. Testimony of Eleanor Coronado, Court Transcript, 2136. Testimony of Dominic Manfredi, ibid., 2048. Although not specifically identified in this context during the court trial, the guests were, most likely, "Tiny" Adams and Marie Louise Adams, two friends of Eleanor Delgadillo Coronado's who were present when the fracas broke out. Testimony of Eleanor Coronado, ibid., 2167.

98. Testimony of Remedios Parra, Court Transcript, 2475. Testimony of Josephine Delgadillo Reyes, ibid., 2314.

99. Testimony of Dominic Manfredi, Court Transcript, 2089. Henry denied that there was a fight at the Sleepy Lagoon or that he was present at the Delgadillo home on the night in question; testimony of Henry Leyvas, ibid., 4410–12. A number of witnesses at the Delgadillo party testified that they thought Henry was holding a weapon in his hand when he struck Cruz Reyes. Yet there are a number of issues that raise serious questions about the reliability of these testimonies. First, there was widespread disagreement among the witnesses as to what the object was (a knife, a stick, or a club). Second, on cross-examination none of the witnesses would conclusively affirm that Henry did indeed hold an object in his hand. Finally, a number of witnesses from among the 38th Street youths, who gave testimonies incriminating their peers at other times, resoundingly denied that Henry held any object in his hands. Thus I have decided to exclude this piece of information in my reconstruction of the events. See the following testimonies from the Court Transcript: Dominic Manfredi, 2056–57; Eleanor Coronado, 2172–73; Josephine Delgadillo Reyes, 2302–3, 2331; Manuel Reyes, 4156; Manuel Delgado, 4163–71; and Lorena Encinas, 5494.

100. Testimony of Eleanor Coronado, Court Transcript, 2136. Testimony of Manuel Reyes, ibid., 4170.

101. Manfredi testified that Leyvas walked toward him with a knife in his hand and raised it to about shoulder level as he neared Manfredi, but no one else corroborated his version. Testimony of Dominic Manfredi, Court Transcript, 2056–59.

102. Testimony of Eleanor Coronado, Court Transcript, 2144. Coronado testified to the Los Angeles County Grand Jury that it was Henry Leyvas who struck Josephine, but she later corrected herself. Testimony of Eleanor Coronado to the Los Angeles County Grand Jury, Grand Jury Transcript, 164; Court Transcript, 2187.

103. Testimony of Eleanor Coronado, Court Transcript, 2147.

104. Testimony of Bertha Aguilar, Court Transcript, 1264–65, 1267–69, 1315–18.

105. Testimony of Manuel Delgado, Court Transcript, 3531, 4692. Henry Leyvas denied letting air out of tires, but Edward Grandpré and Manny Reyes both testified to the contrary. Padilla also denied that he aimed at the cars and testified that he shot at birds sitting on the telephone wires. Manny Reyes and Manuel Delgado, however, testified to the contrary. Testimony of Manuel Reyes to the Los Angeles County Grand Jury, ibid., 4186. Testimony of Manuel Delgado, ibid., 3532, 3555.

106. Testimony of Eleanor Coronado, Court Transcript, 2582.

107. Testimony of Joseph Manfredi, Court Transcript, 2583, 2590, 2592.

108. Testimony of Remedios Parra, Court Transcript, 2470, 2475.

109. Testimony of Manuel Reyes, Court Transcript, 4163.

110. Testimony of Henry Ynostroza, Court Transcript, 3817. Testimony of Eugene Carpio, ibid., 4035.

111. Ruíz initially denied having a club or a rock, although he admitted on cross-examination to beating Parra with a rock. At the same time, Gus Zamora, Henry Ynostroza, Manny Reyes, Eugene Carpio, and Bobby Thompson all testified that Ruíz used a club to beat Parra. María Albino witnessed the fight from her window, about fifty feet away, and testified that she saw someone using a club on a man who had fallen in a ditch. See the following testimonies from the Court Transcript: María Albino, 2397–98; José Chepe Ruíz, 3694–98, 3726; Manuel Reyes, 4163; Remedios Parra, 2535, 2473; Henry Ynostroza, 3817; and Eugene Carpio, 4028.

112. Testimony of Victor Rodman Thompson (aka Bobby Thompson), Court Transcript, 4397–4400. Testimony of Manuel Reyes, ibid., 4167.

113. See the following testimonies from the Court Transcript: Josephine Delgadillo Reyes, 2305; Benny Alvarez, 3244; Josephine Delgadillo Reyes, 2305; and Manuel Reyes, 4151.

114. Testimony of Dominic Manfredi, Court Transcript, 2061, 2068, 2076.

115. Testimony of Henry Ynostroza, Court Transcript, 3816.

116. Testimony of Dominic Manfredi, Court Transcript, 2071.

117. Testimony of Lino Díaz, Court Transcript, 2085–86.

118. Ibid., 2116.

119. Ibid., 107.

120. Testimony of Dora Barrios, Court Transcript, 1491–92.

121. Testimony of Andrew Perales Acosta, Court Transcript, 3563.

122. Ibid., 3535–36. Statement of Garner Brown, reading testimony of Victor Rodman Thompson (aka Bobby Thompson) to the Los Angeles Grand Jury, Court Transcript, 3453–56.

123. Statement of Victor Rodman Thompson, Court Transcript, 3453–55. In his statement given at the Firestone Station, Thompson denied being present at the Delgadillo home for fear of violating the terms of his probation. He asserted, however, that his peers bragged the next day at the pool hall that Chepe Ruíz clubbed a man and that Henry Leyvas used a knife on four men and hit one woman; Court Transcript, 3105, 3108. Manny Delgado's testimony confirmed the details of Thompson's testimony concerning the conduct of Ruíz and Leyvas; Court Transcript, 3535–36.

124. See the following testimonies from the Court Transcript: Ann Kalustian (aka Cummings), 579; Bertha Aguilar, 1316; and Manuel Reyes, 4174.

125. Testimony of Dr. Henry Cuneo, Court Transcript, 4256–63.

126. Ibid., 4256. Testimony of Frank R. Webb, Court Transcript, 169.

### Chapter Four

1. The complete name of the case is *The People in the State of California vs. Gus Zammora et al*. There was, apparently, no significance in naming the case after Gus Zamora (misspelled in the legal documents as "Zammora"). The name was chosen by lottery. McGrath, oral history, 10.

2. Escobar, *Race, Police, and the Making of a Political Identity*.

3. This is amply documented and discussed in ibid.; Escobar, "Chicano Protest and the Law"; Acuña, *Occupied America*, 1st ed., and *Community under Seige*; and Morales, *Ando Sagrando*.

4. Angel Padilla's last name is spelled alternately in the primary documents as "Padillo." I am using the spelling adopted by the Sleepy Lagoon Defense Committee records in his biographical sketch: "Angel Padilla," SLDC Papers, box 4, file 4.

5. Testimony of Angel Padilla, Court Transcript, 3581–86, 3604–06.

6. Joseph Valenzuela's translation. Testimony of Joseph Valenzuela, Court Transcript, 2965, 2973, 2982.

7. Chief of police C. B. Horrall called Ayres's testimony an "intelligent statement of the psychology of the Mexican people," and Sheriff Eugene Biscailuz commented that Ayres's report to the grand jury "fully covered the situation." See C. B. Horall to Ernest W. Oliver, Foreman, Los Angeles County 1942 Grand Jury, 13 August 1942, and E. W. Biscailuz to E. W. Oliver, 20 August 1942, RL Papers. Alice McGrath believes that Ayres was Hispanic and that his middle name was "Durán," but I have been unable to confirm his heritage. McGrath, oral history, 93.

8. "Edward Duran Ayres Report," SLDC Papers, box 5, as cited in Meier and Rivera, *Readings on La Raza*, 127–32.

9. Vernon Rasmussen to Ernest W. Oliver, Foreman, Los Angeles County 1942 Grand Jury, 12 August 1942, RL Papers.

10. See the following testimonies from the Court Transcript: Angel Padilla, 3581; Joseph Valenzuela, 2965, 2973, 2982, 2989, 3983; Benny Alvarez, 3238; Eugene Carpio, 4015; and Manuel Reyes, 4066–68, 4070. Leyvas, "Interview," 22–23; testimony of Henry Leyvas, Court Transcript, 5012–27; "Mexican Trial—Robbin," 20 November [1942], SLDC Papers, box 4, file 4.

11. See the following testimonies from the Court Transcript: Deputy Sheriff M. A. Gallardo, investigator, Bureau of Investigation, 3011, 3034, 3039–40, 3080–81; Clem

Peoples, deputy sheriff, chief of the Criminal Division, 3640, 3637; William L. Drumm, teletype operator for the sheriff's office, 3641–58; Officer N. K. MacVine, 2938, 2950; and Lieutenant Garner Brown, 3861–69.

12. See the following testimonies from the Court Transcript: Henry Leyvas, 5012–32; Angel Padilla, 3572–3616; Deputy Sheriff M. A. Gallardo, 3011–40; Deputy Sheriff Clem Peoples, 3637–40; William L. Drumm, teletype operator for the sheriff's office, 3641–58.

13. Testimony of Angel Padilla, Court Transcript, 3616.

14. Testimony of Henry Leyvas, Court Transcript, 5025–27; "Police Brutality Rocks L.A.: Two Citizens Dead, Third Severely Hurt; D.A. Investigating," *People's Daily World*, 13 January 1943, 1; "Mayor Pledges Probe of L.A. Police Terror: Third Prison Death Reported; City Body Demands Full Inquiry," *People's Daily World*, 14 January 1943, 1, 4.

15. "Nab Boy as Gang General," *Los Angeles Evening Herald and Express*, 7 October 1942, A-11. Carey McWilliams places the date of the grand jury investigation at 8 October 1942 in *North from Mexico*, 238.

16. Bass, *Forty Years*, 128. McGrath, oral history, 38.

17. Almaguer, "Chicano Men," 480.

18. Court Transcript, title page.

19. McGrath, "Education of Alice McGrath," 111.

20. See particularly the prolonged discussion about hair and clothing, Court Transcripts, 797–821. See also "Just Begun to Fight," SLDC Papers, box 1, file 1.

21. McWilliams, "Honorable in All Things," 149.

22. See George Shibley, "Pachucos," SLDC Papers, box 1, file 12; McGrath, oral history, 44; Margolis, "Law and Social Conscience," 141. See also Court Transcript, 797–820.

23. "[Zacsek was] one of these big hat women lawyers, who was a real phony," Ben Margolis remembered about her in "Law and Social Conscience," 141. See, for example, the spirited courtroom debate between the defense lawyers and between the defense, the prosecution, and the judge over the role of the court in providing clean clothing and haircuts to the defendants. Court Transcript, 797–820, 1114.

24. Again, the *Los Angeles Times* was the exception. See "Jury Delves into Boy Gang Terror Wave: Ranch Killing Inquiry Opens," 5 August 1942, 1, 12.

25. See, for example, "Flynn Says Not Guilty: Actor Enters Plea, Asks Early Girl Case Trial," *Los Angeles Evening Herald and Express*, 23 November 1942, A-2.

26. "See Long Inquest in Boy-Gang Death," *Los Angeles Evening Herald and Express*, 7 August 1942, A-3, and "Jury Finds 12 Guilty in Gang Slaying Trial," *Los Angeles Times* [January 1943], as found in SLDC Papers, box 4, file 9.

27. *Los Angeles Bench and Bar*, 14.

28. *Martindale-Hubbell Law Directory*, 1337; *Los Angeles Bench and Bar*, 14. See also Sánchez, *Becoming Mexican American*, 88–91; Starr, *Material Dreams*, 65; Davis, *City of Quartz*, 25, 35, 114–18.

29. *Martindale-Hubbell Law Directory*, 14.

30. McWilliams, "Honorable in All Things," 149.

31. McGrath, oral history, 19. "The Ayres' Law," SLDC Papers, box 1, file 1.

32. Testimony of Lieutenant Garner Brown, Court Transcript, 3847.

33. See, for example, Court Transcript, 2246.

34. Statement of Judge Charles Fricke, Court Transcript, 1416–17.

35. Testimony of Betty Zeiss, Court Transcript, 677.

36. Josephine Gonzales was found in contempt of court for refusing to answer the prosecution's questions. See testimony of Josephine Gonzales, Court Transcript, 787. Valida Dávila to Tom Cullen, 29 October 1942, SLDC Papers, box 4, file 4.

37. Testimony of Ann Kalustian, Court Transcript, 522–24.

38. Ibid., 528.

39. Ibid., 530.

40. Ibid., 582–84.

41. See "Goon Menace Told Trial," *Los Angeles Evening Herald and Express*, 20 October 1942, A-2.

42. "Respondent's Reply Brief," 156–57, as cited in McWilliams et al., "Brief of the Friends of the Court," 9. I am grateful to Alice McGrath for providing me with a copy of this document.

43. McGrath, "Education of Alice McGrath," 227–29, 239–45.

44. McGrath, oral history, 3–4. Although William Julius Wilson, who pioneered the use of this term, focused on African Americans within an urban context, I believe that "underclass" accurately reflects the social and economic station occupied by a significant portion of the Mexican American and African American population in Los Angeles. Like those whom Wilson studied in Chicago, Mexican Americans in Los Angeles constituted the bulk of unskilled laborers in the city and agricultural workers in the rural areas of Los Angeles County. Using the term "underclass" does not preclude "working class" as a category of analysis for Mexican American laborers. Rather, it illustrates the long-term structural relationship many laborers faced in the economy of Los Angeles. See Wilson, *Declining Significance of Race* and *Truly Disadvantaged*. Moore, "Assessment of Hispanic Poverty" and "Is There an Hispanic Underclass?," 265–84. Morales and Bonilla, "Restructuring and the New Inequality," 1–27.

45. Margolis, "Law and Social Conscience," 147–48.

46. McGrath, oral history, 3–4.

47. Testimony of Gus Zamora, Court Transcript, 3727; McGrath, "Education of Alice McGrath," 133–34.

48. Quoting Deputy Sheriff Clem Peoples, "Smashing California's Baby Gangsters," *Sensation* (December 1942), as cited in McWilliams et al., "Brief of Friends of the Court," 6.

49. Clem Peoples, "Smashing California's Baby Gangsters," *Sensation* (December 1942). I am indebted to Joseph Tovares for generously sharing the only known copy of the article. A partial copy is found in SLDC Papers, box 4, file 9.

50. Margolis, "Law and Social Conscience," 124. McGrath, oral history, 55.

51. McCormick, "Activist in the Radical Movement," 64–69. "Group Protests Procedure at Trial of 22 in Slaying," *Los Angeles Daily News*, 27 October 1942, as found in SLDC Papers, box 4, file 9.

52. See Broyles-González, *El Teatro Campesino*, 201–4, 210. Carlos Larralde and Richard Griswold del Castillo, echoing Bert Corona, also argue that historians have slighted the involvement of Luisa Moreno in the Sleepy Lagoon Defense Committee. Citing a 1971 interview with Moreno, Larralde and Griswold del Castillo assert that she was one of the co-founders of the committee and served as co-chair with Carey McWilliams. Although

LaRue McCormick appealed to labor organizers to support the Citizens' Committee for the Defense of Mexican American Youth, neither Moreno nor her union, the United Cannery, Agricultural, Packing and Allied Workers of America, is listed among the twenty-four sponsors named in the first mass mailing by the committee (although Bert Corona and Moreno's husband, Grey Bemis, are listed). Neither is she listed among the officers of the Citizens' Committee for the Defense of Mexican American Youth or the succeeding organization, the Sleepy Lagoon Defense Committee. <www.chicanas.com> cites Francisca Flores as another unsung Chicana activist involved with the Sleepy Lagoon Defense Committee. Flores's nephew, William Flores, confirms that Francisca Flores was active in community issues and provided some translation assistance to the SLDC, but he notes that her involvment with that effort was limited because of her poor health at the time. William Flores believes that Francisca's oral history, which could shed more light on her role, was deposited with the University of California, Los Angeles. Unfortunately, staff in the Special Collections cannot locate the donation. Griswold del Castillo and Larralde, "Luisa Moreno and the Beginnings of the Mexican American Civil Rights Movement in San Diego"; Blea, *Toward a Chicano Social Science*, 80–81; notes from Bill Flores at California State University, Northridge, and Dan Luckenbill of the University of California, Los Angeles, Special Collections, in possession of the author.

53. Broyles-González, *El Teatro Campesino*, 201–4, 210.

54. McGrath, oral history, 17. McWilliams, "Honorable in All Things," 168.

55. *Martindale-Hubbell Law Directory*, 265.

56. McGrath, oral history, 45–46.

57. Ibid., 46.

58. Endore, *Sleepy Lagoon Mystery*, 27–28. "Youth Trial Stalling Trick Hit by Judge," *Los Angeles Daily News*, 30 October 1942, SLDC Papers, box 4, file 9, p. 27, item 133; "'Goons' in Defense Switch," *Los Angeles Evening Herald and Express*, 30 October 1942, SLDC Papers, box 4, file 9, p. 27, item 134.

59. Statement of Anna Zacsek, Court Transcript, 811.

60. Statement of Judge Charles Fricke, Court Transcript, 820.

61. See, for example, testimony of Manuel Delgado, Court Transcript, 4728. Testimony of Garner Brown, ibid., 3848.

62. McGrath, oral history, 46. Margolis, "Law and Social Conscience," 146–48.

63. McWilliams, "Honorable in All Things," 158.

64. Statement of Judge Charles Fricke and George Shibley, Court Transcript, 2385.

65. McGrath, oral history, 19. McGrath, "Education of Alice McGrath," 111.

66. Henry Ynostroza, interviews. See also, Lino Díaz, oral history.

67. Statement of Ben Van Tress, Court Transcript, 5005.

68. Statements of Judge Charles Fricke and George Shibley, Court Transcript, 3841–42, 3861–62.

69. "Lawyer Reminds Jury of War for Fair Deal," *People's Daily World*, 4 January 1943, 4.

70. [Ysmael] Smiles [Parra] to Jaime, 5 November 1943, SLDC Papers, box 4, file 3.

71. "12 Convicted on Two Counts in 'Zoot' Killing," [publisher illegible], SLDC Papers, box 4, file 9, p. 54, item 368.

72. McGrath, "Education of Alice McGrath," 196.

73. "Verdict Hit as Splitting National Unity: 12 Boys Face Life Terms; Five Others Long Sentences," *People's Daily World*, 14 January 1943, 1, 4; "12 Convicted on Two Counts in 'Zoot' Killing," [publisher illegible], SLDC Papers, box 4, file 9, p. 54, item 368.

74. "12 Convicted on Two Counts in 'Zoot' Killing," [publisher illegible], SLDC Papers, box 4, file 9, p. 54, item 371.

75. "Verdict Hit as Splitting National Unity: 12 Boys Face Life Terms; Five Others Long Sentences," 1, 4.

76. There is some evidence that Fricke's verdicts, though harsh, were consistent with the recommendations of the Los Angeles County Grand Jury in "stamping out the 'gang war' menace." See "Indictment of Gang Boys, Adults Urged," [publisher illegible], SLDC Papers, box 4, file 9, p. 54, item 370; "Report of Citizens Committee," 10 December 1942, RL Papers; "Summary of Recommendations and Progress to Date of the Special Committee on Older Youth Gang Activity in Los Angeles and Vicinity," RL Papers; 1943 Los Angeles County Grand Jury, "Findings and Recommendations of the Grand Jury of Los Angeles County for 1943, Based upon its Inquiry into Juvenile Crime and Delinquency in That County," 7, RL Papers.

77. Warne was a senior partner in the Los Angeles firm of Pacht, Pelton, and Warne. McWilliams, "Honorable in All Things," 472. This account on the origins of the Sleepy Lagoon Defense Committee differs markedly from the one Bert Corona offered in García's *Memories of Chicano History*, 114. Corona attributes the origins of the SLDC to El Congreso Nacional del Pueblo de Habla Española, a Mexican American activist group in Los Angeles. However, none of the documents in the Sleepy Lagoon Defense Committee Papers support this claim, although some members of El Congreso were active in certain aspects of the organization.

78. Clore Warne, undated letter [ca. December 1942], SLDC Papers, box 4, file 4.

79. "Try 'Goons:' 24 in 'Sleepy Lagoon' Killing Face Court," *Los Angeles Evening Herald and Express*, 13 October 1942, A-7; "Boy Gang: Complete Jury for Murder Trial," ibid., 14 October 1942, A-2; "Goon Menace Told Trial," ibid., 20 October 1942, A-2; "Girl Stymies 'Goon' Trial," ibid., 21 October 1942, A-13; "22 'Goons' in Court," ibid., 27 October 1942, A-8.

80. *Sensation* (December 1942), as cited in McWilliams et al., "Brief of Friends of the Court," 22. Coronado instead only identified Leyvas as the boy who demanded to know "where are the boys who were going to beat up our gang?" and then struck her sister. "Hectic Scene at Boy Gang Death Inquest: Court Is Heavily Guarded; Free-for-All Fight Told," *Los Angeles Evening Herald and Express*, 11 August 1942, A-2.

81. McWilliams et al., "Brief of Friends of the Court," 22.

82. Clem Peoples, "Smashing California's Baby Gangsters," *Sensation* (December 1942), as cited in McWilliams et al., "Brief of Friends of the Court," 6.

83. See, for example, "Youthful Gang Evil: Vigorous Action Imperative in View of Seriousness of Situation," editorial, *Los Angeles Evening Herald and Express*, 4 August 1942, B-2.

84. The exact 1942 population figure for the city of Los Angeles was placed at 1,635,277, and 3,045,000 for Los Angeles and Orange Counties. "L.A. Gains 131,000 in 2 Years," *Los Angeles Evening Herald and Express*, 2 December 1942, B-3, and "County Population 3 Million," ibid., 2 January 1942, A-14.

85. "Crime Shows Drop in L.A.," *Los Angeles Evening Herald and Express*, 2 January 1942, A-14. For a more complete discussion of juvenile crime in Los Angeles, see Escobar, *Race, Police, and the Making of a Political Identity*, 186–202.

86. See "Youthful Gang Evil: Vigorous Action Imperative in View of Seriousness of Situation," *Los Angeles Evening Herald and Express*, 4 August 1942, B-2.

87. See, for example, "Mayor Tom Bradley," in Terkel, *Good War*, 149.

88. The SLDC report on this event placed it on 12 June 1942. "Mexican Boy Gangs," SLDC Papers, box 7, file 8. See also "Find New Evidence in Gang Murder," *Los Angeles Evening Herald and Express*, 13 August 1942, A-8.

89. "Mexican Boy Gangs," SLDC Papers, box 7, file 8.

90. C. L. Christopher, veteran of the LAPD for twenty years, testified before the Un-American Activities Committee in California that the event took place on 26 July 1942 at "Pomray and Marks." There was no listing for these street names, but there were (and still are) two streets with names very similar—Pomeroy and Mark—that intersect in East Los Angeles across the street from the University of Southern California Medical Center. Thus I will assume that the stenographer misunderstood Christopher's pronunciation of these streets. California Legislature. "'Zoot-Suit' Riots in Southern California," 165.

91. For examples of such reports in the *Los Angeles Evening Herald and Express*, see "Plan Boy Gang Roundup," 13 July 1942, A-5; "Act on 'Boy Gang' Problem: L.A. City, County, Juvenile Chiefs to Hold Parley," 15 July 1942, A-2; "Police 'War' on Boy Gangs: 100 Officers on Special Duty Start Roundup of 300," 23 July 1942, A-2; "Hunt Gang in New Riots," 27 July 1942, A-2; "Boy Gang Arms Seized: Guns, Knives, Chains Taken in Roundup of 250," 10 August 1942, A-2; "Draft Plan to Curtail Boy Gangs," 11 August 1942, A-2; "Offers Boy Gang Antidote," 13 August 1942, A-8; "Nab 29 in Boy Gangs: 13 Arrested after Alleged Attempt to Kidnap Girls," 17 August 1942, A-2; "69 Held in New Gang Roundup: 3 Boys Escape in Auto Chase; Police Avert 'Big Battle,'" 24 August 1942, A-2; "Boxing, Football Urged as Aid in Ending Boy Gangs," 12 October 1942, A-5; "Curfew to Curb L.A. Boy Gangs," 24 November 1942, A-4; "Broad Plan to End Youth Gang Wars," 25 November 1942, A-9; "Clanton St. Gang Reformation Held Up as Example," 27 November 1942, A-10.

92. Clem Peoples, "Smashing California's Baby Gangsters," *Sensation* (December 1942), as cited in McWilliams et al., "Brief of Friends of the Court," 7.

93. "Police 'War' on Boy Gangs: 100 Officers on Special Duty Start Roundup of 300," A-2. Letter from Captain Joseph F. Reed, administrative assistant, to Chief of police C. B. Horrall, n.d., RL Papers, Sleepy Lagoon Material Collection, item 89.

94. Peoples estimated the number of arrested suspects to be at three hundred by Sunday, 9 August 1942. Clem Peoples, "Smashing California's Baby Gangsters," *Sensation* (December 1942), as cited in McWilliams et al., "Brief of Friends of the Court," 7.

95. The *Los Angeles Evening Herald and Express* reported that a mugging took place in a defiant gesture only hours after superior court judge Robert H. Scott "cracked down on the hoodlum coterie" responsible for a riot in Baldwin Park. "New Gang Outrage: Man Robbed, Beaten by East Side Hoodlums," 8 August 1942, A-2.

96. All in the *Los Angeles Evening Herald and Express*: "Brutal Attack on Woman," 8 August 1942, A-2; "3 New Attacks on Women," 28 September 1942, A-3; "3 More

Women Attacked: Husband Slugs, Nabs Suspect Battling with Wife," 26 October 1942, A-2; "2 Women Beaten, Robbed," 28 October 1942, A-8; "Victim of Gang Holdup" and "Robbery: Zoot Suit Boy Held in Woman Slugging," 6 November 1942, A-10; "Attacked: 3 Youths Assault L.A. Mother of 5," 21 December 1942, A-8; and "Nab Love Bandit Suspect: Screams of Woman Lead to Capture," 18 February 1943, A-2.

97. See, for example, "Mother-in-law Tells Saving from Man," *Los Angeles Examiner*, 29 June 1942, 2:8; "Attacks on Women," letter to the editor from J. L. D. of Los Angeles, *Los Angeles Evening Herald and Express*, 30 September 1942, B-2; and "Attacks on Women," letter to the editor from J. L. R. of Los Angeles, 2 November 1942, B-2.

98. Press release to Charles Ellis, 4 November 1943, *Labor Herald*, SLDC Papers, box 1, file 1.

99. "State Acts to Curb L.A. Boy Gangs: Olson Tells Youth Authority to End 'Juvenile War,'" *Los Angeles Evening Herald and Express*, 6 August 1942, A-2.

100. Statements of George Shibley, Esq., and Anna Zacsek, Esq., Court Transcript, 810–11.

101. Statement of George Shibley, Esq., Court Transcript, 798.

102. Statement of Judge Fricke, Court Transcript, 801–2.

103. Statement of Clyde Shoemaker, Esq., Court Transcript, 805.

104. Statement of George Shibley, Court Transcript, 5944–58. McWilliams et al., "Brief of the Friends of the Court," 20–21.

105. Some four thousand Japanese Americans were "transferred" from the Hollenbeck Heights area of Los Angeles to an "assembly center" in Parker, Arizona. All told, more than thirty-four thousand Japanese Americans were removed from Los Angeles County. See "Last Japs in County Going to Camp Today," *Los Angeles Examiner*, 29 May 1942, pt. 2, p. 1.

### Chapter Five

1. Swing jazz actually originated much earlier but did not become a defined moment in music history until 1935.

2. Eastman, "'Pitchin' Up a Boogie'" 84.

3. <http://www.luminet.net/tgort/fdr.htm>

4. "Freedom of Speech," 20 February 1943, 12–16; "Freedom of Worship," 27 February 1943 12–13; "Freedom from Want," 6 March 1943, 12–13; "Freedom from Fear," 13 March 1943, 12–13.

5. For monographs on the American home front, see Winkler, *Home Front U.S.A.* and *Politics of Propaganda*; Dower, *War without Mercy*; Hess, *United States at War*; Polenberg, *War and Society*; Blum, *V Was for Victory*; and Lingeman, *Don't You Know There's a War On?*

6. Erenberg, *Swingin' the Dream*, 35–64.

7. Barnaby Frame, "Gangsters in Zoot Suits," May 1943, n.p., AGM Papers, box 5, file 5.

8. Undated advertisement #2, SLDC Papers, box 1, file 1.

9. Vignati, "Correct Technique for Gentlemen's Trimming and Styling," 6–7. Vignati, [no title], 6–7.

10. Interestingly, hair stylist Davie Layton of Los Angeles gained top honors at the Annual Beauty and Style Show of Hollywood Hair-Stylist's Guild in 1942 for her "Victory Coiffure." Inspired by the military look, Layton's cut was three inches long and tufted up off the neck and above the ears. "It fits with the military theme of everything else," raved chairman of the show Theo Aerto, in "'Victory Coiffure' Awarded Top Honors at Beauty Show," *Los Angeles Times*, 15 June 1942, 1. See also Babette, "Short Hair-Do Acclaimed at Style Show," *Los Angeles Examiner*, 15 June 1942, pt. 2, p. 3.

11. Cruz, "Gang History," 34. Grow, "Keep in Trim with Our Armed Forces," 8–9.

12. Bobby García as quoted by Rodríguez, "Pachuco Yo, Ese," 19–20. Other contemporary names for this style included "Argentinian dovetail," "duck tail," "duck's ass," or "D.A." The pompadour style itself is attributed to the marquise de Pompadour, mistress of Louis XV.

13. See photograph "'Argentine Dovetail' It Is Just Type [*sic*] of Haircut That Goes with Zoot Suit," in "22 'Goons' in Court," *Los Angeles Evening Herald and Express*, 27 October 1942, A-8.

14. A perusal of the fashion section of the *Los Angeles Times*, among other periodicals of the day, is a good way to get a sense of the range and also the boundaries of women's hair fashion. In particular, see 2 June 1942, 12–13; 3 June 1942, 5; 6 June 1942, 5; 7 June 1942, 1, "Myrna Loy," and pt. 3, p. 4, "Dinah Shore." See also photos of young sorority women in "Pansy Ring Claims 52 U.S.C. Co-Eds," *Los Angeles Evening Herald and Express*, 2 June 1942, sec. 2:1.

15. Mary Helen Ponce recalled that the young girls in her Pacoima neighborhood considered the "upsweep" to be a mature-looking hairstyle. Ponce, *Hoyt Street*, 287.

16. See photographs entitled "The Leyvas Family Reacting to Court Decision," in Rodríguez, "Pachuco Yo, Ese," 19; "Romona Gonzalez, 41' [*sic*]," *Lowrider* 2, no. 12 (October 1979): 29; "Frances and Miche Penalber with Friends in 1947 Los Angeles," *Lowrider* 1, no. 12 (1978): 36; "Emily Calleros Valdez, '41 S. Fer," *Lowrider* 2, no. 3 (1979): 36; and "1942, La Dora, El Paul, La Lupe, y 'La Chubby,'" *Lowrider* 2, no. 6 (1979): 22.

17. See photographs in AGM Papers, box 2, file 10: "untitled" [women of the Leyvas family], "Henry Leyvas' Mother," and "Defendants' Parents Meeting."

18. Ruíz, "'Star Struck," 109–29, and Monroy, "Our Children Get So Different Here," 79–108. Although scholars have explored the ways in which young Mexican American women during this period modified popular American hairstyles, there is also the possibility that the Pachuca pompadour may have originated from traditional Mixtec hairstyles found in Oaxaca, Mexico. See Cordry and Cordry, *Mexican Indian Costumes*, 120.

19. Braddy, "Pachucos and Their Argot," 257–58.

20. Typically a radiant cross or some other group symbol such as a spider web. Originally the number of lines extending outward from a simple cross (denoting rays) signaled the amount of time one served in prison, but as the symbol of the radiant cross gained popularity, the rays lost their original significance.

21. Conked hair was cut about two inches long on the top and tapered down around the ears and neck, combed back shiny and smooth after the hair had been chemically straightened. Margarita Obregón Pagán, telephone conversations with author, 27 March 1994; notes in possession of the author. See also Griffith, *American Me*, 66.

22. Griffith, *American Me*, 47, 76–77.

23. "Youthful Gang Secrets Exposed: Young Hoodlums Smoke 'Reefers,' Tattoo Girls, and Plot Robberies," news clipping, n.p., 16 July 1944, MR Papers, box 3, file 10.

24. Ibid.

25. Press release "Jan 43–Nov 43," SLDC Papers, box 1, file 1.

26. Press release to Charles Ellis, *Labor Herald*, from Wayne Parker, 4 November 1943, SLDC Papers, box 1, file 1.

27. Ayres, "Statistics," as cited in Meier and Rivera, *Readings on La Raza*, 127–32.

28. As quoted in an undated press release [cross-referenced to events in 1943], SLDC Papers, file 1, box 1. H. J. O'D. of Los Angeles wrote the *Los Angeles Evening Herald and Express* a detailed letter on both the merits and proper procedure of caning juvenile delinquents—both girls and boys—with birch twigs. "Hoodlums," 21 September 1942, B-2. See also George Offord of Los Angeles, "Punish Attackers," *Los Angeles Evening Herald and Express*, 6 October 1942, A-3.

29. Davenport, "Swing It, Swing Shift!," 24.

30. Ibid., 24, 26. Psychiatrist Ralph Banay read latent feminine qualities in the hat, hair, and shoe styles that usually complemented the zoot. Banay, "Psychiatrist Looks at the Zoot Suit," 84.

31. Bogardus, "Gangs of Mexican American Youth," 56.

32. Himes, "Zoot Suit Riots Are Race Riots."

33. Bogardus, "Gangs of Mexican American Youth," 58; Vigil, *Barrio Gangs*, 40; Cordry and Cordry, *Mexican Indian Costumes*, 120.

34. *New York Times*, 11 June 1943, 21.

35. *Negro Digest* 1 (January 1943): 69–70. Duncan's zoot suit, as pictured in the *New York Times*, is sufficiently different from Gable's costumes in *Gone with the Wind* to be its own unique style.

36. *Newsweek*, 7 September 1943. Shane White, citing an article by Julius J. Adams in *Amsterdam News*, 29 May 1943, also notes that the fashion was common in the 1930s. White and White, *Stylin'*, 215.

37. Malcom X, *Autobiography of Malcolm X*, 34, 69.

38. Pepper and Pepper, *Straight Life*, 41.

39. Green suggests that the zoot suit originated from a combination of sources. "Zoot Suiters," 64–66.

40. The way that Ysmael (Smiles) Parra uses the word "zoot" in a 23 October 1943 letter to Alice Greenfield (McGrath) suggests that it was a jazz slang word that denoted approval: "everything is going along—zoot. (fine)."

41. Other names for the suit included "glad rags" and "drip drapes." See Tyler, "Black Jive and White Repression," 32. See also *Newsweek*, 7 September 1942, 48. Ortega notes in *Caló Orbis* that Harold C. Fox, American clothier and bandleader, coined the term "zoot suit" in 1942, but *Newsweek*, 7 September 1942, 48, attributes the name to a popular song written by Hollywood songwriters in late 1941. Cosgrove suggests that the phrase dates from the 1930s, in "Zoot-Suit and Style Warfare," 78, and there is evidence to support his view in Calloway, *New Cab Calloway's Cat-ologue* and *New Cab Calloway's Hepster's Dictionary*. Citing an 11 June 1943 *New York Times* article, the *Negro Digest* 1 (January 1943): 69–70, identifies "killer diller" as the southern term for the zoot suit.

Bobby García of Los Angeles remembered using only the term "drapes," yet boys living within the immediate vicinity of the 38th Street neighborhood appear to have used the term "zoot suit" exclusively. Rodríguez, "Pachuco Yo, Ese," 20. McWilliams, *North from Mexico*, 242. Chepe Ruíz to Alice Greenfield (McGrath), 18 May 1944, SLDC Papers, box 4, file 2, and Manuel (Manny) Delgado to Alice Greenfield (McGrath), 11 August 1944, SLDC Papers, box 4, file 2.

42. Ortega, *Caló Orbis*, 218, and Santamaría, *Diccionario general de Americanismos*, 116. In *American Me* Griffith defined *tacuche* specifically as referring to the fingertip coat, but I believe that Santamaría's 1942 definition more accurately reflects the idiomatic and historical context of the word: "En algunas partes de Méjico, envoltorio de trapos, lío.— 2. Por extensión, principalmente entre estudiantes, traje en general, vestido." Ortega corroborates this usage in defining the verb *entacucharse* as "to dress one's self up." Likewise, Margarita Obregón Pagán remembers hearing *tacuchado* used to describe one as being "all dressed up" (telephone interview with author, 27 March 1994). Cerda, Cabaza, and Farias define *tejano* usage of *tacuche* as "pants" (*pantalón*), *Vocabulario español de Texas*, 223. Polkihorn defines *tacuche* as "suit" in *Dictionary of Chicano Slang*, 58, as does Cobos, *Dictionary of New Mexico and Southern Colorado Spanish*, 159–60. Santamaría defines *tacuche* as either "outfit" or "a bum" in *Diccionario de Méjicanismos*, 994. See also Galván and Teschner, *Diccionario del Español chicano*, 110.

43. Griffith, *American Me*, 46–47.

44. "A Zoot Suit for My Sunday Gal," as quoted in Chibnall, "Whistle and Zoot," 56. An early music video (called "soundie") of the song "Zoot Suit for My Sunday Gal" is on file at Meyer Media Center, University of California, Los Angeles, entitled "Zoot Suit," #ZVU 108. Terenzio, MacGillivray, and Okudo identify this production as a soundie made in early March 1942, entitled "A Zoot Suit (with a Reat Pleat)" and starring Dorothy Dandridge and Paul White, in *Soundies Distributing Corporation of America*, 70.

45. Malcolm X, *Autobiography of Malcolm X*, 52.

46. "I want to look keen so my dream will say, 'You don't look like the same beau.' So keen she'll scream, 'Here comes my walkin' rainbow," "A Zoot Suit For My Sunday Gal" as quoted in Chibnall, "Whistle and Zoot," 56.

47. In September 1942 the War Production Board specifically ruled against zoot suits; "WPB Swings Down on Zoot Suits," *Los Angeles Evening Herald and Express*, 3 September 1942, B-16.

48. Vibora (aka Snake) as quoted by Rodríguez, "Pachuco Yo, Ese," 20–21.

49. Cruz, "Gang History," 34.

50. McGrath, oral history. See also Bogardus, "Gangs of Mexican American Youth," 55–56.

51. Quotation from *Newsweek*, 7 September 1943, 48. Frame, "Gangsters in Zoot Suits," n.p., May 1943, AGM Papers, box 5, file 5.

52. Bogardus, "Gangs of Mexican American Youth," 55–56.

53. Davenport, "Swing It, Swing Shift!," 24–26; McWilliams, *North from Mexico*, 241; Griffith, *American Me*, 16. Zoot-suited youths were also not permitted to enter a theater on Main Street. See McGrath, "Education of Alice McGrath," 173. McGrath further adds that "among the kids who wore drapes, they made fun of the more extreme drapes" (161).

54. Also known as "jitterbug pants"; Tyler, "Black Jive and White Repression," 33.

55. See "Low Riders Pasados," *Lowrider* 2, no. 2 (1978): 42, and 2, no. 3 (1978): 35; Cruz, "Gang History," 32, 34. On the day that the Sleepy Lagoon boys arrived at the office of Attorney Ben Margolis to thank him formally for his work, none of the boys wore a suit, but Chepe Ruíz wore his drape-shape pants a few inches above his naval held up by wide suspenders, Smiles Parra wore similar pants held up by a thin belt, and Henry Leyvas wore reet pleat pants with no belt at all. The only young men wearing anything close to a zoot on the day of their release from prison were Johnny Matuz and Henry Leyvas, although Bobby Thompson and Chepe Ruíz wore suits with exaggerated shoulders and length. SLDC Papers, box 1, file 10.

56. *Newsweek*, 7 September 1943, 49; Davenport, "Swing It, Swing Shift!," 26, 28; Malcolm X, *Autobiography of Malcolm X*, 52; "Low Riders Pasados," *Lowrider* 2, no. 2 (1978): 42.

57. *Newsweek*, 7 September 1943, 48. See also Malcolm X, *Autobiography of Malcolm X*, 58.

58. Vibora (aka Snake) as quoted by Rodríguez, "Pachuco Yo, Ese," 20–21.

59. I have not been able to trace the trade name of this specific style or the company that made it, but the look of the hat is closest to the sennit or "boater" that was typically made of straw. See Schoeffler and Gale, *Esquire's Encyclopedia of Twentieth Century Men's Fashions*, 323, 325. For examples of the porkpie hat, see ibid., 337, 338. Bogardus, "Gangs of Mexican American Youth," 55–56.

60. Bogardus, "Gangs of Mexican American Youth," 55–56.

61. Malcolm X, *Autobiography of Malcolm X*, 58.

62. Also called *chanclas* from *chanclear*: "to dance." Griffith, *American Me*, 311.

63. McWilliams, *North from Mexico*, 242–43.

64. California Legislature, "'Zoot-Suit' Riots in Southern California," 160.

65. Bobby García as quoted by Rodríguez, "Pachuco Yo, Ese," 19–20.

66. Vibora (aka Snake) as quoted by ibid., 20–21.

67. A *Newsweek* article on the zoot craze mentioned in passing that the "ruke suit" was a female version of the zoot suit; *Newsweek*, 7 September 1942, 48. The only known photograph of this style, taken 11 September 1942 in Los Angeles, shows a blonde woman wearing what looks to be an ordinary drape jacket reaching to midthigh, with a knee-length skirt, BE086453, "Man and Woman in 1940s Zoot Suit Fashions," www.pro.corbis.com. An article carried by the Associated Press described the female zoot suit as a "juke coat . . . cut long to look like the men's"; "WPB Swings Down Beat on Zoot Suits," B-16. For an example of women wearing the *tacuche* with skirts, see the photograph entitled "Beauty Contest?" in *Sensation* (December 1943), 32–33, found in SLDC Papers, box 4, file 9, item 259.

68. Bogardus, "Gangs of Mexican American Youth," 35, reports that these women were also referred to as *cholitas*, a word derived from *cholo*, which generally referred to a darker-skinned worker or an uncouth person. Griffith corroborates Bogardus's general description in *American Me*, 47.

69. Griffith, *American Me*, 47.

70. Leyvas, "Interview," 23.

71. Davenport, "Swing It, Swing Shift!," 24, 26.

72. Leather sandals made in Mexico, also called "zombie shoes." See Griffith, *American Me*, 47. Davenport described the slacks that these women wore as "hip loving," in "Swing It, Swing Shift!," 24, 26.

73. Both Robin Kelley and Larry Neal offer fascinating interpretations on the social significance of the zoot suit for African Americans; Kelley, "'We Are Not What We Seem,'" 86–88; Neal, "Ellison's Zoot Suit," 68–69.

74. Calloway and Rollins, *Of Minnie the Moocher and Me*, 114, as quoted in Tyler, "Black Jive and White Repression," 32.

75. Malcolm X, *Autobiography of Malcolm X*, 142–43, as quoted in Chibnall, "Whistle and Zoot," 59–61.

76. Murray and Murray, oral history; McWilliams, *North from Mexico*, 243; Moore, *Homeboys, Gangs, Drugs and Prison in the Barrios of Los Angeles*, 64, 70–71.

77. Moore, *Homeboys, Gangs, Drugs and Prison in the Barrios of Los Angeles*, 64, 70–71.

78. Chepe Ruíz to Alice Greenfield [McGrath], 18 May 1944, SLDC Papers, file 2, box 4. For Ruíz's full name, see José "Chepe" Vasquez Ruíz to Alice Greenfield [McGrath], 23 April 1943, SLDC Papers, box 4, file 2. McGrath believes that Ruíz's 18 May 1944 letter, as well as letters from Henry Leyvas, were written by a prison scribe. While the handwriting styles and syntax clearly change in letters from Ruíz and Leyvas, it is reasonable to conclude that Ruíz and Leyvas agreed to the sentiments reflected in the letters to which they signed their names.

79. Pepper and Pepper, *Straight Life*, 43.

80. Lipsitz, "Creating Dangerously," xix.

81. Otis, *Upside Your Head*, 24.

82. May, "Rosie the Riveter Gets Married," 139–41; Rupp, *Mobilizing Women for War*, 6–7; Honey, *Creating Rosie the Riveter*, 156.

83. Schrum, "'Teena Means Business,'" 134–63. Schrum notes that *Seventeen* began in 1944, but the actual date may have been as early as 1942.

84. Hartman, *Homefront and Beyond*, 189–91; Evans, *Born for Liberty*, 219–28.

85. As quoted in Evans, *Born for Liberty*, 223; Hartman, *Homefront and Beyond*, 195–96; May, *Pushing the Limits*, 26–27.

86. Ruíz, "Flapper and the Chaperone," 199–226.

87. Ramírez, "Crimes of Fashion," 20–24.

88. Lingeman, *Don't You Know There's a War Going On?*, 154.

89. Hartman, *Homefront and Beyond*, 195–205.

90. Schoeffler and Gale, *Esquire's Encyclopedia of Twentieth Century Men's Fashions*, is an invaluable source for researching white, mostly middle-class men's fashion. For discussion on the English drape suit, see 18–20 and 170–71; peg-top pants, 594–95; the Prince Albert frock coat, 184–85; and the porkpie hat, 342–43, 337–38.

91. Ibid., 184–85. Green notes that Cab Calloway also speculated that the zoot suit started in England, albeit in the 1930s, and was "dumped" on the U.S. market after it did not sell well overseas. "Zoot Suiters," 66. Julius J. Adams also noted the English origins of the zoot suit, attributing the fashion to Edward VII, the duke of Windsor, in *Amsterdam News*, 29 May 1943, as cited in White and White, *Stylin'*, 251.

92. Kimmel, *Manhood in America*, 5–9.

93. See Peretti, *Creation of Jazz*, 124–25; "Detroit Red" in Malcolm X, *Autobiography of Malcolm X*, 84–107; Hobsbawm, *Jazz Scene*, 218.

94. Mary Helen Ponce recalled that young girls in Pacoima loved to window-shop, try on the latest fashions, and spend their earnings on clothing, makeup, and shoes; *Hoyt Street*, 19–22. Ruíz, *Cannery Women, Cannery Lives*, 17.

95. "Time for Sanity," *Los Angeles Times*, 11 June 1943, 1.

96. See Timothy G. Turner, editorial, *Los Angeles Times*, 13 January 1943, as quoted in 1943 press release #9, SLDC Papers, box 1, file 1. Letter to the editor from John J. Phillips of Los Angeles, "As to Hoodlums," *Los Angeles Evening Herald and Express*, 3 September 1942, B-2. Letter to the editor from "Whiskers" of Downey, *Los Angeles Evening Herald and Express*, 24 September 1942, B-2.

97. Biographical sketch: "John Matuz," SLDC Papers, box 4, file 4.

98. Biographical sketch: "Henry Leyvas 2," SLDC Papers, box 4, file 4.

99. Biographical sketch: "Benny Alvarez," SLDC Papers, box 4, file 4.

100. Bogardus, "Gangs of Mexican American Youth," 55–56.

101. Cosgrove, "Zoot-Suit and Style Warfare," 77–91.

102. I owe this insight to David Montgomery of Yale University.

103. Ramírez, "Crimes of Fashion," 18.

104. "Origenes de Pachucos Y 'Malinches,'" *La Opinión*, 26 August 1942, 2.

105. Devlin, "Female Juvenile Delinquency and the Problem of Sexual Authority in America, 1945–1965," 83–106. Although the title of Devlin's article implies a focus on the postwar period, her work also examines the national discourse of juvenile delinquency during the Great Depression and World War II.

106. Ramírez, "Crimes of Fashion," 13.

107. "Black Widow Girls in Boy Gangs; War on Vandals Pushed," *Los Angeles Evening Herald and Express*, 3 August 1942, A1; "Black Legion," *Newsweek*, 24 August 1942; and "Origenes de Pachucos Y 'Malinches,'" *La Opinión*, 26 August 1942, 2. Also "Youthful Gang Secrets Exposed: Young Hoodlums Smoke 'Reefers,' Tattoo Girls, and Plot Robberies," *Los Angeles Times*, 16 July 1944, 2:1, and in MR Papers, box 3, file 10. Frost reports that "How'd you like to go up Cherry Lane with me?" was a common solicitation for sex in El Paso during the war. Frost, *Gentlemen's Club*, 244.

108. That these young women felt personally affected by the reports on Pachucas suggests their readiness to identify as such, even thought they do not in the *Eastside Journal* article.

109. "Mexican American Girls Meet in Protest," *Eastside Journal*, 16 June 1943, as reproduced in Sánchez-Tranquilino and Tagg, "Pachuco's Flayed Hide," 102.

110. This article remains a curious document. The claims of the young women in attendance are at odds with Elizabeth Escobedo's findings in researching the Los Angeles juvenile court records, that Mexican parents regularly turned to the police and the courts in frustration over the sexuality of their daughters. If this protest meeting and those who attended were not staged, the words attributed to the young spokesperson appear to have been heavily edited. Her phrasing resembles the language commonly used by Manuel Ruíz in his campaign to have the word "Mexican" substituted with the more cumbersome phrase "of Mexican extraction." Although it is possible that such a

phrase was in common usage by young Mexican Americans or that she knew and agreed with Ruíz, I have found evidence of such regular usage only among his documents. Waxman's role remains a curious one. Why would these young women turn to him for assistance rather than to Josefina Fierro de Bright, Luisa Moreno, or any number of Mexican American activists or Mexican American political and cultural organizations of the period? That none of the young women were named, and that Waxman's name appears in three of the five short paragraphs, twice identifying him as the editor of the small newspaper, suggest a level of self-promotion behind the meeting and that it may have been convened by Waxman to boost circulation among Mexican American readers.

111. Horace R. Cayton, "Riot Causes: Sex Was an Important Factor Leading to Zoot Suit War on the Coast," *Pittsburgh Courier*, 25 September 1943, 13.

112. Salter, telephone interview; notes in possession of author.

113. Greenfield [McGrath], *Sleepy Lagoon Case*; Endore, *Sleepy Lagoon Mystery*. McWilliams, "Los Angeles' Pachuco Gangs," 76–77; "The Zoot-Suit Riots," 818–20; and "Los Angeles Archipelago," 41–53.

114. See undated press release [ca. 1943], SLDC Papers, box 4, file 4; 10 November 1943 press release draft, ibid., box 1, file 2; 9 November 1943 press release draft, ibid., box 1, file 2; 1943 press release #9, ibid., box 1, file 1; Peter Furst, "Press Blamed for Spread of Zoot-Suit Riot," *P.M.*, 11 June [ca. 1943], SLDC Papers, box 5, file 1.

115. Reprinted in Luckenbill, *Pachuco Era*, 6.

116. Murray and Murray, oral history, 1–2, 14–15.

117. Spanish slang somewhat equivalent to "hick." Originally a common laborer, with idiomatic reference to a darker skin color and rural background.

118. Youths used many other words to denote approval, such as "sharp," "reet," and so on.

119. Redl, "Zoot Suits," 259–62. McWilliams made a similar argument in *North from Mexico*, 243.

120. "Well, the way they dressed, the way they acted [is] what brings out racial prejudice"; Debs, "Oral History Interview," 56–58.

### Chapter Six

1. As quoted in George Seldes, *Lords of the Press*.

2. McWilliams, "Los Angeles' Pachuco Gangs," 76; "Los Angeles Archipelago," 41–53; "Zoot-Suit Riots," 818–20; and *North from Mexico*.

3. Turner and Surace, "Zoot-Suiters and Mexicans," 14–20.

4. Jones also anticipated this thesis, noting that "as occasional gang fights prevailed, the word 'pachuco' lost its original interpretation and became associated with crime and 'the pachuco gangster'"; *Government Riots of Los Angeles, June 1943*, 11.

5. For example, note the informants cited by Braddy, "Pachucos and Their Argot," 255–71.

6. Barker, "Pachuco," 46; Braddy, "Pachucos and Their Argot," 255–71.

7. McWilliams, "Los Angeles' Pachuco Gangs," 76–77. McWilliams received this information from police captain Joseph F. Reed. See "Mexican Boy Gangs" and "Mexican Boy Gangs—Cullen II:I," SLDC Papers, box 7, file 8.

8. Bogardus, "Gangs of Mexican American Youth," 55–66.

9. Griffith, "Who Are the *Pachucos*?," 355, later published as a chapter in her book *American Me*.

10. "Following her graduation from Pomona College in 1933, [Griffith] served in the neighborhood of Los Angeles as a social worker with Mexican families who were on state relief. Later she supervised youth projects for the NYA. Her work here had to do with several hundred Mexican American boys and girls who were engaged in the making of modern ceramics and in other art projects. . . . 'Wanting to give these youngsters' stories as they would give them themselves if they had the chance, I always go to them for the answers. . . . They believe, as I do, 'Us Pachucos wouldn't be so bad if we just had a chance, huh?'" Editor's introductory comments in Griffith, "Who Are the *Pachucos*?," x.

11. Certainly both sides have been argued, neither of which is entirely convincing. For a representation of both, see Braddy, "Pachucos and Their Argot," 255–71. Hernández proposed that the name "Pachuco" evolved from *Paso* (short for El Paso) to *pacho* and then to *pachuco*; *Chicano Satire*, 122 n. 40.

12. Griffith, *American Me*, 46.

13. In the post-1960s era, the hair of so-called Pachucos in the 1940s seems rather short to the untrained eye. They wore their hair long in the front so that it could be combed back and styled behind the head in a duck tail.

14. Barker, "Pachuco," 255–57; Braddy, "Pachucos and Their Argot," 255–71.

15. Quoting *Time* magazine, Endore exempted the *Los Angeles Daily News* and the *Hollywood Citizen-News* from his charge that the Los Angeles press whipped up the mob spirit; *Sleepy Lagoon Mystery*, 41.

16. See Barker, "Pachuco," 46; Braddy, "Pachucos and Their Argot," 255–71; and Gonzalez, "Pachuco."

17. *Los Angeles Times*, 4 August 1942, 1.

18. Hernández also notes that the traditional corrido "Raymundo '*el pachuco*'" contains no reference to *caló*, zoot suits, or any of the other identifying qualities that have come to define the Pachuco of the 1940s; *Chicano Satire*, 122 n. 40.

19. H. F. Henderson and Harry Braverman, "Report of the Special Committee on Problems of Mexican Youth of the 1942 Grand Jury of Los Angeles County," RL Papers. During the 1943 rioting in Los Angeles, Ruíz and his contemporaries also appealed to the federal government for intervention. See 7 June 1943 minutes of the Citizens' Committee for Latin-American Youth, MR Papers, box 3, file 10. Also published in Jones, *Government Riots of Los Angeles, June 1943*, 99.

20. The use of the masculine term "newsmen" is intentional. Reporters who worked the crime beat for the major newspapers in Los Angeles were primarily, if not exclusively, men.

21. McGrath, "Education of Alice McGrath," 218. Even those who worked on the Sleepy Lagoon Defense Committee played with the term "Sleepy Lagoon." Carey McWilliams wrote an undated note to Alice Greenfield [McGrath] ("Mrs. Sleepy Lagoon") wherein he referred to himself as the "Sleepy Goon"; AGM Papers, box 1, file 10.

22. McWilliams, "Honorable in All Things," 164. McWilliams also identifies January 1943 as the moment when the "attack had been resumed" on Mexican American youths by the newspapers. See "Los Angeles Archipelago," 46.

23. McWilliams, "Los Angeles Archipelago," 46. Alice McGrath, who worked extensively with the Sleepy Lagoon boys, speculated that only one or two of the seventeen may have been a Pachuco; McGrath, oral history, July 1992. Notes in possession of the author.

24. Acosta, "Mexican Youth," 1; Bogardus, "Gangs of Mexican American Youth," 55–66; Griffith, "Who Are the *Pachucos*?," 355; McWilliams, "Los Angeles' Pachuco Gangs," 76–77, and "Pachuco Troubles," 5–6; Redl, "Zoot Suits"; "Report Prepared on Pachuco Gang Activities in the City of Los Angeles, Prepared by Dale Drum at the Los Angeles Navy Recruiting Station and Office of Naval Procurement," 18 May 1951, Records of the Eleventh Naval District, file P8-5 "Zoot Suit Gangs"; Sánchez, "Pachucos in the Making"; Tuck, "Behind the Zoot Suit Riots," 313–16, 335.

25. Peoples is also identified as chief criminal deputy in a press release draft prepared by the Sleepy Lagoon Defense Committee dated 7 December 1942, SLDC Papers, box 1, file 2, and as the chief investigator for the sheriff's office in "Mexican Trial—Robbin," n.d., SLDC Papers, box 4, file 4.

26. As noted by Luckenbill, *Pachuco Era*, 3. The term is also attributed to Calloway in "Mexican Boy Gangs," SLDC Papers, box 7, file 8.

27. For example, see Mazón, *Zoot Suit Riots*, 15–30, and Acuña, *Occupied America*, 1st ed., 202–8. Romo traces the pro-interventionist positions that both the *Examiner* and *Times* took during the Mexican Revolution because of the large landholding interests of both Hearst and Harrison Gray Otis, who then owned the *Times*; *East Los Angeles*, 98.

28. The *Los Angeles Examiner* boasted of having the largest daily circulation, 242,000, and the largest Sunday circulation, 651,000; 30 June 1942, sec. 1:9.

29. Alonso, "African-American Street Gangs in Los Angeles." Phillips, *Wallbangin'*. I thank Victor Viesca for calling these citations to my attention.

30. *Los Angeles Times*, 4 August 1942, 1.

31. See Escobar, "Chicano Protest and the Law"; "Mexican Boy Gangs," SLDC Papers, file 8, box 7; undated press release [ca. 1943], SLDC Papers, box 1, file 1. Griffith noted that some Los Angeles policemen were so notorious for planting marijuana cigarettes on "Mexicans" that a few young men took to asking policemen to display their open hands before conducting searches; *American Me*, 330 n. 6.

32. The *Sleepy Lagoon Mystery* sold more than twenty-five thousand copies in the first three months of release; Press release, 20 September 1944, SLDC Papers, box 1, file 1. Endore wrote an earlier version and published it with the Citizens' Committee for the Defense of Mexican American Youth (CCDMAY), which was the organizational predecessor of the Sleepy Lagoon Defense Committee (SLDC). For the sake of clarity, however, I refer to the organized appeal effort as SLDC, unless specifically addressing issues relevant to the CCDMAY.

33. "One Killed and 10 Hurt in Boy 'Wars'; Another Victim Feared Drowned in Flare-up of Juvenile Terrorism," *Los Angeles Times*, 3 August 1942, 1; "Gangs Warned, 'Kid Gloves Off!'; Deputy Sheriff and Police Arrest 34 More Youths and Six Girls," *Los Angeles Times*, 4 August 1942, 1; "Report Prepared on Pachuco Gang Activities in the City of Los Angeles, Prepared by Dale Drum."

34. A description of the article is found in an undated press release [probably 1943], SLDC Papers, file 1, box 1. Joseph Tovares of WGBH in Boston has the only known com-

plete copy. Peoples was also in charge of the preparation of the prosecution testimony in the "Sleepy Lagoon" case and was responsible for the mass arrests of Mexican boys and girls. The SLDC alleged that in 1940 Peoples was removed from the office of chief jailer after an exposé involving him in profitable dealings with "Bugsy" Siegels of "Murder, Incorporated."

35. "Youthful Gang Secrets Exposed: Young Hoodlums Smoke 'Reefers,' Tattoo Girls, and Plot Robberies," news clipping, [n.p.], 16 July 1944, MR Papers, box 3, file 10.

36. *Los Angeles Times*, 9 June 1943, 1.

37. Tuck, *Not with the Fist*, 217. The *Los Angeles Evening Herald and Express* reported on 10 June 1943 that "female mobsters" were amassing to do battle with sailors, but the riot had ended by 8 June 1943, when military authorities confined men to their bases for several days. There were no further indications in the news or in police and military sources that anything came of the alleged plans. See "Girl 'Zoot Suiters' Gird to Join Gangland Battle," A3.

38. "Girl 'Zoot Suiters' Gird to Join Gangland Battle." See also Barnaby Frame, "Gangsters in Zoot Suits," May 1943, n.p., AGM Papers, box 5, file 5.

39. Ramírez, "Crimes of Fashion," 20–24.

40. McWilliams, "Los Angeles' Pachuco Gangs," 76–77.

41. Sánchez, "Pachucos in the Making," 13–20.

42. Tuck, "Behind the Zoot Suit Riots," 313–16. Tuck was case supervisor for the Federal Emergency Relief Administration and State Relief Administration for seven years in communities where a large part of the Mexican population was on relief. She went to Mexico to study the indigent repatriated Mexican. Ibid., 306.

43. Bogardus, "Gangs of Mexican American Youth," 60–61.

44. Ibid., 59.

45. A good example of this is an internal report of the SLDC compiled to study the Mexican problem. See "Mexican Boy Gangs" and "Mexican Boy Gangs—Cullen II:I," SLDC Papers, box 7, file 8.

46. Albee Slade, radio transcript "Our Daily Bread," 18 February 1944, SLDC Papers, box 1, file 6.

47. Perhaps because she knew them best, Alice McGrath strongly disagreed with Endore's characterization of the boys. Carey McWilliams disagreed with Endore's characterization perhaps less than McGrath, but the working relationship within the SLDC was such that each member was free to develop his or her own projects without hindrance from the others. McGrath's only attempt to edit Endore's draft was in his characterization of her role as an "angel of mercy." She preferred that the work focus as much on the plight of the boys as possible, and Endore subsequently deleted her role in the SLDC from the final draft. McGrath, "Education of Alice McGrath," 163–64.

48. Endore, *Sleepy Lagoon Mystery*, 14.

49. Ibid.

50. Ibid., 40. For other sympathetic writings on the Pachuco, see Acosta, "Mexican Youth," 1; Griffith, "Who Are the *Pachucos*?," 355; McWilliams, "Pachuco Troubles," 5–6; Redl, "Zoot Suits"; Sánchez, "Pachucos in the Making"; Tuck, "Behind the Zoot Suit Riots," 313–16.

51. Alice Greenfield [McGrath], "Mexicans Called Their New Home 'Maravilla'—At

First," *Peoples Daily World*, n.d., AGM Papers, box 5, file 1; Alice Greenfield, "Why Lupe Doesn't Go to School . . . ," *People's Daily World*, n.d. (handwritten on document "at time of trial"), AGM Papers, box 5, file 2.

52. For monographs that explore these advances, see Gómez-Quiñones, *Roots of Chicano Politics*, *Mexican American Labor*, and *Chicano Politics*; García, *Memories of Chicano History* and *Mexican Americans*; and Barrera, *Beyond Aztlán*.

53. The State Relief Agency disbanded in July 1942; *Los Angeles Examiner*, 9 July 1942, sec. 1, p. 12.

54. The show aired on 1110 KPAS, 7:15–7:30 P.M., Monday through Friday from the Congress of Industrial Organizations building in Los Angeles. See radio transcript: "Our Daily Bread," 18 February 1944, SLDC Papers, box 1, file 1.

55. Radio transcript: "Our Daily Bread," 5 May 1943, SLDC Papers, box 1, file 6.

56. "Texts of Speeches," SLDC Papers, box 1, file 7.

57. Radio transcript penciled: "Trujillo 10-14-43," SLDC Papers, box 1, file 4; radio transcript: "Our Daily Bread," 18 February 1944, SLDC Papers, box 1, file 6.

58. Radio transcript: "Our Daily Bread," 18 February 1944, SLDC Papers, box 1, file 6.

59. The reaction Anthony Quinn received when he solicited funds for the SLDC from an actor "who had made his reputation playing gangster parts"; *Original Sin*, 82.

60. Endore, *Sleepy Lagoon Mystery*, 7–10.

61. Gilbert, *Cycle of Outrage*, 25.

62. Hearst indeed demanded absolute loyalty from his employees, according to biographer John Winkler, who noted that "[his executives] at times curse him roundly but obey him blindly." Yet Hearst was also a very competitive man who would surely have found it difficult to cut the potential profits of his most lucrative newspaper for the sake of conspiring with his newspaper-publishing rival to attack juvenile delinquency in Los Angeles. Winkler, *W. R. Hearst*, 308.

63. Morrison, *Playing in the Dark*, 17.

### Chapter Seven

1. Routing slip dated 24 October 1942 from port director, San Diego, concerning malicious mischief, possibly by enlisted men of the USS *Kitty*, that resulted in damage being done to the 5th Street Landing, Records of the Eleventh Naval District, file P8-5, 1942, 2/2.

2. See, for example, Harrod, "Study of Deviate Personalities As Found in Main Street of Los Angeles," and DuVall, "Sociological Study of Five Hundred Under-privileged Children." See also Gaspar R. Torres, "Chart of Relationships of Branches of the Latin-American Coordinating Council to L.A. County Coordinating Council and Other Agencies," sec. F, 10 October 1940, 3, MR Papers, box 2, file 11, and "The Alpine Street Project," MR Papers, box 3, file 11.

3. In the days before the American occupation of Los Angeles, Chavez Ravine, named in the 1850s for city councilman Juan Chávez, served as a poor people's burial ground, and in the outbreaks of smallpox in 1850 and 1880 the Chávez farm took in the quarantined animals for the county. Laborers and common folk who could not afford property elsewhere began to settle the area, and by the Second World War small houses fanned out along the hillsides of the ravine and clustered at the bottom of the valley. See WPA,

*Los Angeles*, 174; McWilliams, *North from Mexico*, 224–25; and McGrath, "Education of Alice McGrath," 256–57.

4. The average worth of real estate in the area was around two thousand dollars a house. See Shevky and Williams, *Social Areas of Los Angeles*; United States, Bureau of the Census, "Housing Statistics for Census Tracts: Los Angeles-Long Beach, California."

5. Of the 1,283 occupied dwelling units, 767 (60 percent) were rentals, and the average monthly rent for the area was nineteen dollars.

6. Despite the general pride Mexicans and Mexican Americans exhibited in their cultural identities, a number of Mexican American activists successfully lobbied to have "Mexican" included within the "native white" category of the 1940 census. It was considered a major coup at the time because it was one of the strategies activists adopted during this period in an attempt to ensure that Mexican Americans were indeed recognized as American citizens with full access to citizenship rights. Yet it remains a frustrating artifact for the historian of today in trying to reconstruct the ethnic composition of a given area. Thus I have adopted the following assumptions in my research: that because Mexican migrants followed housing patterns similar to those of other immigrant groups—namely, that friends and relatives tended to live near or with one another—one can deduce with reasonable confidence the ethnicity of the "native whites" living in a particular census block judging by the number of immigrants who also made the area their home. This was probably especially so during the period of enforced housing segregation in Los Angeles. Wherever possible I also utilize impressionistic accounts from the period, such as tourist guides, pamphlets, or memoirs, to corroborate these assumptions.

7. The 1940 U.S. Census reported 918 from Mexico (61 percent of the foreign-born), 286 from Italy (20 percent), 56 immigrants from central Europe (e.g., Yugoslavia, Hungary, Romania, Czechoslovakia), and 45 from Germany—the majority of this last group presumably Jewish (6 percent). Only 1 African American family lived in the ravine in 1940.

8. The 1940 census split the area north from Alpine Street into two tracts: tract 116 took in the area east of Figueroa to Douglas, and tract 115 took in the area west of Figueroa to North Broadway. This division is significant because the statistical information for the two tracts is quite different—tract 116 was the more affluent of the two areas, with a different racial mix and a higher average of school years completed. Because the divide between the affluence and poverty of an area is not often cleanly marked by a single street but gradually spreads over several, I assume that the figures for tract 115 are more accurate for the neighborhoods that are my focus in this work, even though they may fall within the boundaries of tract 116 just east of Figueroa.

9. According to the U.S. Census, the average worth of a house in this area on 1940 was $3,091, and the average cost of rent was $24.00 a month.

10. Harrod, "Study of Deviate Personalities As Found in Main Street of Los Angeles"; WPA, *Los Angeles*. See also Le Roy M. Edwards, Esq., to the Honorable Frank Knox, secretary of the navy, 28 September 1942, Records of the Eleventh Naval District, P8-5, 1942, 2/2.

11. Primarily along Main and 5th Streets. "Navy Bans Sailors from 32 Taverns and Bars," *Los Angeles Times*, 13 June 1943, pt. 1, p. 8.

12. Calculated on the 1940 census figures for census tracts 117, 180, 181, 182, 183, and 185, which include the area west of Figueroa Street to Los Angeles Street and south of Sunset Boulevard to 9th Street. The WPA puts the downtown population at sixty thousand; *Los Angeles*, 150.

13. Only 5 "Asians," no African Americans, and 206 "others" were reported living in this area in 1940.

14. The census recorded 9 African Americans, 54 "Asians," and 228 "others" living in this area. The median years of schooling completed jumped from 8.4 in the predominantly Mexican American sector of Temple Street to 1st Street to 12.1 in the largely Canadian and English area of 5th Street to 9th Street. For the most part, "Asians" and Asian Americans (Japanese nisei, Filipinos, and Chinese) tended to live on farms in the rural areas of Los Angeles. Small business owners in Little Tokyo and New Chinatown lived scattered about the downtown area, showing up in small pockets in areas away from their places of business, west of Figueroa Boulevard around 2nd Street and a few blocks north on Temple Street. However by 1942, with the internment of Japanese Americans, many of their business and homes were quickly purchased or assumed by Mexican Americans and African Americans. See DuVall, "Sociological Study of Five Hundred Under-privileged Children."

15. Kelley, "'We Are Not What We Seem,'" 86–88.

16. "Alpine Street Project." Torres also reported that "our most dangerous areas at the present time are: Hollenbeck, Belvedere, Temple Street, Palos Verdes, Clanton Street. . . . In all the above districts the juvenile delinquency is very high"; "Chart of Relationships of Branches of the Latin-American Coordinating Council to L.A. County Coordinating Council and Other Agencies."

17. Smith, "Negative Interaction," 46.

18. WPA, *Los Angeles*, 145. For an overview of this period from a literary perspective, see also Villa, *Barrio-Logos*, 19–65.

19. "Last Japs in County Going to Camp Today," *Los Angeles Examiner*, 29 May 1942, pt. 2, p. 1.

20. WPA, *Los Angeles*, 174.

21. Godlewska and Smith, *Geography and Empire*, 7.

22. Either North Broadway or New High Street. New Chinatown, created when much of old Chinatown was razed for the construction of the Union Passenger Terminal, was located on North Broadway and College Street. Half a block east of New Chinatown was a Chinese theme park called China City, bounded by Ord Street on the north, Macy Street on the south, New High Street on the west, and Main Street on the east. WPA, *Los Angeles*, 154–55.

23. Urak, Harold William, S2c USN, in Lieutenant Glen A. Litten, USNR, to the Commanding Officer, "Attack on Naval Personnel by 'Zoot-Suiters'—Report on," 10 June 1943, Records of the Eleventh Naval District, P8-5 "Zoot Suit Gangs," 1943, 3/4; hereafter cited as Litten Report.

24. *Los Angeles Examiner*, 17–18 April 1943, as cited in Domer, "Zoot-Suit Riot," 27.

25. As quoted in Griffith, *American Me*, 19.

26. Miller, J. C. P., CM3c, and Bushman, William Howard, S2c V-6 USNR, in Litten Report. Even in the residential areas immediately surrounding the Naval Reserve Ar-

mory, where servicemen were more commonly seen, local youths were no more accommodating. See Robinson, W. L., CM3c V-6 USNR, and Holley, Billie Joe, S2c V-6 USNR, in ibid.

27. Valleta, Domenick, EM3c USN, in Litten Report. Valleta describes young men as "zoot-suiters," but given that a zoot suit is difficult to identify on young men sitting down in a closed car, particularly a West Coast zoot suit, it is likely that "zoot-suiter" was simply a characterization he utilized rather than an accurate description of the young men's clothing. Valleta did not indicate the racial identity of his assailants.

28. Granner, James Jerome, S2c V-6 USNR, in Litten Report.

29. Alice Greenfield [McGrath], "Mexicans Called Their New Home 'Maravilla'—At First," *Peoples Daily World*, n.d., AGM Papers, box 5, file 1. Alice Greenfield [McGrath], "Why Lupe Doesn't Go to School . . . ," *People's Daily World*, n.d. (handwritten on document "at time of trial"), AGM Papers, box 5, file 2.

30. Fregoso, *Bronze Screen*, 29–30.

31. Staples, "Stereotypes of Black Male Sexuality," 466.

32. Donaldson, "What Is Hegemonic Masculinity?," 645–46. See also Hanke, "Theorizing Masculinity with/in Media," 183–203.

33. Meyer, *As Long As They Don't Move Next Door*, 76–77.

34. Bederman, *Manliness and Civilization*, 5.

35. Morín, *Among the Valiant*.

36. Lloyd, Francis Harold, Jr., S2c USN, in Litten Report.

37. See also Mysinger, Kenneth Sinclair, S2c V-6 USNR, in Litten Report; *Los Angeles Examiner*, 11 July 1942, sec. 1:5.

38. Anonymous, "Admiral in Command 11th Naval District, San Diego, California," and 6 March 1944 routing slip "Anonymous Letter."

39. Unsigned letter from San Diego, Calif., 19 February 1944, Records of the Eleventh Naval District, P8-5 "Zoot Suit Gangs," 1943, 3/4.

40. Himes, "Zoot Riots Are Race Riots," 200–201.

41. Thomas, Charles Joseph, S2c USNR, in Litten Report. Similar incidents were reported in Dennis, Roy Marshall, S2c V-6 USN, and two reports filed by King, George Richard, CCM, in ibid.

42. Wells-Barnett, *On Lynchings*; Williamson, *Crucible of Race*.

43. Bederman, *Manliness and Civilization*.

44. See also the complaint filed by Rodli, Kenneth Harold, S2c V-6 USNR, about the attack on Jane Shubin in Boyle Heights by several young men wearing zoot suits, in Litten Report.

45. Boatright, Benny Claire, S2c V-6 USNR, in Litten Report. Boatright reported that the event took place on a Thursday in May 1943. See also the reports filed by Griffie, Donald Edward, S2c V-6 USN, and Miller, J. C. P., CM3c V-6 USNR, in ibid.; WPA, *Los Angeles*, xxi.

46. Miller, J. C. P., CM3c V-6 USNR, Litten Report. See also report filed by Melbye, Harris Arnold, S2c V-6 USNR, on 10 May 1943, in ibid. At least part of the conflict between military men and civilian youths may have been directly linked to gay-bashing. A small but relatively open homosexual community lived in the area surrounding Pershing Square, and a number of gay men or men looking for same-sex activity used the

park for socializing and dating. See Henderson, Dale Corwin, S2c V-6 USNR, in ibid. Harrod, "Study of Deviate Personalities As Found in Main Street of Los Angeles," 24. Berube, *Coming Out under Fire*, 37, 122.

47. Lehne, "Homophobia among Men," 244–45.

48. See, for example, Slater, Richard Lee, S2c V-6 USNR; Valleta, Domenick, EM3c USN; Houston, James Albert, S2c V-6 USNR; Maggard, Cecil, S2c USN; Lee, Charles Gaston, S2c V-6 USNR; and Holley, Billie Joe, S2c V-6 USNR, in Litten Report.

49. Before his involvement in the Sleepy Lagoon trial, Angel Padilla was arrested at least twice for assaulting drunks. Biographical sketch: "Angel Padilla," SLDC Papers, box 4, file 4. McGrath, "Education of Alice McGrath," 242.

50. See reports filed by Templin, Charles Lourn, S2c, and Robbins, Jack Thomas, S2c USN, in Litten Report. See also letter from the commandant, Eleventh Naval District, San Diego, Calif., to all activities in the San Diego area, 21 November 1942, cautioning naval personnel from carrying large sums of money while on liberty because of recent attacks, Records of the Eleventh Naval District, P8-5, 1942, 2/2.

51. See also reports filed by Haynes, Richard Samuel, S2c V-6 USNR, and Perkins, Robert Cleon, S2c V-6 USNR, in Litten Report.

52. The Litten Report gives the exact date as 25 May 1943.

53. See reports filed by Calkins, Robert Lafayette, S2c USNR, and Stetich, Wallace, S2c V-6 USNR, in Litten Report. See also reports filed by Granner, James Jerome, S2c V-6 USNR; Hermann, Richard Ralph, EM1c USN; Bakken, Richard Arthur, S2c V-6 USN, Short, Robert James, S2c USN; and Bushman, William Howard, S2c V-6 USNR, in ibid.

54. California Legislature, "'Zoot-Suit' Riots in Southern California," 170.

55. Edward Duran Ayres, "Statistics," as cited in Meier and Rivera, *Readings on La Raza*.

56. C. B. Horall to Ernest W. Oliver, Foreman, Los Angeles County 1942 Grand Jury, 13 August 1942, and E. W. Biscailuz to E. W. Oliver, 20 August 1942, RL Papers, Sleepy Lagoon Material Collection.

57. Griffith, *American Me*, 18.

58. Ibid. See also "Don McFadden," in Terkel, *Good War*, 147.

59. California Legislature, "'Zoot-Suit' Riots in Southern California," 169–72.

60. Griffith, *American Me*, 19.

61. Adler, "1943 Zoot-Suit Riot."

62. Neither Coleman nor Draper offered a more complete explanation of what they meant by "Indian"—whether the soldier in question was an American Indian or from India. Regardless, he was clearly not a white Anglo Saxon, which indicates that race or color may have been less an issue with civilian youths in the inner city than group affiliation.

63. Coleman, Joe Dacy, S2c USN, and Draper, Homer Charles, S2c V-6 USNR, in Litten Report.

64. See, in Records of the Eleventh Naval District, routing slips dated 17 February 1942, file MM/P13-11 P8-5; 5 March 1942 from C. M. Fitzgerald, district superintendent of the Pullman Company, file P8-5; 15 April 1942 from Ambrose Gherini of San Francisco, file A16-3 P8-5; 21 April 1942 from R. R. Hodgekinson, Department of Police, Newport Beach, file P8-5 N2; 24 April 1942, file L20 P8-5; 1 June 1942 from Philip J. Clowry, A&N

YMCA, San Diego, file P13-5 P8-5; 3 June 1942 from Mrs. Haddel, file P8-5 F/A4; 12 June 1942 from Cincus & NavOp, file P8-5; and 30 November 1942 from Headquarters of the Ninth Service Command, Fort Douglas, Utah, file L20-1 P8-5. See also A. George Fish of the 1944 Grand Jury of San Diego to Rear Admiral W. L. Freidell, 10 June 1944, and Memo #21-44, 7 March 1944, Records of the Eleventh Naval District, file P8-5 1942 2/2.

65. Anonymous, "Admiral in Command 11th Naval District, San Diego, California," and 6 March 1944 routing slip "Anonymous Letter."

### Chapter Eight

1. See, for example, "City, Navy Clamp Lid on Zoot-Suit Warfare," *Los Angeles Times*, 9 June 1943, 1–2; Martin Dickinson, USN (Ret.), commanding officer, memo "To the Commandant of the Eleventh Naval District," 11 June 1943, Records of the Eleventh Naval District, Correspondence Files 1921–47, P8-5, 1943, [1/4].

2. Griffith, *American Me*, and McWilliams, *North from Mexico*. Hearst's shibboleths "Boost circulation. Make the paper pay" and "Get excited when the public is excited" earned him resounding criticism across the country for the aggressive journalism of his many newspapers. Winkler, *W. R. Hearst*, 308. See also Endore, *Sleepy Lagoon Mystery*; radio transcript, 18 February 1944, SLDC Papers, box 1, file 6; "The Ayres' Law," SLDC Papers, box 1, file 1; undated handwritten minutes, SLDC Papers, box 2, file 11; press release draft, 10 November 1943, "Press Blamed for Spread of Zoot Suit Riot," [*P.M.*, 11 June 1943], AGM Papers, box 5, file 5; McWilliams, "The Story behind the 'Zoot War,'" AGM Papers, box 5, file 5; A. L. [Al] Waxman, "Race Incitement to Violence—An Eyewitness Account," *People's Daily World*, 10 June 1943, 1.

3. See also Jiménez, *Mexican American Heritage*, 196–97.

4. Swanberg, *Citizen Hearst*, 531; Winkler, *W. R. Hearst*, 308.

5. Gilbert, *Cycle of Outrage*, 25.

6. King, George Richard, CCM, in Litten Report. King is identified in the report with the designation CCM, which, according to the *Glossary of U.S. Naval Abbreviations*, 5th ed. (April 1949), is the standard abbreviation for "chief carpenter's mate."

7. Watkins, Morris Grant, S2c V-6 USNR, in Litten Report; compare identical phrasing in reported incidents by Judd, Arthur Willis, Jr., on 5 June 1943 and Dennis, Raymond Floyd, V-6 USNR, on 6 June 1943 in ibid.

8. Holmes, as cited in Watkins, Morris Grant, S2c V-6 USNR, in ibid.

9. Herschman, Alvin Louis, S2c V-6 USNR, and Pridmore, Max Udell, S2c USN-I, in ibid.

10. "Swastika on L.A. Street Is Probed" and "Find Mysterious Codes," *Los Angeles Evening Herald and Express*, 28 September 1942, A-3.

11. Rudy Sánchez, "Dear Sir," 6 June 1943, EQ Papers, M349, box 1, file 11. Beatrice Griffith, quoting an unnamed source, places the size of the mob at one hundred; *American Me*, 20. However, naval records indicate that the size of the mob was closer to Rudy Sánchez's estimate of forty to fifty.

12. Sánchez, "Dear Sir."

13. McWilliams, *North from Mexico*, 238.

14. The willful misuse of military property was an offense punishable by court martial; *United States Navy Regulations*, Article 8:15.

15. Rudy Sánchez reported that sailors also carried guns, but I have been unable to corroborate this detail of his account. It would have been difficult to secure the use of military-issue firearms from the armory for unofficial use, particularly outside the compound, although some of the sailors may have carried their own personal firearms. Sánchez, "Dear Sir."

16. These activities seem to have been exclusively male-centered. I have found no evidence in the extant documents that the police officers made any attempts to include young women in their activities. Garcia, Chapman, and Burgoyne were likely working under the auspices of the Coordinating Committee for Latin-American Youth (CCLAY), headed by Mexican American professionals and activists tapped by city officials to help resolve the problem of juvenile delinquency. The CCLAY established a small storefront center at Alpine and Figueroa and held a meeting with numerous youth groups at the Alpine Street School in May 1943. "Narrative Report and Evaluation of the Conditioning Program Undertaken by the Co-ordinating Council of Latin-American Youth with the So-called 'Pachuco' Gangs in Los Angeles, California," n.d., MR Papers; McWilliams, *North from Mexico*, 244.

17. In *American Me* Griffith describes the boys from Alpine Street as "Pachuco," but Rudy Sánchez refers to the group only as "'zuiters'" or "so-called 'zoot zuiters.'" EQ Papers, M349, box 1, file 11.

18. Sánchez, "Dear Sir."

19. Griffith wrote that a sailor shouted up from the street to two boys sitting in a second-story window: "You guys better beat it. There's about a hundred sailors hunting for you up at Alpine." The wording of that quotation is rather odd and further indicates the degree of creativity she employed in her book: Why would someone—a presumably sympathetic person at that—come up to boys already under the protective care of the police and tell them to "beat it" because sailors were hunting for them a mile up the road? He should have said the opposite, such as: "Stay there because people are after you." But for Griffith's reconstruction of the riot she had to place the boys back in the neighborhood at the time the sailors stormed through in order to illustrate her point that the Alpine boys were innocent (and law-abiding) victims of white cruelty. In many ways I am sympathetic to her argument, but Sánchez clearly indicates that they missed the rioting when they arrived in the neighborhood, and the small number of casualties for the first night corroborates this account. Griffith, *American Me*, 20–21; Sánchez, "Dear Sir."

20. Both McWilliams and Griffith wrote that the Alpine boys were assaulted by sailors after police squad cars had dropped them off, but the Sánchez letter does not corroborate this assault. McWilliams, *North from Mexico*, 244; Griffith, *American Me*, 21; Sánchez, "Dear Sir."

21. Sánchez, "Dear Sir."

22. Griffith reported that police at the Los Angeles Central Street Jail received news of the rioting at Alpine as early as 8:00 P.M.; *American Me*, 20.

23. Charles L. Bacon, "Men Returned to Station by Executive Officer, Over Leave,—Report on," 4 June 1943, Records of the Eleventh Naval District, Correspondence Files, 1921–47, P8-5 "Zoot Suit Gangs," 1943, 3/4.

24. See Glen A. Litten, memorandum for the commanding officer, "Men Picked Up

by Shore Patrol, Report on," 4 June 1943, Records of the Eleventh Naval District, P 8-5 (Zoot Suit Gangs), 1943, Correspondence Files 1921–47, [3/4].

25. Bacon, "Men Returned to Station by Executive Officer, Over Leave,—Report on." Bacon dated his report 4 June 1943 and wrote in the present tense, giving the impression that the events he described occurred on that day. However, the report filed that same day by the executive officer Lieutenant Glen A. Litten, USNR, clearly states that the events described by Bacon occurred the previous night, on 3 June 1943.

26. See reports filed by Stanick, Robert Earl, S2c V-6 USNR; Patterson, Richard William, S2c USN; and Hrusa, John Anthony, SM3c V-6 USNR, in Litten Report.

27. Lieutenant Carl T. Cobbs, USN, "Action Regarding 'Zoot Suit' Trouble, Report on," 5 June 1943, Records of the Eleventh Naval District, Correspondence Files, 1921–47, P8-5 "Zoot Suit Gangs," 1943, 3/4.

28. Griffith placed this event on Thursday, 3 June 1943, in *American Me*, 20–21, but the source she cites, *Los Angeles Evening Herald and Express*, clearly places the event on Saturday, 5 June 1943. The reports filed by Lieutenant Carl T. Cobbs, USNR, on 4 June 1943 and Lieutenant Glen A. Litten, C-V(S) USNR, on 5 June 1943 and 10 June 1943 also corroborate this chronology.

29. The Lincoln Heights area, designated on most modern maps of Los Angeles as simply "Boyle Heights," is east of modern-day Chinatown, around the intersection of North Broadway and Daly Street. Cobbs, "Action Regarding 'Zoot Suit' Trouble, Report on." Minutes of the CCLAY, 7 June 1943, 1, 3. Compare handwritten minutes by Manuel Ruíz, executive secretary, with typewritten minutes misdated May 7, 1943, MR Papers, box 3, file 1.

30. McWilliams, *North from Mexcio*, 245–46.

31. Cobbs, "Action Regarding 'Zoot Suit' Trouble, Report on."

32. Ibid.

33. Ibid.

34. Ibid.

35. Ibid.

36. Ibid. McWilliams differed with this interpretation, seeing the arrests merely as token efforts on the part of the LAPD; *North from Mexico*, 246.

37. Dickinson assigned two chief petty officers and twenty-two men per watch for Saturday and Sunday nights, 5–6 June 1943, in Litten Report, 2. Martin Dickinson, commanding officer, "Report on Local Disturbances by the Civilians and Service Personnel," 11 June 1943, and Lieutenant G. A. [Glen] Litten, C-V(S) USNR, "Attack on Naval Personnel by 'Zoot-Suiters'—Report on," 10 June 1943, both in Records of the Eleventh Naval District, Correspondence Files, 1921–47, P8-5 "Zoot Suit Gangs," 1943, 3/4.

38. See, for example, Davis, Claude Jefferson, S2c USN, in Litten Report.

39. Whittier Boulevard begins at Soto Street heading east, running parallel to 4th Street. The only place where Whittier Boulevard intersects with a 4th Street—which is only a side street and not the same major artery—is some twelve miles east of the armory in Montebello and just a few blocks west of the Rio Hondo. Crosland's statement that he was returning to the armory suggests that the incident was located much closer to the downtown area (Crosland, Bobby Gene, USN, in Litten Report, 10 June 1943). Thus I assume that the incident took place somewhere in the half-mile area bordered by

Whittier Boulevard to the south and East 4th Street to the north, South Soto Street to the west and Euclid Avenue to the east, where other confrontations were documented.

40. See also reports by Bengiveno, Chauncy Anthony, RM3c V-6 USNR; Lee, Charles Gaston, S2c USN; and Reynolds, John Tyrell, SK2c V-6 USNR, in ibid.

41. Cruz, "Gang History," 34.

42. "Don McFadden," in Terkel, *Good War*, 146–48; "Jurors Hear 'Zooter' Defend Right to Garb," *Los Angeles Times*, 16 June 1943, 1.

43. McWilliams, *North from Mexico*, 246–47.

44. See Bernius, George Henry, Jr., S2c USN; Smith, Jacque Aubrey, S2c USN, in Litten Report.

45. Report filed by King, George Richard, CCM, in ibid. See also reports filed by Moore, Shirley Timothy, S2c USN; Spencer, Gordon Wayne, S2c V-6 USNR; Bowman, Jack Phillip, S2c V-6 USNR; and Bates, Kenneth Loyd, S2c V-6 USNR, in ibid.

46. "Riot Alarm Sent Out in Zoot War: Servicemen Strip and Beat 50; Five Youth Treated in Hospital," *Los Angeles Times*, 8 June 1943, 1.

47. Litten Report; Dickinson, 11 June 1943 memo "To the Commandant of the Eleventh Naval District"; "The Following Message for Information to the District Patrol Officer, Dictated by Senior Patrol Officer Downtown Los Angeles," Commander Fogg, given by R. O. Smith, CMM, 0045, 8 June 1943, Records of the Eleventh Naval District, Records of the Commandant's Office, Correspondence Files 1921–47, P8-5 "Zoot Suit Gangs," 1943, 3/4.

48. "Riot Alarm Sent Out in Zoot War," 1.

49. Waxman, "Race Incitement to Violence—An Eyewitness Account," 1. This account was likely reprinted from Waxman's own newspaper, *Eastside Journal*.

50. Keith Collins, in *Black Los Angeles*, places the end of the riot closer to 13 June 1943, and a number of scholars have followed his lead. Although sporadic confrontations continued well after 8 June 1943, the large-scale rioting, for all practical purposes, ended when military officials declared Los Angeles off-limits and augmented the shore patrol. McWilliams does not assign a date to the ending of the rioting but closes his narrative with the events of 8 June 1943. See Collins, *Black Los Angeles*, 28; Mazón, *Zoot Suit Riots*, 1; Gutiérrez, *Walls and Mirrors*, 124. Acuña (*Occupied America*, 1st ed.) and Sánchez (*Becoming Mexican American*) have followed McWilliams's interpretive lead in *North from Mexico*, 250–51.

51. Blea posits that Josefina Fierro de Bright "was instrumental in ending the violent racist and sexist conflicts between Chicano citizens and U.S. servicemen after World War II in Los Angeles. By negotiating with Vice President Wallace to declare Los Angeles out of bounds to military personnel, she became the most important person in the termination of the 'zoot suit' conflicts." Unfortunately, Blea cites no evidence, and I have been unable to corroborate from the extant documents that such a scenario was even probable. The president is the commander in chief of the military, not the vice president, and any effort by the vice president to declare Los Angeles off-limits to the military would have to come through the president. I have been unable to locate any record of such an order from President Roosevelt. I have furthermore been unable to discover the outbreak of another zoot suit riot after World War II, as Blea asserts. In addition, Henry Wallace was not vice president during the Truman administration (having been

replaced as vice president in 1944 by Truman) but Alben W. Barkely. Blea's statement, if true, would dramatically alter the historical understanding of Mexican American political activity during this period. Not only would it place Mexican Americans in the role of decisively altering the events and protecting the community from attack, but it would put the resolution of the riot solely in the hands of Fierro de Bright. See Blea, *Toward a Chicano Social Science*, 80–81.

52. "The Following Message for Information to the District Patrol Officer, Dictated by Senior Patrol Officer Downtown Los Angeles"; "City, Navy Clamp Lid on Zoot-Suit Warfare," 1–2.

53. *Newsweek*, 21 June 1943, 36. The source of this information remains unknown, and this figure is the only known estimate of casualties.

54. "A Mexican Youth: We 'Pachucos' Fight for a Free World," photocopied in Dieppa, "Zoot-Suit Riots Revisited," 201. Originally published in *People's Daily World*, 10 June 1943, front page.

55. Astorino, Louis, S2c USN-SV, in Litten Report. See also report filed by Lieutenant Henry A. Turner, USNR, in ibid. The army periodical *Yank* (British edition) reported that "zoot-suit war ended with the zoot-zuiters riding before the city hall waving truce flags, and the Navy allowed the sailors to go on liberty again"; *Yank: The Army Weekly*, 3 June 1943, 15. Many thanks to Grace Aspinall for letting me look at her copy.

56. "Johnny" to Manuel and Claudia Ruíz, MR Papers, box 1, file 3. A cross-reference with Ruíz's response on 20 June 1943 (MR Papers, box 1, file 5) establishes the date of Johnny's letter as 11 June 1943.

57. *Los Angeles Evening Herald and Express*, 5 June 1943, as cited in McWilliams, *North from Mexico*, 245–46. Top-ranking military officials also understood this as part of the motivation for rioting and cautioned servicemen not to take the law into their own hands. See DCGO 11ND Long Beach, "All Units under My Command," 10 June 1943; D. W. Bagley, "Recruit Disorders in Los Angeles," 9 June 1943; and Maxwell Murray, major general, U.S. Army Commanding, "Commanders All Units, Southern California Sector," 11 June 1943, all in Records of the Eleventh Naval District, Correspondence Files, 1921–47, P8-5, 1943, [1/4].

58. Dower's study focused exclusively on Japan, but the public image of Germans and Germany underwent a similar process, though clearly not imbued with the same racial overtones. Germans became "krauts" and symbolized the Old World run amuck with a sophisticated ethnic hatred that bordered on sadism.

59. Edward Duran Ayres, "Statistics," SLDC Papers, box 5, as cited in Meier and Rivera, *Readings on La Raza*, 127–32.

60. Ibid.

61. "Bowron: 'Goon' Gang Protests May Be Inspired," *Los Angeles Evening Herald and Express*, 7 November 1943; "Plot to Create Discord Feared: Enemy Agents May Use Gang Outbreaks to Stir Trouble, Mayor Says," *Los Angeles Times*, 7 November 1943; "Enemy Seeking U.S.-Mexican Rift: Bowron," *Los Angeles Examiner*, 7 November 1943; "No Persecution of Mexican Youths—Bowron," *Los Angeles Daily News*, 7 November 1943; "Gangs May Be Axis Inspired," n.p., n.d., item #300; "Seditious Tirades in L.A. Jail Arouse FBI," n.p., n.d., item #291; "Influences behind Gang Wars Studied Here," n.p., n.d., item #298, all found in SLDC Papers, box 4, file 9.

62. Vega Aircraft Corporation in Burbank, Calif., worked with Boeing and Douglas in a joint project to develop the B-17 "Flying Fortress" bomber. *Los Angeles Examiner*, 5 June 1942, pt. 2, p. 1.

63. The term "character" was probably a substitute for a word or name unsuitable for print. "Collier's reporter follows the sound of revelry by night and learns about swing shifts, zoot suits and some strange people who are herein designated as characters." Davenport, "Swing It, Swing Shift!," 24.

64. Ibid., 28.

65. "Mexican Boy Gangs," SLDC Papers, box 7, file 8. The chief of police vehemently denied any knowledge of this.

66. McWilliams, *North from Mexico*, 247.

67. No doubt had Davenport lived on the West Coast, he would have described the zoot suit in terms of Mexican American youths rather than Filipino laborers.

68. "Zoot Suit Gangsters," dateline 28 November, Los Angeles, *Whittier California News*, n.p., n.d., item #244, SLDC Papers, box 4, file 9.

69. See, for example, the work of the Reverend Revels Clayton in Collins, *Black Los Angeles*.

## Chapter Nine

1. See Leonard, "Years of Hope, Days of Fear"; Dieppa, "Zoot-Suit Riots Revisited."

2. McGrath, "Education of Alice McGrath," 20.

3. "First Lady Traces Zoot Riots to Discrimination," *Los Angeles Times*, 17 June 1943, 1; "Mrs. Roosevelt Blindly Stirs Race Discord," *Los Angeles Times*, 18 June 1943, 4.

4. Manuel Ruíz Reyes to Alice Greenfield [McGrath], 16 June 1943, SLDC Papers, box 4, file 2.

5. Manuel Ruíz to "Johnny," 20 June 1943, MR Papers, box 1, file 5.

6. A[lphonso] V. Rendón to Manuel Ruíz, 5 October 1942, MR Papers, box 3, file 1.

7. Griswold del Castillo, "The International Dimensions of the Zoot Suit Riots." Susan Marie Green argues that the term "Tarzanes" is in reference to the long hair worn by Olympian swimmer turned actor Jonas Weissmuller (aka Johnny Weissmuller), who played Tarzan in the movies from 1932 to 1948. Green, citing Guillermo Hernández, also notes that Mexicans used other names, such as "pisaverdes, catrines, dandies, curritacos, mequetrefes, and petimetres." Green, "Zoot Suiters," 70; Hernández, *Chicano Satire*, 121 nn. 41, 42.

8. Paz, "The Pachuo and Other Extremes," in *Labyrinth of Solitude*, 9–28.

9. Griswold del Castillo, "International Dimensions of the Zoot Suit Riots."

10. Paul Coronel, "The Pachuco Problem," *Mexican Voice* ([July?] 1943), RL Papers. See also unsigned editorial, "A Challenge," in ibid., and T[omás] A. Chacón to Manuel Ruíz, 8 June 1943, MR Papers, box 1, file 2.

11. "Press Telegram" to the *People's Daily World*, 22 October [1942], SLDC Papers, box 1, file 1.

12. Ibid.

13. Press release, 13 January 1943, SLDC Papers, box 1, file 1.

14. McGrath, oral history, 27, 51. This is a different response than the comments she made at an earlier oral history interview, when she speculated that many people did

in fact believe that a fifth column was at work; "Education of Alice McGrath," 152. Her response to my question was so quick and frank that I am inclined to accept her later views on the matter.

15. McGrath, oral history, 91–92.

16. See, for example, press releases, 4 November 1943, 25 March 1944, 28 March 1944, March/May 1944, 9 May 1944, ca. 15 May 1944, 16 May 1944, 7 June 1944, 8 June 1944, 18 August 1944, 20 October 1944, 28 October 1944, in SLDC Papers, box 1, file 1; press release drafts, 9 November 1943, 10 November 1943, 23 October 1944, and undated draft, SLDC Papers, box 1, file 2; and press release draft, 14 October 1943 [written by Rafael Trujillo? Compare press release ca. 15 May 1944], SLDC Papers, box 1, file 1, and box 1, file 4.

17. See Ruíz, "Promise Fulfilled," 51–61; Baca, "Luisa Moreno"; García, *Mexican Americans*; Bert Corona, "Chicano Scholars and Public Issues in the United States in the Eighties."

18. See Wells, "Activist, Interpreter, Statesman"; Gómez, *From Barrio Boys to College Boys*; García, *Mexican Americans*; Gutiérrez, *Walls and Mirrors*; Pagán, "'Who Are These Troublemakers?'"

19. Pagán, "'Who Are These Troublemakers?'"

20. Speaking engagements for Ruíz included the Southern District meeting of the California Probation and Parole Officers Association at the Fred C. Nelles School for Boys, MR Papers, box 1, file 2. Other invitations were Helen Gahagan to Ruíz, 20 April 1944, inviting him for a private discussion; Warren Jefferson Davis, president, the American Academy of Public Affairs (Hollywood), to Ruíz, 7 April 1941; Wesley O. Smith, vice principal of Foshay Jr. High, for the American Legion, Schoolmaster's Post 448 in Los Angeles, to Ruíz, 11 November 1943; V. B. Blakey, assistant manager, Bank of America NT&SA., to Ruíz, 24 October 1944; Vincent B. Claypool, district superintendent, Barstow Union High School, to Ruíz, 12 October 1944; and the president of Occidental College (Los Angeles), to Ruíz, 19 February 1943, MR Papers, box 1, file 2.

21. Copies of the speeches by Eduardo Quevedo and Manuel Ruíz contain, almost point for point, the same agenda outlined by the Coordinating Council for Latin-American Youth around 1943. Both Quevedo and Ruíz were executive members of this organization. See "First Latin-American Organization of Southern California Made Up of Representatives of Persons of Mexican Extraction from Community Level Organizations to Fight for the Following," ca. 1943, EQ Papers, M349, box 1, file 8.

22. Pagán, "'Who Are These Troublemakers?'"

23. Draft, "Latin-American Juvenile Delinquency in Los Angeles—Bomb or Bubble?," MR Papers, box 1, file 6, published in *Crime Prevention Digest* 1 (December 1942). No actual copy of the publication is known to exist.

24. There is a marked tone of reserve in the reports that Ruíz wrote about the success of the CCLAY in organizing youth activities. See "Coordinating Council for Latin American Youth Leadership Training Program," n.d., and "Narrative Report and Evaluation of the Conditioning Program Undertaken by the Coordinating Council of Latin-American Youth with the So-called 'Pachuco' Gangs in Los Angeles," 1942, in MR Papers, box 3, file 14.

25. Alice Greenfield [McGrath] to Bella Joseph, memo, 26 October 1943, SLDC Papers, box 3, file 4.

26. McGrath, oral history, 30–31.

27. McGrath, "Education of Alice McGrath," 100–102.

28. McWilliams, "Honorable in All Things," 111; McGrath, "Education of Alice McGrath," 180–82.

29. McWilliams served during the Culbert Olsen administration, 1938–42. McWilliams, "Honorable in All Things," 95–98.

30. Ibid., 158–60.

31. "Report of the Citizen's Committee," in Meier and Rivera, *Readings on La Raza*, 142.

32. McWilliams, "Honorable in All Things," 158–60.

33. Ibid., 149–50.

34. The name change was never marked by an official announcement, but documents and correspondence from the period indicate that the change occurred as early as 14 September 1943, although press release drafts still utilized the older name as late as 10 December 1943. See press release dated 14 September 1943, SDLC Papers, box 1, file 1, and press release draft, 10 December 1943, ibid., file 2.

35. McGrath, "Education of Alice McGrath," 121.

36. FBI document, AMG Papers, box 2, file 3.

37. McGrath, oral history, 15, 18, 77–78.

38. McGrath had only one semester at Los Angeles Community College. McGrath, "Education of Alice McGrath," 35.

39. McWilliams, "Honorable in All Things," 165–66.

40. McGrath, oral history, 55–57. See also the internal files of the SLDC Papers, box 3, file 4, "Memos." Among the office volunteers were Florence Fletcher, Evelyn Green, and Jeanette Salve. McGrath, "Education of Alice McGrath," 191–95, 206–7.

41. McGrath, oral history, 55–57.

42. Ibid., 30–32. McGrath, "Education of Alice McGrath," 191–93, 236. Adalina Olguín appears to have been the first bilingual office assistant, and María Lerma later filled the role.

43. McGrath, oral history, 30–31. McGrath, "Education of Alice McGrath," 143–44. Even some of the families of the imprisoned youths were reluctant to become greatly involved with the SLDC; McGrath, "Education of Alice McGrath," 171–72.

44. McGrath, "Education of Alice McGrath," 120–23.

45. Ibid., 192.

46. See SLDC Papers, box 4, file 2, "San Quentin Letters."

47. McGrath, "Education of Alice McGrath," 152, 162–65.

48. See press release, 20 September 1944, SLDC Papers, box 1, file 1.

49. Translated works included Franz Blei, *Fascinating Women, Sacred and Profane*, translated by S. Guy Endore (New York: Simon and Schuster, 1928); Andre Durenceau, *Beasts Called Wild*, translated by S. Guy Endore (New York: Farrar and Rinehart, 1930); and *Over-night*, translated from the German by S. Guy Endore (New York: Farrar and Rinehart, 1931). Biographies by Endore included *Casanova: His Known and Unknown Life*

(New York: J. Day, 1929); *The Man from Limbo* (New York: Farrar and Rinehart, 1930); and *The Sword of God: Jeanne d'Arc* (New York: Farrar and Rinehart, 1931). Works of fiction included *The Werewolf of Paris* (New York: Farrar and Rinehart, 1933) and *Babouk* (New York: Vanguard Press, 1934). Endore's screen credits include *Rumba* (Paramount Productions, 1935). His political tracts prior to the *Sleepy Lagoon Mystery* included *The Crime at Scottsboro* (Hollywood: Hollywood Scottsboro Committee, [ca. 1938]); *Let's Skip the Next War, and Win a Free House and Lot* (Hollywood: Hollywood Peace Forum, [ca. 1940]).

50. Endore, *Sleepy Lagoon Mystery*, 46.

51. See, for example, press releases, 13 December 1943, 25 March 1944, 15 May 1944, and 16 May 1944 and undated press release [ca. 16 March 1944], SLDC Papers, box 1, file 1.

52. Henry [Leyvas] to Alice Greenfield, 13 January 1943, SLDC Papers, box 4, file 2.

53. Chepe Ruíz to Alice Greenfield, 4 May 1944, SLDC Papers, box 4, file 2.

54. Undated press release draft, SLDC Papers, box 4, file 2; radio transcript, 18 February 1944, ibid., box 1, file 6; see also Manuel Ruíz [Reyes] to Alice [Greenfield], 28 April 1943, ibid., box 4, file 2.

55. McGrath, "Education of Alice McGrath," 140–42. Elizabeth Escobedo, correspondence with author.

56. Delia [Parra] to Alice [Greenfield], 13 September 1944, SLDC Papers, box 4, file 2. Cross-reference to undated press release, ibid., box 1, file 1; and Ysmael "Smiles" Parra to Alice Greenfield, 12 March 1944, 29 February 1944, and 9 December 1943, ibid., box 4, file 2.

57. McGrath, "Education of Alice McGrath," 58–59.

58. Undated press release [ca. 16 December 1943], SLDC Papers, box 1, file 1.

59. McGrath, "Education of Alice McGrath," 131–32.

60. Undated press release [ca. 16 December 1943], SLDC Papers, box 1, file 1; McGrath, "Education of Alice McGrath," 212.

61. McGrath, "Education of Alice McGrath," 125–26.

62. Press release, [ca. 15 May 1944], SLDC Papers, box 1, file 1.

63. Undated press release draft, "Other Kind of American," SLDC Papers, box 1, file 2; undated press release [ca. 15 May 1944], SLDC Papers, box 1, file 1.

64. McGrath, "Education of Alice McGrath," 186–87.

65. Ibid., 145–46.

66. Press release, early December 1943, SLDC Papers, box 1, file 1. Press release, 13 December 1943, ibid.

67. García, *Memories of Chicano History*, 120–24. McWilliams, "Honorable in All Things," 470.

68. Press release, 4 November 1943, SLDC Papers, box 1, file 1.

69. Undated press release draft, SLDC Papers, box 1, file 2. See also press releases, 28 March 1944, 9 May 1944, 8 June 1944, 18 August 1944, and 23 October 1944, ibid., file 1; press release draft, 9 November 1943, file 2.

70. Press release draft, 10 November 1943, SLDC Papers, box 1, file 2. Press release, 9 May 1944, file 1.

71. Undated press release, [ca. 15 May 1944], SLDC Papers, box 1, file 1. See also press release, 9 May [1944], ibid.

72. McGrath, "Education of Alice McGrath," 178.

73. Ibid., 179.

74. Press releases, 8 June 1944 and 27 July 1944, SLDC Papers, box 1, file 1.

75. See, for example, Smiles [Parra] to Alice [Greenfield McGrath], 11 July 1943 and 25 September 1943, SLDC Papers, box 1, file 1. See also Alice [Greenfield McGrath] to Manny [Delgadillo], 14 August 1944, ibid.

76. Manny Reyes to Alice Greenfield [McGrath], 18 February 1944, SLDC Papers, box 4, file 2; press release, 25 March 1944, ibid., box 1, file 1; McGrath, "Education of Alice McGrath," 148.

77. Press release, 25 March 1944, SLDC Papers, box 1, file 1. Smiles [Parra] to Alice [Greenfield McGrath], 25 January 1943, 16 May 1943, 11 July 1943, and 25 January 1944, ibid., box 4, file 2; McGrath, "Education of Alice McGrath," 166–67.

78. Biographical sketch: Robert Telles, SLDC Papers, box 4, file 4.

79. Smiles [Parra] to Alice [Greenfield McGrath], 9 December 1943, SLDC Papers, box 4, file 2; McGrath, "Education of Alice McGrath," 135–37.

80. Smiles [Parra] to Alice [Greenfield McGrath], 11 July 1943, SLDC Papers, box 4, file 2.

81. McGrath, "Education of Alice McGrath," 200, 211, 248.

82. Ibid., 138–39.

83. Alice Greenfield [McGrath] to Henry Leyvas, care of Warden Duffy, telegram, 4 October 1944, AMG Papers, box 5, file 5.

84. Press release, 20 October 1944, SLDC Papers, box 1, file 1. Press release draft, 23 October 1944, ibid., file 2.

85. Press release, 28 October 1944, SLDC Papers, box 1, file 1.

86. Press release draft, 27 October 1944, SLDC Papers, box 1, file 4.

87. McGrath, oral history.

88. Socorro Díaz Blanchard, interview.

89. Lino Díaz, oral history.

90. California Legislature, "'Zoot-Suit' Riots in Southern California."

91. Jon Watson convincingly argues in "Crossing the Color Lines in the City of Angels" that although the National Association for the Advancement of Colored People in Los Angeles took an active interest in the riot and trial, no long-term changes in policy or ties with Mexican Americans developed.

92. Shibley, "Sleepy Lagoon," 88; Steward, "Attorney George Shibley, Defender of Sirhan, Dies."

93. T. A. Chacon to Manuel Ruíz, 8 June 1943, MR Papers, box 1, file 2.

94. "Coordinating Council for Latin American Youth Leadership Training Program" and "Why a Newspaper Is Necessary for the Coordinating Council for Latin-American Youth," MR Papers, box 3, file 15.

95. The American Jewish Congress, the National Association for the Advancement of Colored People, the American Civil Liberties Union, the Japanese-American Citizens League, and the attorney general of California, Robert W. Kenny, filed briefs in support

of Méndez. See the case of *Méndez v. Westminster* in McWilliams, *North from Mexico*, 280–84; González, *Chicano Education in the Era of Segregation*, 136–56; Wells, "Activist, Interpreter, Statesman," 17.

96. See also Grajeda, "Pachuco in Chicano Poetry," 45–59.

97. The play ran for forty-one performances at the Winter Garden Theater in New York City, from 25 March 1979 to 29 April 1979. <www.ibdb.com> For a more complete discussion about the Zoot Suit production, see Broyles-González, *El Teatro Campesino*, 170–218.

98. Broyles-González, *El Teatro Campesino*, 199.

99. Fregoso, *Bronze Screen*, 32.

100. Ibid., 37.

101. Valdez, "Zoot Suit," in *Zoot Suit and Other Plays*, 26.

102. Grajeda, "Pachuco in Chicano Poetry," 45–59.

103. Romano, "Historical and Intellectual Presence of Mexican Americans," 12–14.

104. Montoya, "José Montoya, Pachuco Artist," 11. Neal, "Malcolm X—an Autobiography" and "Don't Say Goodbye to the Porkpie Hat," in *Hoodoo Hollerin' Bebop Ghosts*, 8–10, 19–24.

105. Acuña, *Occupied America*, 1st ed.; Cosgrove, "Zoot-Suit and Style Warfare"; Chibnall, "Whistle and Zoot," 57. See also Sánchez-Tranquilino and Tagg, "Pachuco's Flayed Hide"; Alvarez, "Power of the Zoot."

106. Gonzales, *I Am Joaquín/Yo soy Joaquín*, 1–22.

107. See, for example, <www.users.muohio.edu/reesr/edl334/style/styles/zoot. html> <www.sleepylagoon.com/LV00B/sleep031.htm>; <www.sleepylagoon.com/R/LV/10x98/1/005.htm>

108. <www.iso.gmu.edu/lsmithc/zoot.html> <www.ssc.wisc.edu/kwehr/211lect8 .pdf> See also <www.suavecito.com/history.htm> <www.brownpride.com/history/history.asp?a=losangeles/zootsuithistory> <www.sleepylagoon.com/H/sltrial.htm> <www.ethnomusic.ucla.edu/estudent/csharp/pachucos.html> <www.swingak.com/doc/his/zootriot.htm>

109. Evans, *Born for Liberty*, 221–29; May, *Pushing the Limits*, 23–37.

110. See, for example, Ortega, *Caló Orbis*, and Vigil, *Barrio Gangs*, 40.

111. Fregoso, *Bronze Screen*, 36.

### Epilogue

1. McGrath, oral history, 84.

2. [Ysmael] "Smiles" [Parra] to Jaime, 5 November 1943, SLDC Papers, box 4, file 4.

3. Bobby Telles estimated that the lead cars in the caravan parked about a quarter of a block from the Delgadillo house. Betty Zeiss estimated that the distance was about forty feet from the gate leading into the Delgadillo courtyard. Ann Kalustian estimated that Benny Alvarez parked about sixty feet from the body, making the distance from Alvarez's car and the courtyard gate one hundred feet. For the purposes of estimating time traveled from where the cars were parked to the courtyard gate, I use Zeiss's figure of forty feet, making a total of eighty feet traveled to and from the gate to their cars. Betty Zeiss stated emphatically that when the group of young people returned to their cars from the Delgadillo home, they were in a hurry but not running. See the following

testimonies from the Court Transcript: Robert Michael Telles, 3765; Betty Zeiss, 472–73, 730; and Ann Kalustian, 564.

4. Testimony of Betty Zeiss, Court Transcript, 477, 496.

5. Ibid., 496.

6. Ibid., 478–79, 480, 482, 693.

7. Gus Zamora also corroborated Zeiss's testimony. See testimony of Gus Zamora, Court Transcript, 3244–45.

8. Testimony of Manuel Reyes, Court Transcript, 4160–61, 4180–85.

9. Testimony of Gus Zamora, Court Transcript, 3721–22.

10. Testimony of Betty Zeiss, Court Transcript, 497.

11. Testimony of Gus Zamora, Court Transcript, 3244.

12. Testimony of Betty Zeiss, Court Transcript, 496, 488, 685; see also testimony of Gus Zamora, Court Transcript, 3244–45; testimony of Robert Michael Telles, Court Transcript, 3780–81; testimony of Manuel Reyes, Court Transcript, 4182.

13. Testimony of Victor Rodman Thompson, Court Transcript, 4397.

14. Ibid., 4398–99.

15. Ibid., 4400.

16. I am grateful to Linda Powell, EMT, for her insights in the probable condition of Díaz when Betty Zeiss and Dora Barrios found him.

17. Ben Van Tress argued this theory before the jury to no avail. See "Mexican Boys Convicted; Win-War Forces Shocked, Map Appeal Fight," *Peoples Daily World*, 14 January 1943, 1, 4.

18. For a complete description of the condition of Díaz's body and the conclusions of the coroner, see testimony of Frank R. Webb, chief autopsy surgeon for Los Angeles County, Court Transcript, 143–69.

19. Testimony of Victor Rodman Thompson, Court Transcript, 4398.

20. As quoted in "People & Events: Lorena Encinas (1922–1991)," Zoot Suit Riots Web site, American Experience, <www.pbs.org/wgbh/amex/zoot/eng_peopleevents/p_en cinas.html>

21. Ibid.

22. Testimony of Eleanor Coronado, Court Transcript, 2134–36; testimony of Remedios Parra, ibid., 2489, 2528–30.

23. Lino Díaz, interview.

24. See judgment of the appellate court, *People v. Zammora* 66 CA 2nd 166; P.2nd 180, 177. Years later McWilliams incorrectly remembered the number of companions with whom Díaz left the party: "he left the party in the company of a friend (who was never called as a witness; very odd circumstances, he was never called)." "Honorable in All Things," 157.

25. "Act to Curb Youth Gangs," *Los Angeles Evening Herald and Express*, 20 July 1942, A-3.

### Appendix

1. See, for example, Acuña, *Occupied America*, 3rd ed., 254.

2. *Pachuquismo*, translated literally, means "Pachuco-ism" and suggests that Pachucos had a distinct and coherent sense of who they were in relation to the larger society.

Luís Valdéz's stage and film productions of *Zoot Suit* are probably the most widely known example of this. Self-styled Pachuco artist José Montoya has toured more locally in the Southwest with his artwork illustrating the teleology between the Pachuco and the Chicano. See "The Traveling Pachuco," *Lowrider* 2, no. 4 (1978): 10–12.

3. McWilliams, *North from Mexico*, 244; Griffith, *American Me*, 20–21; Sánchez, "Dear Sir," 6 June 1943, EQ Papers, 349, box 1, file 11.

4. It is possible that Jones obtained his information from Ruíz himself, with whom he was in direct contact, and mistakenly attributed that information to documents in the Ruíz papers. Compare Jones's endnotes 27, 31, 35, 39, 40, 42, 49, 50–52, 61, 88–91, and 93 with the 7 June 1943 CCLAY handwritten notes and the 7 May 1943 (misdated) typewritten minutes of that meeting in MR Papers, box 3, file 1.

5. For further discussion, see Chapter 4, n. 52.

6. Broyles-González, *El Teatro Campesino*, 183, and *Aguilar v. Universal City Studios, Inc.* 174 Cal. App. 3rd 384 (1985).

7. Gutiérrez, *When Jesus Came the Corn Mothers Went Away*, xxix. Martin, *Keepers of the Game*. Dowd, *Spirited Resistance*.

# BIBLIOGRAPHY

## Oral Histories, Interviews, and Personal Correspondence

Blanchard, Socorro Díaz. Interview by Joseph Tovares while filming "Zoot-Suit Riot" for the PBS series *The American Experience*, Los Angeles, 13 September 1999. Transcript in possession of the author.

Debs, Ernest E. "Oral History Interview with Ernest E. Debs." Oral history transcript, interview by Carlos Vázsquez, 56–58. Oral History Program, University of California, Los Angeles, 1987/[1988?].

Díaz, Lino. Interview by Joseph Tovares while filming "Zoot-Suit Riot" for the PBS series *The American Experience*, Los Angeles, 13 September 1999. Transcript in possession of the author.

———. Oral history interview by author, Anaheim, Calif., 24 July 2000. Transcript in possession of the author.

Encinas, Ted. Correspondence with author. 7 February–24 August 1999. In possession of the author.

Kenney, Robert Walker. "My First Forty Years in California Politics, 1922–1962." Oral history transcript, interview by Doyce B. Nunis. Oral History Program, University of California, Los Angeles, ca. 1964.

Leyvas, Lupe. "Interview." *Lowrider* 2, no. 4 (1979): 22–23.

———. Telephone interview by author. 19 June 1996. Notes in possession of the author.

Leyvas, Rudy. Telephone interview by author. 21 June 1996. Notes in possession of the author.

Margolis, Ben. "Law and Social Conscience." Oral history transcript, interview by Michael S. Balter. Oral History Program. University of California, Los Angeles, 1987.

McCormick, LaRue. "Activist in the Radical Movement, 1930–1960: The International Labor Defense, the Communist Party." Introduction by Dorothy Ray Healey. An interview conducted by Malca Chall. California Women Political Leaders Oral History Project. Regional Oral History Office, Bancroft Library, University of California, Berkeley, 1980.

McGrath, Alice. "The Education of Alice McGrath." Oral history transcript, interview by Michael Balter. Oral History Program, University of California, Los Angeles, ca. 1987.

———. Oral history interview by author, Ventura, Calif., July 1992, May 1996. Transcript in possession of the author.

McWilliams, Carey. "Honorable in All Things." Oral history transcript, interview by

Joel Gardner. Oral History Program, University of California, Los Angeles, ca. 1982.

Murray, Chester, and Arthur Murray. Oral history interview by author, Los Angeles, Calif., 31 July 1992. Transcript in possession of the author.

Salter, Fred. Telephone interview by Desirée García. April 2000. Notes in possession of the author.

Torres, Theresa D. Correspondence with author. 29 January 1999–5 February 1999. In possession of the author.

Ynostroza, Henry. Interviews by Joseph Tovares and author while filming "Zoot-Suit Riot" for the PBS series *The American Experience*, Los Angeles, 13 September 1999. Notes in possession of the author.

Zamora, Mary Jane. Correspondence with author. 7 September 1997–12 January 1998. In possession of the author.

## Archival Collections

National Archives, Pacific Southwest Region, Laguna Niguel, Calif.

Records of the Naval Districts and Shore Establishments, Eleventh Naval District, Headquarters, San Diego, RG 181, Records of the Commandant's Office, Correspondence files 1921–47, file P8-5 1942 [2/2]; P8-5 1943 [1/4], [3/4]

Princeton University, Special Collections, Firestone Library

Fisher, Lloyd H. *The Problem of Violence: Observations on Race Conflict in Los Angeles*. Los Angeles: American Council on Race Relations, [ca. 1945].

Stanford University, Special Collections, Green Library

Manuel Ruíz Papers 295

Eduardo Quevedo Papers M349

University of California at Los Angeles, Special Collections, University Research Library

Guy S. Endore Papers 279

Alice Greenfield McGrath Papers 1490

Carey McWilliams Papers 1319

Carey McWilliams Papers 1243

*People v. Zammora et al.*, 66 C.A. 2d 166; 152 P.2d 180 (1944)

Sleepy Lagoon Defense Committee Papers

University of California at Los Angeles, Chicano Studies Resource Library

Ron López Papers, Sleepy Lagoon Material Collection

## Printed Primary Sources

Acosta, Dan G. "A Mexican Youth: We 'Pachucos' Fight for a Free World." *People's Daily World*, 10 June 1943.

"The Alpine Weekly Gossip." [N.p.], 30 March 1944. Original copy in possession of Alice McGrath.

Ayres, Edward Duran. "Statistics." In *Readings on La Raza: The Twentieth Century*, edited by Matt S. Meier and Feliciano Rivera, 127–33. New York: Hill and Wang, 1974.

Bass, Charlotta A. *Forty Years: Memoir from the Pages of a Newspaper*. Los Angeles: Charlotta A. Bass, 1960.

Bulosan, Carlos. *American Is in the Heart: A Personal History*. Introduction by Carey McWilliams. Seattle: University of Washington Press, 1988.

California Legislature. "'Zoot-Suit' Riots in Southern California." *Second Report: Un-American Activities in California*. Sacramento: 1945.

Calloway, Cab. *The New Cab Calloway's Cat-ologue*. N.p., 1939.

———. *The New Cab Calloway's Hepster's Dictionary: Language of Jive*. New York: Cab Calloway, 1944.

Calloway, Cab, and Bryant Rollins. *Of Minnie the Moocher and Me*. New York: Thomas Y. Crowell, 1976.

Davenport, Walter. "Swing It, Swing Shift!" *Collier's*, 22 August 1942, 24–30.

Dos Passos, John. "San Francisco Looks West: The City in Wartime." *Harper's Magazine* (March 1944): 328–38.

Endore, Guy. *The Sleepy Lagoon Mystery*. Los Angeles: Sleepy Lagoon Defense Committee, 1944.

Grant, Madison. *The Conquest of a Continent; Or, The Expansion of Races in America*. New York: Scribner's, 1933.

———. *The Passing of the Great Race; Or, The Racial Basis of European History*. New York: Scribner's, 1916.

Greenfield, Alice [McGrath]. *The Sleepy Lagoon Case: A Pageant of Prejudice*. Los Angeles: Citizens' Committee for the Defense of Mexican American Youth, 1943.

Griffith, Beatrice. *American Me*. Boston: Houghton Mifflin, 1948.

———. "Who Are the *Pachucos*?" *Pacific Spectator: A Journal of Interpretation* 3 (Summer 1947): 352–60.

Grow, O. W. "Keep in Trim with Our Armed Forces." *Barber's Journal* 45 (May 1942): 8–9.

Gulick, Sydney L. *The American Japanese Problem: A Study of the Racial Relations of the East and the West*. New York: Scribner's, 1914.

Himes, Chester B. "Zoot Riots Are Race Riots." *Crisis* 50 (July 1943): 200–201.

Huntington, Ellsworth. *A Decade of Progress in Eugenics: Scientific Papers of the Third International Congress of Eugenics, Held at American Museum of Natural History, New York, August 21–23, 1932*. Baltimore: Williams and Wilkins Co., 1934.

———. *International Eugenics Congress, Problems in Eugenics: Papers Communicated to the First International Eugenics Congress Held at the University of London, July 24th to 30th, 1912*. London: Eugenics Education Society, 1912.

———. *Scientific Papers of the Second International Congress of Eugenics Held at American Museum of Natural History, New York, September 22–28, 1921*. Baltimore: Williams and Wilkins Co., 1923.

———. *The Second International Exhibition of Eugenics Held September 22 to October 22, 1921, in Connection with the Second International Congress of Eugenics in the American Museum of Natural History, New York*. Baltimore: Williams and Wilkins Co., 1923.

———. *Tomorrow's Children: The Goal of Eugenics, by Ellsworth Huntington in*

Conjunction with the Directors of the American Eugenics Society. New York: Wiley, 1935.

Joyner, W. C. "Immigration Border Patrol." Our Sheriff and Police Journal 31 (June 1936): 23–25.

Kawakami, K. K. The Real Japanese Question. New York: Macmillan, 1921.

Lee, Ulysses, ed. The Negro Problem: A Series of Articles by Representative American Negroes of Today. New York: Arno Press, 1969.

Los Angeles County Grand Jury. "Final Report of the Los Angeles County Grand Jury for the Year 1942: Report of Special Committee on Problems of Mexican Youth of the 1942 Grand Jury of Los Angeles County."

———. "Final Report of the 1943 Los Angeles County Grand Jury: Report of the Special Committee on Racial Problems."

———. "Findings and Recommendations of the Grand Jury of Los Angles County (1943), Based upon Its Inquiry into Juvenile Crime and Delinquency in That County."

Malcolm X, with Alex Haley. The Autobiography of Malcolm X. New York: Grove, 1968.

McGucken, Joseph T., et al. "Report and Recommendations of the Citizens Committee, Los Angeles, June 12, 1943." In Readings on La Raza: The Twentieth Century, edited by Matt S. Meier and Feliciano Rivera, 138–44. New York: Hill and Wang, 1974.

McWilliams, Carey, et al. "Brief of the Friends of the Court." In the District Court of Appeal, Second Appellate District, State of California, Division One, The People of the State of California vs. Gus Zammora et al. In possession of the author.

Meier, Matt S., and Feliciano Rivera, eds. Readings on La Raza: The Twentieth Century. New York: Hill and Wang, 1974.

Mezzrow, Milton. Really the Blues. New York: Random House, 1946.

Mills, H. A. The Japanese Problem in the United States: An Investigation for the Commission on Relations with Japan, Appointed by the Federal Council of the Churches of Christ in America. New York: Macmillan, 1915.

Ponce, Mary Helen. Hoyt Street: An Autobiography. Albuquerque: University of New Mexico Press, 1993.

Quinn, Anthony. The Original Sin: A Self Portrait. Boston: Little, Brown, 1972.

Riley, B. F. The White Man's Burden: A Discussion of the Interracial Question. . . . 1910. New York: Negro Universities Press, 1969.

Shibley, George E. "Sleepy Lagoon: The True Story." Time, 15 January 1979, 88.

Strong, Edward K., Jr., The Second-Generation Japanese Problem. Palo Alto, Calif.: Stanford University Press, 1934.

United States. Bureau of the Census. Fifteenth Census of the United States: 1930, Population. Vol. 3, pt. 1, Washington, D.C.: Government Printing Office, 1932.

———. Fourteenth Census of the United States Taken in the Year 1920. Vol. 3, Population 1920. Washington, D.C.: Government Printing Office, 1922.

———. "Housing Statistics for Census Tracts: Los Angeles–Long Beach, California." Sixteenth Census of the United States, 1940. Washington, D.C.: Government Printing Office, 1943.

———. *Sixteenth Census of the United States: 1940, Population.* Vol. 2, pt. 1, Washington, D.C.: Government Printing Office, 1943.

———. *Sixteenth Census of the United States: 1940, Population.* Vol. 3, *The Labor Force: Occupation, Industry, Employment, and Income*, pt. 2, *Alabama-Indiana.* Washington, D.C.: Government Printing Office, 1943.

———. *Thirteenth Census of the United States Taken in the Year 1910.* Vol. 2, *Population 1910.* Washington, D.C.: Government Printing Office, 1913.

United States Department of Commerce. Weather Bureau. *Climatological Data for the United States by Sections.* 30:6. Washington, D.C.: Government Printing Office, 1943.

*United States Navy Regulations.* Washington, D.C.: Government Printing Office, 1941.

United States War Relocation Authority. *Segregation of Persons of Japanese Ancestry in Relocation Centers.* Washington, D.C.: War Relocation Authority, 1943.

Vignati, John. "Correct Technique for Gentlemen's Trimming and Styling." *Barber's Journal* 45 (November 1942): 6–7.

———. [No title]. *Barber's Journal* 45 (December 1942): 6–7.

Widney, Joseph Pomeroy. *Race Life of the Aryan People.* New York: Funk and Wagnalls, 1907.

———. *The Three Americas: Their Racial Past and the Dominant Racial Factors of Their Future.* Los Angeles: Pacific Publication Co., 1935.

Workers of the Writers' Program of the Works Projects Administration in Southern California. *Los Angeles: A Guide to the City and Its Environs.* New York: Hastings, 1941.

"Zoot Suit for My Sunday Gal." "Soundie" videorecording. Meyer Media Center, University of California, Los Angeles.

## Periodicals

*California Eagle* (Los Angeles)  
*Christian Century*  
*Collier's*  
*Crime Prevention Digest*  
*Eastside Journal*  
*La Opinión* (Los Angeles)  
*Life*  
*Los Angeles Daily News*  
*Los Angeles Examiner*  
*Los Angeles Evening Herald and Express*  

*Los Angeles Times*  
*Lowrider*  
*Mexican Voice*  
*Negro Digest: A Magazine of Negro Comment*  
*Newsweek*  
*Sensation*  
*P.M.*  
*People's Daily World*  
*Time*  
*Yank: The Army Weekly*

## Published Secondary Sources

Acuña, Rodolfo. *Anything but Mexican: Chicanos in Contemporary Los Angeles.* New York: Verso, 1996.

———. *Community under Siege: A Chronicle of Chicanos East of the Los Angeles River, 1945–1975.* Chicano Studies Research Center Publication, Monograph 11. Los Angeles: University of California, 1984.

————. *Occupied America: The Chicano's Struggle toward Liberation*. 1st ed. San Francisco: Canfield Press, 1972.

————. *Occupied America: A History of Chicanos*. 3rd ed. New York: Harper and Row, 1988.

Adler, Patricia Rae. "The 1943 Zoot Suit Riot: Brief Episode in a Long Conflict." In *An Awakened Minority: The Mexican Americans*, edited by Manuel P. Servin, 142–58. Beverly Hills: Glencoe Press, 1974.

Almaguer, Tomás. "Chicano Men: A Cartography of Homosexual Identity and Behavior." In *Men's Lives*, 4th ed., edited by Michael S. Kimmel and Michael A. Messner, 473–86. Boston: Allyn and Bacon, 1998.

————. "Ideological Distortions in Recent Chicano Historiography: The Internal Model and Chicano Historical Interpretation." *Aztlán, Chicano Journal of the Social Sciences and the Arts* 18 (Spring 1987): 7–28.

————. *Racial Fault Lines: The Historical Origins of White Supremacy in California*. Berkeley: University of California Press, 1994.

Alonso, Alejandro A. "African-American Street Gangs in Los Angeles." www.nagia.org/Crips_and_Bloods.htm#_ftn1.

Anderson, E. Frederick. *The Development of Leadership and Organization Building in the Black Community of Los Angeles from 1900 through World War II*. Saratoga, Calif.: Century Twenty One Publishing, 1980.

Arroyo, Luis Leonardo. "Chicano Participation in Organized Labor: The CIO in Los Angeles, 1938–1950." *Aztlán, Chicano Journal of the Social Sciences and the Arts* 6 (Summer 1975): 277–300.

Arroyo, Ronald D. "La Raza Influence in Jazz." *El Grito* 5 (Summer 1972): 80–84.

Avrich, Paul. *The Haymarket Tragedy*. Princeton, N.J.: Princeton University Press, 1984.

Baca, Judith F. "Luisa Moreno: Detail from the Great Wall of Los Angeles." *Pacific Historian* 30 (Summer 1986): cover.

Bachrach, Marion. "The Truth about Los Angeles." *New Masses*, 6 July 1943, 12–13.

Bakan, Michael B. "Way out West on Central: Jazz in the African American Community of Los Angeles before 1930." In *California Soul: Music of African Americans in the West*, edited by Jacqueline Cogdell Dje Dje and Eddie S. Meadows, 23–78. Berkeley: University of California Press, 1998.

Banay, Ralph. "A Psychiatrist Looks at the Zoot Suit." *Probation* 22 (February 1944): 81–85.

Barker, George Carpenter. "Pachuco: An American-Spanish Argot and Its Social Functions in Tucson, Arizona." *Social Science Bulletin* 18 (January 1950): 255–71.

Barrera, Mario. *Beyond Aztlán: Ethnic Autonomy in Comparative Perspective*. New York: Greenwood, 1988.

Barrett, Edward L. *The Tenney Committee: Legislative Investigation of Subversive Activities in California*. Ithaca, N.Y.: Cornell University Press, 1951.

Barron, Clarence W. *The Mexican Problem*. Boston: Houghton Mifflin, 1917.

Bederman, Gail. *Manliness and Civilization: A Cultural History of Gender and Race in the United States, 1880–1917*. Chicago: University of Chicago Press, 1995.

Bennett, David H. *The Party of Fear: From Nativist Movements to the New Right in American History*. Chapel Hill: University of North Carolina Press, 1988.

Berkhofer, Richard. *The White Man's Indian: Images of the American Indian from Columbus to the Present*. New York: Vintage, 1979.

Berube, Allan. *Coming Out under Fire: The History of Gay Men and Women in World War II*. New York: Free Press, 1990.

Blea, Irene I. *La Chicana at the Intersection of Race, Class, and Gender*. New York: Praeger, 1992.

———. *Toward a Chicano Social Science*. New York: Praeger, 1988.

Blum, John Morton. *V Was for Victory: Politics and American Culture during World War II*. New York: Harcourt Brace, 1976.

Bogardus, Emory. "Gangs of Mexican American Youth." *Sociology and Social Research* 28 (September–October 1943): 55–66.

"Boppin' on Central." *Heritage* (Winter 1994): 3–5.

Braddy, Haldeen. "Narcotic Argot along the Mexican Border." *American Speech* 30 (May 1955): 84–90.

———. "The Pachucos and Their Argot." *Southern Folklore Quarterly* 24 (December 1960): 255–71.

———. "Smugglers' Argot in the Southwest." *American Speech* 31 (February 1956): 96–101.

Brandt, Nat. *Harlem at War: The Black Experience in WWII*. Syracuse, N.Y.: Syracuse University Press, 1996.

Broyles-González, Yolanda. *El Teatro Campesino: Theater in the Chicano Movement*. Austin: University of Texas Press, 1994.

Brown, Sterling. *The Negro in American Fiction: Negro Poetry and Drama*. Washington, D.C.: "Associates" in Negro Folk Education, 1937. Reprint, New York: Arno Press and New York Times, 1969.

Burciaga, José Antonio. *Drink Cultura: Chicanismo*. Santa Barbara, Calif.: Capra Press, 1993.

California Youth Authority. *Report of Program and Progress, 1943–1948*. Sacramento, 1948.

Camarillo, Albert. *Chicanos in a Changing Society*. Cambridge: Harvard University Press, 1979.

Candelaria, Cordelia. *Chicano Poetry: A Critical Introduction*. Westport, Conn.: Greenwood, 1986.

Capeci, Dominic J., and Martha Wilkerson. *Layered Violence: The Detroit Rioters of 1943*. Jackson: University of Mississippi Press, 1991.

Carter, Everett. "Cultural History Written with Lightning: The Significance of 'The Birth of a Nation.'" In *Hollywood as Historian: American Film in a Cultural Context*, edited by Peter C. Rollins, 9–19. Lexington: University Press of Kentucky, 1983.

Castañeda, Jorge. "Mexico and California: The Paradox of Tolerance and Democratization." In *The California-Mexico Connection*, edited by Abraham F. Lowenthal and Katrina Burgess, 34–47. Cambridge: Cambridge University Press, 1993.

Cerda, Gilberto, Berta Cabaza, and Juliet Farias, eds. *Vocabulario español de Texas*. Austin, Tex.: University of Austin Press, 1953.

Cervantes, Lorna Dee. "Moonwalkers." In *Emplumada*, 58. Pittsburgh: University of Pittsburgh Press, 1981.

Chesler, Ellen. *Woman of Valor: Margaret Sanger and the Birth Control Movement in America*. New York: Simon and Schuster, 1992.

Chibnall, Steve. "Whistle and Zoot: The Changing Meaning of a Suit of Clothes." *History Workshop: A Journal of Socialist and Feminist Historians* 20 (Autumn 1985): 78–81.

Cobos, Rubén. *A Dictionary of New Mexico and Southern Colorado Spanish*. Santa Fe: Museum of New Mexico Press, 1983.

Collins, Keith E. *Black Los Angeles: The Maturing of a Ghetto, 1940–1950*. Saratoga, Calif.: Century Twenty One, 1980.

Coltharp, Lurline. *The Tongue of the Tirilones: A Linguistic Study of a Criminal Argot*. Tuscaloosa: University of Alabama Press, 1965.

Cooley, John R. *Savages and Naturals: Black Portraits by White Writers in Modern American Literature*. Newark: University of Delaware Press, 1982.

Cordry, Donald, and Dorothy Cordry. *Mexican Indian Costumes*. Austin: University of Texas Press, 1968.

Corona, Bert. "Chicano Scholars and Public Issues in the United States in the Eighties." In *History, Culture, and Society: Chicano Studies in the 1980s*, edited by Mario T. Garcia and Bert N. Corona, 11–18. National Association for Chicano Studies. Ypsilanti, Mich.: Bilingual Press/Editorial Bilingue, 1983.

Cosgrove, Stuart. "The Zoot-Suit and Style Warfare." *History Workshop: A Journal of Socialist and Feminist Historians* 18 (Autumn 1984): 77–91.

Cruz, Manuel. "Gang History: The First LA Gangs." *Lowrider* 2, no. 2 (1978): 32–35.

Daniels, Roger. *The Decision to Relocate the Japanese Americans*. Philadelphia: Lippincott, 1975.

Dash, Norma. *Yesterday's Los Angeles*. Seemann's Historic Cities Series 26. Miami, Fla.: E. A. Seemann Publishing, 1976.

Davis, Mike. *City of Quartz: Excavating the Future in Los Angeles*. New York: Vintage, 1992.

———. "Sunshine and the Open Shop: Ford and Darwin in 1920s Los Angeles." In *Metropolis in the Making: Los Angeles in the 1920s*, edited by Thomas Sitton and William Deverell, 96–122. Berkeley: University of California Press, 2001.

Dawley, Alan. *Struggles for Justice: Social Responsibility and the Liberal State*. Cambridge: Harvard University Press, Belknap Press, 1991.

Delgado, Abelardo. "Stupid America."In *Chicano: Twenty-five Pieces of a Chicano Mind*. Denver: Barrio Publications, 1969. http://xroads.virginia.edu/~UG01/voss/otherpoets.html

Delpar, Helen. *The Enormous Vogue of Things Mexican: Cultural Relations between the United States and Mexico, 1920–1935*. Tuscaloosa: University of Alabama Press, 1992.

Devlin, Rachel. "Female Juvenile Delinquency and the Problem of Sexual Authority in America, 1945–1965." In *Delinquents and Debutantes: Twentieth-Century American*

*Girls' Culture*, edited by Sherrie A. Inness, 83–106. New York: New York University Press, 1998.

Donaldson, Mike. "What Is Hegemonic Masculinity?" *Theory and Society* 22, no. 5 (1993): 645–46.

Dowd, Gregory. *Spirited Resistance: The North American Indian Struggle for Unity, 1745–1815*. Baltimore: Johns Hopkins University Press, 1992.

Dower, John. *War without Mercy*. New York: Random House, 1986.

Doyle, Laura. "Of Race and Woman: Eugenics, Motherhood, and Racial Patriarchy." In *Bordering on the Body: The Racial Matrix of Modern Fiction and Culture*, edited by Laura Doyle, 3–34. New York: Oxford University Press, 1994.

Eastman, Ralph. "'Pitchin' Up a Boogie': African American Musicians, Nightlife, and Music Venues in Los Angeles, 1930–1945." In *California Soul: Music of African Americans in the West*, edited by Jacqueline Cogdell Dje Dje and Eddie S. Meadows, 70–103. Berkeley: University of California Press, 1998.

Ellington, John. *Protecting Our Children from Criminal Careers*. New York: Prentice Hall, 1948.

Ellison, Ralph. "Editorial Comment." *Negro Quarterly* 1 (Winter–Spring 1943): 301.

Engh, Michael E., S.J. "Practically Every Religion Being Represented." In *Metropolis in the Making: Los Angeles in the 1920s*, edited by Thomas Sitton and William Deverell, 201–19. Berkeley: University of California Press, 2001.

Engle, Gary D., ed. *This Grotesque Essence: Plays from the American Minstrel Stage*. Baton Rouge: Louisiana State University Press, 1978.

Erenberg, Lewis A. *Swingin' the Dream: Big Band Jazz and the Rebirth of the Nation*. Chicago: University of Chicago Press, 1998.

Erenberg, Lewis A., and Susan E. Hirsch, eds. *The War in American Culture: Society and Consciousness during World War II*. Chicago: University of Chicago Press, 1996.

Escobar, Edward J. *Race, Police, and the Making of a Political Identity: Mexican Americans and the Los Angeles Police Department, 1900–1945*. Berkeley: University of California Press, 1999.

Evans, Sara M. *Born for Liberty: A History of Women in America*. New York: Free Press, 1989.

Fields, Rick. *How the Swans Came to the Lake: A Narrative History of Buddhism in America*. 3rd rev. ed. Boston: Shambhala Publications, 1992.

Flamming, Douglas. "The Star of Ethiopia and the NAACP: Pageantry, Politics, and the Los Angeles African American Community." In *Metropolis in the Making: Los Angeles in the 1920s*, edited by Thomas Sitton and William Deverell, 145–60. Berkeley: University of California Press, 2001.

Fogelson, Robert M. *The Fragmented Metropolis: Los Angeles, 1850–1930*. Cambridge: Harvard University Press, 1967.

Foley, Neil. "Becoming Hispanic: Mexican Americans and the Faustian Pact with Whiteness." In *Reflexiones 1997: New Directions in Mexican American Studies*, edited by Neil Foley, 53–70. Austin: Center for Mexican American Studies, University of Texas, 1998.

———. *The White Scourge: Mexicans, Blacks, and Poor Whites in Texas Cotton Culture*. Berkeley: University of California Press, 1997.

Ford, John. *Thirty Explosive Years in Los Angeles County*. San Marino, Calif.: Huntington Library, 1961.

Fregoso, Rosa Linda. *The Bronze Screen: Chicana and Chicano Film Culture*. Minneapolis: University of Minnesota Press, 1993.

———. "Hanging Out with the Homegirls? Allison Anders's 'Mi Vida Loca.'" Race in Contemporary American Cinema: Part 4. *Cineaste* 21 (Summer 1995): 36–37.

Frost, H. Gordon. *The Gentlemen's Club: The Story of Prostitution in El Paso*. El Paso, Tex.: Mangan Books, 1983.

Fuller, Elizabeth. *The Mexican Housing Problem in Los Angeles*. Studies in Sociology, Monograph 17. Los Angeles: University of Southern California Press, 1920.

Galván, Roberto, and Richard Teschner, eds. *El diccionario del Español chicano*. Lincoln, Ill.: Voluntad Publishers, 1985.

García, Mario T. *Desert Immigrants: The Mexicans of El Paso, 1880–1920*. New Haven: Yale University Press, 1981.

———. *Memories of Chicano History: The Life and Narrative of Bert Corona*. Berkeley: University of California Press, 1994.

———. *Mexican Americans: Leadership, Ideology and Identity, 1930–1960*. New Haven: Yale University Press, 1989.

García, Mario T., and Francisco Lomeli, eds. *History, Culture, and Society: Chicano Studies in the 1980s*. National Association for Chicano Studies. Ypsilanti, Mich.: Bilingual Press/Editorial Bilingue, 1983.

Gatewood, Willard B. *Aristocrats of Color: The Black Elite, 1880–1920*. Bloomington: University of Indiana Press, 1990.

Gayne, A. R., C. Fries Jr., K. Segerstrom, R. F. Black, and I. F. Wilson. *Geology and Mineral Deposits of the Pachuca—Real del Monte District, State of Hidalgo, Mexico: With a Section on Historical Background by Alan Probert*. Mexico City: Consejo de Recursos Naturales no Renovables Publicación, 1963.

George, Lynell. *No Crystal Stair: African-Americans in the City of Angels*. New York: Verso, 1992.

Gilbert, James. *A Cycle of Outrage: America's Reaction to the Juvenile Delinquent*. New York: Oxford University Press, 1986.

Godlewska, Anne, and Neil Smith, eds. *Geography and Empire*. Oxford, England: Blackwell, 1994.

Gómez, Alma, Cherríe Moraga, and Mariana Romo-Carmona. *Cuentos: Stories by Latinas*. New York: Kitchen Table Press, 1983.

Gómez, Laura E. *From Barrio Boys to College Boys: Ethnic Identity, Ethnic Organizations, and the Mexican American Elite: The Cases of Ernesto Galarza and Manuel Ruiz, Jr*. Working Paper Series, Stanford Center for Chicano Research, No. 25. Stanford, Calif.: Stanford Center for Chicano Research, 1989.

Gómez-Quiñones, Juan. *Chicano Politics: Reality and Promise, 1940–1990*. Albuquerque: University of New Mexico Press, 1990.

———. *Mexican American Labor, 1790–1990*. Albuquerque: University of New Mexico Press, 1994.

———. "Mexican Immigration to the United States, 1848–1980: An Overview." In

*Chicano Studies: A Multidisciplinary Approach*, edited by E. García, F. Lomelí, and I. Ortíz, 56–78. New York: Teacher's College Press, 1984.

———. *Roots of Chicano Politics, 1600–1940*. Albuquerque: University of New Mexico Press, 1994.

Gonzales, Rodolpho "Corky." *I Am Joaquín/Yo soy Joaquín*. New York: Bantam Books, 1972.

González, Gilbert G. *Chicano Education in the Era of Segregation*. Philadelphia: Balch Institute Press, 1990.

———. "Factors Relating to the Property Ownership of Chicanos in Lincoln Heights, Los Angeles." *Aztlán, Chicano Journal of the Social Sciences and the Arts* 2 (Fall 1971): 111–14.

Gonzalez, Rafael Jesus. "Pachuco: The Birth of a Creole Language." *Arizona Quarterly* 23 (Winter 1967), 343–56.

Grajeda, Rafael. "The Pachuco in Chicano Poetry: The Process of Legend-Creation." *Revista Chicano-Riqueña* 8, no. 4 (1988): 45–59.

Gray, Madeline. *Margaret Sanger: A Biography of the Champion of Birth Control*. New York: R. Marek, 1979.

Gregory, James N. *American Exodus: The Dust Bowl Migration and Oakie Culture in California*. New York: Oxford University Press, 1989.

Griswold del Castillo, Richard, and Carlos M. Larralde. "Luisa Moreno and the Beginnings of the Mexican American Civil Rights Movement in San Diego." *Journal of San Diego History* 43 (Summer 1997). www.sandiegohistory.org/journal/97summer/summer97/html.

Griswold del Castillo, Richard, Teresa McKenna, and Yvonne Yarbro-Bejarano. *Chicano Art: Resistance and Affirmation, 1965–1985*. Los Angeles: Wight Art Gallery, University of California, 1991.

Grodzins, Morton. *Americans Betrayed: Politics and the Japanese Evacuation*. Chicago: University of Chicago Press, 1949.

Guerin-Gonzales, Camille. *Mexican Workers and American Dreams: Immigration, Repatriation, and California Farm Labor, 1900–1939*. New Brunswick, N.J.: Rutgers University Press, 1994.

Guevara, Ruben. "The View from the Sixth Street Bridge: The History of Chicano Rock." In *Rock 'n' Roll Confidential Report and Inside the Real World of Rock*, edited by Dave Marsh, 113–26. New York: Pantheon, 1985.

Gutiérrez, David G. *Walls and Mirrors: Mexican Americans, Mexican Immigrants, and the Politics of Ethnicity*. Berkeley: University of California Press, 1995.

Gutiérrez, Ramón. *When Jesus Came the Corn Mothers Went Away: Marriage, Sexuality, and Power in New Mexico, 1500–1846*. Stanford, Calif.: Stanford University Press, 1991.

Guzmán, Ralph C. *The Political Socialization of the Mexican American People*. New York: Arno Press, 1976.

Haley, Lindsey. "Pachuco Boogie." *Lowrider* (June 1985): 34–37.

Hanke, Robert. "Theorizing Masculinity with/in Media." *Communication Theory* 8 (May 1998): 183–203.

Hansen, Arthur A. *Demon Dogs: Cultural Deviance and Community Control in the Japanese-American Evacuation*. Ann Arbor, Mich.: Western Conference of the Association for Asian Studies, 1983.

Harris, Mary G. *Cholas: Latino Girls and Gangs*. New York: AMS Press, 1988.

Hartmann, Susan M. *The Homefront and Beyond: American Women in the 1940s*. Boston: Twayne, 1982.

Hasian, Marouf Arif, Jr. *The Rhetoric of Eugenics in Anglo-American Thought*. Athens: University of Georgia Press, 1996.

Hernández, Guillermo E. *Chicano Satire: A Study in Literary Culture*. Austin: University of Texas Press, 1991.

Hernández-Chávez, Eduardo, et al. *El Lenguaje de los Chicanos: Regional and Social Characteristics*. Arlington, Va.: Center for Applied Linguistics, 1975.

Hess, Gary R. *The United States at War, 1941–1945*. Arlington Heights, Ill.: Harlan Davidson, 1986.

Higham, John. *Strangers in the Land: Patterns of American Nativism, 1860–1925*. New York: Atheneum, 1965.

Hill, Laurence Landreth. *La Reina: Los Angeles in Three Centuries*. Los Angeles: Security Trust and Savings Bank, 1929.

Hobsbawm, Eric J. *The Jazz Scene: Francis Newton*. New York: Da Capo Press, 1975.

Hoffman, Abraham. *Unwanted Mexican Americans in the Great Depression: Repatriation Pressures, 1929–1939*. Tucson: University of Arizona Press, 1977.

Honey, Maureen. *Creating Rosie the Riveter: Class, Gender, and Propaganda during World War II*. Amherst: University of Massachusetts Press, 1984.

Housing Authority of the City of Los Angeles. *Now We Plan*. Los Angeles: Housing Authority of the City of Los Angeles, 1940.

Howser, Fred N. "Report on Juvenile Deliquency in Wartime Los Angeles." Mimeograph. County of Los Angeles, 1943.

Hoxie, Frederick E. *A Final Promise: The Campaign to Assimilate the Indians, 1880–1920*. Lincoln: University of Nebraska Press, 1984.

Hylan, Arnold. *Los Angeles before the Freeways, 1850–1950*. Los Angeles: Dawson's Book Shop, 1981.

Irons, Peter H. *Justice at War*. New York: Oxford University Press, 1983.

Jackson, Kenneth T. *Crabgrass Frontier: The Suburbanization of the United States*. New York: Oxford University Press, 1985.

Jackson, Peter, and Susan J. Smith, eds. *Social Interaction and Ethnic Segregation*. London: Academic Press, 1981.

Jacobson, Matthew Frye. *Barbarian Virtues: The United States Encounters Foreign Peoples at Home and Abroad, 1876–1917*. New York: Hill and Wang, 2000.

James, Thomas. *Exile Within: The Schooling of Japanese Americans, 1942–1945*. Cambridge: Harvard University Press, 1987.

Jiménez, Carlos M. *The Mexican American Heritage*. 2nd ed. Berkeley, Calif.: TQS Publications, 1994.

Jones, Soloman James. *The Government Riots of Los Angeles, June 1943*. San Francisco: R and E Research Associates, 1973.

Jonnes, Jill. *Hep-Cats, Narcs, and Pipe Dreams: A History of America's Romance with Illegal Drugs*. New York: Scribner's, 1996.

Keating, Stephen J. "Understanding the Minority Group Deliquent." *California Youth Authority Quarterly* 1 (Winter 1948): 26–36.

Keller, Gary D. *Chicano Cinema: Research, Reviews, Resources*. Hispanic Research Center, Arizona State University. Tempe, Ariz.: Bilingual Review Press, 1985.

Keller, Morton. *Affairs of State: Public Life in Late Nineteenth Century America*. Cambridge: Harvard University Press, Belknap Press, 1977.

Kelley, Robin D. G. "'We Are Not What We Seem': Rethinking Black Working-Class Opposition in the Jim Crow South." *Journal of American History* 80 (June 1993): 75–112.

Kennedy, David M. *Birth Control in America: The Career of Margaret Sanger*. New Haven: Yale University Press, 1973.

Kimmel, Michael S. *Manhood in America: A Cultural History*. New York: Free Press, 1996.

Kimmel, Michael S., and Michael A. Messner. *Men's Lives*. 4th ed. Boston: Allyn and Bacon, 1998.

Klein, Norman M., and Martin J. Schiesl. *Twentieth Century Los Angeles: Power, Promotion, and Social Conflict*. Claremont, Calif.: Regina Books, 1990.

Knight, Alan. *The Mexican Revolution*. Vol. 2, *Counter-Revolution and Reconstruction*. Lincoln: University of Nebraska Press, 1990.

Knobel, Dale T. *America for the Americans: The Nativist Movement in the United States*. New York: Twayne, 1996.

Kuhl, Stefan. *The Nazi Connection: Eugenics, American Racism, and German National Socialism*. New York: Oxford University Press, 1994.

Lears, T. J. *Fables of Abundance: A Cultural History of Advertising in America*. New York: Basic Books, 1994.

———. *No Place of Grace: Antimodernism and the Transformation of American Culture, 1880–1920*. New York: Pantheon, 1981.

Lears, T. J. Jackson, and Richard W. Fox, eds. *The Culture of Consumption: Critical Essays in American History, 1880–1980*. New York: Pantheon, 1983.

Lee, Alfred McClung, and Norman D. Humphrey. *Race Riot, Detroit 1943*. New York: Octagon Books, 1968.

Lehne, Gregory K. "Homophobia among Men: Supporting and Defining the Male Role." In *Men's Lives*, edited by Michael S. Kimmel and Michael A. Messner, 4th ed., 237–49. Boston: Allyn and Bacon, 1998.

Leonard, William T. *Masquerade in Black*. Metuchen, N.J.: Scarecrow Press, 1986.

Lewontin, R. C., Steven Rose, and Leon J. Kamin. *Not in Our Genes: Biology, Ideology, and Human Nature*. New York: Pantheon, 1984.

Lhamon, W. T., Jr. *Raising Cain: Blackface Performance from Jim Crow to Hip Hop*. Cambridge: Harvard University Press, 1998.

Lingeman, Richard. *Don't You Know There's a War On? The American Home Front, 1941–1945*. New York: Putnam, 1970.

Lipsitz, George. *Class and Culture in Cold War America: A Rainbow at Midnight*. South Haley, Mass.: Bergin and Garvey, 1982.

————. "Creating Dangerously: The Blues Life of Johnny Otis." Introduction to Johnny Otis, *Upside Your Head! Rhythm and Blues on Central Avenue*. Hanover, N.H.: Wesleyan University Press, 1993.

————. "Land of a Thousand Dances: Youth, Minorities, and the Rise of Rock and Roll." In *Recasting America: Culture and Politics in the Age of Cold War*, edited by Lary May, 217–72. Chicago: University of Chicago Press, 1989.

List, Christine. *Chicano Images: Refiguring Ethnicity in Mainstream Film*. New York: Garland, 1996.

*Los Angeles Bench and Bar*. Centennial ed., 1949–50. Los Angeles: Wilson and Sons, 1950.

Los Angeles Committee for Interracial Progress. *Los Angeles Committee for Interracial Progress: Origin and Functions*. Los Angeles: The Committee, 1945.

Lowenthal, Abraham F., and Katrina Burgess. *The California-Mexico Connection*. Cambridge: Cambridge University Press, 1993.

Luckenbill, Dan. *The Pachuco Era: Catalog of an Exhibit, University Research Library, September–December 1990*. Los Angeles: University of California, Department of Special Collections, University Research Library, 1990.

MacCann, Donnarae, and Gloria Woodard, eds. *The Black American in Books for Children: Readings in Racism*. 2nd ed. Metuchen, N.J.: Scarecrow Press, 1985.

Macleod, David I. *Building Character in the American Boy: The Boy Scouts, YMCA, and Their Forerunners, 1870–1920*. Madison: University of Wisconsin Press, 1983.

Madrid-Barela, Arturo. "In Search of the Authentic Pachuco: An Interpretive Essay." *Aztlán, Chicano Journal of the Social Sciences and the Arts* 4 (Spring 1973): 31–59.

Martin, Calvin. *Keepers of the Game: Indian-Animal Relationships and the Fur Trade*. Berkeley: University of California Press, 1978.

*The Martindale-Hubbell Law Directory*. 74th annual ed. Vol. 1. Summit, N.J.: Martindale-Hubble, 1942.

Martínez, Oscar J. *Border Boom Town: Ciudad Juarez since 1848*. Austin: University of Texas Press, 1978.

Matthews, Donald G. "The Southern Rite of Human Sacrifice." *Journal of Southern Religion* 3 (2000). <http://jsr.as.wvu.edu/jsrlink3.htm>

Maurer, David W. "The Argot of the Underworld Narcotic Addict." *American Speech* 11 (April 1936): 128–36.

————. "Teen-age Hophead Jargon." *American Speech* 27 (February 1952): 23–31.

May, Elaine Tyler. *Pushing the Limits: American Women, 1940–1961*. New York: Oxford University Press, 1994.

————. "Rosie the Riveter Gets Married." In *The War in American Culture*, edited by Lewis A. Erenberg and Susan E. Hirsch, 128–43. Chicago: University of Chicago Press, 1996.

Mazón, Mauricio. *The Zoot Suit Riots: The Psychology of Symbolic Annihilation*. Austin: University of Texas, 1984.

McCarthy, Thomas J. "Report from Los Angeles." *Commonweal*, 25 June 1943, 243–44.

McDonagh, Edward C. "Status Levels of Mexicans." *Sociology and Social Research* 33 (July 1949): 449–59.

McWilliams, Carey. "The Los Angeles Archipelago." *Science and Society* 10 (Winter 1946): 46.

———. "Los Angeles' Pachuco Gangs." *New Republic*, 18 January 1943, 76–77.

———. *North from Mexico: The Spanish-Speaking People of the United States*. Philadelphia: Lippincott, 1949.

———. "Pachuco Troubles." *Inter-American* 2 (August 1943): 5–6.

———. "The Story behind the 'Zoot War.'" *P.M.*, 12 June 1943, 1.

———. "The Zoot Suit Riots." *New Republic*, 21 June 1943, 818–20.

Melendez, Rudolph. *Pachuco Mark*. New York: Grossmont Press, 1976.

Meyer, Michael C., and William L. Sherman. *The Course of Mexican History*. New York: Oxford University Press, 1987.

Meyer, Stephen Grant. *As Long As They Don't Move Next Door: Segregation and Racial Conflict in American Neighborhoods*. Lanham, Md.: Rowman, 2000.

Milkman, Ruth. *Gender at Work: The Dynamics of Job Segregation by Sex during World War II*. Urbana: University of Illinois Press, 1987.

Monroy, Douglas. "'Our Children Get So Different Here': Film, Fashion, Popular Culture, and the Process of Cultural Syncretization in Mexican Los Angeles, 1900–1935." *Aztlán, Chicano Journal of the Social Sciences and the Arts* 19:1 (1988–90): 79–108.

———. *Rebirth: Mexican Los Angeles from the Great Migration to the Great Depression*. Berkeley: University of California Press, 1999.

Montejano, David. *Anglos and Mexicans in the Making of Texas, 1836–1986*. Austin: University of Texas, 1987.

———. "Anglos and Mexicans in the Twenty First Century." Occasional Paper No. 3, Julian Samora Research Institute, Michigan State University, August 1992.

Montoya, José. "El Louie." *Rascatripas* 2 (1970). Reprinted in *Aztlán, Chicano Journal of the Social Sciences and the Arts* 4 (Spring 1973): 53–55.

———. "José Montoya, Pachuco Artist." *Lowrider* 2, no. 4 (1978): 11.

Moore, Joan W. "An Assessment of Hispanic Poverty: Does an Hispanic Underclass Exist?" *Tomas Rivera Center Report* 2, no. 1 (1988).

———. *Going Down to the Barrio: Homeboys and Homegirls in Change*. Philadelphia: Temple University Press, 1991.

———. "Is There an Hispanic Underclass?" *Social Science Quarterly* 70 (June 1989): 265–84.

Moore, Joan W., et al. *Homeboys, Gangs, Drugs and Prison in the Barrios of Los Angeles*. Philadelphia: Temple University Press, 1978.

Morales, Armando. *Ando Sagrando (I Am Bleeding): A Study of Mexican American–Police Conflicts*. La Puente, Calif.: Perspectiva Publications, 1972.

Morales, Rebecca, and Frank Bonilla. "Restructuring and the New Inequality." In *Latinos in a Changing U.S. Economy*, edited by Rebecca Morales and Frank Bonilla, 1–27. Newbury Park, Calif.: Sage, 1993.

Morín, Raul. *Among the Valiant: Mexican Americans in WW II and Korea*. Los Angeles: Borden Publishing, 1963.

Morrison, Toni. *Playing in the Dark: Whiteness and the Literary Imagination*. Cambridge: Harvard University Press, 1992.

Navarrette, Ruben, Jr. *A Darker Shade of Crimson: Odyssey of a Harvard Chicano*. New York: Bantam Books, 1993.

Neal, Larry. "Don't Say Goodbye to the Porkpie Hat." In *Hoodoo Hollerin' Bebop Ghosts*, 19–24. Washington, D.C.: Howard University Press, 1974.

———. "Ellison's Zoot Suit." In *Ralph Ellison: A Collection of Critical Essays*, edited by John Hersey, 68–69. Englewood Cliffs, N.J.: Prentice Hall, 1974.

———. "Malcolm X—an Autobiography." In *Hoodoo Hollerin' Bebop Ghosts*, 8–10. Washington, D.C.: Howard University Press, 1974.

Nelson, John Herbert. *The Negro Character in American Literature*. College Park, Md.: McGrath, 1926.

Nelson, Victor Folke. "Addenda to 'Junker Lingo.'" *American Speech* 8 (October 1933): 34.

Newby, I. A. *The Development of Segregationist Thought*. Homewood, Ill.: Dorsey Press, 1968.

Nicolaides, Becky. *My Blue Heaven: Life and Politics in the Working-Class Suburbs of Los Angeles, 1920–1965*. Chicago: University of Chicago Press, 2002.

Noriega, Chon, ed. *Chicanos and Film: Representation and Resistance*. Minneapolis: University of Minnesota Press, 1992.

Oles, James. *South of the Border: Mexico in the American Imagination, 1914–1947*. Washington, D.C.: Smithsonian Institution Press, 1993.

Ortega, Aldofo. *Caló Orbis: Semiotics of a Chicano Language Variety*. New York: Peter Lang, 1991.

Otis, Johnny. *Upside Your Head! Rhythm and Blues on Central Avenue*. Hanover, N.H.: Wesleyan University Press, 1993.

Pagán, Eduardo Obregón. "Los Angeles GeoPolitics and the Zoot-Suit Riot, 1943." *Journal of Social Science History* 24 (Spring 2000): 223–56.

Painter, Nell Irvin. *Standing at Armageddon: United States, 1877–1919*. New York: W. W. Norton, 1987.

Pallen, Agnes. "Mexicans in Los Angeles." *Los Angeles Times*, 3 May 1925.

Pascoe, Peggy. "Miscegenation Law, Court Cases, and Ideologies of 'Race' in Twentieth-Century America." *Journal of American History* 83 (June 1996): 44–69.

Paz, Octavio. *Labyrinth of Solitude, The Other Mexico, and Other Essays*. New York: Grove, 1985.

Pepper, Art, and Laurie Pepper. *Straight Life: The Story of Art Pepper*. Updated version. New York: Da Capo Press, 1994.

Peretti, Burton W. *The Creation of Jazz: Music, Race, and Culture in Urban America*. Urbana: University of Illinois Press, 1992.

Perkins, Clifford Alan. *Border Patrol: With the U.S. Immigration Service on the Mexican Boundary, 1910–1954*. El Paso: Texas Western Press, 1978.

Phillips, Susan A. *Wallbangin': Graffiti and Gangs in L.A.* Chicago: University of Chicago Press, 1999.

Placéncia, Luis F. B. "Low Riding in the Southwest: Cultural symbols in the Mexican Community." In *History, Culture, and Society: Chicano Studies in the 1980s*, ed. Mario T. García and Francisco Lomeli, 141–75. National Association for Chicano Studies. Ypsilanti, Mich.: Bilingual Press/Editorial Bilingue, 1983.

Platt, Anthony M. *The Child Savers: The Invention of Delinquency*. Chicago: University of Chicago Press, 1977.

Polenberg, Richard. *War and Society: The United States, 1941–1945*. Philadelphia: Lippincott, 1972.

———, ed. *America at War: The Home Front, 1941–1945*. Englewood Cliffs, N.J.: Prentice Hall, 1968.

Polkihorn, Harry, Alfredo Velasco, and Malcolm Lambert. *El libro de caló: The Dictionary of Chicano Slang*. Mountainview, Calif.: Florentino Press, 1986.

Ponce, Mary Helen. *Hoyt Street: An Autobiography*. Albuquerque: University of New Mexico Press: 1993.

"Portent of Storm." *Christian Century*, 23 June 1943, 735–36.

Porter, Roy, and David Keller. *There and Back: The Roy Porter Story*. Baton Rouge: Louisiana State University Press, 1991.

Public Administration Service. *The Organization and Administration of the Housing Authority of the City of Los Angeles*. Boston: Public Administration Service, 1941.

Rak, Mary Kidder. *Border Patrol*. Boston: Houghton Mifflin, 1938.

Ramírez, Catherine. "Crimes of Fashion: The Pachuca and Chicana Style Politics." *Meridians: Feminism, Race, Transnationalism* 2 (March 2002): 1–35.

Redl, Fritz. "Zoot Suits: An Interpretation." *Survey Monthly* 79 (October 1943): 259–62.

Ríos-Bustamante, Antonio. "Latino Participation in the Hollywood Film Industry, 1911–1945." In *Chicanos and Film: Representation and Resistance*, edited by Chon Noriega, 21–32. Minneapolis: University of Minnesota Press, 1992.

Ríos-Bustamante, Antonio, and Pedro Castillo. *An Illustrated History of Mexican Los Angeles, 1781–1985*. Chicano Studies Research Center Publication, Monograph 12. Los Angeles: University of California, 1986.

Rischin, Moses. "Continuities and Discontinuities in Spanish-Speaking California." In *Ethnic Conflict in California History*, edited by Charles Wollenberg, 43–60. Los Angeles: Tinnon-Brown, 1970.

Rodríguez, Luís J. *Always Running: La Vida Loca—Gang Days in L.A*. Willimantic, Conn.: Curbstone Press, 1994.

Rodríguez, Roberto. "Pachuco Yo, Ese." *Lowrider* 2, no. 4 (1979): 19–20.

Romano, Octavio. "The Historical and Intellectual Presence of Mexican Americans." *El Grito* 2 (Winter 1969): 12–14.

Romo, Ricardo. *East Los Angeles: History of a Barrio*. Austin, Tex.: University of Austin Press, 1983.

———. "Southern California and the Origins of Latino Civil Rights Activism." *Western Legal History* 3 (Summer/Fall 1990): 299–406.

———. "The Urbanization of Southwestern Chicanos in the Early Twentieth Century." In *New Directions in Chicano Scholarship*, edited by Ricardo Romo and Raymund Paredes, 183–208. Chicano Studies Monograph Series. La Jolla: University of California, San Diego, 1978.

Rosales, F. Arturo. *Pobre Raza! Violence, Justice, and Mobilization among México Lindo Immigrants, 1900–1936*. Austin: University of Texas Press, 1999.

Rosenau, James N. "Coherent Connection or Commonplace Contiguity?" In

*California-Mexico Connection*, edited by Abraham F. Lowenthal and Katrina Burgess, 3–33. Cambridge: Cambridge University Press, 1993.

Rosenthal, Michael. *The Character Factory: Baden-Powell and the Origins of the Boy Scout Movement*. New York: Pantheon, 1986.

Ruíz, Vicki L. *Cannery Women, Cannery Lives: Mexican Women, Unionization, and the California Food Processing Industry, 1930–1950*. Albuquerque: University of New Mexico Press, 1987.

———. "The Flapper and the Chaperone: Cultural Constructions of Identity and Heterosexual Politics among Adolescent Mexican American Women, 1920–1950." In *Delinquents and Debutantes: Twentieth-Century American Girls' Culture*, edited by Sherrie A. Inness, 199–226. New York: New York University Press, 1998.

———. "A Promise Fulfilled: Mexican Cannery Workers in Southern California." *Pacific Historian* 30 (Summer 1986): 51–61.

———. "'Star Struck': Acculturation, Adolescence, and the Mexican American Woman, 1920–1950." In *Building with Our Hands: New Directions in Chicana Studies*, edited by Adela De La Torre and Beatríz M. Pesquera, 109–29. Berkeley: University of California Press, 1993.

———. "Texture, Texts, and Context: New Approaches in Chicano Historiography." *Mexican Studies/Estudios Mexicanos* 2 (Winter 1986): 145–52.

Rupp, Leila J. *Mobilizing Women for War: German and American Propaganda, 1939–1945*. Princeton, N.J.: Princeton University Press, 1978.

Sánchez, George I. "Pachucos in the Making." *Common Ground* 4 (Autumn 1943): 13–20.

Sánchez, George J. *Becoming Mexican American: Ethnicity, Culture, and Identity in Chicano Los Angeles, 1900–1945*. New York: Oxford University Press, 1993.

Sanchez, Thomas, *Zoot-Suit Murders: A Novel*. New York: Dutton, 1978.

Sanchez-Tranquilino, Marcos, and John Tagg. "The Pachuco's Flayed Hide: The Museum, Identity, and Buenas Garras." In *Cultural Studies*, edited by Lawrence Grossberg, Cary Nelson, and Paula Treichler, 556–70. London: Routledge, 1992.

Santamaría, Francisco J. *Diccionario de Méjicanismos*. 2nd ed. Mexico City: Editorial Porrua, 1974.

———. *Diccionario general de Americanismos*. Mexico City: Editorial Pedro Robredo, 1942.

Saragoza, Alex M. "The Significance of Recent Chicano-Related Historical Writings: An Appraisal." *Ethnic Affairs* 1 (Fall 1987): 25–62.

Schapps, Myra. *High Walls and Open Gates: A Report Submitted to the California Department of Corrections and Social Welfare*. Sacramento: California Department of Social Welfare, 1959.

Schoeffler, O. E., and William Gale, eds. *Esquire's Encyclopedia of Twentieth Century Men's Fashions*. New York: McGraw-Hill, 1973.

Schrum, Kelly. "'Teena Means Business': Teenage Girls' Culture and Seventeen Magazine, 1944–1950." In *Delinquents and Debutantes: Twentieth-Century American Girls' Culture*, edited by Sherrie A. Inness, 134–63. New York: New York University Press, 1998.

Schwendinger, Herman, and Julia R. "Delinquency and the Collective Varieties of Youth." *Crime and Social Justice* 5 (Spring–Summer 1976): 7–25.

Selden, Steven. *Inheriting Shame: The Story of Eugenics and Racism in America*. New York: Teacher's College Press, 1999.

Seldes, George. *Lords of the Press*. New York: J. Messner, 1946.

Shevky, Eshrev, and Marilyn Williams. *The Social Areas of Los Angeles*. Berkeley: University of California Press, 1949.

Sitton, Thomas, and William Deverell, eds. *Metropolis in the Making: Los Angeles in the 1920s*. Berkeley: University of California Press, 2001.

Smith, Gary, and George Otero. *Teaching about Cultural Awareness*. Denver: University of Denver, 1985.

Smith, John David, ed. *Racial Determinism and the Fear of Miscegenation, Post 1900: Race and "the Negro Problem."* New York: Garland, 1993.

———. *Racist Southern Paternalism: General Statements of "the Negro Problem."* New York: Garland, 1993.

Smith, Page. *Democracy on Trial: The Japanese-American Evacuation and Relocation in World War II*. New York: Simon and Schuster, 1995.

Smith, Susan J. "Negative Interaction: Crime in the Inner City." In *Social Interaction and Ethnic Segregation*, edited by Peter Jackson and Susan J. Smith, 35–58. London: Academic Press, 1981.

Sorell, Victor Alejandro. "Articulate Signs of Resistance and Affirmation in Chicano Public Art." In *Chicano Art: Resistance and Affirmation, 1965–1985*, edited by Richard Griswold del Castillo, Teresa McKenna, Yvonne Yarbro-Bejarano, 16–24. Los Angeles: Wight Art Gallery, University of California, 1991.

Spaulding, Charles B. "Housing Problems of Minority Groups in Los Angeles County." *Annals of the American Academy of Political and Social Science* 246 (November 1946): 220–25.

Staples, Robert. "Stereotypes of Black Male Sexuality: The Facts behind the Myths." In *Men's Lives*, 4th ed., edited by Michael S. Kimmel and Michael A. Messner, 466–71. Boston: Allyn and Bacon, 1998.

Starke, Catherine Juanita. *Black Portraiture in American Fiction: Stock Characters, Archetypes, and Individuals*. New York: Basic Books, 1971.

Starr, Kevin. *Inventing the Dream: California through the Progressive Era*. New York: Oxford University Press, 1985.

———. *Material Dreams: Southern California through the 1920s*. New York: Oxford University Press, 1990.

Steward, Jill. "Attorney George Shibley, Defender of Sirhan, Dies." *Los Angeles Times*, 5 July 1989.

Swanberg, W. A. *Citizen Hearst: A Biography of William Randolph Hearst*. New York: Scribner's, 1961.

Takaki, Ronald T. *Double Victory: A Multicultural History of America in World War II*. Boston: Little, Brown, 2000.

———. *Iron Cages: Race and Culture in Ninteenth-Century America*. Rev. ed. New York: Oxford University Press, 2000.

Terenzio, Maurice, Scott MacGillivray, and Ted Okudo. *The Soundies Distributing Corporation of America: A History and Filmography of Their "Jukebox" Musical Films of the 1940s*. Jefferson, N.C.: McFarland and Co., 1991.

Terkel, Studs. *The Good War: An Oral History of World War Two*. New York: Pantheon, 1984.

Toll, Robert C. *Blacking Up: The Minstrel Show in Nineteenth Century America*. New York: Oxford University Press, 1974.

Trombetta, Jim. "'Zoot' Suit and Its Real Defendants." *Calendar*, 11 October 1981, 4.

Tuck, Ruth D. "Behind the Zoot Suit Riots." *Survey Graphic: Magazine of Social Interpretation* 32 (August 1943): 313–16, 335.

———. *Not with the Fist: Mexican Americans in a Southwest City*. New York: Harcourt Brace, 1946.

Turner, Ralph H., and Samuel J. Surace. "Zoot-Suiters and Mexicans: Symbols in Crowd Behavior." *American Journal of Sociology* 62 (July 1956): 14–20.

Tyler, Bruce M. "Black Jive and White Repression." *Journal of Ethnic Studies* 16 (Winter 1989): 31–66.

Valdez, Luís. *Zoot Suit and Other Plays*. Houston: Arte Publico Press, 1992.

Vigil, James Diego. *Barrio Gangs: Street Life and Identity in Southern California*. Austin: University of Texas Press, 1988.

Villa, Raúl Homero. *Barrio-Logos: Space and Place in Urban Chicano Literature and Culture*. Austin: University of Texas, 2000.

Villanueva, Tino. "Pachuco Remembered." In *Hay Otra Voz Poems (1968–1971)*. New York: Editorial Mensaje, 1972.

Villareal, José Antonio. *Pocho*. New York: Anchor, 1989.

Warren, Kenneth W. *Black and White Strangers: Race and American Literary Realism*. Chicago: University of Chicago Press, 1993.

Watson, Jon. "Crossing the Color Lines in the City of Angels: The NAACP and the Zoot-Suit Riot of 1943." *Journal of Contemporary History* 4 (June 2002). <www.sussex.ac.uk/Units/HUMCENTR/usjch/jwatson4html>

Weaver, John D. *Los Angeles: An Enormous Village, 1781–1981*. Santa Barbara, Calif.: Capra Press, 1980.

Weber, Devra. *Dark Sweat, White Gold: California Farm Workers, Cotton, and the New Deal*. Berkeley: University of California Press, 1994.

Wells-Barnett, Ida B. *On Lynchings: Southern Horrors, a Red Record, Mob Rule in New Orleans*. New York: Arno Press, 1969.

White, Shane, and Graham White. *Stylin': African American Expressive Culture from Its Beginnings to the Zoot Suit*. Ithaca, N.Y.: Cornell University Press, 1998.

Williamson, Joel. *The Crucible of Race: Black-White Relations in the American South since Emancipation*. New York: Oxford University Press, 1984.

Wilson, William Julius. *The Declining Significance of Race: Blacks and Changing American Institutions*. Chicago: University of Chicago Press, 1978.

———. *The Truly Disadvantaged: The Inner City, the Underclass, and Public Policy*. Chicago: University of Chicago Press, 1987.

Winkler, Allan M. *The Home Front U.S.A.: America during World War II*. Arlington Heights, Ill.: Harlan Davidson, 1986.

————. *The Politics of Propaganda: The Office of War Information, 1942–1945*. New Haven: Yale University Press, 1978.

Winkler, John Kennedy. *W. R. Hearst: An American Phenomenon*. New York: Simon and Schuster, 1928.

Yatsushiro, Toshio. *Politics and Cultural Values: The World War II Japanese Relocation Centers*. New York: Arno Press, 1978.

Yavno, Max, and Lee Shippey, *The Los Angeles Book*. Boston: Houghton Mifflin, 1950.

"Zoot-Suit Riots: 125 Hurt in Los Angeles Fights." *Life*, 21 June 1943, 30–31.

## Dissertations, Theses, and Unpublished Papers

Adams, Karen M. "Black Images in Nineteenth-Century American Painting and Literature: An Iconological Study of Mount, Melville, Homer and Mark Twain." Master's thesis, Emory University, 1977.

Alvarez, Luis Alberto. "The Power of the Zoot: Race, Community, and Resistance in American Youth Culture, 1940–1945." Ph.D. diss., University of Texas at Austin, 2001.

Böger, Gerd. "A Content Analysis of Selected Children's Books on the Negro and on Japan." Master's thesis, Michigan State University, 1966.

Carlson, Julie Ann. "A Comparison of the Treatment of the Negro in Children's Literature in the Periods 1929–1938 and 1959–1968." Master's thesis, University of Connecticut, 1969.

de Graff, Lawrence Brooks. "Negro Migration to Los Angeles, 1930 to 1950." Ph.D. diss., University of California, Los Angeles, 1962.

Dieppa, Ismael. "The Zoot-Suit Riots Revisited." Ph.D. diss., University of Southern California, 1973.

Domer, Marilyn. "The Zoot-Suit Riot: A Culmination of Social Tensions in Los Angeles." Master's thesis, Claremont Graduate School, 1955.

DuVall, Everett W. "A Sociological Study of Five Hundred Under-privileged Children." Ph.D. diss., University of Southern California, 1936.

Escobar, Edward Joseph. "Chicano Protest and the Law: Law Enforcement Responses to Chicano Activism in Los Angeles, 1850–1936." Ph.D. diss., University of California, Riverside, 1983.

Escobedo, Elizabeth. "The Female Zooter: Sexuality and Mexican Identity in World War II Los Angeles." Paper presented at the annual meeting of the National Association of Chicana and Chicano Scholars, Chicago, 2002.

Gomes, Glenn Michael. "Violence on the Home Front: The 1943 Los Angeles 'Zoot Suit' Riots." Master's thesis, University of California, Davis, 1973.

Gonzalez, Alfredo Guerra. "Mexicano/Chicano Gangs in Los Angeles: A Sociohistorical Case Study." Ph.D. diss., University of California, Berkeley, 1981.

Green, Susan Marie. "Zoot Suiters: Past and Present." Ph.D. diss., University of Milwaukee, 1997.

Griswold del Castillo, Richard. "The International Dimensions of the Zoot Suit Riots." Unpublished manuscript in author's possession.

Harrod, Merrill Leonard. "A Study of Deviate Personalities As Found in Main Street of Los Angeles." Master's thesis, University of Southern California, 1939.

Harvey, Louise. "The Delinquent Boy in an Urban Area, 1945." Master's thesis, University of Southern California, 1947.

Johnson, Beulah V. "The Treatment of the Negro Woman as a Major Character in American Novels, 1900–1950." Ph.D. diss., New York University, 1955.

Leonard, Kevin Allen. "Years of Hope, Days of Fear: The Impact of World War II on Race Relations in Los Angeles." Ph.D. diss., University of California, Davis, 1992.

Mazón, Mauricio. "Social Upheaval in World War II: Zoot-Suiters and Servicemen in Los Angeles, 1943." Ph.D. diss., University of California, Los Angeles, 1976.

Pagán, Eduardo Obregón. "'Who Are These Troublemakers?': The Mexican American Middle Class Reacts to Pachucos, 1940–1944." Paper presented at the annual meeting of the Organization of American Historians, Anaheim, Calif., 1993.

Ramírez, Catherine Sue. "The Pachuca in Chicana/o Art, Literature and History: Reexamining Nation, Cultural Nationalism and Resistance." Ph.D. diss., University of California, Berkeley, 2000.

Scott, Robin Fitzgerald. "The Mexican American in the Los Angeles Area, 1920–1950: From Acquiescence to Activity." Ph.D. diss., University of Southern California, 1971.

Ward, Hazel Mae. "The Black Woman as Character: Images in the American Novel, 1852–1953." Ph.D. diss., University of Texas at Austin, 1977.

Wells, Christopher W. "Activist, Interpreter, Statesman: A Political Biography of Manuel Ruíz, Jr." Honors thesis, Williams College, 1995.

# INDEX

173, 176, 179, 180, 192, 204, 208, 209, 221

*Eastside Journal*, 123, 132, 179, 204

Eckstine, Billy, 53

*El Congreso del Pueblo de Habla Espa-
ñola. See* Congress of Spanish-
Speaking People

Eleventh Naval District Headquarters,
San Diego, 158, 166

Ellington, Duke, 53

El Monte Legion Stadium, 53

Elson, Eugene, 206

Emerson, Lloyd, 73

Encinas, Lorena, 203, 222, 224

Encinas, Luís "Louie," 224–25

Encinas, Theodore "Ted," 224

Endore, Guy, 8, 9, 124, 126, 128, 133,
138–39, 141, 201–2, 214

Erenberg, Lewis, 98, 100

Escobar, Edward, 8, 15, 31, 71

Eugenics, 24–25, 36, 106

Evans, Sara, 217

Fierro de Bright, Josefina, 85–86, 140,
196, 198, 205, 250 (n. 52), 260 (n. 110)

Filipinos, 93, 107, 185, 193, 231

Fisher, Lloyd H., 51

Flynn, Errol, 80

Foley, Neil, 12, 13, 33

Folsom Prison, 208

42nd Street neighborhood, 63

Frame, Barnaby, 101

Fregoso, Rosa Linda, 155, 214, 216–17

Freirson-McEvere, 108

Fricke, Charles W., 74, 80–89 passim,
96–97, 205, 208–9. See also *People v.
Zammora et al.*

Gable, Clark, 108

Gallardo, Miguel, 73

Gamma Eta Gamma, 32

García, Bobby, 115

Gastelum, Richard, 89

Gillespie Furniture, 56

Godlewska, Anne, 154

Gonzales, Josephine, 57, 61–63, 82, 222

Gonzales, Juanita "Jenny," 57, 61–63, 203

Goodman, Benny, 98

Gordon, Dexter, 118

Grandpré, Edward "Turkey," 77, 89

Granner, James Jerome, 155

Grant, Madison, 24

Great Depression, 3, 98, 107, 129

Griffith, Beatrice, 36, 104–15 passim,
129, 163, 171, 215, 230–31

Griffith, D. W., 25

Gutíerrez, David, 13, 26

Gutíerrez, Ramón, 232

Hairstyles popular among Los Angeles youth: G.I. cut, 101; Lamar or
ducktail, 100–102, 106, 121; Pachuca
pompadour, 102, 104, 106; reactions
to, 96–97, 100–106

Hancock, Hunter, 53

Hartman, Susan, 40, 119

Hawkins, Coleman, 52

Hayworth, Rita, 205

Hearst, William Randolph, 8, 86, 126,
138, 141, 167–68, 216

Henderson, Fletcher, 98

Henson, Jimmy, 52

Herrera, Joe, 77

Himes, Chester B., 108, 158, 239 (n. 52)

Hipsters, 17, 37, 99, 104, 110, 114, 116–18,
120, 125, 132–33; manhood and, 120–
21; and opposition to war, 11; origin
of term, 39; and use of marijuana and
opium, 39, 121

Hopkinson, Raymond T., 73

Horne, Lena, 205

Horrall, Clemence B. (also known as
C. B. Horrall), 132–33, 162

Hoxie, Frederick, 26

"Huggy Boy," 53

Hunt, Harry, 77

Hunt, Myron, 28

Hunter, Patsy, 118